EU Environmental Law

ELGAR EUROPEAN LAW

Founding Editor: John Usher, *formerly Professor of European Law and Head, School of Law, University of Exeter, UK*

European integration is the driving force behind constant evolution and change in the laws of the member states and the institutions of the European Union. This important series will offer short, state-of-the-art overviews of many specific areas of EU law, from competition law to consumer law and from environmental law to labour law. Whilst most books will take a thematic, vertical approach, others will offer a more horizontal approach and consider the overarching themes of EU law.

Distilled from rigorous substantive analysis, and written by some of the best names in the field, as well as the new generation of scholars, these books are designed both to guide the reader through the changing legislation itself, and to provide a firm theoretical foundation for advanced study. They will be an invaluable source of reference for scholars and postgraduate students in the fields of EU law and European integration, as well as lawyers from the respective individual fields and policymakers within the EU.

Titles in the series include:

Judicial Review in EU Law
Alexander H. Türk

EU Intellectual Property Law and Policy
Catherine Seville

EU Private International Law
Second Edition
Peter Stone

EU Labour Law
A.C.L. Davies

EU Public Procurement Law
Second Edition
Christopher H. Bovis

EU Internet Law
Andrej Savin

EU Consumer Law and Policy
Second Edition
Stephen Weatherill

EU Private International Law
Third Edition
Peter Stone

EU Intellectual Property Law and Policy
Second Edition
Catherine Seville

EU Environmental Law
Geert Van Calster and Leonie Reins

EU Environmental Law

Geert Van Calster

Professor, KU Leuven, Belgium; Monash University, Australia; King's College London, UK, and Member of the Bar of Belgium

Leonie Reins

Assistant Professor, Tilburg Institute for Law, Technology and Society, Tilburg University, the Netherlands

ELGAR EUROPEAN LAW

Cheltenham, UK • Northampton, MA, USA

© Geert Van Calster and Leonie Reins 2017

Copyright cover photo: KJ Garnett, euperspectives.com

All rights reserved. No part of this publication may be reproduced, stored in a retrieval system or transmitted in any form or by any means, electronic, mechanical or photocopying, recording, or otherwise without the prior permission of the publisher.

Published by
Edward Elgar Publishing Limited
The Lypiatts
15 Lansdown Road
Cheltenham
Glos GL50 2JA
UK

Edward Elgar Publishing, Inc.
William Pratt House
9 Dewey Court
Northampton
Massachusetts 01060
USA

Paperback edition 2018

A catalogue record for this book
is available from the British Library

Library of Congress Control Number: 2016953910

This book is available electronically in the **Elgar**online
Law subject collection
DOI 10.4337/9781782549185

Printed on 30% PCR Stock
ISBN 978 1 78254 917 8 (cased)
ISBN 978 1 78254 918 5 (eBook)
ISBN 978 1 78811 944 3 (paperback)
Printed and bound by Thomson-Shore, Inc.

Typeset by Servis Filmsetting Ltd, Stockport, Cheshire

Copyright image: Irina Chrennikowa

To the memory of Prof Marc Pallemaerts, gentle giant of environmental law

Geert Van Calster

To my family

Leonie Reins

Contents

List of figures and table	xiii
Preface	xiv
Table of cases	xv
Table of legislation	xx

1	Setting the context			1
	I	History and development		1
	II	Sources of European environmental law		4
	III	Heads of power or "competences"		6
	IV	Objectives of the EU's environmental policy		8
		A	Sustainable development as a Union objective	9
		B	High level of environmental protection	10
		C	The quality of the environment and its legislation	12
		D	The right to the protection of the environment	12
		E	Protecting human health	13
		F	Promoting measures at international level to deal with regional or worldwide environmental problems, and in particular combating climate change	13

PART I BASICS/FRAMEWORK OF EUROPEAN ENVIRONMENTAL LAW

2	Principles of European environmental law		17
	I	Subsidiarity and proportionality	19
	II	The integration principle	22
	III	Sustainable development	24
	IV	Precautionary principle	28
	V	Prevention principle	33
	VI	Rectification of damage at source	35
	VII	Polluter pays principle	36
3	Environmental law-making in the EU			40
	I	Actors		40
		A	The European Parliament	40
		B	The Council of the European Union	42

				Page
		C	The European Commission	42
		D	The Court of Justice of the European Union	43
		E	The Committee of the Regions and the Economic and Social Committee	45
		F	Other actors	47
	II	(Legal) instruments		50
		A	Delegated and implementing acts	52
		B	Other legal instruments	52
		C	Vertical and horizontal legislation	53
	III	Legal basis		54
	IV	The environmental guarantee		61
		A	Overall meaning and context	61
		B	The conditions for the guarantee to apply	62
	V	Decision-making process		66
4	Implementation and enforcement			69
	I	Implementation of environmental law		69
		A	Legal implementation	69
		B	Non-legal instruments aiming at better implementation	71
	II	Primacy and direct effect		73
	III	The infringement procedure		75
		A	Imposing fines on unwilling Member States	77
	IV	European citizens as EU environmental law enforcers		79
5	Public participatory rights			81
	I	Implementation of the Aarhus Convention in the EU Member States		82
		A	Access to environmental information	83
		B	Participation in environmental decision making	92
		C	Access to justice	93
	II	Application of the Aarhus Convention to Union institutions and bodies		95
		A	Access to environmental information	96
		B	Public participation	100
		C	Access to justice	101
6	Additional tools in implementing European environmental law			108
	I	Environmental management systems		108
		A	Main provisions and duties for companies registering under EMAS	109
	II	Permitting and best available techniques		112
		A	Obligations of the Member States	113

		B	Best available techniques	118
	III	EU labelling		119
		A	EU Ecolabel	120
		B	EU Energy Label	123
	IV	Green public procurement		126

7	Environmental and Strategic Impact Assessments			130
	I	Environmental Impact Assessment		130
		A	Basic principles	130
		B	Splitting of projects, incremental projects, cumulative assessment	134
		C	Obligations of the Directive	137
		D	Transboundary projects	141
		E	The relationship between the EIA Directive and the Aarhus Convention	143
	II	Strategic Environmental Assessment		144
		A	The relationship between the EIA and SEA Directives	145
		B	The provisions of the Directive	147
		C	Guidance	149

8	Environmental liability and environmental crime		150
	I	Environmental liability	150
	II	Environmental crime	157

9	State aid and competition law			161
	I	State aid		161
		A	Regulatory framework	161
		B	Antecedents of the Commission's Guidelines – the troublesome introduction of the polluter pays principle	168
		C	"Indirect" aid: tax relief, reductions in charges and various tax benefits	171
	II	Competition law and the environment		175
		A	Eco-Emballages	176
		B	DSD	177

PART II SUBSTANTIVE LEGISLATION

10	Biodiversity and nature conservation			181
	I	Natura 2000 network and the Wild Birds and Habitats Directive		183
		A	The Wild Birds Directive	183

		B	The Habitats Directive	185
		C	Relation between the Habitats Directive and the EIA Directive	204
	II	Soil		206
		A	The Soil Thematic Strategy	208
		B	European Soil Charter and other European legislation indirectly addressing soil	209
	III	Invasive alien species		213
11	Water protection legislation and policy			215
	I	The Water Framework Directive and integrated river basin management		217
		A	Common implementation strategy	220
	II	Adaptation to climate change: floods, droughts and water scarcity		221
		A	Floods	221
		B	Droughts and water scarcity	222
	III	Drinking water		224
	IV	Bathing water		225
	V	Groundwater		227
	VI	Water pollution		228
	VII	Protection of the marine environment		229
12	Noise pollution legislation and policy			231
	I	The Environmental Noise Directive		231
	II	Sector specific regulation and harmonisation		233
		A	Noise from motors in vehicles	234
		B	Agricultural and forestry tractors	236
		C	Two- or three-wheel vehicles and quadricycles	236
		D	Protection of workers from exposure to noise at work	237
		E	Outdoor use equipment	238
		F	Noise emission by aircraft	240
13	Air pollution legislation and policy			242
	I	Air quality		242
		A	The Air Quality Directive	242
		B	The Fourth Daughter Directive	246
	II	National emission ceilings		246
	III	Sector specific regulation and harmonisation		247
		A	Transport emissions	247
		B	The Paints Directive	252

14	Climate change legislation and policy			253
	I	Adaptation		254
	II	Mitigation		256
		A	The European Emissions Trading System	257
		B	Emissions from land transport	261
15	Waste legislation and policy			264
	I	EU waste policy		264
		A	General policy orientation	264
		B	The 2003 Communication "Towards a thematic strategy on the prevention and recycling of waste"	265
		C	2011 thematic strategy and beyond	268
		D	The "circular economy package"	272
	II	The definition of waste		272
	III	Table: relevant EU waste law		275
16	Chemicals legislation and policy			277
	I	REACH		277
		A	Registration	278
		B	Authorisation	286
	II	Regulation on the Classification, Labelling and Packaging of Substances and Mixtures ("CLP Regulation")		290
		A	Harmonised criteria	291
		B	Obligations to classify, label and package	292
		C	Harmonised classification and labelling	294
	III	The Biocidal Products Regulation ("BPR")		295
		A	Active substances	295
		B	Biocidal products	297
		C	Treated articles	298
		D	Data protection and data sharing	298
	IV	Genetically modified organisms		299
		A	The GMO Directive: authorisation	300
		B	Traceability and labelling	302
		C	Genetically modified food and feed	304
		D	Regulatory developments	306
17	Trade and the environment			308
	I	Introduction		308
	II	Mutual recognition, positive and negative harmonisation		310
		A	The New Approach – including the emphasis on "minimum harmonisation"	311

	B	Community pre-emption – or the exhaustive effect of community legislation	311
	C	The Compassion case – taking exhaustion too far	312
	D	The environmental guarantees of Articles 114 and 193 TFEU	315
III		Second-guessing of national environmental priorities?	316
IV		PreussenElektra, Essent 1 and Essent 2	317
	A	PreussenElektra	318
	B	Ålands Vindkraft and Essent 1: a clear preference for market-based renewable energy support	320
	C	Essent 2	324
V		Restrictions on the use of lawfully marketed products and the EU's internal market	326

Index   331

Figures and table

FIGURES

6.1	EU Ecolabel	121
6.2	EU energy label	124
7.1	The EIA procedure	132
7.2	The relationship between the EIA and SEA Directive	146
16.1	Hazard pictogram	292

TABLE

15.1	Relevant EU waste law	275

Preface

For use both as a handbook and as a general introduction for professionals and students, *EU Environmental Law* addresses the reality of legal practice throughout the EU. Environmental law in Member States is for a large part regulated by the EU, making it ever less 'national'. Increasingly, moreover, business and personal links have a European angle to them. Sustainable development and growth has become fundamental, not only to industry, but also to society in general. Consequentially European environmental regulation is becoming more complex and interrelated, making it an emerging field of study for European law graduates, and an area of increasing exposure to the legal profession. This book gives readers a thorough overview of core European environmental law, with a section on the basic framework and principles, as well as on substantive law issues, providing insight into legislation in the different sectors and into the most topical developments. Other volumes of European environmental law provide an extensive overview and are, amongst others, Jan H. Jans and Hans H.B. Vedder, *European Environmental Law: After Lisbon* (Groningen: Europa Law Publishing, 2012); Ludwig Krämer, *EU European Environmental Law* (London: Sweet & Maxwell, 2012). Lee and Scott also provide analyses of selected issues: M. Lee, *EU Environmental Law: Governance and Decision-making Modern Studies in European Law* (Oxford and Portland, OR: Hart Publishing, 2014) and J. Scott, *EC Environmental Law* (London: Longman, 1998).

Our special thanks to Lieselot Mariën, Colienne Linard, Christophe Schelfaut, Alec van Vaerenbergh and Sofia Sjögren for their help in researching and writing some sections of this volume.

Table of cases

EUROPEAN CASES

C-106/77, *Amministrazione delle Finanze dello Stato v Simmenthal SpA*, [1978] ECR 629 73
C-106/84 *Commission v Denmark*, [1986] ECR 833 173
C-106/89 *Marleasing v Comercial Internacional de Alimentación*, [1990] ECR I-4135 75
C-110/05 *Commission v Italy*, [2009] ECR I-519 328
C-112/15 *Kodbranchens Fallesrad*, ECLI:EU:C:2016:185 312
C-115/09 Bund für Umwelt und Naturschutz Deutschland, Landesverband Nordrhein-Westfalen, [2011] ECR I-3673 88
C-120/78 *Rewe v Bundesmonopolverwaltung für Branntwein*, [1979]ECR I-649 .... 167, 310, 321
C-121/03 *Commission v Spain*, ECLI:EU:C:2005:512 219
C-125/88 *Criminal proceedings against H.F.M. Nijman*, [1989] ECR 3533 ...... 65, 316
C-127/02 *Waddenvereniging and Vogelbeschermingsvereniging*, [2004] ECR I-7405 .... 189, 204
C-128/09 *Boxus and Others*, [2011] ECR I-9711 131
C-13/77 *Inno v Atab* [1977] ECR 2115 175
C-131/93 *Commission v Germany*, [1994] ECR I-3303 .... 65, 316
C-137/14 *Commission v Germany* ECLI:EU:C:2015:683 94
C-140/79 *Chemial Farmaceutici SpA v DAF SpA.*, [1981] ECR 1 174
C-142/05 *Aklagaren v Percy Mickelsson and Joakim Roos*, [2009] ECR I-4723 328
C-142/07 *Ecologistas en Acción-CODA v Ayuntamiento de Madrid*, [2008] ECRI-6097 134
Joined Cases 142/80 and 143/80 *Amministrazione delle Finanze dello Stato v Essevi SpA and Carlo Salengo*, [1981] ECR 1413 173
C-152/89 *Commission v Luxembourg*, [1991] ECRI-3141 173
C-155/91 *Commission v Council*, [1993] I-939 .... 55, 56
C-166/07, *Parliament v Council*, [2009] ECR I-7135 .... 55, 56
C-166/97 *Commission v France*, [1999] ECR I-1719 184
C-174/82 *Criminal proceedings against Sandoz BV*, [1983] ECR 2445 ..... 65, 316, 317
C-176/03, *Commission v Council* ("Environmental crimes"), [2005] ECR I-7879 .... 55, 56, 80,158
C-180/96 *United Kingdom v Commission*, [1998] EHR I-226 29
C-182/10, *Solvay and Others*, ECLI:EU:C:2012:82 .... 134, 187, 196
Joined Cases C-1/90 and C-176/90 *Aragonesa de Publicidad Exterior SA and Publiva SAE v Departamento de Sanidad y Seguridad Social de la Generalitat de Cataluna*, [1991] ECR I-4151 .... 65, 316
C-1/96 *R v MAFF, ex parte Compassion in World Farming*, [1998] ECR I-1251 312
C-198/01 *Fiammiferi* [2003] ECR I-08055 175

xv

C-2/07 *Abraham and Others*, [2008] ECR I-1197.. 131
C-203/80 *Casati* [1981] ECR 2595... 80, 158
C-204/09 *Flachgas Torgau GmbH v Federal Republic of Germany*, ECLI:
EU:C:2012:71... 84
C-204/12 *Essent Belgium*, ECLI:EU:C:2014:2192 320
C-205/08 *Umweltanwalt von Kärnten*, [2009] ECR I-11525 134
C-213/96 *Outokumpu*, ECLI:EU:C:1998:155 172
C-215/06 *Commission v Ireland*, [2008] ECR I-4911 134
C-217/97 *Commission v Germany* ECLI:EU:C:1999:395.. 90
C-226/08 *Stadt Papenburg*, ECLI:EU:C:2010:10 204
C-226/97 *Lemmens* [1998]ECR I-3711 .... 80, 158
C-227/82 *Criminal proceedings against Leendert van Bennekom*, [1983]
ECR 3883 .... 65, 313, 316
C-235/02 Criminal proceedings against Saetti and Frediani, ECLI:EU:C:2004:26 .. 273
C-237/07 Janecek, ECR [2008] I- 6221... 245
Joined Cases C- 241/12 and C- 242/12 Criminal proceedings against Shell
Nederland Verkoopmaatschappij BV and Belgian Shell NV, ECLI:EU:C:2013:
821 273
C-242/87 *Commission v Council* ("ERASMUS"),[1989] ECR I-1425 .... 55, 56
C-244/12 *Salzburger Flughafen*, [2013] ECLI:EU:C:2013:203................................ 136
C-247/84 *Criminal proceedings against Léon Motte*, [1985] ECR 3887 314
C-247/85 *Commission v Belgium*, ECR [1987] 3029 183
C-25/62 *Plaumann & Co. v Commission*, [1963] ECR 95 102
C-251/78, *Denkavit*, [1979] ECR 3369.. 315
C-252/85 *Commission v France*, [1988] ECR I -2243 184
C-255/08 *Commission v Netherlands*, [2009] ECR I-167 140
C-256/10 Barcenilla Fernández and Macedo Lozano, ECR [2011] I- 4083.............. 238
C-258/11 *Sweetman v An Bord Pleanala*, ECLI:EU:C:2013:220............................. 191
C-260/11 *Edwards and Pallikaropoulos* ECLI:EU:C:2013:221........................ 94, 143
C-262/85 *Commission v Italy*, [1987] ECR I-3073 184
C-263/08 *Djurgarden – Lilla Värtans Miljöskyddsförening*,[2009] ECR I-9967...... 143
C-266/09 *Stichting Milieu and Others v College voor de toelating van
gewasbeschermingsmiddelen en biociden*, ECLI:EU:C:2010:779.................. 84, 88
C-26/62 *NV Algemene Transportonderneming van Gend en Loos v Netherlands
Inland Revenue Administration*, [1963] ECR 3 73
C-267/86 *Van Eyke v Aspa* [1988] ECR 4769... 175
Joined cases C-267/91 and C-268/91 *Keck and Mithouard*, [1993] ECRI-6097167, 328
C-27/03 *Commission v Belgium* ECLI:EU:C:2004:418 79
C-275/09 *Brussels Hoofdstedelijk Gewest and Others*, [2011] ECR I-1753 131
C-277/83 *Commission v Italy*, [1985] ECR 2049 173
C-279/12 *Fish Legal et al v Information Commissioner et al.* ECLI:EU:C:2013:539 85
C-287/98 *Linster*, [2000] ECR I-6917.. 131
C-2/90 *Commission v Belgium*, [1992] ECR I-4431 35
C-290/03 *Diane Barker v London Borough of Bromley*, [2006] ECRI-3949 135
C-293/94 *Criminal proceedings against Jacqueline Brandsma*, [1996] ECR I-3159
.... 65, 316
C-294/83 *Les Verts v Parliament*, [1986] ECR I-1339... 167
C-295/10 *Valčiukienė and Others* [2011] ECR I-8819 145
C-300/89, *Commission v Council* ("Titanium Dioxide"), [1991] ECRI-2867 ...... 55, 57
C-301/12 *Cascina Tre Pini*, ECLI:EU:C:2014:214 203

Table of cases

C-302/86, *Commission v Denmark*, [1988] ECR 4607... 66, 317
C-304/05 *Commission v Italy*, ECLI:EU:C:2007:532 196
C-32/05 *Commission v Luxembourg*, ECR [2006] I-11323..................................... 219
C-320/03 *Commission v Austria*, [2005] ECR I-9871 327
C-321/95P *Stichting Greenpeace v Commission*, [1998] ECR I-1651 103
C-322/88 *Grimaldi* [1989] ECR I-4407... 51
C-332/04 *Commission v Spain*, [2006] ECR I-40... 133
C-333/08 *Commission v France* [2010] ECR I-757 30
Joined Cases C-38/90 and C-151/90 *Lomas and Others*, [1992] ECR I-1781 314
C-340/02 *Commission v France* [2005] ECR I-6263 76
C-343/9 *Afton Chemical* [2010] ECR I-7027 19
C-344/04 IATA and ELFAA [2006] ECR I-403... 11
C-347/89 *Freistaat Bayern v Eurim-Pharm GmbH*, [1991] ECR I-1747........... 65, 316
C-347/97 *Braathens Sverige AB v Riksskatteverket*, [1999] ECRI-3419 165
C-35/76 *Simmenthal*, [1976] ECR 1871 315
C-353/98 *P Laboratoires pharmaceutiques Bergaderm a.o. v Commission* [2000] ECR 5291 29
C-355/90 *Commission v Spain – Santona Marshes*, [1993] ECR I-4221................. 184
C-36/11 *Pioneer Hi Bred Italia*, ECLI:EU:C:2012:534 302
C-36/98 *Spain v Council*, ECLI:EU:C:2001:64.. 56
C-361/10 *Danske Svineproducenter*, [2011] ECR I-13721 312
C-366/10, *Air Transport Association of America and Others*, [2011]ECR I 13755
.... 167, 260
C-368/10 *Commission v Netherlands*, ECLI:EU:C:2012:284................................. 129
C-376/98 *Germany v Parliament and Council*, ("Tobacco Advertising I"), [2000] ECR I-8419... 55, 56
C-379/98 *PreussenElektra*, ECLI:EU:C:2001:160... 318
C-381/07 *Association nationale pour la protection des eaux et rivieres*, EHR [2008] I-8281... 216
C-385/07 *Der Grüne Punkt – Duales System Deutschland GmbH v Commission*, [2009] ECR I-06155... 178
C-392/96 *Commission v Ireland*, [1999] ECR I-5901 134
C-399/14 *Grüne Liga Sachsen and Others*, ECLI:EU:C:2016:10............................ 186
C-400/96 *Criminal proceedings against Jean Harpegnies*, [1998] ECR I-5121 65, 316
C-401/12 P *Council v Vereniging Milieudefensie and Stichting Stop Luchtverontreiniging Utrecht* ECLI:EU:C:2015:4 104
C-404/09 *Commission v Spain*, ECR [2011] I-11853.. 192, 194
C-404/13 *ClientEarth*, ECLI:EU:C:2013:805... 245
C-416/10 *Križan and Others*, ECLI:EU:C:2013:8 44
C-418/04 *Commission v Ireland*, ECLI:EU:C:2007:780... 189
Joined Cases C- 418/97 and C- 419/97 Arco Chemie v VROM and Vereniging Dorpsbelang Hees et al v provincie Gelderland, ECLI:EU:C:2000:318.............. 273
C-420/11 *Jutta Leth*, ECLI:EU:C:2013:166... 131
C-41/11 *Inter-Environnement Wallonie and Terre Wallonne* ECLI:EU:C:2012:103 145
C-422/05 *Commission v Belgium*, ECLI:EU:C:2007:342 312
C-427/07 *Commission v Ireland*, [2009] I-627... 133
C-43/10, *Nomarchiaki Aftodioikisi Aitoloakarnanias*, ECLI:EU:C:2011:253 .. 197, 218
C-435/97 *WWF and Others* [1999] ECR I-5613 131
C-440/05 *Commission v Council*, [2007] ECR I-9097... 158
C-442/09 *Bablok and Others*, ECR [2011] I-7419 305

C-448/01 *EVN and Wienstrom*, [2003] ECR I-14527...129
C-44/95 *R v Secretary of State for the Environment, ex parte RSPB*, [1996] I-3805..184
C-45/86 *Commission v Council* ("Generalised Tariff Preferences"), [1987] ECR-01493..55, 56
C-45/91 *Commission v Greece* [1992] ECR I-2509...77
C-461/13 *Bund für Umwelt und Naturschutz Deutschland*, ECLI:EU:C:2015:433..219
C-463/11 *L v M.*, ECLI:EU:C:2013:247..147
C-473/10 *Commission v Hungary*, ECLI:EU:C:2013:113...44
C-473/98 *Kemikalieninspektionen v Toolex Alpha A.B.*, ECLI:EU:C:2000:379.......312
C-48/14 *Parliament v Council*, ECLI:EU:C:2015:91...56, 57
C-492/14 *Essent Belgium*, ECLI:EU:C:2016:732...324, 325
C-50/09 *Commission v Ireland*, [2011] ECR I-873..137
C-508/09 *Commission v Belgium*, ECLI:EU:C:2011:115...189
C-513/99 *Concordia Bus Finland*, [2002] ECR I-7213..129
C-515/11 *Deutsche Umwelthilfe* ECLI:EU:C:2013:523..87
C-521/12 *Briels*, ECLI:EU:C:2014:330..192
C-524/09, *Ville de Lyon v Caisse des dépôts et consignations* ECLI:EU:C:2010:822...89
C-530/11 *Commission v United Kingdom* ECLI:EU:C:2014:67...................................95
C-531/13 *Marktgemeinde Straßwalchen and Others*, ECLI:EU:C:2015:79.............136
C-533/11 *Commission v Belgium* ECLI:EU:C:2013:659...78
C-534/13 *Fipa Group and Others*, ECLI:EU:C:2015:140.....................................17, 153
C-552/07 *Commune de Sausheim v Pierre Azelvandre* ECLI:EU:C:2009:96.............89
C-558/07 *S.P.C.M. and Others*, ECR [2009] I-5783..280
C-56/93 *Belgium v Commission*, [1996] ECR I-723..163
C-560/08 *Commission v Spain*, ECR [2011] I-199...138
C-567/10 *Inter-Environnement Bruxelles and Others*, ECLI:EU:C:2012:159..........145
C-573/12 *Alands Vindkraft*, ECLI:EU:C:2014:2037...320
C-58/10 to C-68/10, *Monsanto and Others*, ECR [2011] I-7763...............................306
C-583/11 P *Inuit Tapiriit Kanatami and Others v Parliament and Council*, ECLI:EU:C:2013:625..103
C-6/64 *Costa v ENEL* [1964] ECR I-1141..55, 73
C-612/13 P *ClientEarth v Commission* ECLI:EU:C:2015:486....................................98
C-66/06 *Commission v Ireland*, [2008] ECR I-158..140
Joined Cases 67, 68, and 70/85, *Gebroeders Van Der Kooy et al. v Commission*, [1988] ECR 219..163
C-67/97 *Criminal proceedings against Ditlev Bluhme*, [1998] ECR I-8033.............316
C-68/96 *Grundig Italiana SpA v Minestero delle Finanze*, [1997] ECR I-3797.......173
C-71/10 *Office of Communications v Information Commissioner*, ECLI:EU:C:2011:525..88
C-71/14 *East Sussex County Council v Information Commissioner, Property Search Group et al.*, ECLI:EU:C:2015:656...90
C-72/95 *Kraaijeveld and Others*, [1996] ECR I-5403..131
C-76/08 *Commission v Malta*, [2009] ECR I-8213...76
C-77/09 *Gowan Comércio Internacional e Serviços*, [2010] ECR I-13533...............33
C-87/02 *Commission v Italy*, [2004] ECR I-5975..140
Joined Cases C-89/85, C-104/85, C-114/85, C-116/85, C-117/85, C-125/85, C-126/85, C-127/85, C-128/85 and C-129/85 *A. Ahlström Osakeyhtiö and others v Commission of the European Communities (Wood Pulp)*, [1994] ECR I-99.......167

C-9/00 Palin Granit Oy, ECLI:EU:C:2002:232 273
C-9/90 *Francovich and Bonifaci v Italy* [1991] ECR I-5357 78
C-90/94 *Haahr Petroleum v Abenra Havn and Others*, ECLI:EU:C:1997:368 173
C-92/78 *Simmenthal v Commission*, [1979] ECR 777... 102
C-94/03 *Commission v Council* ("Rotterdam PIC Convention"), ECLI:EU:C: 2006:2 .... 55, 56
T-1/10 RENV *PPG and SNF v ECHA*, ECLI:EU:T:2014:616 287
T-13/99 *Pfizer Animal Health v Council*, [2002] ECR II-3305 29
T-134/13 *Polynt and Sitre v ECHA*, ECLI:EU:T:2015:254 19
T-135/3 *Hitachi Chemical Europe and Others v ECHA*, ECLI:EU:T:2015:253 19
T-198/12 *Germany v Commission*, ECLI:EU:T:2014:251.................................. 30, 66
T-331/06 *Evropaiki Dynamiki v EEA*, [2010] ECR II-136 129
T-93/10 *Bilbaina de Alquitranes and Others v ECHA*, ECLI:EU:T:2013:106 288
T-94/10 *Rütgers Germany and Others v ECHA*, ECLI:EU:T:2013:107................... 287
T-95/10 *Cindu Chemicals and Others v ECHA*, ECLI:EU:T:2013:108 287
T-96/10 *Rütgers Germany and Others v ECHA* ECLI:EU:T:2013:109................... 287
T-351/02 *Deutsche Bahn AG v Commission of the European Communities*, [2006] ECR II-1047... 164
T-545/11 *Stichting Greenpeace Nederland and PAN Europe v Commission*, ECLI:EU:T:2013:523 98

NATIONAL CASES

R (Seiont, Gwyrfai and Llyfni Anglers' Society) v Natural Resources Wales [2016] EWCA Civ 797.. 151
HS2 Action Alliance Ltd, R (on the application of) v The Secretary of State for Transport & Anor [2014] UKSC 3 (22 January 2014)....................................... 149
Alyson Austin v Miller Argent (South Wales) Ltd, [2013] EWHC 2622 144
UK Supreme Court in Healthcare at Home Limited (Appellant) v The Common Services Agency (Respondent) (Scotland), [2014] UKSC 49.............................. 128
Dutch Council of State (Raad van State) 11 June 2014, ECLI:NL:RVS:2014:2120.......
Fish Legal v IC & Ors (Information rights: Information rights: practice and procedure) [2015] UKUT 52 (AAC) (19 February 2015) 87

INTERNATIONAL CASES 112

Trail Smelter Arbitrage, *United States v Canada*, Arbitral Tribunal, Montreal, 16 April 1938 and 11 March 1941, 3 United Nations Reports of International Arbitral Awards, 1905.3 156
US v Canada, 3 RIAA (1941) 1907 34
The Corfu Channel Case (United Kingdom v Albania); Assessment of Compensation, 15 XII 49, International Court of Justice (ICJ), 15 December 1949 156

Table of legislation

DIRECTIVES

Directive of 23 October 1962 on the approximation of the rules of the Member States concerning the colouring matters authorized for use in foodstuffs intended for human consumption, [1959] L 62/279 314

Directive 65/65 of 26 January 1965 on the approximation of provisions laid down by Law, Regulation or Administrative Action relating to proprietary medicinal products, [1965] OJ 22/369 224

Directive 67/548 of 6 November 1967 on the approximation of laws, regulations and administrative provisions relating to the classification, packaging and labelling of dangerous substances, [1967] OJ 196/1, ... 281

Directive 70/156 on the approximation of the laws of the Member States relating to the type-approval of motor vehicles and their trailers, [1970] OJ L 42/1 234

Directive 70/157 of 6 February 1970 on the approximation of the laws of the Member States relating to the permissible sound level and the exhaust system of motor vehicles, [1970] OJ L 42/16 234

Directive 70/220 of 20 March 1970 on the approximation of the laws of the Member States relating to measures to be taken against air pollution by gases from positive-ignition engines of motor vehicles, [1970] OJ L 76/1. 248

Directive 73/350/EEC of 7 November 1973 adapting to technical progress the Council Directive of 6 February 1970 on the approximation of the laws of the Member States relating to the permissible sound level and the exhaust system of motor vehicles [1973] OJ L 321/33 235

Directive 75/440 of 16 June 1975 concerning the quality required of surface water intended for the abstraction of drinking water in the Member States, [1976] OJ L 194/26 215

Directive 76/160 of 8 December 1975 concerning the quality of bathing water, [1975] OJ L 31/1 215

Directive 76/464 of 4 May 1976 on pollution caused by certain dangerous substances discharged into the aquatic environment of the Community, [1976] OJ L 129/23 .. 215

Directive 78/659 of 18 July 1978 on the quality of fresh waters needing protection or improvement in order to support fish life, [1987] OJ L 222/1 215

Directive 79/409 on the conservation of wild birds, [1979] OJ L 103/1 .. 183

Directive 79/923 of 30 October 1979 on the quality required of shellfish waters, [1979] OJ L 281/47 215

Directive 80/68 of 17 December 1979 on the protection of groundwater against pollution caused by certain dangerous substances, [1980] OJ L 20/43 215

Directive 80/777 of 15 July 1980 on the approximation of the laws of the Member States relating to the exploitation and marketing of natural mineral waters, [1980] OJ L 229/1 224

Directive 81/334/EEC of 13 April 1981 adapting to technical progress Council Directive 70/157/EEC on the approximation of the laws of the Member States relating to the permissible sound level and the exhaust system of motor vehicles, [1981] OJ L 131/6 235

Directive 84/372/EEC of 3 July 1984 adapting to technical progress Council Directive 70/157/EEC on the approximation of the laws of the Member States relating to the permissible sound level and the exhaust system of motor vehicles [1984] OJ L 196/47 235

Directive 84/424/EEC of 3 September 1984 amending Directive 70/157/EEC on the approximation of the laws of the Member States relating to the permissible sound level and the exhaust system of motor vehicles [1984] OJ L 238/31 235

Directive 84/532 of 17 September 1984 on the approximation of the laws of the Member States relating to common provisions for construction plant and equipment, [1984] OJ L 300/11 234

Directive 84/533/EEC of 17 September 1984 on the approximation of the laws of the Member States relating to the permissible sound power level of compressors [1984] OJ L 300/123 239

Directive 84/534/EEC of 17 September 1984 on the approximation of the laws of the Member States relating to the permissible sound power level of tower cranes,, [1984] OJ L 300/130 239

Directive 84/535/EEC of 17 September 1984 on the approximation of the laws of the Member States relating to the permissible sound power level of welding generators, [1984] OJ L 300/142 239

Directive 84/536/EEC of 17 September 1984 on the approximation of the laws of the Member States relating to the permissible sound power level of power generators, [1984] OJ L 300/149 239

Directive 85/406/EEC of 11 July 1985 adapting to technical progress Council Directive 84/533/EEC on the approximation of the laws of the Member States relating to the permissible sound power level of compressors, [1985] OJ L 233/11 . 239

Directive 85/408/EEC of 11 July 1985 adapting to technical progress Council Directive 84/536/EEC on the approximation of the laws of the Member States relating to the permissible sound power level of power generators, [1985] OJ L 233/18 239

Directive 86/662/EEC of 22 December 1986 on the limitation of noise emitted by hydraulic excavators, rope- operated excavators, dozers, loaders and excavator- loaders, [1986] OJ L 384/1 240

Directive 87/405/EEC of 25 June 1987 amending Directive 84/534/EEC on the approximation of the laws of the Member States relating to the permissible sound power level of tower crane, [1987] OJ L 220/60 .. 239

Directive 89/391 on the introduction of measures to encourage improvements in the safety and health of workers at work, [1989] OJ L 183/1 59

Directive 89/514/EEC of 2 August 1989 adapting to technical progress Council Directive 86/662/EEC on the limitation of noise emitted by hydraulic excavators, rope- operated excavators, dozers, loaders and excavator- loaders, [1989] OJ L 253/35 240

Directive 89/665 on the coordination of the laws, regulations and administrative provisions relating to the application of review procedures to the award of public supply and public works contracts, [1989] OJ L 395/33 128

Directive 91/271 concerning urban waste-water treatment, [1991] OJ L 135/40 .... 79, 216, 228
Directive 91/414 concerning the placing of plant protection products on the market, [1991] OJ L 230/57, 98
Directive 91/676 of 12 December 1991 concerning the protection of waters against pollution caused by nitrates from agricultural sources, [1991] OJ L 375/1 .... 216, 228
Directive 91/689 on hazardous waste, [1991] OJ L 377/20 37
Directive 92/43 on the conservation of natural habitats and of wild fauna and flora, [1992] OJ L 206/7 153
Directive 92/81 on the harmonisation of the structures of excise duties on mineral oils [1992] OJ L 316/12... 164
Directive 92/97/EEC of 10 November 1992 amending Directive 70/157/EEC on the approximation of the laws of the Member States relating to the permissible sound level and the exhaust system of motor vehicles, OJ L 371, 19.12.1992, pp. 1–31 235
Directive 94/62on packaging and packaging waste [1994] OJ L 365/10 37
Directive 95/27/EC of 29 June 1995 amending Council Directive 86/662/EEC on the limitation of noise emitted by hydraulic excavators, rope- operated excavators, dozers, loaders and excavator- loaders, [1995] OJ L 168/14 240
Directive 96/20/EC of 27 March 1996 adapting to technical progress Council Directive 70/157/EEC relating to the permissible sound level and the exhaust system of motor vehicles [1996] OJ L 92/23 235
Directive 96/29/Euratom of 13 May 1996 laying down basic safety standards for the protection of the health of workers and the general public against the dangers arising from ionising radiation, [1996] OJ L 159/1 279
Directive 96/61 of 24 September 1996 concerning integrated pollution prevention and control, [1996] OJ L 257/26 .... 23, 112, 216
Directive 96/62 of 27 September 1996 on ambient air quality assessment and management, [1996] OJ L 296/55 .... 242, 319
Directive 97/68 of 16 December 1997 on the approximation of the laws of the Member States relating to measures against the emission of gaseous and particulate pollutants from internal combustion engines to be installed in non- road mobile machinery, [1998] OJ L 59/1, ... 247
Directive 98/8/EC of 16 February 1998 concerning the placing of biocidal products on the market, [1998] OJ L 123/1 295
Directive 98/70 of 13 October 1998 relating to the quality of petrol and diesel fuels and amending Directive 93/12, [1998] OJ L 350/58, as lastly amended by Directive 2011/63 of 1 June 2011 amending, for the purpose of its adaptation to technical progress, Directive 98/70 relating to the quality of petrol and diesel fuels, [2011] OJ L 147/15... 247
Directive 98/83 of 3 November 1998 on the quality of water intended for human consumption, [1998] OJ L 330/32 224
Directive 1999/13 on the limitation of emissions of volatile organic compounds due to the use of organic solvents in certain activities and installations, [1999] OJ L 85/1 36
Directive 1999/30 of 22 April 1999 relating to limit values for sulphur dioxide, nitrogen dioxide and oxides of nitrogen, particulate matter and lead in ambient air, [1999] OJ L 163/41, ... 242
Directive 1999/31 on the landfill of waste, [1999] OJ L 182/1 37
Directive 1999/62 of 17 June 1999

on the charging of heavy goods vehicles for the use of certain infrastructures, [1999] OJ L 187/42 263

Directive 1999/94 of 13 December 1999 relating to the availability of consumer information on fuel economy and CO_2 emissions in respect of the marketing of new passenger cars, [2000] OJ L 12/16 262

Directive 1999/101 of 15 December 1999 adapting to technical progress Council Directive 70/157/EEC relating to the permissible sound level and the exhaust system of motor vehicles, [1999] OJ L 334/41 235

Directive 2000/14 of 8 May 2000 on the approximation of the laws of the Member States relating to the noise emission in the environment by equipment for use outdoors, [2000] OJ L 162/1 238

Directive 2000/60 of 23 October 2000 establishing a framework for Community action in the field of water policy, [2000], OJ L 327/1 .... 18, 27, 93

Directive 2000/69 of 16 November 2000 relating to limit values for benzene and carbon monoxide in ambient air, [2000] OJ L 313/12 ... 242

Directive 2001/18/EC of 12 March 2001 on the deliberate release into the environment of genetically modified organisms, [2001] OJ L 106/1 .... 58, 62, 300

Directive 2001/37/EC on the approximation of the laws, regulations and administrative provisions of the Member States concerning the manufacture, presentation and sale of tobacco, [2001] OJ L 194/26 60

Directive 2001/42 of 27 June 2001 on the assessment of the effects of certain plans and programmes on the environment [2001] OJ L 197/30 .... 27, 93, 144, 145

Directive 2001/77/EC of the European Parliament and of the Council of 27 September 2001 on the promotion of electricity produced from renewable energy sources in the internal electricity market, [2001] OJ L 283/33 320

Directive 2001/83/EC of 6 November 2001 on the Community code relating to medicinal products for human use, [2001] OJ L 311/67 224

Directive 2001/813 October 2001 on national emission ceilings for certain atmospheric pollutants, [2001] OJ L 309/22 246

Directive 2002/3 of 12 February 2002 relating to ozone in ambient air, [2002] OJ L 67/14 242

Directive 2002/30 on the establishment of rules and procedures with regard to the introduction of noise-related operating restrictions at Community airports, [2002] OJ L 85/40 58

Directive 2002/49 of 25 June 2002 relating to the assessment and management of environmental noise – Declaration by the Commission in the Conciliation Committee on the Directive relating to the assessment and management of environmental noise, [2002] OJ L 189/12 231

Directive 2003/4/EC of 28 January 2003 on public access to environmental information and repealing Council Directive 90/313/EEC, [2003] OJ L 41/26 .... 53, 81, 82

Directive 2003/10 of 6 February 2003 on the minimum health and safety requirements regarding the exposure of workers to the risks arising from physical agents (noise) (Seventeenth individual Directive within the meaning of Article 16(1) of Directive 89/391/EEC), [2003] OJ L 42/38 and repealing Directive 86/188 of 12 May 1986 on the protection of workers from the risks related to exposure to noise at work, [1986] OJ L 137/28 237

Directive 2003/35/EC of 26 May 2003 providing for public participation in respect of the drawing up of certain plans and programmes relating to the environment and amending with regard to public participation and access to justice Council Directives 85/337/EEC and 96/61/EC,[2003] OJ L 156/17. 82

Directive 2003/87 of 13 October 2003 establishing a scheme for greenhouse gas emission allowance trading within the Community and amending Directive 96/61, [2003] OJ L 275/32 257

Directive 2003/96 restructuring the Community framework for the taxation of energy products and electricity, [2003] OJ L 283/5158, 164

Directive 2003/98 on the re-use of public sector information, [2003] OJ L 345/90 83

Directive 2004/17 coordinating the procurement procedures of entities operating in the water, energy, transport and postal services sectors, OJ [2004] L134/1 128

Directive 2004/18 on the coordination of procedures for the award of public works contracts, public supply contracts and public service contracts, [2004] OJ L 134/114 128

Directive 2004/26 of 21 April 2004 amending Directive 97/68 on the approximation of the laws of the Member States relating to measures against the emission of gaseous and particulate pollutants from internal combustion engines to be installed in non- road mobile machinery, [2004] OJ L 146/1 263

Directive 2004/35 on environmental liability with regard to the prevention and remedying of environmental damage, [2004] OJ L 143/56 .... 18, 150

Directive 2004/42 of 21 April 2004 on the limitation of emissions of volatile organic compounds due to the use of organic solvents in certain paints and varnishes and vehicle refinishing products and amending Directive 1999/13, [2004] OJ L 143/87 252

Directive 2004/107 of 15 December 2004 relating to arsenic, cadmium, mercury, nickel and polycyclic aromatic hydrocarbons in ambient air, [2005] OJ L 23/3 .... 243, 246

Directive 2005/29 concerning unfair business-to- consumer commercial practices in the internal market, [2005] OJ L 149/22 119

Directive 2006/7/EC of 15 February 2006 concerning the management of bathing water quality and repealing Directive 76/160/EEC, [2006] OJ L 64/37 225

Directive 2006/21 on the management of waste from extractive industries and amending Directive 2004/35, [2006] OJ L 102/15 155

Directive 2006/93 of 12 December 2006 on the regulation of the operation of aeroplanes covered by Part II, Chapter 3, Volume 1 of Annex 16 to the Convention on International Civil Aviation, second edition (1988), [2006] OJ L 374/1 241

Directive 2006/118/EC of the European Parliament and of the Council of 12 December 2006 on the protection of groundwater against pollution and deterioration, [2006] OJ L 372/19 227

Directive 2007/2 establishing an Infrastructure for Spatial Information in the European Community, [2007] OJL 108/1 83

Directive 2007/34/EC of 14 June 2007 amending, for the purposes of its adaptation to technical progress, Council Directive 70/157/EEC concerning the permissible sound level and the exhaust system of motor vehicles, [2007] OJ L 155/49 234

Directive 2007/60 of 23 October 2007 on the assessment and management

of flood risks, [2007] OJ L 288/27 221
Directive 2008/50 of 21 May 2008 on ambient air quality and cleaner air for Europe, [2008] OJ L 152/1 242
Directive 2008/56 of 17 June 2008 establishing a framework for community action in the field of marine environmental policy, [2008] OJ L 164/19 229
Directive 2008/52 on certain aspects of mediation in civil and commercial matters, [2008] OJ L 136/3 81
Directive 2008/99/EC of 19 November 2008 on the protection of the environment through criminal law, [2008] OJ L 328, 6.12.2008, pp. 28–37 157
Directive 2008/101 of 19 November 2008 amending Directive 2003/87 so as to include aviation activities in the scheme for greenhouse gas emission allowance trading within the Community, [2009] OJ L 8/3 .. 259
Directive 2009/28 of 23 April 2009 on the promotion of the use of energy from renewable sources and amending and subsequently repealing Directives 2001/77 and 2003/30, [2009] OJ L 140/16. .... 256, 322
Directive 2009/29 of 23 April 2009 amending Directive 2003/87 so as to improve and extend the greenhouse gas emission allowance trading scheme of the Community, [2009] OJ L 140/63. 258
Directive 2009/31 on the geological storage of carbon dioxide, [2009] OJ L 140/114................................. 155
Directive 2009/41/EC of 6 May 2009 on the contained use of genetically modified micro-organisms, [2009] OJ L 125/75 59
Directive 2009/54/EC of the European Parliament and of the Council of 18 June 2009 on the exploitation and marketing of natural mineral waters, [2009] OJ L 164/45 224
Directive 2009/63 of 13 July 2009 on certain parts and characteristics of wheeled agricultural or forestry tractors, [2009] OJ L 214/23......... 236
Directive 2009/76 of 13 July 2009 relating to the driver- perceived noise level of wheeled agricultural or forestry tractors, [2009] OJ L 201/18... 236
Directive 2009/81 on the coordination of procedures for the award of certain works contracts, supply contracts and service contracts by contracting authorities or entities in the fields of defence and security, and amending Directives 2004/17/EC and 2004/18/EC, [2009] OJ L 216/76 . 128
Directive 2009/147 on the conservation of wild birds [2010] OJ L 20/7 153
Directive 2010/30 on the indication by labelling and standard product information of the consumption of energy and other resources by energy-related products, [2010] OJ L 153/1 .... 60, 123
Directive 2010/31 on the energy performance of buildings, [2010] OJ L 153/13 .... 60, 256
Directive 2010/75 on industrial emissions (integrated pollution prevention and control), [2010] OJ L 334/1 723, 54, 92, 112, 228, 256, 267
Directive 2011/92 on the assessment of the effects of certain public and private projects on the environment, [2012] OJ L 26/1 .... 54, 92, 130
Directive 2012/13 of 4 July 2012 on waste electrical and electronic equipment [2012] OJ L 197/38....... 27
Directive 2012/18 on the control of major-accident hazards involving dangerous substances, amending and subsequently repealing Council Directive 96/82/EC, [2012] OJ L 197/1 54
Directive 2012/27 of 25 October 2012 on energy efficiency, amending Directives 2009/125 and 2010/30 and repealing Directives 2004/8 and 2006/32, [2012] OJ L 315/1 ... 256
Directive 2012/33 of 21 November 2012 amending Council Directive

1999/32 as regards the sulphur content of marine fuels, [2012] OJ L 327/1 251

Directive 2013/30 on safety of offshore oil and gas operations and amending Directive 2004/35/EC, [2013] OJ L 178/66 155

Directive 2013/51/Euratom of 22 October 2013 laying down requirements for the protection of the health of the general public with regard to radioactive substances in water intended for human consumption, [2013] OJ L 296/12 .. 57

Directive 2014/25 of 26 February 2014 on procurement by entities operating in the water, energy, transport and postal services sectors and repealing Directive 2004/17, [2014] OJ L 94/243 127

Directive 2014/40 of 3 April 2014 on the approximation of the laws, regulations and administrative provisions of the Member States concerning the manufacture, presentation and sale of tobacco and related products and repealing Directive 2001/37/EC, [2014] OJ L 127/1 60

Directive 2014/52 of 16 April 2014 amending Directive 2011/92 on the assessment of the effects of certain public and private projects on the environment, [2014], OJ L 124/1 . 130

Directive 2015/412 of 11 March 2015 amending Directive 2001/18/EC as regards the possibility for the Member States to restrict or prohibit the cultivation of genetically modified organisms (GMOs) in their territory, [2015] OJ L 68/1 59

REGULATIONS

Regulation 1836/93 of 29 June 1993 allowing voluntary participation by companies in the industrial sector in a Community eco-management and audit scheme, [1993] OJ L 168/1 109

Regulation 258/97 concerning novel foods and novel food ingredients, [1997] OJ L 43/1 304

Regulation 1049/2001 regarding public access to European Parliament, Council and Commission documents, [2001] OJ L 145/43 82, 96

Regulation 178/2002 laying down the general principles and requirements of food law, establishing the European Food Safety Authority and laying down procedures in matters of food safety, [2002] OJ L 31/1 33

Regulation 1406/2002, OJ [2002] L 208/1 49

Regulation 1829/2003 of 22 September 2003 on genetically modified food and feed, [2003] OJ L 268/1 ... 58, 304

Regulation 1830/2003 concerning the traceability and labelling of genetically modified organisms and the traceability of food and feed products produced from genetically modified organisms, [2003] OJ L 268/24. 59, 299, 301, 305

Regulation No 65/2004 of 14 January 2004 establishing a system for the development and assignment of unique identifiers for genetically modified organisms, [2004] OJ L 10/5 304

Regulation 1013/2006 of 14 June 2006 on shipments of waste, [2006] OJ L 190/1 .... 23, 159

Regulation 1083/2006 of 11 July 2006 laying down general provisions on the European Regional Development Fund, the European Social Fund and the Cohesion Fund and repealing Regulation (EC) No 1260/1999, [2006], OJ L 210/25 ... 147

Regulation 1367/2006 on the application of the provisions of the Aarhus Convention on Access to Information, Public Participation in Decision-making and Access to Justice in Environmental Matters to Community institutions and bodies, [2006] OJ L 264/13 .... 54, 82, 104

Table of legislation

Regulation 1907/2006 of 18 December 2006 concerning the Registration, Evaluation, Authorisation and Restriction of Chemicals (REACH), establishing a European Chemicals Agency, [2009] OJ L 36/84 .... 49, 277

Regulation 614/2007 concerning the Financial Instrument for the Environment (LIFE+), [2007] OJ L 149/1 54

Regulation No 715/2007 of 20 June 2007 on type approval of motor vehicles with respect to emissions from light passenger and commercial vehicles (Euro 5 and Euro 6) and on access to vehicle repair and maintenance information, [2007] OJ L 171/1 249

Regulation No 216/2008 of 20 February 2008 on common rules in the field of civil aviation and establishing a European Aviation Safety Agency, and repealing Council Directive 91/670, Regulation No 1592/2002 and Directive 2004/36/EC, [2008] OJ L 79/1 240

Regulation No 1272/2008 of 16 December 2008 on classification, labelling and packaging of substances and mixtures, amending and repealing Directives 67/548 and 1999/45, and amending Regulation (EC) No 1907/2006, [2008] OJ L 353/1 290

Regulation 73/2009 of 19 January 2009 establishing common rules for direct support schemes for farmers under the common agricultural policy and establishing certain support schemes for farmers, amending Regulations 290/2005, 247/2006, 378/2007 and repealing Regulation 1782/2003, [2009] OJ L 30/16 211

Regulation 401/2009 on the European Environment Agency and the European Environment Information and Observation Network, [2009] OJ L126/13 .... 48, 54

Regulation No 443/2009 of 23 April 2009 setting emission performance standards for new passenger cars as part of the Community's integrated approach to reduce CO_2 emissions from light- duty vehicles, [2009] OJ L 140/1 .... 248, 261

Regulation No 595/2009 of 18 June 2009 on type- approval of motor vehicles and engines with respect to emissions from heavy duty vehicles (Euro VI) and on access to vehicle repair and maintenance information and amending Regulation No 715/2007 and Directive 2007/46 and repealing Directives 80/1269, 2005/55 and 2005/78, [2009] OJ L 188/1.. 250, 263

Regulation 1221/2009 on the voluntary participation by organisations in a Community eco-management and audit scheme (EMAS), repealing Regulation (EC) No 761/2001 and Commission Decisions 2001/681/EC and 2006/193/EC [2009] OJ L 342/1 .... 54, 108

Regulation No 1222/2009 of 25 November 2009 on the labelling of tyres with respect to fuel efficiency and other essential parameters, [2009] OJ L 342/46 262

Regulation 66/2010 on the EU Ecolabel, [2010] OJ L 27/1 ..... 54, 120

Regulation No 168/2013 of 15 January 2013 on the approval and market surveillance of two- or three- wheel vehicles and quadricycles, [2013] OJ L 60/52 236

Regulation (EU) No 182/2011 of 16 February 2011 laying down the rules and general principles concerning mechanisms for control by Member States of the Commission's exercise of implementing powers, [2011] OJ L 55/13 70

Regulation 304/2011 of 9 March 2011 concerning use of alien and locally absent species in aquaculture, [2011] OJ L 88/1 213

Regulation 566/2011 as regards access to vehicle repair and maintenance information, [2008] OJ L 199/1 36

Regulation 619/2011 of 24 June 2011 laying down the methods of sampling and analysis for the official control of feed as regards presence of genetically modified material for which an authorisation procedure is pending or the authorisation of which has expired, [2011] OJ L 166/9 304

Regulation 1169/2011 on the provision of food information to consumers, [2011] OJ L 304/18 58

Regulation No 459/2012 of 29 May 2012 amending Regulation No 715/2007 of Regulation No 692/2008 as regards emissions from light passenger and commercial vehicles (Euro 6), [2012] OJ L 142/16. 250

Regulation 528/2012 concerning the making available on the market and use of biocidal products, [2012] OJ L 167/1 .... 58, 295

Regulation No 601/2012 of 21 June 2012 on the monitoring and reporting of greenhouse gas emissions pursuant to Directive 2003/87, [2012] OJ L 181/30 258

Regulation No 598/2014 of 16 April 2014 on the establishment of rules and procedures with regard to the introduction of noise-related operating restrictions at Union airports within a Balanced Approach and repealing Directive 2002/30/ EC, [2014] OJ L 173/65 240

Regulation 1143/2014 on the prevention and management of the introduction and spread of invasive alien species, [2014] OJ L 317/35 214

1. Setting the context

I. HISTORY AND DEVELOPMENT

European environmental law has a long history.[1] At the founding stage of what we call today the European Union (EU), in the 1950s, environmental concerns were not on the agenda. Neither the European Coal and Steel Community Treaty (ECSC), nor the 1957 Treaty of Rome which established the European Economic Community (EEC) contained any policy or legal provisions directly related to the environment. The only notion which created an indirect link to the issue was contained in the preamble of the EEC Treaty stating that "the High Contracting Parties . . . affirm as the essential objective of their efforts the constant improvement of the living and working conditions of their peoples" (Recital 3 of the EEC Treaty).

"Living and working conditions" is a direct reference to public health and occupational health and safety (OHS) and a sign of the anthropocentric approach to environmental law which typifies its early development. Arguably, environmental awareness at the international and European level generally started in the 1970s, when people around the world realised that economic growth and environmental concerns are closely interlinked. Consequently a wave of actions, policies and legislation emerged. A pivotal moment was the publication of the Club of Rome's *Limits to Growth* in 1972.[2] An important milestone in the (international) history of environmental law was the United Nations Conference on the Human Environment (the Stockholm Conference) in 1972 and, as a result, the

---

[1] A synopsis of the history of European environmental law is also provided by C. Hey, "EU Environmental Policies: A short history of the policy strategies", in European Environmental Bureau, *EU Environmental Policy Handbook*, 18–30, available at http://www.eeb.org/publication/chapter-3.pdf. For a detailed analysis of the history of European law please refer to the contributions in P. Craig and G. de Búrca (eds), *The Evolution of EU Law*, Oxford: Oxford University Press, 2011.

[2] D.H. Meadows, D.L. Meadows, J. Randers and W.W. Behrens III, *Limits to Growth*, New York: New American Library, 1972.

creation of the United Nations Environment Programme (UNEP), as well as the Stockholm Declaration.[3]

The process of realising the relevance of environmental concerns started with the European institutions announcing the need for an environmental action programme. This announcement by the European Commission in 1970, suggested that a programme was needed for the "protection and improvement of the environment". The Commission called for "the power to issue provisions governing these [environmental] matters which would be directly applicable in each Member State and which, once adopted, would supersede the existing national provisions or fill gaps in national legislation".[4]

The "programme of action" was formally adopted in 1973 as a joint declaration of the Council and the Commission.[5] Despite its non-binding character, it laid the foundation for the environmental law and policy to come.

Not having a special legal basis for environmental measures, Article 235 EEC (the at that time Article on "implied powers") and Article 100a (legislation necessary for the realisation of what was then called the Common Market (later: "internal market")) served to fulfil this purpose. An important milestone was the introduction of a legal basis on the environment into the EEC Treaty by the Single European Act in 1986. From that time, Environmental Title VII, Articles 130r to 130t formed the explicit legal basis for environmental law. However, for the provisions on the internal market in Article 100a, majority voting was necessary following the Single European Act. Unanimous voting was required under the environmental title (see also Chapter 3 V on decision-making). This difference goes some way to explaining the tendency to keep on introducing legislation on the environment under the internal market provisions of the Treaty, even after a specific Environment Title was introduced.

The Maastricht Treaty (the Treaty on European Union; TEU) in 1992 renamed the EEC Treaty to the "Treaty on the European Community", or the European Community Treaty (ECT). It introduced qualified majority voting in environmental matters in Article 130r ECT as a general rule. Measures of a fiscal nature, as well as measures affecting town and country planning and some aspects of land use, as well as measures

---

[3] Declaration of the United Nations Conference on the Human Environment, U.N. Doc. A/Conf.48/14/Rev. 1 (1973); 11 I.L.M. 1416 (1972).
[4] European Commission, First communication of the Commission about the Community's policy on the environment, 22 July 1971, SEC (71) 2616.
[5] Declaration of 22 November 1973 on the programme of action of the European Communities on the environment, [1973] OJ C 112/1.

relating to energy security and sources were still subject to unanimous voting under Article 130s ECT.

The Maastricht Treaty also promoted environmental objectives to the level of the overall objectives of the Community (now Union), in particular by including a reference to the environment in Articles 2 (promotion of "a sustainable and non-inflationary growth respecting the environment") and Article 3k (establishment of a stand-alone policy area "in the sphere of the environment"). This change promoted the environment as a "key priority" into the Union's objectives and recognised for the first time the need for an integrated, horizontal environmental policy throughout the Union, as well as the need for sustainable growth. The introduction of the "environmental guarantee" and the inclusion of the precautionary principle stresses this interpretation.[6] Further, the role of the European Parliament was strengthened through the inclusion of the co-decision procedure (see Chapter 3 V).

The introduction of the Amsterdam Treaty in 1997 can be considered a second milestone in the history and development of European environmental law.[7] The principle of sustainable development, already implicitly present in The Maastricht Treaty, was made a Union objective, in the same way as the principle of a high level of environmental protection (Article 2 ECT), which now had a "constitutional status" under European law. Union environmental legislation from Amsterdam onwards was now subject to an improved co-decision-making procedure. Further, the environmental guarantee in Article 100a was enhanced, even if no "right to a protection of the environment" was established (it does exist in some Member States, as further discussed below in Chapter 1 IV C). Additional improvements were the promotion of the integration principle to a general European law principle and the horizontal application of the subsidiarity and proportionality principles with regard to environmental aspects in decision making. The Treaty renumbered Articles 130r–130s ECT to Articles 174–176 ECT.

The subsequent 2001 Treaty of Nice, introduced only minor changes to Article 175.

The most important change in the environmental area in the Lisbon Treaty in 2007 was the introduction of a separate legal basis on energy issues. Energy was formerly addressed by the provisions of the internal market (Article 114 Treaty on the Functioning of the European Union

---

[6] As further discussed below in Chapter 1 IV C.
[7] See also G. Van Calster and K. Deketelaere, "Amsterdam, the IGC and greening the EU Treaty", 7 *European Environmental Law Review*, 1 (1998), 12–25.

(TFEU)), competition or under the environmental title. Article 194 TFEU has now introduced a separate legal basis. Under Article 194, energy policy needs to be developed having "regard for the need to preserve and improve the environment". Additionally, Article 191(1) TFEU now includes an explicit reference to climate change in the objectives of environmental policy, even if this is a rather cosmetic change: the environmental legal basis has been frequently used as a basis for climate change legislation in the past. Further changes under Lisbon are the new Article 4(2)(e) TEU which lists "environment" under the area as a shared competence and recognises in Article 13 TFEU (formerly adopted as a Protocol to Amsterdam Treaty) animal welfare as an area of Union concern. Regarding public participation, Article 11(4) TEU establishes the possibility for European citizens to invite the Commission to submit a legislative proposal.[8]

To conclude, the area of European environmental law and policy emerged over the years from an area of "no interest" to one of the key areas of EU law, having cross-cutting horizontal effects to other policy areas.

II. SOURCES OF EUROPEAN ENVIRONMENTAL LAW

The EU legal order is complex. The Union has its own legal personality and is itself an actor under international law and thus bound by treaties and conventions to which it is a party (see Article 216(2) TFEU). Further, the EU has its own body of law.[9]

Firstly, *primary* EU law consists of the laws written down in treaties (for example the Treaty on European Union, the Treaty on the Functioning of the European Union and the Charter of Fundamental Rights of the European Union) and the general principles of EU law (for example Supremacy and the Principle of Direct Effect, further discussed in Chapter 4 II).

Secondly, the European institutions may subsequently create legislation on the basis of and under the conditions (including voting majorities etc.) provided for in primary law. Such legislation is called *secondary law*.

---

[8] See also on the "citizen's initiative", M. Lee, "The Environmental Implications of the Lisbon Treaty", 10 *Environmental Law Review* 2 (2008), 131–138, at 135.

[9] See for the different sources of EU law and their hierarchy, K. Lenaerts and P. Van Nuffel, *European Union Law*, London: Sweet & Maxwell, 2013, 817ff.

There are two groups of secondary legislation. The first group consists of the binding acts which are listed in Article 288 TFEU, namely regulations, directives and decisions, as well as recommendations and opinions. Included in the second group of non-binding instruments, which are not listed under Article 288 TFEU, are declarations, resolutions and communications of the European institutions, as well as other actions and acts of these Institutions. Even though they are not binding, they are often used by the courts in interpreting Union law and thus have a strong moral value. All instruments are further explained in Chapter 4 I.

A third source of European environmental law is the *case law of the European Court of Justice* (ECJ).[10] The judgments on the interpretation or validity of Union law are applicable *ex tunc* (from the outset) and *erga omnes* (binding for everyone). The position of ECJ case law within the European legal order is ambiguous. On the one hand it cannot be seen as being at the same level as secondary law, since it can interpret the latter. On the other hand the ECJ does not have the competence to assess the validity of primary law, hence it is not quite equal to primary law.

Fourthly, the obligations arising under international law prevail over Union secondary legislation.[11]

It is noteworthy that the internal division of competence between the EU and the Member States extends to the international stage:[12] the Union has the exclusive competence to negotiate and conclude international agreements. Mixed agreements are those where the Union and the Member States have joint competence. Article 191(4) TFEU explicitly specifies that, taking into account the division of competences, the Union and the Member States "shall cooperate with third countries and with the competent international organizations". The need for international

---

[10] Since the Treaty of Lisbon, some confusion has crept in on the exact acronym for the European Courts. The "Court of Justice of the European Union" (CJEU) is the collective term for the EU's judicial arm (see Article 19 TEU), consisting of three separate courts. The predominant court of relevance of questions of EU private international law is the Court of Justice (CJ), formerly known as the European Court of Justice (ECJ). Most, if not all, of the relevant cases reach the CJEU via the preliminary review procedure (leading national courts to ask "Luxembourg" (where the Court is based) for its authoritative view on a matter of interpretation). It would seem that while "CJ" would be the most correct form of reference [see also Francis Jacobs in the House of Lords' Select Committee on the EU, http://www.publications.parliament.uk/pa/ld201011/ldselect/ldeucom/128/12805.htm#n8 (para 9)], common form is to continue using "ECJ". Which is what we decided to do in current volume.
[11] Case C-344/04 *IATA and ELFAA* [2006] ECR I-403.
[12] Referred to as the *in fori interno in fori externo* principle.

cooperation in the area of environmental law is therefore explicitly recognised in the Treaty.

In areas of shared competence, Member States' and the Union's rights and duties arising under an international treaty are detached from each other. Only when secondary legislation transposing the international legislation exists does the Commission enforce the convention and, consequently, the Member States are bound to comply with this legislation. If the convention is only declared by a Council decision, and not transposed into EU secondary law, the convention is not directly binding on the Member States. However, they do have the option to adhere to the convention themselves and transpose it into national law.[13]

Finally, a newer source of EU environmental law are the Environmental Action Programmes. The first five action programmes, from a legal point of view, were mere political statements, even though they were always considered an important basis for environmental policymaking. However, the Maastricht Treaty created a Treaty basis for the adoption of action programmes (Article 130s(3)). In Article 192(3) TFEU the Lisbon Treaty finally included that general action programmes "setting out priority objectives to be attained" are to be adopted by the European Parliament and the Council, following a Commission proposal by the ordinary legislative procedure. Thus, starting from the 7th Environmental Action Programme these have been adopted as formal legal acts. The action programmes commonly establish mid-term and long-term goals and create synergies with other long-term strategies of European environmental law. The implementation measures to achieve the goals outlined in the action programmes are adopted independently. It is fair to say that one cannot find additional hard "law" in the programmes.

III. HEADS OF POWER OR "COMPETENCES"

"Heads of power" is translated in EU jargon as "competences" or "competencies". There are generally three categories of competence in the EU: exclusive, non-exclusive and supportive.[14] In accordance with

---

[13] For the relationship between international law and European law please refer to K. Lenaerts and P. Van Nuffel, *European Union Law*, London; Sweet & Maxwell, 2013, 861ff, as well as G. De Baere, *Constitutional Principles of EU External Relations*, Oxford: Oxford University Press, 2008.

[14] See also K. Lenaerts and P. Van Nuffel, *European Union Law*, London: Sweet & Maxwell, 2013, 124ff.

Article 2(1) TFEU, if the Union has exclusive competence in a specific area, "only the Union may legislate and adopt legally binding acts, the Member States [are] able to do so themselves only if so empowered by the Union or for the implementation of Union acts".

Member States therefore are not allowed to adopt legislation in these areas, even if they go beyond the measures taken by the Union. Regarding the area of the environment, the Union only has exclusive competence to regulate the conservation of marine biological resources under the common fisheries policy (Article 3(1)(d) TFEU). By contrast, in the area of a shared competence,

> the Union and the Member States may legislate and adopt legally binding acts in that area. The Member States shall exercise their competence to the extent that the Union has not exercised its competence. The Member States shall again exercise their competence to the extent that the Union has decided to cease exercising its competence. (Article 2(2) TFEU)

Three fundamental principles are crucial in determining the division of competences between the Union and the Member States: the principles of subsidiarity (Article 5(3) TEU) and proportionality (Article 5(4) TEU; these principles are further discussed in Chapter 2) as well as the principle of attributed powers or "conferral" (Article 5(2) TEU and Article 4(1) TEU), meaning that only the EU has those powers which have been expressly attributed to it. The principal of conferral establishes whether an EU competence exists at all.[15] The principles of subsidiarity and proportionality determine the extent to which the Union can exercise the competence (see Article 5(1) TEU).

Article 4(2)(e) TFEU includes "environment" (as well as "energy" under Article 4(2)(i) TFEU) as an area of shared competence. Hence with deference to the subsidiarity and proportionality principle, the institutions have to justify why an environmental matter is better regulated on a Union wide basis rather than at a national level (for a detailed explanation see Chapter 1 III).

Further, the Union has a supportive competence to carry out actions, as well as support, coordinate or supplement the actions of the Member States amongst others in the area of protection and improvement of human health (Article 6(a) TFEU).

For legislation based on Article 192 TFEU, Article 193 TFEU opens up the possibility for Member States to introduce more stringent measures.

---

[15] For in-depth discussion please refer to K. Lenaerts and P. Van Nuffel, *European Union Law*, London: Sweet & Maxwell, 2013, 112ff.

This is referred to as the environmental guarantee under the environmental title. A similar provision is included in the internal market provisions (Article 114 TFEU), as discussed in Chapter 3 III.

IV. OBJECTIVES OF THE EU'S ENVIRONMENTAL POLICY

Article 3 TEU establishes the overall objectives and aims of the EU. The third paragraph contains several references regarding the environment: "[The Union] shall work for the sustainable development of Europe . . . and a high level of protection and improvement of the quality of the environment." Accordingly, the Union's overall objectives in the area of the environment are threefold: sustainable development; a high level of protection; and improvement of the quality of the environment.

The preamble of the TEU underlines this intention "taking into account the principle of sustainable development . . . and environmental protection". However, there is no further reference in the Treaty of what specifically these objectives entail. There is neither definition nor specification for either "sustainable development and high level protection" or "quality of the environment". Nor is there a definition of the "environment" itself. The overall aims are further supplemented and specified by the provisions of Article 191 TFEU. Article 191(1) lists the following objectives for environmental policy making:

a) *preserving, protecting and improving the quality of the environment*,
b) protecting *human health*,
c) prudent and *rational utilisation of natural resources*,
d) promoting measures at *international level* to deal with regional or worldwide environmental problems, and in particular combating *climate change*. (Emphasis added)

The second paragraph further specifies that "Union policy on the environment shall aim at a high level of protection taking into account the diversity of situations in the various regions of the Union".

The objectives under Article 191 are not listed in hierarchical order; they are equally important. This is further underlined by Article 11 TFEU, which requires the integration and promotion of environmental protection requirements and sustainable development into the definition and implementation of all Union policies and activities. Notwithstanding the inclusion of the protection of human health as a focal point for EU environmental policy, Article 191 clearly indicates that the policy is not purely anthropocentric. Moreover, the reference to prudent and rational utilisation of natural resources also indicates the immediate link with energy policy.

Article 191(3) specifies the criteria which have to be "taken into account" in environmental law making:

- available scientific and technical data,
- environmental conditions in the various regions of the Union,
- the potential benefits and costs of action or lack of action,
- the economic and social development of the Union as a whole and the balanced development of its regions.

There are many indications in Article 191 which prima facie may suggest the proscribed use of "best available technique" (BAT; see more in Chapter 6 II). However, in reality not all, indeed very little, EU environmental law imposes the duty to employ whatever best technology is available on the market, regardless of cost. While the precautionary principle (further discussed in Chapter 2 IV) supports the use of BATs, other principles pull it in another direction. In particular, the many bells and whistles surrounding the principle of a high level of environmental protection lead to BATNEEC (best available technology not entailing excessive costs) rather than BAT being the standard reference in many European environmental laws. Moreover, the very principle of sustainable development aims to balance environmental, economical and social development.

In contrast with, for instance, the provisions on the internal market where "quantitative restrictions on imports [and exports] and all measures having equivalent effect shall be *prohibited*" (emphasis added) (Article 34, [35] TFEU), the environmental title does not contain an explicit prohibition of environmental pollution. Hence, unlike in the internal market area, the environmental objectives cannot be enforced in and of themselves on grounds of the Treaty basis. They require transposition and elaboration using secondary law to become enforceable. This interpretation is supported by the notion that "proposals" (employed in Article 114) refers to specific measures, not, as in Article 191, to "policy" as a whole.

A. Sustainable Development as a Union Objective

The first objective listed under Article 3 TEU is the achievement of sustainable development. Its introduction into the Amsterdam Treaty in 1999 was a milestone in European environmental law-making. It is further strengthened in the 7th indent of the Preamble to the TEU: "Determined to promote economic and social progress for their peoples, taking into account the principle of sustainable development and within the context of the accomplishment of the internal market . . ."

The principle and its importance are further strengthened in Article 191 and in the integration principle in Article 11 TFEU.

However, as for most key concepts and terms of European environmental law, no definition of sustainable development is provided in primary law. Nor do the various strategies on sustainable development contain a specific overarching definition.[16] As a consequence the legal operation and enforceability of the principle can be questioned (for a discussion of the principle of sustainable development see also Chapter 2 III). This remains the case even if one can assume that the integration of sustainable development in the EU's objectives is directly linked to the developments in international environmental law (the Rio Conference and its aftermath), where the concept and its consequences have arguably been further clarified.

B. High Level of Environmental Protection

The second paragraph of Article 191 TFEU complements the aims by including a reference to the high level of protection.[17] However, much like Article 3 TEU, Article 191 TFEU does not define the various elements either. For example, there is no indication of what a "high level of protection" entails and how it can be achieved.[18] One possible way of determination is to look at the current long-term strategies and policy in the environmental area, such as at the Environmental Action Programmes, as discussed in Chapter 1 II. The 7th Union Environment Action Programme, for example, identifies amongst others the protection, conservation and enhancement of the Union's natural capital; as well

---

[16] For example the 2001 strategy, "A sustainable Europe for a better world: a European Union strategy for sustainable development", COM (2001) 264 or the 2009 review thereof (COM (2009) 400).

[17] For the nuances and discussion of the objective in the various areas of European environmental law please refer to the contributions in R. Macrory, *Reflections on 30 Years of EU Environmental Law: A High Level of Protection?*, The Avosetta Series 7, Groningen: Europa Law Publishing, 2006.

[18] For a more detailed discussion refer to D. Misonne, "The Importance of Setting a Target: The EU Ambition of a High Level of Protection", 4 *Transnational Environmental Law* 1 (2015), 11–36.

as changing the Union into a resource-efficient, green and competitive low-carbon economy as the objectives.[19]

Further, the ECJ held that a high level of environmental protection has to be balanced against economic interests.[20] Article 191 TFEU itself clearly indicates that the Union's quest for a high level of environmental protection is not imposed dogmatically. A variety of considerations in Article 191 indicate nuances in this principle.

First of all, Article 191 TFEU obliges the institutions to take the differing situations in the Union into account. On the one hand, from a technical point of view, Article 191(2) TFEU refers to the "environmental conditions in the various regions of the Union". Indeed, Member States' geography, even within one and the same State, differs to such an extent that it would not make sense to impose the same standards and rules upon all Member States. "Differing situations" within the Union may also be taken in a socio-economic meaning.

A second nuance of the high level of protection may be found in the reference to the "economic and social development of the Union as a whole and the balanced development of its regions". This consideration traditionally receives less attention in the European Commission's proposals; however, it invariably surfaces during Council discussions. This often triggers protest by observers and activists. It is, however, in line with the principles included in Article 191 TFEU.

The cost/benefit analysis prescribed by Article 191 TFEU has to be understood both in a technical (environmental) sense and from an economic point of view.

A practical example of the application of a high level of environmental protection objective are two rulings by the General Court regarding the "substances of very high concern" (SVHC) under the Registration, Evaluation, Authorisation and Restriction of Chemicals (REACH) Regulation.[21] In these judgments the court expanded the Commission's and European Chemicals Agency's (ECHA's) powers to include SVHCs on the candidate list which triggers additional information requirements. The Court found this to be in line with the Regulation's objective of a high level of environmental protection.[22]

---

[19] For the other objectives see also Article 1 of Decision No 1386/2013 of 20 November 2013 on a General Union Environment Action Programme to 2020 "Living well, within the limits of our planet", OJ L 354, 28.12.2013, at 171–200.
[20] Case C-343/09 *Afton Chemical* [2010] ECR I-7027.
[21] Case T-134/13 *Polynt and Sitre v ECHA*, ECLI:EU:T:2015:254, as well as case T-135/13 *Hitachi Chemical Europe and Others v ECHA*, ECLI:EU:T:2015:253.
[22] Case T-135/13, at 46 and 112, as well as Case T-134/13, at 46 and 106.

C. The Quality of the Environment and its Legislation

Any effort to increase the quality of legislation and, thus, the quality of the environment should of course be welcomed. Concrete means of a technical nature include a far-reaching duty of the Commission to report on the effectiveness of existing legislation; built-in reviews of the provisions; varying provisions over time; and so on. Reporting duties are widely used in the Union's environmental legislation, as are multi-annual programmes. The latter are used, for example, for emission standards, which remain valid for only a number of years (often five years). The legislation concerned then provides either for indicative values for the second and subsequent periods, or merely provides for new legislative initiatives to fill the gap after the initial period. This and other techniques prevents the Union from resting on its laurels, once legislation in a particular field has been issued.

D. The Right to the Protection of the Environment

In the past, some Member States tabled proposals to include a "right to a clean and healthy environment" in the Treaty. The Treaty does include some provisions with respect to fundamental rights and non-discrimination, including a procedure for action in the event of a breach by a Member State of the principles on which the Union is founded. However, so far, the Treaty does not contain a right to the protection of the environment. The calls for the inclusion of such right flounded on the confusion with which it is surrounded. Comparative analysis shows that quite a number of Member States (Austria, Belgium, Finland, Germany, Greece, the Netherlands, Portugal, Spain) have a constitutional basis for environmental protection. This imposes a duty on the State to take regulatory action to protect and improve the environment. Whether such right has to be seen as a "human" or "fundamental" right with respect to the environment is far from certain.

The international discourse in this respect is confusing. Principle 1 of the Rio Declaration may be a good example of the difficulties surrounding the issue. Because so many States were represented at this Conference, the Rio proceedings do carry considerable weight in the debate. Principle 1 reads: "Human beings are at the centre of concerns for sustainable development. They are entitled to a healthy and productive life in harmony with nature." This is far less radical than what was stated in the Declaration of Stockholm: "Man has the fundamental right to freedom, equality and adequate conditions of life, in an environment of a quality that permits a life of dignity and well-being, and he bears a solemn responsibility to protect and improve the environment for present and future generations...."

One of the stumbling blocks for the recognition of a "human" or "fundamental" right for the protection of the environment is the condition that its contents be sufficiently precise (as with all other human rights). In other words, in order to sustain such a right, its content should be the same, regardless of the (historical and geographic) circumstances.

As for the environment, the situation is unclear: what sort of a fundamental right is it? Are we all entitled to a clean environment, or a healthy one, or one which generally suits human beings? How about the rights of the environment itself? Some activists claim that the concept of "human rights" and of "sustainable development" might be irreconcilable, in light of the essentially anthropocentric character of the former.

Some authors stress the fact that a right to environmental protection is self-enforcing. It could, for instance, accelerate the development of instruments such as environmental impact assessments, or access to justice. However valid this argument may be, in our view one should be careful not to confirm the existence of the human right itself, by arguing that it is self-enforcing.

E. Protecting Human Health

This objective refers to human health only and not to animal health. Interestingly, Article 13 TFEU on animal welfare states that animals are sentient beings and that animal welfare requirements have to be taken into account to the policies on "agriculture, fisheries, transport, internal market, research and technological development and space"; it does not list environmental policy. Whilst one may argue that animal health and animal welfare are included under the broad interpretation of the word "environment" and thus need to be respected in environmental policy objectives, the case remains that animal welfare legislation in the EU tends to be adopted under the agriculture title of the Treaty.

F. Promoting Measures at International Level to Deal with Regional or Worldwide Environmental Problems, and in Particular Combating Climate Change

This objective was included in the Maastricht Treaty and establishes that the environment is not limited to Union territory but expands to the international level to deal with transboundary, regional and worldwide environmental problems. The reference to climate change was integrated into the provision after Lisbon and emphasises the Union's strong belief that it may take the necessary measures to deal with this international concern. The competences of the Union at the international level are described in Chapter 1 III.

PART I

Basics/framework of European environmental law

2. Principles of European environmental law

Legal principles and scholarship on this subject have a long history. A multitude of definitions and theories have been put forward over the years. Legal philosophers such as Ronald Dworkin[1] and Robert Alexy[2] have written extensively on legal rules and principles. It is generally accepted that a rule does not contain legal value.[3]

European environmental law principles may not have practical legal force in and of themselves.[4] They are transposed into secondary law.[5] It is their (incorrect) application and interpretation in conjunction with secondary law that gives rise to citizens and corporations calling upon the principles to support their individual positions. Hence despite their trumpeted value as "principles", in the law in practice, individual citizens or corporations need transposition of said principles in secondary law to argue that such secondary law has infringed the principles.

A clear application of this reality is the recent ECJ judgment in Case C-534/13, a case with an impossibly long series of applicants and defendants.[6] The main issue that arose was whether national (Italian) legislation, under which no provision is made for the authorities to require owners of polluted land who have not contributed to that pollution to

---

[1] R. Dworkin, *Taking Rights Seriously*, Cambridge, MA: Harvard University Press, 1977.

[2] R. Alexy, "Zum Begriff des Rechtsprinzips", *Rechtstheorie – Beiheft 1 Argumentation und Hermeneutik in der Jurisprudenz*, Berlin: Duncker und Humblot, 1979 and R. Alexy, *Theorie der Grundrechte*, Suhrkamp, 1985.

[3] Winter, on the contrary, argues that principles are not operative in themselves and need to be transposed and implemented though specific tools or measures in order to become effective. He argues further that they help to interprete a legal norm and assess whether the norm is in general compatible with Union law. See: G. Winter, "The Legal Nature of Environmental Principles in International, EC and German Law", in: R. Macrory and I. Havercroft (eds), *Principles of European Environmental Law*, Groningen: Europa Law Publishing, 2004, at 13f.

[4] See the discussion of case law throughout this chapter, especially in relation to the precautionary principle.

[5] Winter, *supra* note 3 at 19.

[6] C-534/13 *Fipa Group and Others*, ECLI:EU:C:2015:140.

carry out preventive and remedial measures, and the sole obligation imposed concerns the reimbursement of the measures undertaken by those authorities, is compatible with the "polluter pays" principle, the precautionary principle and the principles that preventive action should be taken and that environmental damage should be rectified at source as a matter of priority. The ECJ emphasised the role of Directive 2004/35 in this context.[7] It held that the Directive does not hold against such absence, and in line with previous case law, it recalled that the environmental principles of the Treaty

> do no more than define the general environmental objectives of the European Union, since Article 192 TFEU confers on the European Parliament and the Council of the European Union, acting in accordance with the ordinary legislative procedure, responsibility for deciding what action is to be taken in order to attain those objectives... Consequently, since Article 191(2) TFEU, which establishes the "polluter pays" principle, is directed at action at EU level, that provision cannot be relied on as such by individuals in order to exclude the application of national legislation – such as that at issue in the main proceedings – in an area covered by environmental policy for which there is no EU legislation adopted on the basis of Article 192 TFEU that specifically covers the situation in question... Similarly, the competent environmental authorities cannot rely on Article 191(2) TFEU, in the absence of any national legal basis, for the purposes of imposing preventive and remedial measures... (at 39–41)

Of note, however, is that within specific secondary law even vague principles can take on quite a bite. For instance in the *BUND* case, the ECJ held that the Water Framework Directive[8]

> establishes common principles and an overall framework for action in relation to water protection and coordinates, integrates and, in a longer perspective, develops the overall principles and the structures for protection and sustainable use of water in the European Union. The common principles and overall framework for action which it lays down are to be developed subsequently by the Member States by means of the adoption of individual measures in accordance with the timescales laid down in the directive. (at 34)

In the area of European environmental law one can differentiate between general principles which also apply to the environment; specific

---

[7] Directive 2004/35 of 21 April 2004 on environmental liability with regard to the prevention and remedying of environmental damage, [2004] OJ L 143/56.

[8] Directive 2000/60 of 23 October 2000 establishing a framework for Community action in the field of water policy, [2000], OJ L 327/1.

environmental law principles; and, for both, between substantive and procedural principles.

General principles applicable to environmental matters are the subsidiarity and proportionality principles included in Article 5(3) TEU, as well as the integration principle in Article 11 TFEU and the principle of sustainable development referred to in Articles 3 and 5 TEU and 11 TFEU. Specific European environmental law principles are included in Article 191(2) TFEU. The Article reads:

> Union policy on the environment shall aim at a high level of protection taking into account the diversity of situations in the various regions of the Union. It shall be based on the precautionary principle and on the principles that preventive action should be taken, that environmental damage should as a priority be rectified at source and that the polluter should pay.

Hence, the following principles are included:

- The precautionary principle
- The prevention principle
- The rectification at source principle
- The polluter pays principle

The principles referred to above are substantive principles of environmental law,[9] meaning that they address the content of the legislation and policy. Procedural principles of environmental law, such as access to information, participation in decision-making and justice, will be further discussed in Chapter 5. Objectives of the EU's environmental policy have been discussed in Chapter 1.

I. SUBSIDIARITY AND PROPORTIONALITY

The subsidiarity principle[10] is included in Article 5(3) TEU and reads:

> Under the principle of subsidiarity, in areas which do not fall within its exclusive competence, the Union shall act only if and in so far as the objectives of the proposed action cannot be sufficiently achieved by the Member States, either at central level or at regional and local level, but can rather, by reason of the scale or effects of the proposed action, be better achieved at Union level.

---

[9] See for a detailed analysis also Macrory (ed.), *supra* note 3.
[10] For a detailed discussion of the role of the subsidiarity principle, the requirements and the application in European law please refer to K. Lenaerts and P. Van Nuffel, *European Union Law*, London: Sweet & Maxwell, 2013, 131–140.

The principle was originally introduced as a principle for environmental policy only. It was promoted under the Maastricht Treaty in Article 3b to become a general European law principle for determining the competences between Member States and the Union. That it is only applicable in the area of non-exclusive competences is imposed by Article 5 itself and is self-evident. For exclusive competences, there is no question of competing Member States competences needing to be balanced. The overall aim of the subsidiarity principle (originally a principle of political theory, in particular the division of responsibilities between the State and charitable organisations in social policy) is to determine the best level (national or European) at which to take a measure.

The Lisbon Treaty added a new reference to the central, regional or local level for proposed actions, thus emphasising the aim to determine measures at the best possible level of regulation, ensuring that these measures are as close as possible to the citizens.

The subsidiarity principle imposes two criteria which both have to be met for an action at the Union level to be justified. Firstly, the "objectives of the proposed action cannot be sufficiently achieved by [actions of] the Member States" and secondly and simultaneously, they can be better achieved at Union level "by reason of the scale or effects of the proposed action". A proposal of Union action in the area of the environment thus always has to justify why the intended action will be more effective if taken at the Union level and why actions at the national level are not sufficient to achieve a specific aim.

This is supported by the second paragraph of Article 5(3) TEU which refers to Protocol No. 2 to the TEU (originally adopted as Protocol No. 30 on the application of the Principles of Subsidiarity and Proportionality under the Amsterdam Treaty) and states that "The institutions of the Union shall apply the principle of subsidiarity as laid down in the Protocol on the application of the principles of subsidiarity and proportionality. National Parliaments ensure compliance with the principle of subsidiarity in accordance with the procedure set out in that Protocol."

Whilst the Treaty prescribes (and the Commission thoroughly prepares) an objective assessment of the various strands of the subsidiarity principle, the weighing and balancing of the impact of the principle for a given policy proposal arguably comes down to a political assessment. Member States need to be convinced, on the basis of the preparatory work, that Union action is warranted in the sector concerned. The exact decision-making process involving the national parliaments and the Union institutions is laid down in Articles 4 and 6 of the Protocol. Accordingly, since the Lisbon Treaty national parliaments play a core role in *ex ante* enforcement of the principle. Article 6 of the Protocol states that within eight weeks from the date of transmission of a draft legislative act, parliaments can send a reasoned opinion to the institutions involved in drafting the act, stating why they consider that the draft in question does not comply with the principle of subsidiarity. The institutions involved then have to review the draft piece of legislation and decide whether to maintain, amend or withdraw the act (Article 7(2) of the Protocol). This procedure is also referred to as the "yellow card procedure". If the proposal is maintained, the Commission forwards it together with a reasoned opinion to the EU legislator, which then has to decide according to a specific decision-making process laid out in Article 7(3)(a) and (b) of the Protocol (also referred to as the "orange card procedure"). Article 8 of the Protocol states further that the ECJ has jurisdiction in actions on grounds of infringement of the principle by a legislative act.

One popular example for the application of the subsidiarity principle and the debate between national parliaments and the Union institutions was the discussion whether an environmental liability regime should be implemented as a Union measure,[11] as well as the protracted (and now stalled) negotiations on an EU soil directive. As for environmental liability, action at the European level was eventually taken, after consensus that the EU was the right level of regulation from a subsidiarity point of view. This is in contrast, for instance, with local noise standards which were abandoned by the Commission following the 1992 Edinburgh Declaration on subsidiarity.

The principle of subsidiarity has to be read in conjunction with the principle of proportionality.[12] Paragraph 4 of Article 5 TEU states that "under the principle of proportionality, the content and form of Union action shall not exceed *what is necessary to achieve the objectives* of the Treaties" (emphasis added).

Thus, the proportionality principle determines the extent of EU action, once the subsidiarity test is met. The three underlying aspects are (a) the sustainability or appropriateness between the means and the end of a measure, (b) the necessity of the action to achieve the proposed Union objective (in the area of the environment the objectives under Article 191 TFEU) and (c) the proportionality of the measure itself (*stricto sensu*),

---

[11] See for example European Commission, "White paper on environmental liability", COM (2000) 66, as well as G. Van Calster and L. Reins, "The ELD's background", in: L. Bergkamp and B. Goldsmith (eds), *The EU Liability Directive*, Oxford: Oxford University Press, 2013, 9–30.

[12] For a detailed discussion of the role of the proportionality principle, the requirements and application in European law please see also K. Lenaerts and P. Van Nuffel, *European Union Law*, London: Sweet & Maxwell, 2013, 141–147.

meaning whether the measure is disproportionate in respect of the goal intended.[13]

According to Article 5 of the Protocol, the draft legislative act has to contain

> [an] assessment of the proposal's *financial impact* and, in the case of a directive, of its *implications for the rules* to be put in place by Member States, including, where necessary, the regional legislation. [Further drafts] shall take account of the need for any *burden*, whether financial or administrative, falling upon the Union, national governments, regional or local authorities, economic operators and citizens, to be *minimised and commensurate* with the objective to be achieved. (Emphasis added)

Thus, the Protocol, as well as the Treaty provision itself, establishes criteria which have to be met to fulfil the principle and against which Union action has to be balanced, and which include financial as well as normative requirements.

II. THE INTEGRATION PRINCIPLE

This principle was formally introduced under the environmental title (Article 130r and later 174 Treaty establishing the European Community (TEC)) of the Treaty and was subsequently promoted to Article 3d, later 6 TEC which is now Article 11 TFEU.

Article 11 TFEU states that: "Environmental protection requirements must be integrated into the definition and implementation of the Union's policies and activities, in particular with a view to promoting sustainable development."

The principle therefore requires that legislation in other policy areas be modified or amended in its substantive content in order to meet environmental protection requirements, where necessary.[14] The reference to "Union's policies and activities" aims at the different policy areas, namely agriculture, cohesion policy, development, economic recovery plan, employment, energy, enterprise, fisheries, internal market, research, trade and external relations, transport and economic and financial affairs.

---

[13] T.I. Harbo, "The Function of the Proportionality Principle in EU Law", 16 *European Law Journal*, 2 (2010), at 165.

[14] For a description of the origins and history of the integration principle please see L. Kraemer, "The Genesis of EC Environmental Principles", in: R. Macrory (ed.), *Principles of European Environmental Law*, The Avosetta Series 4, Groningen: Europa Law Publishing, 2004, 33–38.

These areas were identified in the Commission Communication on "A strategy for integrating environment into EU policies – Partnership for Integration"[15] in 1998 (also referred to as the Cardiff process).

There are two layers of integration.

First, there is the "narrow" or "vertical" interpretation of the principle, meaning that environmental law and policy have to be integrated. One example is the Directive concerning integrated pollution prevention and control[16] (IPPC Directive) which has now been recast as the Industrial Emissions Directive[17] and establishes one integrated permit for the environmental performance of a plant, taking into account all environmental aspects, and levels such as air and noise pollution, water and land use, waste generation and energy efficiency.

The second layer, the broad interpretation of the principle, is explicitly addressed in the Treaty provision: the integration and implementation of environmental requirements and objectives in to other (even "conflicting") areas, thus a "horizontal" integration into the sectors and areas mentioned above.

An early example of integration in the area of competition is the internal market integration strategy, adopted in 2001 (as subsequently reviewed), which increasingly also refers to environmental objectives.[18] The adoption of European legislation on public procurement, eco-labelling and eco-taxation are the result of the practical implementation of this strategy. In addition, any EU trade agreement is subject to a Sustainability Impact Assessment (SIA), which is carried out *ex ante* and assesses the economic, social and environmental implications of a trade negotiation.

The principle of integration aims at the integration of environmental aspects in both procedural and substantive law. Procedural integration is evident, for example in the abovementioned SIAs in order to promote environmental aspects in the area of trade, as well as the Environmental Impact Assessments (EIAs) which have to be carried out under the EIA Directive for certain projects (see Chapter 7). An example of integration into substantive legislation is the Regulation on shipments of waste[19]

---

[15] European Commission, "A strategy for integrating environment into EU policies – partnership for integration", COM (1998) 333.

[16] Directive 96/61 of 24 September 1996 concerning integrated pollution prevention and control, [1996] OJ L 257/26.

[17] Directive 2012/75 of 24 November 2010 on industrial emissions, [2010] OJ L334/17.

[18] See for example European Commission, "A single market for 21st century Europe", 20.11.2007, COM (2007) 724.

[19] Regulation 1013/2006 of 14 June 2006 on shipments of waste, [2006] OJ L190/1.

which includes legal rules in order to protect the environment with regard to trade measures.

The principle of environmental integration is incorporated in two further provisions of the Treaty, namely in Article 13 on animal welfare and Article 194 on energy. Further, in Article 37 the EU Charter on Fundamental Rights also contains a reference to the principle of integration similar to the provisions in Article 11 and 191 TFEU: "A high level of environmental protection and the improvement of the quality of the environment must be integrated into the policies of the Union and ensured in accordance with the principle of sustainable development."

III. SUSTAINABLE DEVELOPMENT

Sustainable development was initially an international law concept, addressed for the first time in the 1972 Stockholm Declaration on the Human Environment and formally introduced and defined in the 1987 Report of the World Commission of Environment and Development (WCED).[20] It was subsequently promoted in various international conventions, treaties and declarations, such as the UN Climate Change Convention, the Convention on Biological Diversity and the 1992 Rio Declaration on Environment and Development, where sustainable development was included as principle 4.

Sustainable development has been defined and interpreted in various ways. The definition provided in the Brundtland Report is one of the most important and often cited ones. There, sustainable development is defined as "development that meets the needs of the present without compromising the ability of future generations to meet their own needs". Much cited as it may be, this is a definition which despite its success is somewhat wanting, for it arguably does not sufficiently highlight the intra-generational element of sustainable development. That is, the need to ensure that various groups within the same generation equally enjoy access to the world's resources. Accordingly, environmental protection, economic development and social equity and equality are three sides of the same coin. The principle includes a social, an environmental, as well as an economic objective. It aims at both intra-generational (within a generation) and *inter*generational (amongst/between generations) justice.

---

[20] Often also referred to as the Brundtland Report.

At the European level, the principle of sustainable development[21] was originally introduced into the Treaties by the Amsterdam Treaty in 1997 in Articles 2, 3 and 6 ECT. It became not only a key principle but also an "overarching long-term goal of the EU".[22] The main provision on sustainable development is included in Article 11 TFEU. It reads: "Environmental protection requirements must be integrated into the definition and implementation of the Union's policies and activities, in particular with a view to promoting sustainable development."

The principle therefore is more than a European environmental law principle. It requires the integration of the concept into other policy areas. Further, being part of the integration principle (as discussed above), the principle is both a general and also a material or substantive law principle. The fact that it is included in several sections and titles in the TEU as well as in the TFEU acknowledges the requirement included in Article 11 TFEU but also stresses the outstanding character of the principle within the Union's policy and legal framework.

Firstly, it is included in the preamble to the TEU as well as in Articles 2(3) and (5) TEU. Paragraph 3 states:

> The Union shall establish an internal market. It shall work for the sustainable development of Europe based on balanced economic growth and price stability, a highly competitive social market economy, aiming at full employment and social progress, and a high level of protection and improvement of the quality of the environment. It shall promote scientific and technological advance.

This combines the idea of sustainable development with the internal market and stresses the economic aspect of the concept. This is further underlined by the reference to the concept in the economic and monitory policy area. Article 119(3) TFEU states that activities of the Member States and the Union in this area "shall entail compliance with the following guiding principles: stable prices, sound public finances and monetary conditions and a sustainable balance of payments".

Furthermore, paragraph 5 of Article 3 TEU adds that:

---

[21] For further reading on sustainable development and its status in the EU, please refer to M. Pallemaerts and A. Azmanova (eds), *European Union and Sustainable Development: Internal and External Dimensions*, Brussels: VUB Press, 2006, as well as P.M. Barnes and T.C. Hoerber (eds), *Sustainable Development and Governance in Europe: The Evolution of the Discourse on Sustainability*, London: Routledge, 2013.

[22] European Commission, "Mainstreaming sustainable development into EU policies: 2009 review of the European Union strategy for sustainable development", COM (2009) 400.

In its relations with the wider world, the Union shall uphold and promote its values and interests and contribute to the protection of its citizens. It shall contribute to peace, security, the sustainable development of the Earth, solidarity and mutual respect among peoples, free and fair trade, eradication of poverty and the protection of human rights, in particular the rights of the child, as well as to the strict observance and the development of international law, including respect for the principles of the United Nations Charter.

This paragraph stresses the social angle of the concept and underlines its "worldwide" dimension and the fact that it is not only a European concern and objective. This function is further expressed in Article 21 TEU on the Union's external action. Article 21 lays down guiding principles on which the Union's action on the international level shall be based, as well as the overall objectives pursued. These are amongst others to "foster the sustainable economic, social and environmental development of developing countries, with the primary aim of eradicating poverty" (Article 21(2)(d) TEU) and to "help develop international measures to preserve and improve the quality of the environment and the sustainable management of global natural resources, in order to ensure sustainable development" (Article 21(2)(f) TEU).

The principle thus contains a constitutional dimension through the requirement of integration into other policy areas, as well as an external dimension stressing the inclusion of sustainable development as foreign policy goals, especially in the areas of trade and development.

Despite its being omnipresent in primary law, the principle as such is not defined in the Treaty. The definition repeatedly used by the European institutions is indeed the one put forward in the Brundtland Report, as for example in the 2001 Strategy on Sustainable Development, in the reviewed 2009 version[23] and in the Draft Declaration on Guiding Principles for Sustainable Development.[24] However, interpretation and the exact definition might depend on the exact policy area and act of secondary legislation. The principle is frequently referred to in preambles of directives and in the subject matter, stressing that the aim of the specific legislation promotes or contributes to sustainable development. This is, for example, the case in the industry and waste policy area in the Waste Electrical and

---

[23] European Commission, "A sustainable Europe for a better world: a European Union strategy for sustainable development", 15.5.2001, COM (2001) 264, as well as Council of the European Union, "Review of the EU sustainable development strategy", Brussels, 9.6.2006, 10117/06.

[24] European Commission, "Draft Declaration on Guiding Principles for Sustainable Development", 25.5.2005, COM (2005) 658.

Electronic Equipment Directive,[25] in the area of water legislation, the Water Framework Directive[26] and regarding horizontal environmental law the Strategic Environmental Assessment Directive.[27] The absence of a definition in the Treaties raises the issue of the legal value of the principle. It is, without any reservation, of some legal importance; however, the precise content and role remains unclear and vague, which raises questions about the legal enforceability of the principle and might lead some to conclude that it is a policy action instrument, rather than a legal concept or principle.

An important non-binding instrument for interpretation and practical application of the sustainable development principle at the European level is the European Union Strategy for Sustainable Development originally published in 2001 and revised twice in 2006 and 2009.

The original strategy analyses the main threats to sustainable development and establishes an action plan to face these challenges. The 2006 renewal of the strategy reinforces the commitments to sustainable development and restructured the strategy to give it a stronger focus. It establishes detailed key objectives and policy guiding principles. It further identifies seven "key challenges and corresponding targets, operational objectives and actions", namely:

- Climate change and clean energy
- Sustainable transport
- Sustainable consumption and production
- Conservation and management of natural resources
- Public health
- Social inclusion, demography and migration
- Global poverty and sustainable development challenges

The 2009 revision specifically addresses the economic and financial crises which started in 2008 and adds another layer of difficulty to the concept. It calls for the European institutions to "turn the crisis into an opportunity to address financial and ecological sustainability".[28]

---

[25] Directive 2012/13 of 4 July 2012 on waste electrical and electronic equipment [2012] OJ L 197/38.
[26] Directive 2000/60 of 23 October 2000 establishing a framework for Community action in the field of water policy, [2000] OJ L 327/1.
[27] Directive 2001/42 of 27 June 2001 on the assessment of the effects of certain plans and programmes on the environment [2001] OJ L 197/30.
[28] European Commission, "Mainstreaming sustainable development into EU

IV. PRECAUTIONARY PRINCIPLE

Principle 15 of the Rio Declaration states: "In order to protect the environment, the precautionary approach shall be widely applied by States according to their capabilities. Where there are threats of serious or irreversible damage, lack of full scientific certainty shall not be used as a reason for postponing cost-effective measures to prevent environmental degradation."

The precautionary principle is not only a central principle in international law (albeit disputed at this level), but also in European environmental law.[29] At the international level, even if it is recognised by international agreements, such as the World Trade Organization (WTO) Agreement on Sanitary and Phytosanitary Measures (SPS Agreement), the principle arguably cannot be called an undisputed general principle of international law or international customary law as yet. At the EU level, its status is more definite. It is included in Article 191(2) TFEU and had its origin in the German legal system at the beginning of the 1980s as the *Vorsorgeprinzip*.[30] The principle was inserted into the Treaty of Maastricht. It is a legal tool used to achieve the environmental goals, especially to achieve a high level of environmental protection. There is no explicit definition of the principle given in the Treaty provisions itself, nor in secondary law; the main guidance and interpretation document in this regard is a soft law instrument, namely a Commission Communication from 2000.[31] It was designed to ease trade tensions with the United States[32] and is arguably the highest profile exercise of translating the principle into specific guidelines.[33]

The missing legal definition is presumably one reason for the ongoing

---

policies: 2009 review of the European Union strategy for sustainable development", 24.7.2009, COM (2009) 400.

[29] For a detailed discussion of the principle please refer to N. de Sadeleer, *Environmental Principles: From Political Slogans to Legal Rules*, Oxford: Oxford University Press, 2005, 91–223.

[30] For a description of the origins and history of the precautionary principle please see L. Kraemer, "The Genesis of EC Environmental Principles", in: R. Macrory (ed.), *Principles of European Environmental Law*, The Avosetta Series 4, Groningen: Europa Law Publishing, 2004, 38f.

[31] European Commission, "The precautionary principle", 2.2.2000, COM (2000) 1.

[32] See E. Fisher, "Precaution, Precaution Everywhere: Developing a 'Common Understanding' of the Precautionary Principle in the European Community", 9 *Maastricht Journal of European and Comparative Law*, 1 (2002), at 7–28.

[33] G. Van Calster, "The Law(s) of Sustainable Development". Available at SSRN: http://ssrn.com/abstract=1147544 or http://dx.doi.org/10.2139/ssrn.1147544, last consulted 21.11.2015.

debate which surrounds the principle and its application, even if the Commission states in its Communication that the absence of a definition does not lead to legal uncertainty. On the contrary, there it says that the "Community authorities' practical experience with the precautionary principle and its judicial review make it possible to get an ever-better handle on the precautionary principle."[34] And indeed, the principle has been applied by the European institutions, for example in the area of nanotechnology,[35] and by the European courts several times, and is further commonly applied in secondary law. The ECJ gave legal effect to the principle[36] and it has been expressly used in the area of health protection,[37] especially regarding food law. In *BSE*[38] (1996), although it expressly referred to the principle, the ECJ upheld the export ban on beef. The court held: "Where there is uncertainty as to the existence or extent of risks to human health, the institutions may take protective measures without having to wait until the reality and seriousness of those risks become fully apparent."[39] In *Bergaderm*,[40] the Court referred explicitly to the principle for the first time.

In *Pfizer*[41] the Court of First Instance (CFI; now the General Court) introduced some limitations to the application of the principle. It held:

> a preventive measure cannot properly be based on a purely hypothetical approach to the risk, founded on mere conjecture which has not been scientifically verified. Rather, it follows from the Community Courts' [now Union's

---

[34] COM (2000) 1, at 9.

[35] G. Van Calster, "Risk Regulation, EU Law and Emerging Technologies: Smother or smooth?", 2 *NanoEthics* 1 (2008), 61–71.

[36] For a detailed discussion of the ECJ case law in regard to the precautionary principle, see A. Alemanno, "The Shaping of the Precautionary Principle by European Courts", in: L. Cuocolo and L. Luparia (eds), *Valori Constituzionali e Nuove Politiche del Dritto*, Cahiers Europèens, Halley, 2007, at 11–24.

[37] de Sadeleer, *Environmental Principles: From Political Slogans to Legal Rules*, 119. One of the first cases on the precautionary principle addressed the prohibition of substances in foodstuff and the prohibition of imports of the latter on grounds of public health. See case ECJ, C-227/82 *Van Bennekom*, [1983] ECR I- 3883, at 37ff.

[38] ECJ, C-180/96 *United Kingdom v Commission*, [1998] EHR I-226.

[39] Ibid., paragraph 99.

[40] ECJ, Case C-353/98 *P Laboratoires pharmaceutiques Bergaderm a.o. v Commission* [2000] ECR 5291.

[41] T-13/99 *Pfizer Animal Health v Council*, [2002] ECR II-3305. For a detailed discussion of the case see G. Van Calster, "Note under case T-70/99, Alpharma Inc. v. Council of the European Union (Alpharma), 11 September 2002 and case T-13/99, Pfizer animal health SA v. Council of the European Union (Pfizer)", 12 *Review of European Community & International Environmental Law*, 1 (2003), 109–111.

Court] interpretation of the precautionary principle that a preventive measure may be taken only if the risk, although the reality and extent thereof have not been "fully" demonstrated by conclusive scientific evidence, appears nevertheless to be adequately backed up by the scientific data available at the time when the measure was taken.[42]

In *Commission v France* the ECJ further suggested

a correct application of the precautionary principle presupposes, first, identification of the potentially negative consequences for health of the proposed use of the substance at issue, and, secondly, a comprehensive assessment of the risk to health based on the most reliable scientific data available and the most recent results of international research. Where it proves to be impossible to determine with certainty the existence or extent of the alleged risk because of the insufficiency, inconclusiveness or imprecision of the results of studies conducted, but the likelihood of real harm to public health persists should the risk materialise, the precautionary principle justifies the adoption of restrictive measures, provided they are non-discriminatory and objective.[43]

Germany v Commission[44] dealt with the burden of proof under the precautionary principle. On 1 March 2012, the European Commission only partially (and temporarily) granted Germany approval for upholding stricter limits on maximum values for lead, barium, arsenic, antimony, mercury, nitrosamines and nitrosatable substances in toys. The ECJ stood with Germany only in its appeal against the European Community's (EC's) decision on values for lead: this decision was internally inconsistent (acknowledgement of higher public health protection in the German measures while at the same time an unfounded (and vague) limitation in time for those German measures). However, for all other substances, the ECJ rejected Germany's appeal. In doing so it emphasised the burden of proof which the precautionary principle implies (often misrepresented by opponents of the principle). The review of the available scientific evidence showed first of all the challenges associated with the different methods employed by Germany and the EC. The latter's measures employed migration limits (migration being the amount of toxic substances not just released from the product but effectively absorbed by the human body), while Germany's measures relied on bioavailability (the amount of chemical substances released from the product and available for human absorption, even if not all of the substances are necessarily effectively absorbed).

---

[42] *Pfizer*, paragraphs 143–144.
[43] ECJ, Case C-333/08 *Commission v France* [2010] ECR I-757, at 92 and 93.
[44] ECJ, Case T-198/12 *Germany v Commission*, ECLI:EU:T:2014:251

The ECJ allows Member States to have divergent opinions on risk compared to those of the EC; however, the Member State concerned needs to show that the national measures better protect human health and do so in a proportionate way. The crucial shortcoming in Germany's proof turned out to be that its exposure scenarios were, in the view of the ECJ, unrealistic (and not supported by further scientific reporting): they imply simultaneous exposure of a child to all possible toy safety directive scenarios: dry, brittle, powder-like or pliable toy material; *and* liquid or sticky toy material; *and* scraped-off toy material.

Criticism of the application of the principle in the EU often relates to the wide room for manoeuver institutions have in applying the principle. Representatives of this position got food for thought in *Gowan*.[45] The Commission relied on the precautionary principle as a justification for restrictions imposed on the use of fenarimol, regardless of a favourable assessment by the relevant committees and of a favourable draft proposal by the Commission. The Court found no "manifest error of assessment" of the Commission.[46]

Secondary law examples of the use of the principle are the inclusion of the principle in the Annex of the IPPC Directive with reference to BAT (see more in Chapter 6 II), the Water Framework Directive and in the area of food safety. For example, Article 7 of Regulation 178/2002[47] incorporates the precautionary principle as follows:

1. In specific circumstances where, following an assessment of available information, the possibility of harmful effects on health is identified but scientific uncertainty persists, provisional risk management measures necessary to ensure the high level of health protection chosen in the Community may be adopted, pending further scientific information for a more comprehensive risk assessment.
2. Measures adopted on the basis of paragraph 1 shall be proportionate and no more restrictive of trade than is required to achieve the high level of health protection chosen in the Community, regard being had to technical and economic feasibility and other factors regarded as legitimate in the matter under consideration. The measures shall be reviewed within a reasonable period of time, depending on the nature of the risk to life or health

---

[45] Case C-77/09 *Gowan Comércio Internacional e Serviços*, [2010] ECR I-13533.

[46] For a detailed discussion of the case see A. Alemanno, "Case C-79/09, Gowan Comércio Internacional e Serviços Lda v. Ministero della Salute, Judgment of the Court of Justice (Second Chamber) of 22 December 2010", 48 *Common Market Law Review* 4, 2011.

[47] Regulation 178/2002 laying down the general principles and requirements of food law, establishing the European Food Safety Authority and laying down procedures in matters of food safety, [2002] OJ L 31/1.

identified and the type of scientific information needed to clarify the scientific uncertainty and to conduct a more comprehensive risk assessment.

The precautionary principle therefore is a tool for risk assessment and management. The example above shows that in cases where scientific uncertainties remain after the assessment of an activity, the precautionary principle opens the door for risk managers and policymakers to take precautionary measures to reduce potential harm to health and the environment. The Commission Communication establishes conditions and limits for its application. Accordingly, an action under the precautionary principle is only justified if the following three conditions are met:[48]

- identification of potentially adverse effects,
- evaluation of the scientific data available, and
- evaluation of the extent of scientific uncertainty.

Once a measure is deemed necessary under the precautionary principle, the following six criteria[49] have to be met which limit and balance a precautionary action. They derive from the general principles of risk management.

Actions or measures have to be:

- *proportional* in order to achieve the appropriate level of protection. Thus it must generally not aim at zero risk, even if this might be required in some cases. Less restrictive alternatives shall be considered,
- *non-discriminatory*. Comparable situations shall not be treated differently and different situations not in the same way,
- *consistent* with measures adopted in similar circumstances or using similar approaches,
- *based on an examination of the benefits and costs of action or lack of action*, meaning that they have to be subject to an economic cost/benefit analysis and negative and positive consequences, and the overall cost has to be taken into account on a short- and long-term basis,
- *subject to examination of scientific developments*, taking into account the overall societal risks and review in the light of new scientific findings.

---

[48] COM (2000) 1, p. 13ff.
[49] Ibid., p. 17ff.

Only if all criteria are fulfilled is an action considered to be in line with the precautionary principle.

The EU and its Member States view risk analysis as a linear process, in which the various steps of a risk analysis process (risk identification, risk assessment, risk management and risk communication) are neatly divided. Importantly, the EU assigns the responsibility and the main lead in each of these steps to different professional groupings. Whilst the steps of risk identification, and certainly that of risk assessment, are the responsibility of scientists, the step of risk management is very firmly seen as a *political* step, in which elected politicians on both the national scene and the European scene take the lead. This preponderant role of politicians in risk management makes the process, so its critics say, prone to being susceptible to scaremongering, and to recourse to the precautionary principle. Hence it is more likely that the general outlook on life and risk is the determinant for the regulatory approach of these States, rather than their belief as to whether the precautionary principle as part of law is legally binding or not.[50]

Of note is the distinction obvious, at least in theory, between the precautionary and prevention principles. The prevention principle had already been introduced in 1987 through the Single European Act, thus before the precautionary principle. The precautionary principle applies to *potential* risks, that is, risks which cannot be qualified or quantified as yet because of a lack of scientific data or knowledge. By contrast, the prevention principle is referred to in situations where the likelihood that a risk occurs is quantifiable.

V. PREVENTION PRINCIPLE

In the same way as the precautionary principle, the prevention principle is included in Article 191(2) TFEU. In contrast with the precautionary principle, it is an undisputed principle of public international law. It is at least indirectly included in several international agreements and treaties, such as for example in the International Convention for the Prevention of Pollution from Ships (MARPOL) and the Convention on Biological Diversity (CBD). Further, it is included as principle 21 in the 1972 Stockholm Declaration. Its status under international law is solid and more recognised than the principle of precaution. It is an application of

---

[50] G. Van Calster, "Risk Regulation, EU Law and Emerging Technologies: Smother or Smooth?", 2 *Nanoethics* 1 (2008), 61–71.

sic utere tuo ut alienum non laedas, as recognised for example in the *Trail Smelter* arbitration.[51] At the European level, before being included in the 1987 Single European Act, the principle was already apparent in various Environmental Action Programmes, starting from the first one in 1972. It is therefore a long-established and often applied principle of European environmental law.[52]

The principle does not address *potential* risks on grounds of scientific uncertainty but rather risks which are known and likely to occur while carrying out a certain activity (or as a result of inaction).[53] However, similarly to the precautionary principle, the application of the prevention principle is subject to two main thresholds, namely the actual relationship between the probability and the extent of damage, and a cost–benefit analysis.[54] The former aims at ensuring that the risk is considered with the required due diligence and ensures that a balance is struck with regard to the level and intensity of intervention and prevention.[55] The latter ensures that the risk is balanced against the economic effects of regulatory intervention (or lack thereof), mid- as well as long term.[56]

Even more than the precautionary principle, the prevention principle has its origins in waste and pollution legislation. The recast of the IPPC Directive, the Industrial Emissions Directive (IED) Directive, is a main tool in implementing the principle in secondary legislation. "Prevention" is the overall topic of the Directive, as the title and the explicit reference to the principle in recital 2 of the preamble suggest. The second sentence of the subject matter in Article 1 states clearly: "It also lays down rules designed to prevent or, where that is not practicable, to reduce emissions into air, water and land and to prevent the generation of waste, in order to achieve a high level of protection of the environment taken as a whole."

---

[51] *US v Canada*, 3 RIAA (1941) 1907. For further information on international environmental law principles in general see G. Van Calster, *supra* note 50.

[52] See also L. Kraemer, "The Genesis of EC Environmental Principles", in: R. Macrory (ed.), *Principles of European Environmental Law*, The Avosetta Series 4, Groningen: Europa Law Publishing, 2004, at 38; as well as for a detailed discussion de Sadeleer, *Environmental Principles: From Political Slogans to Legal Rules*: 61–90.

[53] See also on the distinction between precaution and prevention, L. Kraemer, "The Genesis of EC Environmental Principles", in: R. Macrory (ed.), *Principles of European Environmental Law*, The Avosetta Series 4, Groningen: Europa Law Publishing, 2004, at 39.

[54] de Sadeleer, *Environmental Principles: From Political Slogans to Legal Rules*: 80f.

[55] Ibid.

[56] See above under the precautionary principle.

This is also the main objective of the 2005 Thematic Strategy on the Prevention and Recycling of Waste,[57] which is currently under review.[58] Another field where the principle of prevention serves as a main underlying principle is the field of EIA procedures, further discussed in Chapter 7.

VI. RECTIFICATION OF DAMAGE AT SOURCE

The rectification of damage at source principle is included with the other environmental law principles in Article 191(2) and was introduced at the same time as the inclusion of the environmental legal basis by the Single European Act.[59] The principle is closely interlinked with the prevention principle, in the sense that it steps in once the application of the prevention principle has failed and the damage has occurred and has been identified.[60] The principle of rectification of damage at source aims at combating the damage at a very early stage, namely, as the name suggests, at the source.[61]

This component of the principle was stressed by the ECJ. In its judgment justifying a national ban for hazardous waste imports, the court held:

> The principle that environmental damage should as a matter of priority be remedied at source, ... entails that it is for each region, municipality or other local authority to take appropriate steps to ensure that its own waste is collected, treated and disposed of; it must accordingly be disposed of as close as possible to the place where it is produced, in order to limit as far as possible the transport of waste.[62]

Traditionally, the main tool to implement this principle is the introduction of emission standards for a certain activity. These standards are available

---

[57] European Commission, "Taking sustainable use of resources forward: a thematic strategy on the prevention and recycling of waste", 2005, COM (2005) 666.

[58] European Commission, "Report on the thematic strategy on the prevention and recycling of waste", 19.1.2011, COM (2011) 13.

[59] For a description of the origins and application of the principle L. Kraemer, "The Genesis of EC Environmental Principles", in: R. Macrory (ed.), *Principles of European Environmental Law*, The Avosetta Series 4, Groningen: Europa Law Publishing, 2004, at 41–43.

[60] For its relationship with the prevention principle see also de Sadeleer, *Environmental Principles: From Political Slogans to Legal Rules*: 75.

[61] For a more detailed discussion of the principle please refer also to J. De Cendra de Larragan, *Distributional Choices in EU Climate Change Law and Policy: Towards a Principled Approach?* Alphen aan den Rijn: Kluwer Law International, 2011, at 148–151.

[62] Case C-2/90 *Commission v Belgium*, [1992] ECR I-4431, para 34.

for a multitude of activities, such as for all types of cars and commercial vehicles,[63] as well as for industrial emissions from various sectors.[64] The recent, more flexible trend is to combine the strict emission standards with quality objectives or "emission rectification of damage at source principle standards", also often referred to as the "combined approach". This is, for example, the case in European water policy (further discussed in Chapter 11). The main piece of legislation in this policy area, the Water Framework Directive, combines emission maximum values and quality standards in order to achieve a good ecological and chemical status of the waters covered by the Directive.

VII. POLLUTER PAYS PRINCIPLE

The polluter pays principle has its origins in the Organisation for Economic Co-operation and Development (OECD). At the international level it is included as principle 16 in the Rio Declaration and reads: "National authorities should endeavour to promote the internalization of environmental costs and the use of economic instruments, taking into account the approach that the polluter should, in principle, bear the cost of pollution, with due regard to the public interest and without distorting international trade and investment."

It is further explicitly recognised as a binding principle in several international conventions and treaties such as in Article 2 of the 1992 Helsinki Convention on the Protection and Use of Transboundary Watercourses and International Lakes. At the European level, nominally at least, it forms one of the pillars of European environmental policy.[65] The polluter pays principle was included in the EU Treaties by the 1986 Single European Act. Prior thereto, it was incorporated in the EU's Environmental Action Programmes,[66] and served as a basis for several instruments of EU secondary legislation, especially in the waste

---

[63] See for example Commission Regulation 566/2011 as regards access to vehicle repair and maintenance information, [2008] OJ L 199/1.

[64] Directive 1999/13 on the limitation of emissions of volatile organic compounds due to the use of organic solvents in certain activities and installations, [1999] OJ L 85/1.

[65] N. de Sadeleer, *Environmental Principles: From Political Slogans to Legal Rules*: 27, as well as L. Kraemer, "The Genesis of EC Environmental Principles", in: R. Macrory (ed.), *Principles of European Environmental Law*, The Avosetta Series 4, Groningen: Europa Law Publishing, 2004, 43ff.

[66] The principle first featured in the 1973–1976 programme, and directly or indirectly in all programmes thereafter.

management sector.⁶⁷ During its 40 years of existence, the polluter pays principle evolved from a principle to avoid distortions of competition to an instrument of pollution control.⁶⁸ In the same way as the rectification of damage at source principle, the polluter pays principle steps in once the application of the prevention principle has failed and the damage has occurred. And where no effective preventive measures are taken, the polluter pays principle is applied in order to make the polluter pay for the environmental damage that ensues.⁶⁹

The polluter pays principle aims at internalising externalities (costs of production which are not directly reflected in the price of a product). Today, it functions as a legal basis for several acts of secondary legislation, especially in the area of waste management, for example for the directive on hazardous waste, the packaging and packaging waste directive and the landfill of waste directive.⁷⁰

Importantly, the principle in its core form takes no stance as to whether environmental pollution ought to be reduced or indeed stamped out.⁷¹ It "simply" calls for there to be put a price on pollution, so that the negative environmental externality of production will be included in the companies' (or indeed individuals') costs structure. In a *Coase* approach,⁷² this will then lead to the pollution being caused by the companies for which it brings the most benefit. Companies which can use the activity that causes the pollution to add significant economic value, even if they have to pay for the pollution, will continue to engage in that activity (but for the "right" price, i.e. taking account of the pollution they cause). Naturally, for activities which are considered harmful to such a degree that they

---

⁶⁷ For example, Directive 91/689 on hazardous waste, [1991] OJ L 377/20; Directive 94/62on packaging and packaging waste [1994] OJ L 365/10; Directive 1999/31 on the landfill of waste, [1999] OJ L 182/1; G. Van Calster, "European Union", in: R. Seerden et al. (eds), *Public International Law in the European Union and the United States – A Comparative Analysis*, Comparative Environmental Law & Policy Series, The Hague: Kluwer Law International, 2002, at 465ff.

⁶⁸ Annex I Nr. 1, Council Recommendation 75/436 regarding cost allocation and action by public authorities on environmental matters, [1975] OJ L 194/1 as well as de Sadeleer, *Environmental Principles: From Political Slogans to Legal Rules*: 33.

⁶⁹ L. Bergkamp, "The Proposed EC Environmental Liability Regime and EC Law Principles", in: J Hamer (ed.), *Environmental Liability in the EU*, Trier: Europaeische Rechtsakademie, 2002, at 26ff.

⁷⁰ Directive 91/689 on hazardous waste [1991] OJ L 377/20; Directive 94/62 on packaging and packaging waste [1994] OJ L 365/10; and Directive 1999/31 on the landfill of waste, [1999] OJ L 182/1.

⁷¹ See also M. Lee, *EU Environmental Law*, Oxford: Hart, 2005, at 185ff.

⁷² R.H. Coase, "The Problem of Social Cost", 3 *J. Law & Econ.* (1960) 1.

ought to be phased out, pricing the pollution at high levels will help to encourage industry to seek less harmful alternatives.[73]

Despite dating back to 1975, the first soft law instrument on the polluter pays principle, the recommendation regarding cost allocation and action by public authorities on environmental matters, still serves as one of the main instruments for guidance on the principle. Accordingly, the reasoning behind the principle is

> charging to polluters the costs of action taken to combat the pollution which they cause encourages them to reduce that pollution and to endeavor to find less polluting products or technologies thereby enabling a more rational use to be made of the resources of the environment. Moreover it satisfies the criteria of effectiveness and equitable practice.[74]

The main instruments brought forward to implement the principle are standards and charges or a combination thereof.[75] *Standards* may take the forms of environmental quality standards, product standards, process standards, installation design standards and operation standards. *Charges* have two main functions. They serve as an incentive for polluters to reduce pollution, and they have a redistribution function for cumulative pollution, ensuring that the polluter pay its share of the overall pollution cost.[76]

Simply assessed, the polluter pays principle grants a right to pollute and attaches a price to it. However, what seems at first sight to be logical and straightforward is in fact not that easy to apply and implement in practice. The polluter pays principle is riddled with challenges, the most obvious one of which relates to it not being easy to calculate the economic value of pollution. This is particularly so in those instances where damage is caused which has no immediate human health impact (e.g. certain damage to biodiversity). Moreover, even in those instances where damage can be quantified and has already occurred, the application of the principle as a legal reasoning raises the question of who the actual polluter is (especially in cases of diffuse pollution and damage, as well as cumulative and chain pollution). Further, the polluter either may not be traceable or may have gone bankrupt/wound up the business. What if the polluter had already paid for its pollution?[77]

---

[73] G. Van Calster, *supra* note 33.
[74] Annex I Nr. 1, Council Recommendation 75/436/Euratom, ECSC, EEC of 3 March 1975 regarding cost allocation and action by public authorities on environmental matters.
[75] Ibid., Nr. 4(a).
[76] Ibid., Nr. 4(b).
[77] N. de Sadeleer, *Environmental Principles: From Political Slogans to Legal Rules*: 38ff.

The biggest obstacle to full roll-out of the principle, however, remain political nerves. By way of example, the differing environmental and public health impact of road transport versus rail/inland waterway transport is well documented (and could actually be fairly specifically calculated), yet countries hesitate to force the full environmental costs of road transport upon the sector.[78]

---

[78] G. Van Calster, *supra* note 33.

3. Environmental law-making in the EU

I. ACTORS

Article 13 of the TEU states that the Union has one institutional framework which "shall aim to promote its values, advance its objectives, serve its interests, those of its citizens and those of the Member States, and ensure the consistency, effectiveness and continuity of its policies and actions". The Article further lists the seven Union institutions.[1] For European environmental law, the most relevant institutions are the European Parliament, the Council of the European Union, the European Commission and the Court of Justice of the European Union.

Two advisory bodies, the Committee of the Regions and the Economic and Social Committee, as well as several decentralised agencies are actors of fluctuating relevance in the area of European environmental law and policy.

A. The European Parliament

The European Parliament represents the "Union's citizens" (Article 14(1) TEU) and has 766 members plus the president.[2] The members are elected by popular vote every five years and reflect the population of the Member States. The Parliament has three overall functions. Firstly, it has an advisory function, being entitled to advise on any question relating to the Union and to adopt resolutions. Further, the Parliament has budgetary, control and supervisory functions. Lastly, it has decision-making power in some policy areas. The Parliament does not have full legislative power over all subject matters. The legislative procedure depends on the legal basis of the subject area (the Treaty provisions). Decision-making power takes the

---

[1] For a detailed discussion of the actors of the EU, please refer to K. Lenaerts and P. Van Nuffel, *European Union Law*, London: Sweet & Maxwell, 2013, 452–566.
[2] Due to the accession of Croatia the Members of the European Parliament will be reduced from 766 to 751; applicable for the elections in 2014.

form of facultative consultation, compulsory consultation and co-decision making under Article 294 TFEU (the ordinary legislative procedure, the fullest legislative power; see also further Chapter 3 V) or consent. Hence the Parliament has the right to accept, amend or reject legislation coming from other institutions; however, it cannot initiate legislation. It can only invite the Commission to introduce a legislative proposal, although the Commission is not bound to take up this invitation (Article 17(1) TEU).

Rule 183 of the Parliament's Rules of Procedures[3] establishes the standing committees of the Parliament and explains the set-up. There are 20 standing committees. With 71 (69 before the accession of Croatia) members, the committee of Environment, Public Health and Food Safety is the largest legislative committee. Its powers and responsibilities are the following:

1. environmental policy and environmental protection measures, in particular concerning:
   (a) air, soil and water pollution, waste management and recycling, dangerous substances and preparations, noise levels, climate change, protection of biodiversity,
   (b) sustainable development,
   (c) international and regional measures and agreements aimed at protecting the environment,
   (d) restoration of environmental damage,
   (e) civil protection,
   (f) the European Environment Agency,
   (g) the European Chemicals Agency;
2. public health, in particular:
   (a) programmes and specific actions in the field of public health,
   (b) pharmaceutical and cosmetic products,
   (c) health aspects of bioterrorism,
   (d) the European Medicines Agency and the European Centre for Disease Prevention and Control;
3. food safety issues, in particular:
   (a) the labelling and safety of foodstuffs,
   (b) veterinary legislation concerning protection against risks to human health; public health checks on foodstuffs and food production systems,
   (c) the European Food Safety Authority and the European Food and Veterinary Office. (Annex VII No. VII of the Rules of Procedure).

Rule 188 defines the duties of the Committees and establishes that "standing committees shall examine questions referred to them by Parliament . . . ". Thus the committees are entitled to deliver opinions, reports and

---

[3] Rules of Procedure of the seventh parliamentary term from February 2013.

amendments to issues of their subject matter. The Environmental committee, for example, delivered an opinion on current challenges and opportunities for renewable energy on the European internal energy market.[4]

The European Parliament's impact on the development of EU environmental policy cannot be overstated.

B. The Council of the European Union

The Council of the European Union (often called the "Council of Ministers" (its previous name), "EU Council" (not to be confused with the "Council of the EU") or simply the "Council") represents the national governments at ministerial level. The Council together with the European Parliament are the main legislators, acting usually on a Commission proposal. It also exercises budgeting and coordination functions, especially in the area of the common foreign and security policy (Article 16 TEU). The Council further coordinates Member States' policies, including in the area of the environment. Eight different Council groups exist, depending on the subject, one of them being the Environment Council. It is composed of the environment ministers of the Member States and meets about four times a year. Decisions are taken by the co-decision procedure with the Parliament by qualified majority voting (see further Chapter 3 V). Besides adopting Union legislation, the Council can also conclude international agreements on behalf of the Union. One example in the area of the environment is the EU's membership of the United Nations Framework Convention on Climate Change (UNFCCC).

C. The European Commission

The European Commission is the "guardian of the Treaties" (Article 17 TEU) and the "neutral" Union institution representing the Union interest. The overall functions of the European Commission are listed in Article 17(1) TEU. Accordingly, the Commission

> shall promote the general interest of the Union and take appropriate initiatives to that end. It shall ensure the application of the Treaties, and of measures adopted by the institutions pursuant to them. It shall oversee the application of Union law under the control of the Court of Justice of the European Union. It shall execute the budget and manage programmes. It shall exercise coordinating, executive and management functions, as laid down in the Treaties. With the exception of the common foreign and security policy, and other cases provided for in the Treaties, it shall ensure the Union's external representation. It

---

[4] Opinion 2012/2259(INI), dated 25 February 2013.

shall initiate the Union's annual and multiannual programming with a view to achieving interinstitutional agreements.

It thus has four overall tasks: firstly the monitoring of the compliance with Union law, by the other institutions, individuals and firms (for example competition law and state aid) and by the Member States (Article 258 TFEU). Secondly, the Commission has an executive role and the power of implementation (Article 290 and 291 TFEU), together with the Council and the Member States. Further, it can deliver opinions and recommendations. Lastly, the Commission is the representative of the Union in legal transactions within each Member State and in international transactions.

The Commission is organised in Directorate-Generals (DGs).[5] For environmental issues, besides the DGs "Climate Action" (CLIMA), DG "Maritime Affairs and Fisheries" (MARE) and DG "Energy" (ENER), DG "Environment" (ENV) is, unsurprisingly, of special importance. Previously referred to as "DG XI", the overarching aim of DG Environment is to "protect, preserve and improve the environment for present and future generations". The DG prepares relevant policy and specific legislative proposals. It is also responsible, together with the legal service of the Commission, for the correct application of legislation on the environment and it represents the EU at international meetings relating to environmental matters, including the Conventions of the Parties of Multilateral Environmental Agreements to which the EU is a party. Within DG Environment, the different policy areas are established along the main subjects which are dealt within several units in six directorates: Policy; Circular Economy and Green Growth; Natural Capital; Quality of Life; Implementation and Support to Member States; Global Sustainable Development.

D. The Court of Justice of the European Union

According to Article 19 TFEU, the "Court of Justice of the European Union" includes the Court of Justice, the General Court and specialised courts. It "shall ensure that in the interpretation and application of the Treaties the law is observed" (Article 19(1)). Since the Treaty of Lisbon, some confusion has crept in on the exact acronym for the European Courts. The CJEU has the power to

---

[5] See Article 19 of the Rules of Procedure of the Commission, [2000] OJ L 308.

(a) rule on actions brought by a Member State, an institution or a natural or legal person;
(b) give preliminary rulings, at the request of courts or tribunals of the Member States, on the interpretation of Union law or the validity of acts adopted by the institutions;
(c) rule in other cases provided for in the Treaties. (Article 19 para. 3 TEU).

Accordingly, there are five types of cases that can be brought before the court (further discussed in Chapter 4).

These are firstly preliminary ruling requests by national courts according to Article 267 TFEU concerning the interpretation of the Treaties and validity and interpretation of acts of the institutions.[6] National courts can refer to the Court of Justice to clarify an issue of European law in order to ensure effective and uniform application of European law.

Further, actions for failure to fulfil an obligation according to Articles 258 to 260 TFEU concern cases where a Member State does not comply with Union law.[7] Such an action can be brought to the court by the Commission or a Member State after having given the concerned Member State the opportunity to reply and address the failure. If an infringement is found, the Member State concerned has to address the failure without delay, otherwise the Court might impose a fixed or periodic penalty.

Actions for annulment review the legality of a Union measure adopted by an institution, body, office or agency of the Union, according to Article 263 TFEU. Individuals, companies or organisations may also bring such an action before the European courts; however, their standing is quite limited, as further discussed in Chapter 5. Normally, the General Court has jurisdiction at the first instance, unless actions are brought by Member States against the European Parliament or the Council or brought by one Union institution against another institution, in which case the Court of Justice has exclusive jurisdiction.

Actions regarding a failure to act are set out in Article 265 TFEU and review the lawfulness of a failure to act by the institution, body, office or agency of the Union. A prerequisite is that the institution has been called upon to act. Should the ECJ side with the applicant, the failure to act needs to be remedied. The criteria for jurisdiction of the courts are the same as for the actions for annulment.

There is no special court for environmental matters in the EU, in contrast with a number of Member States which have specialised environmental

---

[6] See for example Case C-416/10 *Križan and Others*, not yet published in ECR.
[7] Case C-473/10 *Commission v Hungary*, not yet published in ECR.

courts in their administrative and general court systems.[8] There is, however, a certain degree of specialisation in environmental matters among the Advocate Generals (AGs) at the Court, who assist the Court with the legal analysis required in each case. Key case law of the Court will be discussed in the individual chapter of the subject matter.

E. The Committee of the Regions and the Economic and Social Committee

In accordance with Article 13(4) TEU, the Committee of the Regions and the Economic and Social Committee are the two advisory bodies to the European Parliament, the Council and the Commission. Their precise mandate is further specified in Articles 300ff. TFEU.

The Committee of the Regions

The Committee of the Regions consists of representatives of regional and local bodies who either hold an electoral mandate or are politically accountable to an elected assembly. In practice, the Committee has 353 members representing all 28 Member States.[9] The members are regional presidents, mayors or elected representatives of regions and cities, which are appointed for five years (Article 305 TFEU). Even though the members of the Committee of the Regions must be accountable to the national institutions in some form, they shall not be bound by the mandate and are completely independent and act in the Union's general interest (Article 300(4)), in the same way as the members of the Economic and Social Committee.

The Committee of the Regions was first introduced by the Maastricht Treaty in 1993 and its role has been continuously extended. The Amsterdam Treaty included amongst others the environment as falling under the Committee's competences and the Lisbon Treaty added the areas of climate change and energy. Further, the Lisbon Treaty explicitly recognised

---

[8] See for example H.T. Anker, O.K. Fauchald, A. Nilsson and L. Suvantola, "The Role of Courts in Environmental Law – A Nordic Comparative Study", 9 *Nordic Environmental Law Journal* 33 (2009), 9–33; as well as G. Pring and C. Pring, *Greening Justice: Creating and Improving Environmental Courts and Tribunals*, 2009 addressing the issue from a global perspective, available at http://www.eufje.org/images/DocDivers/Rapport%20Pring.pdf, last consulted 21.11.2015; and R. Macrory, "The Long and Winding Road – Towards an Environmental Court in England and Wales", 25 *Journal of Environmental Law* 3 (2013), 1.

[9] In Article 305 TFEU, the maximum amount of Members of the Committee of the Region is limited to 350 members. However, after the accession of Croatia the number was augmented to 353 as an interim measure.

territorial cohesion in addition to social cohesion and solidarity as a Union objective (Article 3(3) TEU), which strengthens the role of the Committee in the legislative procedure. The Commission, the Council or the European Parliament have to consult the Committee in all areas of its competence and in all cases which concern cross-border cooperation (Article 307 TFEU). Besides giving opinions upon consultation by the abovementioned Union institutions, the Committee can also submit opinions on its own initiative in areas which it deems necessary. Further, in all areas where the Economic and Social Committee is consulted on a legislative initiative, the Committee of the Regions has to be informed of this request and may draft an opinion as well, in the case where regional interests are involved (Article 307 TFEU). Article 192(3) TFEU also adds that, regarding the adoption of environmental action programmes, the Committee of the Regions and the Economic and Social Committee have to be consulted.

Further, according to Article 8 of Protocol No. 2 to the TFEU,[10] the Committee of the Regions has the right to bring legal actions (also for annulment) to discipline the application of the principles of subsidiarity and proportionality before the Court of Justice, in the areas where the Committee has competence, thus also including environmental issues. One of its core functions is to supervise the correct application of the subsidiarity principle and to ensure that the actions taken by the Union are as close to the citizens as possible. Legal standing for the Committee was only introduced with the Lisbon Treaty, hence it is too early to say what the impact of this new power might be.

The Committee has six distinct Commissions that draft opinions and resolutions relating to their subject matter, which are subsequently discussed and submitted for adoption to the Plenary Assembly. One of the six Commissions is the Commission "Environment, Climate Change and Energy" (ENVE), which is competent in the areas of environment policy, climate change adaptation and mitigation, renewable energy and space policies.

Economic and Social Committee
The Economic and Social Committee has the same role in the legislative procedure as the Committee of the Regions. It has to be consulted by the Commission, the Council or the European Parliament in its areas of competence (mandatory consultation)[11] and in all cases the institutions

---

[10] Protocol No. 2 on the Application of the Principles of Subsidiarity and Proportionality.
[11] For instance, regarding the procedure on access to genetic resources. References: CESE 2313/2012 – NAT/582, COM (2012) 576 – 2012/278 (COD).

consider necessary. The Economic and Social Committee can also issue opinions on own initiative (Article 304 TFEU).[12] It consists of (currently 353) representatives from employers, employees and several civil society interest groups (representing the economic, civil, professional and social sector). As with the members of the Committee of the Regions, the total amount of the members cannot exceed 350[13] and they are also appointed for 5 years (Article 301(1) and Article 302(1) TFEU).

The Committee was introduced by the 1957 Treaty of Rome with the aim to provide a forum for the discussion of issues relating to the establishment of the single market. However, its function and competence were systematically extended by the Single Act and the Treaties of Maastricht and Amsterdam which added the regional and environmental areas to the Economic and Social Committee's competence. Further, the latter also added the consultation option to be addressed by the European Parliament besides the Council and the Commission.

Similar to the Committee of the Regions, the Economic and Social Committee is divided into six sections, preparing the opinions and reports for adoption by the Committee. One of them is the section on Agriculture, Rural Development and the Environment (NAT), which also deals with climate change and sustainable development policies besides the specific issues on waste, air quality, biodiversity, forestry, fisheries management and control, food safety, civil protection and animal health and welfare.

It is fair to say that due to the non-binding character of the opinions of both Committees, and their absence in the formal legislative procedure, their true impact is more limited than their size and workload may suggest.

F. Other Actors

The European Investment Bank

Unlike the European Central Bank, the European Investment Bank (EIB), located in Luxembourg, is not an institution of the EU. Its members are the Member States (Article 308 TFEU). Its purpose is included in Article 309 TFEU to: "contribute, by having recourse to the capital market and utilising its own resources, to the balanced and steady development of the internal market in the interest of the Union". The bank operates on a non-profit basis and finances projects relating to the environment.

---

[12] For instance, "Prevention and reduction of food waste". References: CESE 1917/2012 – NAT/570, Own-initiative.
[13] Ibid.

It has therefore established Environmental and Social Principles and Standards[14] which serve as reference criteria for the financing of a project. These principles and standards focus on the impacts a specific project will have on biodiversity, in regard to climate change, and on the social component of sustainable development.[15]

The European Environment Agency
The European Environment Agency (EEA) is *not* an EU institution. Its membership is wider than the Member States of the EU.[16] Located in Copenhagen, the EEA was established by Regulation 401/2009[17] and aims to set up a European Environment Information and Observation Network (Eionet). In order to achieve the environmental objectives of the Treaty, the EEA's function is to provide:

(a) objective, reliable and comparable information at European level enabling them to take the requisite measures to protect the environment, to assess the results of such measures and to ensure that the public is properly informed about the state of the environment, and to that end;
(b) the necessary technical and scientific support.[18]

These general functions are further specified in Articles 2 and 3 of the Regulation and range around the following priority areas (Article 3(2)):

(a) air quality and atmospheric emissions;
(b) water quality, pollutants and water resources;
(c) the state of the soil, of the fauna and flora, and of biotopes;
(d) land use and natural resources;
(e) waste management;
(f) noise emissions;
(g) chemical substances which are hazardous for the environment;
(h) coastal and marine protection.

---

[14] The EIB Statement of Environmental and Social Principles and Standards, 2009, available at http://www.eib.org/attachments/strategies/eib_statement_esps_en.pdf; last consulted 8.9.2015.

[15] The European Bank for Reconstruction and Development (EBRD), which is *not* affiliated with the EU, has similar provisions to ensure the environmental soundness of their financing decisions.

[16] All 28 European Member States, as well as Iceland, Liechtenstein, Norway, Switzerland and Turkey are members of the EEA. Further, the following countries are cooperating countries: Albania, Bosnia and Herzegovina, the former Yugoslav Republic of Macedonia, Montenegro, Serbia and Kosovo.

[17] Regulation 401/2009, OJ [2009] L 126/13.

[18] See Article 1(2) of the Regulation.

The EEA acts mainly upon requests from the European institutions and its advisory bodies but also serves civil society, the industry sector and non-governmental organisations as a source of environmental information.

The European Maritime Safety Agency

The European Marine and Safety Agency (EMSA) was established in 2002 through Regulation 1406/2002.[19] Its overall aim is to ensure "a high, uniform and effective level of maritime safety" and to prevent pollution by ships. The main task of the agency is to assist the Union's institutions and the Member States with technical and scientific assistance. Further, the Agency monitors the implementation of the Regulation in the Member States and provides assistance in this regard. It also evaluates the effectiveness of the current measures in place.

European Chemicals Agency

The European Chemicals Agency (ECHA) was established by Regulation 1907/2006[20] as one part of the Union's regulatory system on the Registration, Evaluation, Authorisation and Restriction of Chemicals (REACH). The agency is a key actor in all components of the regime: it receives the registration of the chemicals through the registration dossier, evaluates the latter together with the Member States, controls the authorisation and can request the restriction of a chemical.

The ECHA consists of different committees. Below, the function of three of these committees in the REACH system will be highlighted. The functions of the ECHA in the other chemicals legislation will be discussed in the relevant chapters.

The *Committee for Risk Assessment* (RAC) prepares ECHA opinions related to the risks of substances to human health and the environment in the authorisation and restriction procedures under REACH. With regard to the restriction procedure, the Committee evaluates whether a proposed restriction is appropriate in reducing the risk to human health and the environment. This includes the assessment of comments submitted by third parties. In the context of the authorisation procedure, RAC assesses the risk arising from the uses of the substance when an application for authorisation is submitted. This includes an assessment of the appropriateness and effectiveness of the risk management measures as described

---

[19] Regulation 1406/2002, OJ [2002] L208/1.
[20] Regulation 1907/2006 of 18 December 2006 concerning the Registration, Evaluation, Authorisation and Restriction of Chemicals (REACH), establishing a European Chemicals Agency, [2009] OJ L 36/84.

in the authorisation application and, if relevant, of the risks posed by possible alternatives. Third party contributions linked to the application are also assessed.

The *Committee for Socio-economic Analysis* (SEAC) prepares ECHA opinions related to the socio-economic impact of possible legislative actions on chemicals in the REACH restriction and authorisation processes. The final decisions on these issues are taken by the European Commission through a regulatory committee procedure.

The *Member State Committee* (MSC) participates in several REACH processes such as evaluation and authorisation. The MSC is responsible for resolving divergences of opinions among Member States and on proposals for the identification of Substances of Very High Concern (SVHCs). The Committee provides opinions on the ECHA's draft recommendation for the authorisation list (Annex XIV) and draft Community Rolling Action Plan (CoRAP) for the substance evaluation process. If an agreement is not reached within the MSC, the matter is referred to the European Commission for a decision.

There are other, more specialised agencies with specific roles, which will be referred to when required in the context of the individual subject matter.

II. (LEGAL) INSTRUMENTS

The European institutions can create "secondary" legislation on the basis of primary legislation. There are two groups of secondary legislation. The first group consists of the acts which are listed in Article 288 TFEU, namely regulations, directives, decisions, recommendations and opinions.[21] The second group are discussed below under "Other legal instruments".

A *regulation* is "generally applicable" which means that it does not require transposition into national legislation. Member States, in other words, do not need to draft their own, national legislation to give effect to European regulations. Regulations are in their entirety directly applicable in all national systems of Member States. They are often very detailed and can relate to both legislative and implementing issues (see further below).

A *directive*, by contrast, is only binding on the result to be achieved. It is up to the Member States and the national authorities to determine

---

[21] For a detailed analysis of these measures please refer to K. Lenaerts and P. Van Nuffel, *European Union Law*, London: Sweet & Maxwell, 2013, at 893ff.

the form and methods to achieve the prescribed result. Since they are not directly applicable, they *do* need to be transposed into national law. The Water Framework Directive, for example, which establishes the general aim to achieve "good ecological status and a good chemical status" by 2015 (Article 4), as well as a general framework regarding the characteristics of river basin districts (Article 5) and for strategies on the pollution of water (Article 16), determines that such a status is to be achieved and generally that the river basin approach needs to be employed to achieve it; however, it leaves the exact means open for Member States to decide. The Directive only establishes general guidance and administrative measures which the individual Member States have to take in order to fulfil the aim.

Directives are important legislative tools for the harmonisation of EU law (regulations on the contrary aim at unification of the laws of the Member States), since they create an overall framework and only bind the Member States by the result prescribed and not by the exact means. Further, directives do not contain obligations to individuals, only to Member State bodies. Through the implementation into national law, from measures enacted by authorities, rights and obligations for citizens do arise (see also "Direct effect" further discussed in Chapter 4 II). Directives also have both legislative and implementing functions (discussed further below).

A *decision* is binding in its entirety and has a general scope of application. But, unlike a regulation, a decision may only be addressed to specific parties and in that case is only binding upon them. They can be addressed to Member States, individuals or companies, and they usually have an individual scope. One example is Decision 2455/2001 establishing the list of priority substances in the field of water policy which is addressed to Member States (Article 5) and adds an Annex X to the Water Framework Directive including a list of priority (hazardous) substances which pose a significant risk to the aquatic environment. Decisions are drafted by either the Commission or the Council (sometimes together with the Parliament).

Recommendations and opinions are not binding ("soft law") instruments; however, they still have a legal effect.[22] They are a general tool for the European institutions to publish their view and perception of a specific subject and to indicate a desired course of action without creating legal obligations. The Recommendation of the European Parliament and of the Council of 4 April 2001, as reviewed in 2007, for example, provides for minimum criteria for environmental inspections in the Member States.[23]

---

[22] See also Case C-322/88 *Grimaldi* [1989] ECR I-4407.
[23] European Commission Communication on the review of Recommendation

Further, opinions are often used by the European institutions and advisory bodies to comment on a situation or developments in the Union or a Member State or on a legislative proposal, for example the opinion of the Committee of the Regions on the seventh Environment Action Programme.[24]

A. Delegated and Implementing Acts

The Treaty of Lisbon created a new hierarchy of norms through the introduction of delegated and implementing acts. The first level are the legislative acts as described above; delegated and implementing acts form a lower category of legal acts to supplement the legislative acts with further rules, details and most often technical requirements or amend non-essential elements of a legislative act (Articles 290 and 291 TFEU). The objectives, content, scope and duration of the delegation of power are explicitly defined in the legislative act. The system replaced the former "comitology" procedure with the "Right of Scrutiny" (RoS) which was used in the pre-Lisbon era (from 2006 onwards) in order for the Commission to exercise its implementing powers conferred on it by the EU legislator. In particular the Parliament found it unacceptable that a legislative act, which was previously adopted under co-decision, could be amended without any further involvement of Parliament. The latest procedure as it stands pays regard to this fact. As it is still relatively new it remains to be seen whether the new set-up really addresses this long-standing issue.[25]

B. Other Legal Instruments

The second group of legal instruments is composed of acts which are not listed under Article 288 TFEU. These are in the main declarations, resolutions, communications, and conclusions, as well as green and

---

2001/331/EC providing for minimum criteria for environmental inspections in the Member States, Brussels, 14.11.2007, COM (2007) 707.

[24] Opinion of the Committee of the Regions on "Towards a 7th Environment Action Programme: better implementation of EU environment law" (2013/C 17/07).

[25] See for a detailed discussion and explanation of delegated and implementing acts: European Institute of Public Administration, *Delegated & Implementing Acts: The New Comitology*, 2013, available at http://www.eipa.eu/files/repository/product/20130904094203_Comitology_Brochure5EN_web.pdf, last consulted 27.10.2015.

white papers. Green papers are generally published with the intention of starting a discussion and consultation process on a specific issue within the entire Union. For example the green paper "Adapting to climate change in Europe" (COM (2007) 354) lists challenges for European society and European public policy resulting from climate change and proposes several general options for EU action.

Green papers are commonly followed by white papers which contain proposals for specific action. The white paper on "Adapting to climate change: Towards a European framework for action" (COM (2009) 147) as a follow-up from the green paper lists specific proposals for action, for example regarding knowledge building, the integration into other policy areas and financing.

None of these acts is binding; however, they still have a legal effect since they are often used as guidelines for interpretation of EU law by the ECJ and the Court of First Instance.

C. Vertical and Horizontal Legislation

A different way of classifying secondary Union environmental law (legislation under the format of regulations and directives) is by distinguishing between non-sectoral (or "horizontal"), and sectoral (or "vertical") legislation. The former by and large deals with issues of a procedural nature, and applies throughout the whole spectrum of environmental problems and challenges. The latter, by contrast, applies to specific environmental issues.

Under non-sectoral EU environmental law, one can classify the legislation applicable to public participation, access to environmental information and access to justice (further discussed in Chapter 5), namely the Directive on public access to environmental information.[26] The Directive provides for public participation in respect of the drawing up of certain plans and programmes relating to the environment[27] and the Regulation on the application of the provisions of the Aarhus Convention on Access to Information, Public Participation in Decision-making and Access to Justice in Environmental Matters to Community institutions

---

[26] Directive 2003/4 on public access to environmental information and repealing Council Directive 90/313/EEC, [2003] OJ L 41/26.

[27] Directive 2003/35 providing for public participation in respect of the drawing up of certain plans and programmes relating to the environment and amending with regard to public participation and access to justice Council Directives 85/337/EEC and 96/61/EC – Statement by the Commission, [2003] OJ L 156/17.

and bodies.[28] Other examples are Directive 85/337 on environmental impact assessment, as codified by Directive 2011/92;[29] the Seveso Directive on emergency planning and reporting concerning the use of dangerous substances;[30] the Industrial Emissions Directive;[31] Regulation 1221/2009 on the Eco management and audit scheme;[32] Regulation 66/2010 on the the EU Ecolabel;[33] Regulation 614/2007 on a financing instrument for the environment (LIFE);[34] and Regulation 933/1999 on the European Environment Agency, lastly amended by Regulation 401/2009.[35]

Sectoral environmental law will be discussed in Part II of this volume.

III. LEGAL BASIS

The legal basis of a Union measure is important not only to determine the extent of competence the Union has, but also for the decision-making procedure and the involvement of the EU institutions. However, the institutions (and the Commission in particular, which is the institution with the sole right of initiative in the environmental area) obviously cannot simply pick a legal basis which suits them. All power in the EU is attributed power, meaning that the EU can only exercise those powers specifically attributed to it by the Treaties, and under the terms and conditions so specified by the Articles in the Treaties.

---

[28] Regulation 1367/2006 on the application of the provisions of the Aarhus Convention on Access to Information, Public Participation in Decision-making and Access to Justice in Environmental Matters to Community institutions and bodies, [2006] OJ L 264/13.

[29] Directive 2011/92 on the assessment of the effects of certain public and private projects on the environment, [2012] OJ L 26/1.

[30] Directive 2012/18 on the control of major-accident hazards involving dangerous substances, amending and subsequently repealing Council Directive 96/82/EC, [2012] OJ L 197/1.

[31] Directive 2010/75 on industrial emissions (integrated pollution prevention and control), [2010] OJ L 334/17.

[32] Regulation 1221/2009 on the voluntary participation by organisations in a Community eco-management and audit scheme (EMAS), repealing Regulation (EC) No 761/2001 and Commission Decisions 2001/681/EC and 2006/193/EC, [2009] OJ L 342/1.

[33] Regulation 66/2010 on the EU Ecolabel, [2010] OJ L 27/1.

[34] Regulation 614/2007 concerning the Financial Instrument for the Environment (LIFE+), [2007] OJ L 149/1.

[35] Regulation 401/2009 on the European Environment Agency and the European Environment Information and Observation Network, [2009] OJ L 126/13.

In the area of environmental protection, the legal basis chosen by the Commission to justify the introduction of environmental protection, prior to the existence of an explicit environmental title, continues to serve as the foundation for such policy even after the introduction of a specific title. Hence the ECJ generally employs the centre of gravity or *accessorium sequitur principale* approach[36] to decide which of the legal bases (these may incidentally also involve trade policy, agriculture, etc.) is the correct one in a particular case. It is the main object and purpose of the proposed measure which determines the legal basis that needs to be used.[37]

The principle of supremacy of Union law determines that, in a case where Union law conflicts with national law, Union law prevails and hence cannot be amended by national law.[38] The principle of attributed powers or "conferral" (Article 5(2) TEU and Article 4(1) TEU), requires that every Union action needs a legal basis to be justified.[39]

After the introduction of a legal basis on the environment in the Single European Act (1987), the issue arose as to which legal basis should be employed for the adoption of legislation in the environmental area: Article 114 TFEU (previously 95 EC), the standard legal base for legislation adopted within the framework of the internal market, or Article 191 ff. TFEU (previously 174 EC) which make up the environmental title of the Treaty.[40] As noted above, the Commission had to justify introducing

---

[36] Case C-300/89, *Commission v Council* ("Titanium Dioxide"), [1991] ECR I-2867. See also M. Schemmel and B. de Regt, "The European Court of Justice and the Environmental Protection Policy of the European Community", 17 *Boston College International and Comparative Law Review* 53 (1994); R. van Ooik, "Cross-pillar Litigation before the ECJ: Demarcation of Community and Union Competences", 4 *European Constitutional Law Review* (2008), 399–420.

[37] See cases ECJ, C-45/86 *Commission v Council* ("Generalised Tariff Preferences"), [1987] ECR-01493; C-242/87 *Commission v Council* ("ERASMUS"), [1989] ECR I-1425; Case 155/91 *Commission v Council*, [1993] I-939; C-376/98 *Germany v Parliament and Council*, ("Tobacco Advertising I"), [2000] ECR I-8419; C-176/03, *Commission v Council* ("Environmental crimes"), [2005] ECR I-7879; C-94/03 *Commission v Council* ("Rotterdam PIC Convention"), [2006] ECR I-1; and C-166/0, *Parliament v Council,* [2009] ECR I-7135.

[38] As established by the Court of Justice in Case 6–64 *Costa v ENEL* [1964] ECR I-1141; see also K. Lenaerts and P. Van Nuffel, *European Union Law*, London: Sweet & Maxwell, 2013, 754ff.

[39] See further K. Lenaerts and P. Van Nuffel, *European Union Law*, London: Sweet & Maxwell, 2013, 112ff.

[40] See further D. Benson and A. Jordan, "A Grand Bargain or an incomplete contract?: European Union Environmental Policy after the Lisbon Treaty", 17 *European Energy and Environmental Law Review* 5 (2008), 280–290.

environmental legislation by reference to the negative impact on the internal market of diversity in national environmental laws. Even after the introduction of an environmental title in the Treaty, this reasoning still exists, and consequently, so does the potential for recourse to Article 114 TFEU as a legal basis.

ECJ case law with respect to the choice between Articles 114 and 191 (in particular, *Commission v Council*[41]) and, generally, the case law on determining the correct legal basis where a dual legal basis solution would not be possible, for instance due to the incompatibility of the procedures involved, effectively employs the *accesorium sequitur principale* rule. Where the procedures are divergent, the act must be based on a single legal basis, namely that required by its main or predominant purpose or component (where legislative procedures are identical, the act may potentially be based upon both Articles).[42]

Interestingly, the case of *Spain v Council*[43] has also followed the *accesorium sequitur principale* rule for choosing the correct procedure within Article 192 TFEU (in particular with a view to deciding the majority required).

It is noteworthy that the choice between Articles 114 and 193 TFEU may be important in particular vis-à-vis the possibility for Member States to adopt unilateral measures. In the case of Article 193 TFEU, they have a freer hand.

As established above, the legal basis of a measure is determined by the main objective and content of the measure intended ("predominant legal basis"),[44] as well as on the more specific legal basis. For example, in *Parliament v Council*[45] the Court held that the legal basis regarding measures on radioactive substances in water intended for human consumption

---

[41] Case 155/91, [1993] ECR I-939.
[42] See cases C-45/86 *Commission v Council* ("Generalised Tariff Preferences"), [1987] ECR-01493; C-242/87 *Commission v Council* ("ERASMUS"), [1989] ECR I-1425; Case 155/91 *Commission v Council*, [1993] I-939; C-376/98 *Germany v Parliament and Council* ("Tobacco Advertising I"), [2000] ECR I-8419; C-176/03 *Commission v Council* ("Environmental crimes"), [2005] ECR I-7879; C-94/03 *Commission v Council* ("Rotterdam PIC Convention"), [2006] ECR I-1; and C-166/07 *Parliament v Council*, [2009] ECR I-7135.
[43] Case C-36/98 *Spain v Council*, ECLI:EU:C:2001:64.
[44] Case C-155/91 *Commission v Council*, ECLI:EU:C:1993:98; on the evolution of the ECJ case law on legal bases see K. St Clair Bradley, "Powers and Procedures in the EU Constitution: Legal Bases and the Court", in: P. Craig and G. de Búrca (eds), *The Evolution of EU Law*, Oxford: Oxford University Press, 2011, at 89–94.
[45] C-48/14 *Parliament v Council*, ECLI:EU:C:2015:91.

(Directive 2013/51/Euratom[46]) was indeed Article 31 Euratom Treaty and not as argued by the European Parliament Article 191 TFEU, as the Euratom Treaty "constitutes a more specific legal basis for protecting the health of populations against radioactive substances in water intended for human consumption than the general legal basis resulting from Article 192(1) TFEU".[47]

Article 296 TFEU further specifies that "legal acts shall state the reasons on which they are based and shall refer to any proposals, initiatives, recommendations, requests or opinions required by the Treaties". Where a measure's aim and content relates to more than one provision in the Treaty, the measure must be based on both of them ("multiple legal bases").

One interesting case in this regard is *Titanium Dioxide*.[48] The institutions did not agree on whether to base the Directive on waste from the titanium dioxide industry on Article 130s TEC (now Article 192 TFEU) or on Article 100a TEC (now Article 114 TFEU). Multiple legal bases were not possible since the decision-making procedures of these legal bases differed. The ECJ ruled that the correct legal basis was Article 100a TEC (now 114 TFEU) on the grounds that amongst others environmental protection must be included in all other Union policies by virtue of the integration principle – where the presence of an impact on environmental policy cannot trigger the environmental title, for in essence all EU policy by default (as a result of the integration principle) is "environmental law".

This case already indicates that in the area of environmental law, different legal bases are possible, depending on the specific issue of the measure. Common legal bases used regarding environmental related law and policy are:

1. Article 43 TFEU on a common agricultural policy. This Article for instance commonly functions as the legal basis for issues on agriculture in order to establish a common agricultural policy amongst the Member States. Directive 91/414 on plant protection products, for example, is based on this Treaty provision.[49]

---

[46] Directive 2013/51/Euratom of 22 October 2013 laying down requirements for the protection of the health of the general public with regard to radioactive substances in water intended for human consumption, [2013] OJ L 296/12.
[47] C-48/14 at 37.
[48] Case C-300/89 *Commission v Council*, [1991] ECR I-2867.
[49] Directive 91/414 concerning the placing of plant protection products on the market, [1991] OJ L 230/1.

2. Article 100 TFEU on transport. This Article serves as a legal basis for transport and environmental matters. For example, Directive 2002/30 on the establishment of rules and procedures with regard to the introduction of noise-related operating restrictions at airports.[50]
3. Article 113 TFEU on taxes. This Article is commonly used as a basis for indirect taxation regarding environmental measures aiming at harmonisation of Member State legislation and implementing the polluter pays principle. One example is the Energy Taxation Directive,[51] which is also aimed at protecting the environment (see for example recitals 6, 11, 29).
4. Article 114 TFEU on the internal market. The internal market provision in this Article provides the legal basis regarding environmental measures removing distortions of competition. As established in Chapter 1, before the introduction of a separate legal basis for environmental issues, the internal market served extensively as a basis in this regard. In the same way as the environmental title, it includes a direct reference to environmental issues. A difference is that under the environmental title, the policy "*shall contribute*" to fulfil the objectives and "*aim* at a high level of protection", whereas under Article 114(3) the Commission proposals "*will* take as a base a high level of protection". Thus the requirement to establish a high level of protection is stricter under the internal market than under the environmental provisions.

To date the internal market provisions often serve as a legal basis for measures relating to food[52] and the making available on the market and use of products which can be harmful to the environment and human health[53] as well as regarding genetically modified organisms (GMOs).[54] The Article also includes an environmental

---

[50] Directive 2002/30 on the establishment of rules and procedures with regard to the introduction of noise-related operating restrictions at Community airports, [2002] OJ L 85/40.

[51] Directive 2003/96 restructuring the Community framework for the taxation of energy products and electricity, [2003] OJ L 283/51.

[52] Regulation 1169/2011 on the provision of food information to consumers, [2011] OJ L 304/18.

[53] For example Regulation 528/2012 concerning the making available on the market and use of biocidal products, [2012] OJ L 167/1.

[54] In fact, all legal instruments on GMOs are based on amongst others Article 114 TFEU (or the older versions thereof): Directive 2001/18/EC of 12 March 2001 on the deliberate release into the environment of genetically modified organisms, [2001] OJ L 106/1; Regulation (EC) No 1829/2003 of 22 September 2003 on genetically modified food and feed, [2003] OJ L 2681; Regulation (EC) No 1830/2003

guarantee. GMOs are one area where the safeguard clause is currently applied by Member States. Article 23 of Directive 2001/18 reads:

> Where a Member State, as a result of new or additional information made available since the date of the consent and affecting the environmental risk assessment or reassessment of existing information on the basis of new or additional scientific knowledge, has detailed grounds for considering that a GMO as or in a product which has been properly notified and has received written consent under this Directive constitutes a risk to human health or the environment, that Member State may provisionally restrict or prohibit the use and/or sale of that GMO as or in a product on its territory . . .

5. Article 153 on social policy. This Article obliges the Union to support the activities of the Member States amongst others in improvement "of the working environment to protect workers' health and safety". Within this context measures can also relate to environmental issues, as for example within the framework of the OHS Directive.[55] Within this Framework Directive, several individual directives have been passed, addressing, for example, exposure to chemical agents and chemical safety, exposure to physical hazards and exposure to biological agents.[56]

6. Article 182 TFEU on research and technological development. The research and development provisions in Article 182 TFEU serve as a legal basis for the adoption of multi-annual framework programmes (FPs) with the objective to strengthen the scientific and technological base. In the 7th framework programme, projects are commonly also granted on environmental matters, in order to "better understand and cope with issues such as climate change and identify environmentally friendly technologies in order to improve

---

concerning the traceability and labelling of genetically modified organisms and the traceability of food and feed products produced from genetically modified organisms, [2003] OJ L 268/24; Directive 2009/41/EC of 6 May 2009 on the contained use of genetically modified micro-organisms, [2009] OJ L 125/75; and Directive (EU) 2015/412 of 11 March 2015 amending Directive 2001/18/EC as regards the possibility for the Member States to restrict or prohibit the cultivation of genetically modified organisms (GMOs) in their territory, [2015] OJ L 68/1.

[55] Directive 89/391 on the introduction of measures to encourage improvements in the safety and health of workers at work, [1989] OJ L 183/1.

[56] See for an overview of the individual directive, European Agency for Safety and Health at Work (EU-OSHA), available at https://osha.europa.eu/en/legislation/directives/exposure-to-chemical-agents-and-chemical-safety/ last consulted 27.10.2015.

our management of both natural and man-made resources".[57] The budget for the period from 2007 to 2013 is 1890 million euros for research on environmental matters only.

7. Article 194 TFEU on energy. This Article (established in the Lisbon Treaty) further serves as a legal basis relating to energy issues; however, it explicitly mentions the preservation and improvement of the environment. One example for a measure taken on this basis which also supports environmental issues is Directive 2010/31 on the energy performance of buildings,[58] as mentioned several times throughout the preamble of the Directive and the text itself (see for example recitals 24 and 26 of the Directive). Another example is Directive 2010/30 on the labelling of energy products.[59] Before the inclusion of the Energy title into the Treaty, energy issues were dealt with under the internal market or environmental basis.

8. Article 207 TFEU on common commercial policy. This Article can serve as a basis for actions relating to trade in goods and services in connection with the environment. An example was the Tobacco Products Directive[60] which was based on Article 133 TEC (now Article 207 TFEU) and Article 95 TEC (now 114 TFEU). The revised version, Directive 2014/40,[61] is based on Articles 53(1), 62 and 114.

9. Articles 196, 214 and 222 TFEU on civil protection, humanitarian aid and solidarity. The so-called solidarity clause in Article 222 TFEU can possibly act as a legal basis relating to matters on the environment. It asks for Member States' solidarity in the event of a terrorist attack or a natural or man-made disaster, even if there is no definition of what exactly these terms cover. The clause was introduced in the Lisbon Treaty following the terrorist attacks in Madrid in March 2004 and can serve as a basis for actions in case

---

[57] European Commission, "Research and Innovation", available at http://ec.europa.eu/research/fp7/index_en.cfm?pg=env, last consulted 27.10.2015.

[58] Directive 2010/31 on the energy performance of buildings, [2010] OJ L 153/13.

[59] Directive 2010/30 on the indication by labelling and standard product information of the consumption of energy and other resources by energy-related products, [2010] OJ L 153/1.

[60] Directive 2001/37/EC on the approximation of the laws, regulations and administrative provisions of the Member States concerning the manufacture, presentation and sale of tobacco, [2001] OJ L 194/26.

[61] Directive 2014/40 of 3 April 2014 on the approximation of the laws, regulations and administrative provisions of the Member States concerning the manufacture, presentation and sale of tobacco and related products and repealing Directive 2001/37/EC, [2014] OJ L 127/1.

of a natural or man-made environmental disaster or as a result of a terrorist attack in this regard. So far no action has been taken.

Article 196 TFEU on civil protection (also newly established in the Lisbon Treaty) supports the need for Member State cooperation to improve the effectiveness of systems for prevention and protection against natural or man-made disasters and to "support and complement the Member States' action at the local and regional level".

Finally, Article 214 TFEU on humanitarian aid extends the solidarity and cooperation to third countries, providing "ad hoc assistance and relief and protection".

However, so far no actions in relation to environmental matters have been taken based on any of these Articles.

10. Article 192 TFEU on Environment. As mentioned above, Article 192 TFEU is the dominant and most explicit legal basis (*lex specialis*) for environmental matters. It contains in paragraph 2 the possibility to include a safeguard clause in legislation allowing the Member States to take provisional measures for "non-economic environmental reasons".

IV. THE ENVIRONMENTAL GUARANTEE

A. Overall Meaning and Context

Arguably considerably more so than in the context of other EU policies, Member States seek to resort to unilateral measures to protect their environmental interests, or their ethical interests, such as in the case of animal welfare. Part of this tendency may be explained by the perceived "North–South" divide in environmental proactivity (the reality of which is, however, uncertain). The suggestion of a North–South divide implies that, almost by definition, the environmental standard reached in harmonising legislation does not meet with the expectations of the "greenest" Member States. To achieve their environmental goals, these States can have recourse to the environmental safeguard clause of Article 114(4–6) TFEU, or, as the case may be, to the safeguard clause of Article 193 TFEU (depending on the legal basis of the legislation at issue).

We would suggest that the environmental safeguards contained in Articles 114 and 193 TFEU have not (yet) received the widespread application that was predicted at the time of their conception. Over and above the rather dramatic step of employing the environmental guarantee, Article 191(2) as well as Article 114(10) establish the less dramatic but not less effective possibility of the inclusion of a "safeguard clause" in

Union harmonisation measures, allowing Member States to take additional measures. The use of such a safeguard clause effectively cements the potential for different national measures in Union legislation itself. Safeguard measures can only be provisional, meaning limited in time, and they generally have to be notified to, approved by and followed up by the European Commission. This has, for example, been the practice of several Member States in the context of Directive 2001/18 on GMOs.[62]

B. The Conditions for the Guarantee to Apply

Article 193 TFEU includes the environmental title's "environmental guarantee". The environmental guarantee is so-called for it was introduced in the Amsterdam Treaty,[63] to reassure the more environmentally proactive Member States that they would not have to give up their environmental laws in the face of what was thought to be the potential for European environmental law to become watered down. Indeed, prior to Maastricht, as noted above, environmental law was subject to unanimity: Member States which considered a proposed European environmental law too lax could simply block it. With the introduction of qualified majority voting, this was no longer an option. Measures adopted under the environmental guarantee must be stricter than the provisions under EU law, and they have to be "compatible" with the Treaty provisions (Article 193 sentence 2). The most relevant Treaty provisions against which the national measures need to be tested are the Treaty Articles on disguised quantitative restrictions, as established in Articles 34 and 36 TFEU. Stricter measures must be notified to the Commission (Article 193 sentence 3). Common examples for these more stringent standards are for example the introduction of stricter emission standards or stricter water quality standards as required by the Water Framework Directive.[64]

The other main legal basis for environmental law, Article 114, also provides for an environmental guarantee. Article (4–6) TFEU reads:

---

[62] Directive 2001/18 on the deliberate release into the environment of genetically modified organisms and repealing Council Directive 90/220/EEC, [2001] OJ L 106/1.

[63] See also G. Van Calster and K. Deketelaere, "Amsterdam, the IGC and greening the EU Treaty", 7 *European Environmental Law Review* 1 (1998), 12–25.

[64] For further detail on the environmental guarantee, see L. Kraemer, *EU Environmental Law*, 7th Edition, London: Sweet & Maxwell, 2012, at 114–120, and see N. de Sadeleer, *EU Environmental Law and the Internal Market*, Oxford: Oxford University Press, 2014, Chapter 7.

4. If, after the adoption of a harmonisation measure by the European Parliament and the Council, by the Council or by the Commission, a Member State deems it necessary to maintain national provisions on grounds of major needs referred to in Article 36, or relating to the protection of the environment or the working environment, it shall notify the Commission of these provisions as well as the grounds for maintaining them.
5. Moreover, without prejudice to paragraph 4, if, after the adoption of a harmonisation measure by the European Parliament and the Council, by the Council or by the Commission, a Member State deems it necessary to introduce national provisions based on new scientific evidence relating to the protection of the environment or the working environment on grounds of a problem specific to that Member State arising after the adoption of the harmonisation measure, it shall notify the Commission of the envisaged provisions as well as the grounds for introducing them.
6. The Commission shall, within six months of the notifications as referred to in paragraphs 4 and 5, approve or reject the national provisions involved after having verified whether or not they are a means of arbitrary discrimination or a disguised restriction on trade between Member States and whether or not they shall constitute an obstacle to the functioning of the internal market.

In the absence of a decision by the Commission within this period the national provisions referred to in paragraphs 4 and 5 shall be deemed to have been approved.

When justified by the complexity of the matter and in the absence of danger for human health, the Commission may notify the Member State concerned that the period referred to in this paragraph may be extended for a further period of up to six months.

Article 193 TFEU provides: "The protective measures adopted pursuant to Article 192 shall not prevent any Member State from maintaining or introducing more stringent protective measures. Such measures must be compatible with the Treaties. They shall be notified to the Commission."

Article 114(6), refers specifically to three conditions: the national measures must not constitute a means of arbitrary discrimination, or a disguised restriction on trade between Member States. Further, the Amsterdam Treaty added the condition that the measures must not constitute an obstacle to the functioning of the internal market. In other words, the "environmental guarantee" of Article 114, and the room for unilateral action left by Article 193, both embed Member States' unilateral action in the environmental area (after harmonisation) in internal market rationale.[65] Neither of them creates a presumption in favour of environmental protection. The condition provided for in Article 114, that

---

[65] See for an extensive analysis of this issue, G. Van Calster, *International and EC trade law – The Environmental Challenge*, London: Cameron May, 2000. See also Chapter 17 on trade and the environment.

the measures concerned must not constitute an obstacle to the functioning of the internal market, has been interpreted by the Commission as a proportionality requirement.[66] Any national measure derogating from a harmonisation measure constitutes a measure that is likely to affect the internal market. The Commission therefore considers that, in the context of Article 114(6), the concept of "obstacle to the functioning of the Internal Market" has to be understood as a disproportionate effect in relation to the pursued (environmental or health) objective.

The element "disproportionate effect in relation to the pursued (environmental or health) objective" does take the Commission onto dangerous ground. In two of its decisions which struck down national invocations of Article 114(4),[67] the decisions were based on the absence of sound scientific evidence to support the claim of the Member States concerned, not on a perceived disproportionate impact on the internal market (following the dismissal of the requests based on the former consideration, the Commission did not assess the latter element). In one negative decision, the Commission held that the evidence produced was not new, and had in fact been taken into account in the harmonising legislation.[68] In five decisions which gave the go-ahead for stricter national measures,[69] the Commission considered the internal market not to be disproportionately affected, on the basis of market studies which did not reveal considerable impact of the national measures on the internal market of the products in question.

The decisions in which it was decided to reject Member States' invocation of the environmental guarantee are controversial, as can be expected, and one of them at least (the condemnation of Denmark's legislation on foodstuffs) has been received with outright hostility in the Member State concerned. One can imagine that decisions will be all the more controversial should the Commission hold that whilst scientific evidence supports the environmental or public health claims of a particular Member State, market studies show a "disproportionate" impact on the internal market.

---

[66] See the first Commission Decisions applying the Article in OJ [1999] L 329. The Commission approved five of seven requests to impose stricter rules after Community harmonisation.

[67] Denmark (use of sulphites, nitrites and nitrates in foodstuffs), [1999] OJ L 329/1, and Germany (classification, packaging and labelling of dangerous substances), [1999] OJ L 329/100.

[68] Commission decision 2001/570, limitations on the marketing and use of organostannic compounds (Germany), [2001] OJ L 202/37.

[69] Creosote: the Netherlands [1999] OJ L 329/25; Germany [1999] OJ L 329/43; Sweden [1999] OJ L 329/63; and Denmark [1999] OJ L 329/82; and concerning PCPs in the Netherlands [1999] OJ L 329/15.

Such a decision would amount to a direct condemnation of a State's policy choices, as it would tell them that the very level of protection which it seeks is too high, vis-à-vis the objectives of the internal market.

This role of the Commission "second-guessing" Member States' internal policy objectives arguably sits uneasily with the application of Article 34 TFEU on the prohibition of quantitative restrictions on imports by the Court of Justice. In a convincing number of cases, the ECJ has expressly held that the setting of the level of protection is up to the Member States themselves, in the absence of Union harmonisation.[70] The proportionality test to which the national measures are then subject would seem to condemn manifestly unreasonable measures only,[71] and obliges Member States to cooperate with the authorities in other Member States, to avoid unnecessary delays in and obstacles to free movement.[72]

However, the Court has left the door open for speculation, since it often adds to the recognition that it is up to the Member States themselves to set their desired level of protection for "the requirements of the free movement of goods."[73] Moreover, the much-cited *Danish Bottles* case has

---

[70] See for example Joined Cases C-1/90 and C-176/90 *Aragonesa de Publicidad Exterior SA and Publiva SAE v Departamento de Sanidad y Seguridad Social de la Generalitat de Cataluña*, [1991] ECR I-4151, at 16; Case C-347/89 *Freistaat Bayern v Eurim-Pharm GmbH*, [1991] ECR I-1747, at 26; Case 125/88 *Criminal proceedings against H.F.M. Nijman*, [1989] ECR 3533, at 14; Case C-131/93 *Commission v Germany*, [1994] ECR I-3303, at 16; Case 174/82 *Criminal proceedings against Sandoz BV*, [1983] ECR 2445, at 15 *et seq.* (in particular at 19, where the Court upholds a "wide discretion" for the Member States, in the absence of scientific certainty); Case 227/82 *Criminal proceedings against Leendert van Bennekom*, [1983] ECR 3883, at 36 *et seq.* (similar "wide discretion" for the Member States, in the absence of scientific certainty); Case C-293/94 *Criminal proceedings against Jacqueline Brandsma*, [1996] ECR I-3159, at 11; and recently in Case C-400/96 *Criminal proceedings against Jean Harpegnies*, [1998] ECR I-5121, at 33. In addition, the Commission reportedly takes the same view: for example Opinion AG Fennelly in Case C-67/97 *Criminal proceedings against Ditlev Bluhme*, [1998] ECR I-8033, at 20.

[71] See Joined Cases C-1/90 and C-176/90, at 17.

[72] This duty of cooperation, which is also expressed in Article 20 TEU (previously Article 10 EC), refers for instance to the mutual recognition of scientific analysis and laboratory tests.

[73] See, e.g. in Case 174/82, note 70 above, at 24, where the Court subsequently found the national blanket ban to market a product, unless the manufacturers supply proof that a particular additive was safe, to be unlawful; it held that national authorities are obliged to assess the merits of each case, taking into account all relevant information. See G. Van Calster, *International and EC Trade law – The environmental challenge*, London, Cameron May, 2000, for a more extensive analysis of this particular issue.

caused confusion. The Court reviewed Danish legislation which limited the marketing of the packaging of beers and soft drinks to those which were returnable and which were sold in previously approved containers. The marketing of non-approved albeit returnable containers was limited to 3000 hectolitres (hl) per producer per year. That the Danish system amounted to a quantitative restriction to trade was not contested. The ECJ found that the very obligation to use reusable containers and to organise a recovery system, including the use of mandatory deposits, was not *in se* contrary to the rules with respect to the free movement of goods.[74] However, it did find against the obligation for foreign producers either to use approved containers, or to limit their export quantity to 3000 hl of reusable, non-approved containers. The ECJ found that even though the use of non-approved but reusable containers did not guarantee the same level of environmental protection as the use of approved containers, the former nevertheless also served to protect the environment. This tilted the balance of proportionality, even though the use of non-approved containers is not just a less trade-restrictive means, it is also a less environmentally effective means. The Court did not assess in particular whether the Danish measures were indistinctly applicable, but focused instead solely on the issue of proportionality. This is remarkable, since the "indistinctly applicable test" is the standard first tier of the Rule of Reason under free movement of goods case law.

The controversial nature of any EC decision on the environmental guarantee is perfectly illustrated by *Germany v Commission* (toys),[75] reviewed above under the precautionary principle.

V. DECISION-MAKING PROCESS

The Treaty does not usually establish one general decision-making procedure for the adoption of all acts. The most often used procedure is now the "ordinary" decision-making procedure (formerly known as "co-decision"). The Lisbon Treaty simplified the decision-making procedure within the Union to one ordinary legislative procedure and several special legislative procedures.[76]

As established above, the decision-making procedure is determined

---

[74] Case 302/86, *Commission v Denmark*, [1988] ECR 4607, at 13.
[75] ECJ, Case T-198/12 *Germany v Commission*, ECLI:EU:T:2014:251.
[76] See also at length K. Lenaerts and P. Van Nuffel, *European Union Law*, London: Sweet & Maxwell, 2013, 647–676.

by the individual legal basis and established in the Treaty provisions. Article 192 TFEU lays down the decision-making procedure in environmental matters. According to paragraph 1 "The European Parliament and the Council, acting in accordance with the ordinary legislative procedure and after consulting the Economic and Social Committee and the Committee of the Regions, shall decide what action is to be taken by the Union in order to achieve the objectives referred to in Article 191." Thus for most environmental matters the standard decision-making procedure applies (as it also does for the adoption of action programmes, according to Article 192(3) TFEU).

The Lisbon Treaty did not change this main decision-making procedure, which is outlined in Article 294 TFEU. It has three stages. In the "first reading", the Commission submits a legislative proposal to the Parliament which either approves or amends the proposal and forwards it to the Council. The latter either accepts all amendments and adopted acts by the Parliament or does not accept all amendments and adopts a common position by qualified majority voting (QMV, discussed further below).

If there are no amendments made by the Parliament, the Council may either adopt the act by QMV or may adopt a common provision by QMV and refer it back to the Council.

If the Parliament is inactive for the following three months, the act is deemed to be adopted. Further, in a second reading, the Parliament has three possibilities. Firstly, it can formally adopt the act with the majority of its members. The act is then adopted as changed by the Council. Secondly, the Parliament can reject the act with the majority of its members and thirdly it can amend it with the majority of its members and refer it back to the Council and the Commission. The Council in that case can, if the Commission supports these amendments, adopt the amended act by QMV or send it to the Conciliation Committee (further explained below). When the Commission does not support the amendments made during the second reading in the Parliament, the Council can still adopt the amended act but this time by unanimity or send it to the Conciliation Committee. The Conciliation Committee is composed of an equal number of members of the European Parliament and Council representatives, and functions as a mediator in order to reach an agreement on a joint text. The latter has to be approved by the majority of the members of the Parliament and by QMV in the Council within six weeks, otherwise the act will finally not be adopted.

Finally, Article 192 TFEU requires consultation of the Economic and Social Committee as well as the Committee of the Regions. The Committees give their opinion in a non-binding form.

The Council is the central legislative organ in the Union's decision-making process. There are generally four different types of voting: consensus, unanimity, simple majority (of the Members or of the votes cast) and QMV. As established above, the unanimity and the QMV are of importance for decision making in environmental matters. Unanimity is the straightforward requirement that all Member States in the Council have to agree on the specific matter. The Lisbon Treaty simplified the QMV and establishes in Article 16 TEU that from the 1 November 2014 onwards, a QMV on a Commission proposal is

> defined as at least 55 % of the members of the Council, comprising at least fifteen of them and representing Member States comprising at least 65 % of the population of the Union. A blocking minority must include at least four Council members, failing which the qualified majority shall be deemed attained.

Article 238(2) TFEU contains further provisions in this regard.

The ordinary legislative procedure is applicable for most actions aimed at achieving the environmental objectives of Article 191 TFEU. However, paragraph 2 specifies that a special legislative procedure shall apply to:

(a) provisions primarily of a fiscal nature;
(b) measures affecting:
 – town and country planning,
 – quantitative management of water resources or affecting, directly or indirectly, the availability of those resources,
 – land use, with the exception of waste management;
(c) measures significantly affecting a Member State's choice between different energy sources and the general structure of its energy supply.

In these areas, the Council has to act unanimously after consultation with the European Parliament, the Economic and Social Committee and the Committee of the Regions. However, the Council, acting unanimously on a proposal from the Commission and after consulting the European Parliament, the Economic and Social Committee and the Committee of the Regions, may make the ordinary legislative procedure applicable to these matters.

4. Implementation and enforcement

Implementation and enforcement have always been one of the key challenges in environmental law. For a variety of reasons, the Commission has had a hard task to ensure correct and timely implementation of legislation in the Member States. Even when directives are formally transposed, their effects may not be felt for years due to unenthusiastic enforcement.

Reasons for enforcement problems abound: the principal recourse to directives rather than directly enforceable regulations, giving Member States room for manoeuvre which often leads to implementation delays; the technical nature of the legislation involved; the qualification of a number of environmental goods as being part of the common heritage, hence not triggering direct enforcement action by individuals (the so-called "tragedy of the commons"); the over-emphasis of Union environmental law on the specific environmental challenges posed by heavy industry, sidelining the concerns of small and medium-sized enterprises and hence causing resentment with grass roots industrial activity; the lack of sufficient resources allocated by Member States to environmental protection; and so on.

I. IMPLEMENTATION OF ENVIRONMENTAL LAW

A. Legal Implementation

Implementation of legislation is generally undertaken by the Member States. Article 4(3) TEU states that "the Member States shall take any appropriate measure, general or particular, to ensure fulfillment of the obligations arising out of the Treaties or resulting from the acts of the institutions of the Union." Further, "Member States shall adopt all measures of national law necessary to implement legally binding Union acts" (Article 291(1) TFEU). Thus the general rule for the implementation of Union law is the implementation by the national authorities of the Member States (*administration communautaire indirect*). Article 17(1)

TEU adds that the Commission "simply" oversees the application of Union law. This system of implementation is also referred to as "executive federalism".[1]

The concept of executive federalism is also employed with regard to the implementation of environmental law, as reinforced in Article 192(4) TFEU, which reads "without prejudice to certain measures adopted by the Union, the Member States shall finance and implement the environment policy". The exception is the implementation by the Commission or the Council, if explicitly provided for: "Where uniform conditions for implementing legally binding Union acts are needed, those acts shall confer implementing powers on the Commission, or, in duly justified specific cases . . . on the Council" (Article 291(2)); also referred to as the conferral of executive powers on the Commission or Council.[2] In these cases, the basic act must expressly contain a provision conferring the implementing powers to one of the two institutions.

Regulation 182/2011 establishes the rules and general principles concerning mechanisms for control by Member States of the Commission's exercise of implementing powers.[3] This Regulation adopts the new "comitology" framework by the European Parliament and the Council. It establishes the examination and advisory procedures (Articles 4 and 5 of the Regulation) and committees assisting the Commission (Recital 6 and Article 3 of the Regulation). The Committees mainly consist of representatives of the Member States and occasionally scientists and representatives from business and industry. It is chaired by a Commission representative without voting rights. There are currently around 300 such committees

For environmental matters, the "examination" procedure applies (Article 2(b)(iii)), meaning that the individual committee has to deliver a positive opinion for the Commission to be able to adopt an implementing act (Article 5(2)). If a negative opinion is issued, adoption is not possible. If no opinion is delivered, the Commission has to amend the draft implementing act (Article 5(3)) (note therefore the difference between a negative opinion being issued, and no opinion being issued at all).

---

[1] See also, K. Lenaerts and P. Van Nuffel, *European Union Law*, London: Sweet & Maxwell, 2013, 688ff.

[2] See for a detailed explanation of the system, K. Lenaerts and P. Van Nuffel, *European Union Law*, London: Sweet & Maxwell, 2013, 694ff.

[3] Regulation (EU) No 182/2011 of 16 February 2011 laying down the rules and general principles concerning mechanisms for control by Member States of the Commission's exercise of implementing powers, [2011] OJ L 55/13.

Adoption is then subject to further conditions laid down in paragraph 4 of the Regulation.

A 2012 Commission Communication[4] "Improving the delivery of benefits from EU environment measures: building confidence through better knowledge and responsiveness"[5] confirms the overall challenges in ensuring better implementation of EU environmental law. It lists eight objectives aimed at improving knowledge on implementation. It focuses on better communication and information exchange between the local authorities, citizens, national authorities and the Union's institutions. Many of these themes have reoccurred since the very first issuance of such a communication. Key aspects are the establishment of more effective information systems for implementation, building upon the Shared Environmental Implementation System (SEIS) in order to "modernise and simplify the collection, exchange and use of the data and information" and to replace the currently centralised systems.[6] This system should work in line with the development of Structured Implementation and Information Frameworks (SIIFs) for the major environmental laws – one imagines this is also a reference to the EU Network for the Implementation and Enforcement of Environmental Law (IMPEL), the earlier informal network of contacts between national environmental enforcement officials, which has since received more formal backing from the institutions.[7] Further, the Commission emphasises the increasing role of the European Environmental Agency (EEA), Eurostat (the statistical office of the EU) and the Joint Research Centre, in monitoring and data collection in order to improve implementation and EU-level environmental legislation, as well as to build confidence in the information gathered at national, regional and local levels.[8] Much earlier attempts to turn the Agency into a pan-European enforcement institution have failed.

B. Non-legal Instruments Aiming at Better Implementation

Non-legal instruments and measures such as the Technical Platform for Cooperation on the Environment as set up by DG Environment and the Committee of the Regions aim to improve implementation through

---

[4] Building on the 2008 "Communication on implementing European Community Environmental Law", COM (2008) 773.
[5] COM (2012) 95.
[6] COM (2008) 46 at 1.
[7] COM (2012) 95 at 5.
[8] COM (2012) 95 at 6.

dialogue and information exchange between the representatives and stakeholders of the regions and Union officials.[9]

Another example is the aforementioned IMPEL, an international non-profit association aimed at "promoting the effective implementation and enforcement of EU environmental law".[10] The organisation is composed of environmental authorities and associations based in the EU or in an EEA, European Free Trade Association (EFTA) or candidate country. The objective of the association is to ensure a more effective application of the Union's environmental law and especially to promote information exchange and capacity building between environmental authorities (at a local, regional or national level); to carry out joint enforcement projects; and to produce guidance, tools and common standards for implementation best practice.[11] The association is doing so by carrying out specific projects which are conducted by experts employed by an environmental authority. Projects are either related to the cluster "Improving permitting, inspection and enforcement" or "Transfrontier Shipments of Waste (TFS)" and the cluster "Better regulation (practicability and enforceability)".[12]

Similar to IMPEL, the EU Forum of Judges for the Environment (EUFJE) is an international non-profit association aimed at "promote[ing], in the perspective of sustainable development, the implementation of National, European and international Environmental Law".[13] Every judge interested in environmental law who is a member of the ECJ, the European Court of Human Rights or a court or tribunal of an EU or EFTA Member State can join. The aim of the association is to share experience on judicial training in environmental law and foster the knowledge of environmental law among judges. The association does so by initiating and promoting studies and by publishing reviews or monographs.[14]

Furthermore, DG Environment is currently carrying out a stakeholder consultation on the revision of the EU legal framework on environmental inspections in order to establish a structured approach and a level playing

---

[9] See also Committee of the Regions, "New cooperation platform to support Europe's local authorities in delivering 7th Environment Action Programme", available at http://cor.europa.eu/en/news/pr/Pages/cooperation-platform-environment-action-programme.aspx, last consulted 27.10.2015.

[10] See Article 3 para.1 IMPEL Statute, available at http://impel.eu/wp-content/uploads/2013/02/IMPEL-Statute-web-version-06-Dec-2012.pdf, last consulted 27.10.2015.

[11] See Article 3(3) IMPEL Statute.

[12] See Articles 3(3), 10 and 11 IMPEL Statute.

[13] See Articles 1 and 3 EUFJE Statute, available at http://www.eufje.org/EN/presentation/bylaws, last consulted 27.10.2015.

[14] See Article 3 EUFJE Statute.

field for environmental inspections, as well as to broaden the scope of the environmental acquis which is subject to explicit provisions on inspections.[15] The 7th Environmental Action Programme focuses on national and regional authorities to improve implementation.[16]

II. PRIMACY AND DIRECT EFFECT

The ECJ has contributed in decisive fashion to defining the EU as a Union governed by the rule of law by laying down two essential rules: the *direct effect* of Union law in the Member States; and the *primacy* (also called supremacy) of Union law over national law. Of those decisions, the *van Gend en Loos* (1963),[17] *Costa v E.N.E.L.* (1964)[18] and *Simmenthal* (1978)[19] judgments are the most important.

Costa v E.N.E.L. amounts to a forceful statement[20] of the transfer of sovereignty from the Member States to the Union. The Court held that

> (b)y contrast with ordinary international treaties, the EEC Treaty has created its own legal system which, on the entry into force of the Treaty, became an integral part of the legal systems of the Member States and which courts are bound to apply. By creating a Community of unlimited duration, having its own institutions, its own legal personality, its own legal capacity and capacity of representation on the international plane and, more particularly, real powers stemming from a limitation of sovereignty or a transfer of powers from the States to the Community, the Member States have limited their sovereign rights, albeit within limited fields, and have thus created a body of law which binds both their nationals and themselves.

Simmenthal put the principle of primacy, or supremacy, of Union law over national law, in even clearer terms: provisions of Union law

---

[15] European Commission, "Consultation on Revision of the EU legal framework on environmental inspections", available at http://ec.europa.eu/environment/consultations/inspections_en.htm, last consulted 21.11.2015, as well as the Consultation document itself at 5.
[16] Decision No 1386/2013 of 20 November 2013 on a General Union Environment Action Programme to 2020 "Living well, within the limits of our planet" [2013] OJ L 354/171, at 57.
[17] Case 26/62 *NV Algemene Transportonderneming van Gend en Loos v Netherlands Inland Revenue Administration*, [1963] ECR 3.
[18] Case C-6/64 *Flaminio Costa v E.N.E.L*, [1964] ECR 585.
[19] Case C-106/77, *Amministrazione delle Finanze dello Stato v Simmenthal SpA*, [1978] ECR 629.
[20] J.-V. Louis, *The Community Legal Order*, Luxembourg: Office for Official Publications of the European Communities, 1990, at 11.

are an integral part of, and take precedence in, the legal order applicable in the territory of each of the Member States.[21] ... every national court must, in a case within its jurisdiction, apply Community law in its entirety and protect rights which the latter confers on individuals and must accordingly set aside any provisions of national law which may conflict with it, whether prior or subsequent to the Community rule.[22]

In *Van Gend en Loos*, after recalling the historic circumstances in which the Union was created, and referring to the preamble of the Treaty and to the founding fathers' intention, the Court held that

the Community constitutes a new legal order of international law for the benefit of which the States have limited their sovereign rights, albeit within limited fields, and the subjects of which comprise not only Member States but also their nationals. Independently of the legislation of Member States, Community law therefore not only imposes obligations on individuals but is also intended to confer upon them rights which become part of their legal heritage.[23]

Direct effect of EU law increases the level of enforcement and compliance with it, because a private individual can go to his national court and ask it to set aside provisions of national law that are contrary to EU law.[24] For there to be direct effect, the provisions of EU law must be sufficiently clear, precise and unconditional to confer rights and obligations directly on individuals.

Supremacy and direct effect are closely related, but not interchangeable.[25] All regularly adopted provisions of Union law take precedence over national law that is incompatible with them. But not all Union provisions enjoy the direct effect necessary for individuals to be able to invoke these provisions directly in proceedings in their national courts. Advocate-General Mayras formulated a three-tier test for determining whether a provision of Union law may have direct effect:[26] the provision must impose a clear and precise obligation on Member States; it must be unconditional, that is, subject to no limitations (if the limitations are, however, exactly defined, this does not prevent there being direct effect); and a Member

---

[21] Ibid., at 17.
[22] Ibid., at para. 21.
[23] Note 17 above.
[24] J.-V. Louis, *supra*, note 20, p. 110.
[25] See in-depth, K. Lenaerts and P. Van Nuffel, *European Union Law*, London: Sweet & Maxwell, 2013, 754 and 809–813.
[26] In his opinion in Case 41/74 *Van Duyn v Home Office*, [1974] ECR 1337, as summarised in *Law of the European Communities*, gen. ed. David Vaughan, London: Butterworths, 1986, vol. 1, 413–414.

State must not be left with any real discretion as to the application of the rule in question. In the absence of direct effect, the individual has three options left at his disposal (these options are somewhat simplified in what follows). If the adversary in the national procedure is a public authority, the individual can rely on the provisions of a directive which has not been properly implemented (otherwise, the authority could profit from its lack of correct implementation); if the adversary is not a public authority, national courts are under a duty to apply national law to the greatest extent possible in line with Union law (based on the *Marleasing* case[27]); finally, if neither of the preceding options is available, the individual may seek damages from the Member State concerned for failure properly to implement Union law.

III. THE INFRINGEMENT PROCEDURE

According to official Commission statistics,[28] 334 infringements in the environmental sector were identified in 2014 (353 in 2013 and 296 in 2012). Most of them (189 infringements) were related to poor application of a directive and/or its transposing legislation. Within the environmental sector, the waste (31 per cent), nature (19 per cent) and water (20 per cent) sector contained the most cases.

The action for infringement of Union law by a Member State is laid out in Articles 258–260 TFEU.[29] The origins for an infringement action taken by the Commission against a Member State can either be a complaint by citizens,[30] a petition or question from the European Parliament (Article 227 TFEU)[31] or be based on the Commission's own initiative.

---

[27] C-106/89 *Marleasing v Comercial Internacional de Alimentación*, [1990] ECR I-4135.

[28] All data retrieved from http://ec.europa.eu/environment/legal/law/statistics.htm, last consulted 27.10.2015.

[29] See also K. Lenaerts and I. Maselis, *Procedural law of the European Union*, Oxford: Oxford University Press, 2014, 159–214. For a detailed analysis please also refer to S. Andersen, *The Enforcement of EU Law: The Role of the European Commission*, Oxford: Oxford University Press, 2012.

[30] In 2009, the Secretariat General of the Commission established a central registry (CHAP), where all complaints and enquiries are now collected and registered. See also Commission Communication, "Updating the handling of relations with the complainant in respect of the application of Union law", COM (2012), for more information about the citizens' complaints procedure.

[31] Article 227 TFEU provides that any citizen of the Union, and any natural or legal person residing or having their registered office in a Member State, shall

There are generally three types of infringements: non-communication, non-conformity or bad application.

Article 258 TFEU provides the basis for an infringement procedure of Union law brought to court by the Commission against a Member State, Article 259 TFEU for an action by one Member State against another. Both procedures foresee an attempt to settle the dispute informally by firstly issuing a formal letter warning the Member State concerned and stating the failure to fulfil an obligation and a possible action before the ECJ (Article 258(1)). If the Member State concerned fails to resolve the issue after the lapse of a certain amount of time, the Commission can issue a reasoned opinion that indicates the grounds for the infringements and possibly (there is no formal requirement) includes solutions to cure the infringement.

The reasoned opinion marks the beginning of the time period within which the Member State has to comply. If the State concerned does not comply with the opinion within the period laid down by the Commission, the latter may bring the matter before the CJEU (Article 258(2)). If the ECJ finds that a Member State has failed to fulfil an obligation under Article 258 or 259 TFEU, the Member State is required to take the necessary measures to comply with the judgment of the Court (Article 260(1) TFEU). After the infringement procedure, if the Member State concerned still does not comply with the Union law and the ECJ's judgment, Article 260(2) TFEU establishes a procedure which can result in a financial penalty for the Member State. This sanction can be a lump sum and/or a penalty payment.[32] Of importance, especially regarding infringement cases in the area of environmental legislation, is Article 279 TFEU allowing the Court of Justice to prescribe any necessary interim measures before a final judgment on grounds of Article 260 TFEU. Especially in the field of environmental protection, the time lapse between the submission of the case to the ECJ and the actual judgment (one and a half to two years is not exceptional) may lead to irreparable damage. The possibility of interim measures therefore is a very powerful instrument. A case where it was applied was *Commission v Malta*[33] regarding the Wild Birds Directive. The Court ordered Malta to refrain from adopting any measures applying

---

have the right to address, individually or in association with other citizens or persons, a petition to the European Parliament on a matter which comes within the Union's fields of activity and which affects him, her or it directly.

[32] Regardless of the explicit wording "lump sum or penalty payment" of the Treaty provision, the ECJ held that, in practice, both a lump sum *and* a penalty payment can be imposed on a Member State (see Case C-340/02 *Commission v France* [2005] ECR I-6263).

[33] Case C-76/08 *Commission v Malta*, [2009] ECR I-8213.

the derogation in Article 9 referring to the urgency of the measure and the absence of another satisfactory solution.

Under the Lisbon Treaty two changes were introduced to the system in Article 260 TFEU. Firstly, according to Article 260(2) TFEU it is no longer required to issue a reasoned opinion with the second round of infringement proceedings. Thus, if the Commission thinks that a Member State has not complied with an ECJ judgement, it can refer the matter to the Court after having sent a letter of formal notice the Member State concerned asking the latter to submit its observations (first pre-litigation procedural step). If the Member State does not comply with this request, the Commission can refer the matter directly to the Court. In practice, this speeds up the procedure which now "only" takes about 8 to 18 months. The second change relates to the imposition of fines on unwilling Member States and is discussed below.

A. Imposing Fines on Unwilling Member States

The very first judgment ordering a Member State to pay a penalty payment for non-compliance concerned the implementation of an environmental directive by Greece. Greece was ordered to pay EUR 20,000.00 per day on the basis of its failure to comply with a judgment of 7 April 1992,[34] concerning the drawing up and implementation of plans necessary for the disposal of waste and toxic and dangerous waste from the area concerned without endangering human health or without harming the environment.

Article 260 TFEU (ex-Article 228 EC) was introduced by the Maastricht Treaty and provides that the Commission, if it considers that the state concerned has not taken the measures necessary to comply with the Court's judgment,

> may bring the case before the Court after giving that State the opportunity to submit its observations. It shall specify the amount of the lump sum or penalty payment to be paid by the Member State concerned which it considers appropriate in the circumstances. If the Court finds that the Member State concerned has not complied with its judgment it may impose a lump sum or penalty payment on it.

Whilst the Commission is explicitly committed to the principles of proportionality and equal treatment of all Member States in the application of Article 260 TFEU, it accepts that the amount of the penalty payment should reflect the Member State's ability to pay. Thus the Commission

---

[34] Case C-45/91 *Commission v Greece* [1992] ECR I-2509.

concludes that the deterrent effect is achieved by applying a special factor in its calculations based on the Member State's gross domestic product (GDP) and the weighting of votes in Council. The higher the GDP and the greater the votes in Council, the higher the penalty payment sought.[35] The significance of the *Greece* judgment lies in particular in the role of Article 260 TFEU as a complement to the doctrine of state liability for damages for breach of Union law, developed at the European Court.[36] The conditions surrounding the application of this latter doctrine are such as to render its application problematic in the environmental sphere. Noteworthy in this respect is the pre-condition for its application that the Union law at issue confer rights upon individuals. Penalty payments do not suffer from this requirement.

Significant though the judgment is, however, it does also highlight problems inherent in Article 260 TFEU. Notable in this respect is the inevitable question of delay. The Commission's application was lodged on 14 November 1997, and judgment handed down on 4 July 2000. Yet the penalty payment imposed was declared to run from the date of delivery of the present judgment. Alongside the issue of delay is that relating to the Commission's capacity to demonstrate before the Court, for a second time, a failure to comply with Union law obligations. That the Commission was precluded from seeking such a remedy when at first it initiates an action under Article 258 TFEU was such as to render this procedure burdensome and highly resource intensive.

The practice before the Lisbon Treaty regarding infringement proceedings under Article 258 TFEU was that the Commission, after having obtained a declaratory judgment that a Member State has failed to fulfil its obligation, had to apply a second time to the Court in order to request the imposition of a lump sum and penalty payment. The Lisbon Treaty substantially changed the provision in this regard. It is now possible for the Commission to propose the imposition of a lump sum or penalty payment to the Court at the stage of the infringement proceedings itself, which means in the same judgment establishing the Member State's failure to fulfil its obligations.

An example is *Commission v Belgium*.[37] According to the EC, Belgium

---

[35] See for more information and the concrete factors representing the payment capacity of the Member States' GDP and the number of votes it has in the Council, Commission Communication, "Updating of data used to calculate lump sum and penalty payments to be proposed by the Commission to the Court of Justice in infringement proceedings", COM (2012) 6106.
[36] Case 6–9/90 *Francovich and Bonifaci v Italy* [1991] ECR I-5357.
[37] Case C-533/11 *Commission v Belgium* ECLI:EU:C:2013:659.

had failed to comply with the Court's judgment in Case C-27/03[38] concerning the failure to transpose the Urban Waste Water Directive[39] within the given time limit. The Commission proposed a penalty payment of EUR 55,836.00 for Belgium to pay each day of delay in complying with the judgment, from delivery of the judgment in the present case until the date on which the judgment in Case C-27/03 has been complied with. The Court in its final judgment set the amount of the lump sum to EUR 10 million, recognising that "the Kingdom of Belgium agreed to substantial investments in order to comply with the judgment in *Commission* v *Belgium* and has made considerable progress" (at 59) and "has fully cooperated with the Commission during the proceedings" (at 60).

IV. EUROPEAN CITIZENS AS EU ENVIRONMENTAL LAW ENFORCERS

The role of the European citizen, too, in implementation and enforcement of European environmental law is referred to in the Communication. Access to justice and better complaint handling and mediation at the national level are two cornerstones to improve the responsiveness of the Union at the local and regional level.[40] In practice, the European citizen is the first and foremost enforcer of EU environmental law, via primacy and direct effect (see Chapter 4 II), supplemented with a preliminary review by the ECJ.

The Commission has further strengthened citizens' role as an enforcer in its recent initiatives on collective settlements and class actions.[41] The Recommendation[42] promotes supplementary private enforcement of rights in the form of collective redress explicitly in the area of environment protection.[43] The Commission refers to the provisions of the Aarhus Convention and encourages a wide access to justice in environmental matters (Recital 23). The overall purpose of the recommendation

---

[38] Case C-27/03 *Commission v Belgium* ECLI:EU:C:2004:418.
[39] Directive 91/271 concerning urban waste-water treatment, [1991] OJ L 135/40.
[40] COM (2012) 95, at 6–8.
[41] European Commission, "Towards a European Horizontal Framework for Collective Redress", COM (2013) 401, at 4 and 10.
[42] Commission Recommendation of 11 June 2013 on common principles for injunctive and compensatory collective redress mechanisms in the Member States concerning violations of rights granted under Union Law, [2013] OJ L 201/60.
[43] Recital 7 of the Recommendation.

is to "facilitate access to justice, stop illegal practices and enable injured parties to obtain compensation in mass harm situations caused by violations of rights granted under Union law, while ensuring appropriate procedural safeguards to avoid abusive litigation" (Article 1). The Recommendation outlines general common principles regarding injunctive and compensatory redress in relation to standing, admissibility information on a collective redress action, legal cost reimbursement of winning parties and funding, as well as more a specific principle regarding the two actions.

The difficult birth of the Environmental Crime Directive[44] and its criticism on the grounds of subsidiarity issues, but especially the annulment of the Council's Framework Decision[45] by the ECJ, stresses the role national governments and especially citizens have in enforcement. The ECJ amongst others reasoned that "as a general rule, neither criminal law nor the rules of criminal procedure fall within the Community's competence".[46] In 2013 the Commission introduced a legislative proposal to establish a European Public Prosecutor's Office (EPPO), mostly regarding financial issues.[47] After significant criticism by the Member States, the Commission, however, amended these plans.[48]

The Mediation Directive,[49] too, is a possible tool for resolving environmental conflicts. It has not been applied much in practice as yet.

---

[44] Directive 2008/99 on the protection of the environment through criminal law, [2008] OJ L 328/28.

[45] Case C-176/03 *Commission v Council* [2005] ECR I-7879.

[46] Case C-176/03 *Commission v Council* [2005] ECR I-7879, at 47 and also Case 203/80 *Casati* [1981] ECR 2595, para. 27 and Case C-226/97 *Lemmens* [1998] ECR I-3711, at 19.

[47] European Commission, Proposal for a Council Regulation on the establishment of the European Public Prosecutor's Office, COM (2013) 534.

[48] See for a more detailed analysis, S. Peers, "Fundamental Rights and the European Public Prosecutor's Office: an uncomfortable silence", available at http://eulawanalysis.blogspot.fr/2015/04/fundamental-rights-and-european-public.html, last consulted 10.11.2015.

[49] Directive 2008/52 on certain aspects of mediation in civil and commercial matters, [2008] OJ L 136/3.

5. Public participatory rights

On 25 June 1998, the United Nations Economic Commission for Europe (UNECE) Convention on Access to Information, Public Participation in Decision-Making and Access to Justice in Environmental Matters ("Aarhus Convention") was adopted. In its objective the Aarhus Convention states that

> in order to contribute to the protection of the right of every person of present and future generations to live in an environment adequate to his or her health and well-being, each Party shall guarantee the rights of access to information, public participation in decision-making, and access to justice in environmental matters in accordance with the provisions of this Convention.

The Convention thus establishes three pillars of public participatory rights: (1) the right of access to information, (2) participation in decision making, and (3) access to justice. The EU adopted the Convention on 17 February 2005 through Decision 2005/370[1] and has adhered to it since May 2005. In order to transpose the requirements into Union law, the institutions passed several pieces of legislation, reflecting the three pillars. Given its role in the external environmental relations of the Member States, the EU has adopted legislation which applies to the Member States and to the EU institutions.

Secondary law aimed at transposing the Aarhus provisions for the *Member States* is:

- Directive 2003/4[2] of the European Parliament and of the Council of 28 January 2003 on public access to environmental information

---

[1] Decision 2005/370 on the conclusion, on behalf of the European Community, of the Convention on access to information, public participation in decision-making and access to justice in environmental matters, [2005] OJ L 124/1.

[2] Directive 2003/4/EC of 28 January 2003 on public access to environmental information and repealing Council Directive 90/313/EEC, OJ L 41, 14.2.2003, pp. 26–32.

- Directive 2003/35[3] of the European Parliament and of the Council of 26 May 2003 providing for public participation in respect of the drawing up of certain plans and programmes relating to the environment.

Regarding the third pillar of Aarhus, access to justice, the EU has no competence to outline provisions in this regard vis-à-vis the Member States. The implementation of the third pillar of the Convention is left to the Member States. However, access to justice to the EU institutions is regulated at a European level.

Secondary law applicable to the *Union institutions* is:

- Regulation 1049/2001 regarding public access to European Parliament, Council and Commission documents[4]
- Regulation 1367/2006 on the application of the provisions of the Aarhus Convention to Community institutions and bodies[5] renders the provisions of the Aarhus Convention binding on the European institutions.

I. IMPLEMENTATION OF THE AARHUS CONVENTION IN THE EU MEMBER STATES

Before looking at the individual pillars in detail, it is noteworthy that the Commission makes a somewhat peculiar recourse to the principle of proportionality in relation to the obligations arising for Union institutions. The principle is referred to in both Directives.[6] In the recitals it is stated that the Directives do not go beyond what is necessary to adhere to the Aarhus

---

[3] Directive 2003/35/EC of 26 May 2003 providing for public participation in respect of the drawing up of certain plans and programmes relating to the environment and amending with regard to public participation and access to justice Council Directives 85/337/EEC and 96/61/EC, OJ L 156, 25.6.2003, pp. 17–25.

[4] Regulation 1049/2001 regarding public access to European Parliament, Council and Commission documents, [2001] OJ L 145/43.

[5] Regulation 1367/2006 on the application of the provisions of the Aarhus Convention on Access to Information, Public Participation in Decision-making and Access to Justice in Environmental Matters to Community institutions and bodies, [2006] OJ L 264/13.

[6] Recital 32 of Directive 2003/4/EC of 28 January 2003 on public access to environmental information, [2003] OJ L 41/26, and recital 12 of Directive 2003/35 providing for public participation in respect of the drawing up of certain plans and programmes relating to the environment, [2003] OJ L 156/17.

Convention. In other words the Commission limits itself to those obligations which are required as a minimum, by the Convention. It presents this as if it were required by the principle of proportionality. However, this principle, like the principle of subsidiarity (both included in the same Article of the EU Treaty), serves as a protection for Members States' powers. Given that Member States obviously have no power to interfere in how the Union institutions themselves carry out their obligations under the Convention, the principle of proportionality has little calling in relation to the obligations as applied by the institutions. This also explains why the Member States argue that the Commission in this area displays a lack of ambition, in contrast with what it requires of the Member States.

A. Access to Environmental Information

Directive 2003/4 transposes the provisions relating to the first pillar of the Aarhus Convention, on access to environmental information. The Directive builds upon earlier Community law instruments on access to environmental information. The overall objectives are to firstly guarantee the right of access to environmental information held by or for public authorities (so-called "passive" transparency, seen from the point of view of the authorities) and secondly to ensure that environmental information is made public, especially through the use of electronic sources and the Internet (Article 1 of the Directive, as well as Article 7) (so-called "active" transparency, given that the Member States have to take active steps to ensure the organisation of information).

It obliges the Member States to actively and systematically disseminate environmental information which is relevant to their function and to assist applicants to find the relevant information (Articles 3(5) and Article 7 of the Directive). Further, it lays the groundwork for active distribution of environmental information and is the basis of the European framework for sharing environmental information and monitoring activities.[7]

Environmental information

"Environmental information" is defined as in Aarhus (Article 2 of the Convention). Hence it is defined very broadly and subject to a

---

[7] The framework is set up through Directive 2007/2 establishing an Infrastructure for Spatial Information in the European Community, [2007] OJ L 108/1 ("INSPIRE Directive"), Directive 2003/98 on the re-use of public sector information, [2003] OJ L 345/90 ("PSI Directive") and the Communication from the Commission – Towards a Shared Environmental Information System ("SEIS"), COM (2008) 46.

far-reaching application. This is confirmed by the ECJ, which considered a procedure for authorisation of a plant protection product to be "environmental information", as defined by the Directive.[8] It includes general information regarding the state of environmental elements (air, water biodiversity, etc.), factors (substances, noise, radiation, emissions, etc.) and human health and safety (contamination of food chains, cultural sites, etc.). Further, it covers environmental administrative measures such as policies, legislation, environmental plans and programmes and reports of implementation of these measures, especially relating to implementation of environmental legislation. Cost–benefit and economic analyses in relation to the measures also fall under the scope of environmental information (Article 2(1) of the Directive, as well as Article 7(2)). Regarding the quality of the environmental legislation, Member States have to ensure that the information is up to date, accurate and comparable (Article 8).

Public authority
The term "public authority", too, is to be interpreted in a broad manner (Article 2(2)) of the Directive). The Directive states that "public authority" shall mean:

> (a) government or other public administration, including public advisory bodies, at national, regional or local level; (b) any natural or legal person performing public administrative functions under national law, including specific duties, activities or services in relation to the environment; and (c) any natural or legal person having public responsibilities or functions, or providing public services, relating to the environment under the control of a body or person falling within (a) or (b).

Member States may provide that this definition shall not include bodies or institutions when acting in a judicial or legislative capacity.

The definition clearly captures all government or other public administration and natural or legal persons performing or having public responsibilities or functions, including advisory bodies.

How broad this latter exclusion needs to be applied, is disputed.

In *Flachgas Torgau* the ECJ held that ministers participating in the legislative process may be exempt for the time of the process.[9]

---

[8] Case C-266/09 *Stichting Milieu and Others v College voor de toelating van gewasbeschermingsmiddelen en biociden*, at 43, ECLI:EU:C:2010:779.
[9] Case C-204/09 *Flachgas Torgau GmbH v Federal Republic of Germany*, ECLI:EU:C:2012:71.

Fish Legal[10] concerns private companies which manage a public service relating to the environment (water and sewage services). The dispute centres on whether the management of that service is of such a nature that, even though the companies concerned are private, they have to be regarded as "public authorities" for the purposes of Directive 2003/4 and, in consequence, must comply with the request for information addressed to them by two private individuals. In England and Wales, water and sewerage services may be provided only by companies which have been appointed by the Secretary of State or (now) by Ofwat (the economic regulator of the water industry in England and Wales) as water supply and/or sewerage providers for a particular area of England or Wales. Only a limited company may be appointed as a water or sewerage provider. The companies are run by boards of directors, accountable to the shareholders. The companies are run in accordance with normal commercial principles, as set out in their memoranda and articles of association, with the aim of generating profits for distribution to shareholders as dividends and for reinvestment in the business. The companies are subject to the rules binding upon all other public limited companies or limited companies. They receive no public subsidy. Neither borrowing nor investment decisions are directly dictated by government or any other public body. Nor is any borrowing by the companies backed by the State. Accordingly, each company's funds are generated by charges to customers, the sale of shares and other rights issues, borrowing through the capital markets at normal commercial rates, and other commercial activities such as the sale of land and other assets.

Where access was sought by a non-profit-making organisation and by a natural person to information held by companies which the national authority did not regard as "public authorities" for the purposes of Directive 2003/4, as described above, AG Cruz Villalon opined that

> admittedly, the concept in question is not relevant solely in the context of EU law; on the contrary, it comes within the ambit of an international convention – the Aarhus Convention – which is binding on the European Union and in the light of which Directive 2003/4 must be construed. Obviously, that directive is not decisive when it comes to the interpretation of the Aarhus Convention but it is decisive for the purposes of ensuring that the European Union meets its obligations in relation to that convention, since it can only do justice to them if it is able to ensure that, in the context of the European Union, the concept of "[n]atural or legal persons performing public administrative functions under national law", as used in Article 2(2)(b) of the Aarhus Convention, is uniformly construed in all the Member States.

---

[10] Case C-279/12 *Fish Legal et al v Information Commissioner et al.*, ECLI:EU:C:2013:539.

Despite the need for autonomous interpretation, the specific EU provision under consideration itself refers to national law: Article 2(2)(b): "any natural or legal person performing public administrative functions *under national law*, . . ." (emphasis added). The AG suggests that this provision should be read purely in a factual sense: EU law cannot determine which persons or institutions actually perform those functions in each Member State; that is for the Member State to decide. However, it is for EU law alone to establish what those functions are and in what they consist. Put differently, "since certain functions are defined under EU law as "public administrative functions", it will then be necessary to determine, *in accordance with national law*, which bodies – in addition to the public authorities in the strict sense – may perform such functions and are therefore covered by Article 2(2)(b) of Directive 2003/4" (emphasis in the original).

The AG then defines "public administrative functions" within the context of the provision, as "functions by virtue of which individuals have imposed on them a will the immediate effectiveness of which, albeit subject to review, does not require their consent." He suggests that

> Article 2(2)(b) refers to individuals who, by virtue of a formal, express delegation of authority, exercise with some degree of autonomy certain official powers, whereas Article 2(2)(c) encompasses individuals who, without substantive autonomy, are instruments of the State for the purposes of the latter's actions in the sphere of private relationships as a mere individual. Accordingly, both cases involve the State, either because an individual exercises public authority which is the monopoly of the State or because an individual allows the State (directly or via an intermediary) to act through him as an individual governed by private law.[11]

Finally the AG reviews how far the duty of information (and transparency) goes, and distinguishes two possible situations:[12]

> (i) the situation of bodies or persons whose activities are limited to the management of a service under conditions which mean that they must be regarded as public authorities for the purposes of Directive 2003/4; and (ii) the situation of bodies or persons who, in addition to managing a service under such conditions, also perform other, completely unconnected, activities, an example being bodies or persons who also manage a service relating to the environment in another territory but under free competition conditions and without it being possible to classify them as "public authorities" for the purposes of Directive 2003/4.

---

[11] At 103.
[12] At 117ff. Footnotes omitted.

As far as the persons or bodies in situation (i) are concerned, the question is answered by Directive 2003/4 itself, Article 3(1) of which provides that "Member States shall ensure that public authorities are required, in accordance with the provisions of this Directive, to make available environmental information held by or for them to any applicant . . ." In short, Directive 2003/4 imposes on the State – both the State *stricto sensu* and a "public authority" in the broader sense of Article 2(2)(b) of Directive 2003/4 – the obligation to permit access to environmental information held by it, regardless of the capacity in which it obtained that information: in other words, both where that information is the result of exercising its imperium and where it is the result of its activities as a body governed by private law.

As far as the persons or bodies in situation (ii) are concerned, it is my view that they do not warrant the same treatment. They may be regarded as public authorities only to the extent that they perform activities relating to the environment in circumstances which may be classified as "control" within the meaning of Article 2(2)(c) of Directive 2003/4; in other words, in so far as they act "under the control" of the public authorities. Aside from that, they are merely individuals and, as such, are not subject to the requirement laid down in Article 3(1) of the Directive.

I accept that, as the parties have observed, the foregoing may, in certain circumstances, give rise to a "hybrid" situation which is difficult to handle in practice. In so far as that is the case, it is my opinion that, in the light of the spirit of Directive 2003/4 and its objective of promoting access to information held by the public authorities in the broadest sense of the term, situations of uncertainty should always be resolved in favour of the person requesting information.

The ECJ, in its judgment generally agreed with the AG. For EU law, the Court's judgment is of great importance. "Public authorities" is a concept which is used extensively in EU law. While formally opined vis-à-vis the environmental information irective, it is clear that the analysis of the AG may be of general use for EU law and consequently will have an impact on the ever-increasing trend of privatisation and outsourcing of public functions. The referring court held on substance in February 2015 that water companies are public authorities because they have "special powers".[13]

In *Deutsche Umwelthilfe*[14] the court dealt with the extent of the power of the Member States to exclude bodies acting in a legislative capacity from the definition of "public authority" under the directive. The Court held that

> the option given to Member States by that provision of not regarding "bodies or institutions acting in a . . . legislative capacity" as public authorities, required to allow access to the environmental information which they hold, may not be

---

[13] *Fish Legal v IC & Ors* (Information rights: Information rights: practice and procedure) [2015] UKUT 52 (AAC) (19 February 2015).
[14] Case C-515/11 *Deutsche Umwelthilfe* ECLI:EU:C:2013:523.

applied to ministries when they prepare and adopt normative regulations which are of a lower rank than a law.

In its reasoning, the Court clarified that

> as regards the aims of the directive, only the smooth running of the process for the adoption of legislation and the particular characteristics of the legislative process which ensure that the public is usually adequately informed justify the fact that those bodies acting in a legislative capacity or participating in the legislative process should be exempt from the obligations to provide information imposed by that directive.

As previously interpreted by the Court in analogy in *Bund für Umwelt und Naturschutz Deutschland, Landesverband Nordrhein-Westfalen*.[15]

Grounds for refusal of access
Under Article 3 of the Directive, public authorities are requested to grant access to environmental information to an applicant upon request within a time frame ranging from one to two months, without him having to state an interest (for the definition of "interest" see this chapter, below). Exceptions to this general rule of granting access shall be interpreted in a restrictive way, taking into account the particular case[16] and the public interest served by disclosure. This should be balanced against the interest served by refusal.[17] The Court further specified that while balancing the public interests, authorities might cumulatively take into account a number of the grounds for refusal set out in Article 4(2).[18]

Limitations to public access to environmental information are provided for in Article 4 of the Directive.[19] Requests for information can only be refused if they relate amongst others to confidentiality of public authority proceedings, personal data or commercial or industry information, the course of justice, international relations, public security or defence or intellectual property rights. This list is exhaustive, hence Member States are not allowed to add further derogations for refusal. However, they do not have to transpose all requirements into national law, since Member

---

[15] Case C-115/09 *Bund für Umwelt und Naturschutz Deutschland, Landesverband Nordrhein-Westfalen*, [2011] ECR I-3673, at 41.
[16] As confirmed by the ECJ in Case C-266/09 *Stichting Milieu and Others v College voor de toelating van gewasbeschermingsmiddelen en biociden*, at 59.
[17] As also stressed in Case C-71/10 *Office of Communications v Information Commissioner*, at 22.
[18] Case C-71/10 *Office of Communications v Information Commissioner*, at 32.
[19] Using the same wording as Article 4(3–5) of the Convention.

States are allowed to introduce measures providing broader access to information than established by the Directive (see also Recital 24 of the preamble to the Directive).

The application of this article proves to be challenging in practice, especially regarding the relation with sector-specific *lex specialis*.[20] As a general rule, *lex specialis* overrules the access provisions of the Directive; however, most sector specific directives refer to Directive 2003/4 and thus apply these general access provisions or specify the individual scope of application.[21] For example, regarding the interpretation of the exception of "international relations, public security or national defence" in Article 4(2)(b), the Court has held that Member States cannot invoke the exception provision of "public security" of Directive 2003/4 in order to refuse access to information which should be in the public domain under the provisions of Directive 2001/18 (the "GMO Directive").[22] Thus, the transparency requirements of the GMO Directive (more precisely Articles 9, 25(4) and 31(3)), the *lex specialis*, overrule the *lex generalis* (Directive 2003/4), which includes public security as a possible derogation for access to information rights.

Further, where a request deals with information regarding emissions into the environment, it is generally assumed that the public interest served by disclosure prevails over the interest served by refusal. Concerning emissions, the grounds of refusal are further limited and access to the information may only be refused on grounds of intellectual property rights, international relations, public security or national defence or course of justice. In *Ville de Lyon v Caisse des dépôts et consignations*,[23] the Court dealt with the question whether data on greenhouse gas emissions allowance trading are considered to be "information on emissions into the environment" within the meaning of Article 4 of Directive 2003/4, against whose supply "the confidentiality of commercial or industrial information" could not be invoked. The Court held that these data did not have to be made publicly accessible since they fall exclusively under the specific rules governing public reporting and confidentiality contained in Directive 2003/87 and in Regulation 2216/2004.[24]

---

[20] Report on the experience gained in the application of Directive 2003/4 on public access to environmental information, COM (2012) 774, at 9.
[21] Ibid.
[22] Case C-552/07 *Commune de Sausheim v Pierre Azelvandre* ECLI:EU:C:2009:96 at 50, as well as opinion of AG Sharpston, ECLI:EU:C:2008:772, delivered on 22 December 2008, at 56.
[23] Case C-524/09, *Ville de Lyon v Caisse des dépôts et consignations* ECLI:EU:C:2010:822.
[24] Ibid., at 41.

Charging for access

Article 5 of Directive 2003/4 provides that *in situ* access to information, for example to public registers, has to be free of charge. Further, charges for supplying any environmental information must be "reasonable". In C-217/97 *Commission v Germany*[25] (based on an earlier version of the Directive), the ECJ held that "any interpretation of what constitutes 'a reasonable cost' for the purposes of Article 5 of the directive which may have the result that persons are dissuaded from seeking to obtain information or which may restrict their right of access to information must be rejected" (at 47) and that consequently

> the term "reasonable" for the purposes of Article 5 of the directive must be understood as meaning that it does not authorise Member States to pass on to those seeking information the entire amount of the costs, in particular indirect ones, actually incurred for the State budget in conducting an information search. (at 48)

This led to further specification in what is now Recital 18 of the Directive, which reads

> Public authorities should be able to make a charge for supplying environmental information but such a charge should be reasonable. This implies that, as a general rule, charges may not exceed actual costs of producing the material in question. Instances where advance payment will be required should be limited. In particular cases, where public authorities make available environmental information on a commercial basis, and where this is necessary in order to guarantee the continuation of collecting and publishing such information, a market-based charge is considered to be reasonable; an advance payment may be required. A schedule of charges should be published and made available to applicants together with information on the circumstances in which a charge may be levied or waived.

In *East Sussex County Council*,[26] the question under consideration was the application of the Directive's reasonableness test, in particular its "objective" character, seen in the light of English statutory law which allows local authorities to specify access (and other) fees providing that the amount "shall not exceed an amount which the public authority is satisfied is a reasonable amount". Application in that case[27] is made by a property

---

[25] C-217/97 *Commission v Germany* ECLI:EU:C:1999:395.
[26] Case C-71/14 *East Sussex County Council v Information Commissioner, Property Search Group et al.*, ECLI:EU:C:2015:656 (Opinion AG Sharpston 16 April 2015, ECLI:EU:C:2015:234).
[27] See, for background to the application, the referring tribunal's brief, available at http://goo.gl/M4ci2j, last consulted 21.4.2015.

search group with a view to commercial conveyancing. AG Sharpston in April 2015 opined that even for commercial applicants, authorities' hands are quite tied. In particular,

- that Article 5(2) of Directive 2003/4 does not authorise a public authority to recover, through a charge for supplying information, all or part of the costs of establishing and maintaining a database in which it has organised the environmental information it holds and which it uses to answer requests for information of the type listed in a questionnaire such as that at issue in the main proceedings.
- that a charge which does not exceed a reasonable amount within the meaning of Article 5(2) of Directive 2003/4 is a charge which: (i) is set on the basis of objective factors that are known and capable of review by a third party; (ii) is calculated regardless of who is asking for the information and for what purpose; (iii) is set at a level that guarantees the objectives of the right of access to environmental information upon request and thus does not dissuade people from seeking access or restrict their right of access; and (iv) is no greater than an amount that is appropriate to the reason why Member States are allowed to make this charge (that is, that a member of the public has made a request for the supply of environmental information) and directly correlated to the act of supplying that information; that
- In particular, a charge of a "reasonable amount" under Article 5(2) of Directive 2003/4 is to be based on the costs actually incurred in connection with the act of supplying environmental information in response to a specific request. That will include the costs of staff time spent on searching for and producing the information requested and the cost of producing it in the form requested (which may vary). However, it is not permissible for such a charge also to seek to recover overheads such as heating, lighting or internal services. And that
- Article 5(2) of Directive 2003/4 requires public authorities to ensure that their charges do not exceed a reasonable amount, judged by the yardstick of what a "reasonable amount" means objectively under EU law. That does not, as such, preclude a rule of national law according to which a public authority must satisfy itself that a charge levied meets that standard. However the Member States have to ensure that there is (first) administrative and (then) judicial review of whether a public authority's decision on what constitutes a reasonable charge is in conformity with the autonomous EU law meaning of what is "reasonable" under Article 5(2) of Directive 2003/4.

In other words: the current wording in the relevant English statute, in the view of the AG, does not infringe the Directive. It does in our view at least, however, add a layer of complication: for the authority's *subjective* finding of reasonableness subsequently has to be checked, in two tiers of appeal (administrative *casu quo* judicial), against the Directive's *objective* standard.

Article 6 of the Directive provides the right to effective remedy. Access to justice has to be granted to applicants who are of the opinion that their specific request has been ignored or wrongfully refused. Two types of appeal are provided for: administrative review and review by court or another impartial body of law. Paragraph 1 specifies that such a procedure must be expeditious, as well as free of charge or inexpensive.

B. Participation in Environmental Decision Making

Directive 2003/35 provides for public participation in respect of the drawing up of certain plans and programmes relating to the environment. It further amends Directives 85/337 on the assessment of the effects of certain public and private projects on the environment[28] and Directive 1996/61 concerning integrated pollution prevention and control.[29] The Directive implements the provisions relating to public participation under the Aarhus Convention. It provides for public participation in respect of the drawing up of certain plans and programmes relating to the environment and the improvement thereof, and in regard to access to justice (Article 1 of the Directive). Accordingly, the public has to be given early and effective opportunities to participate in preparation, modification and review of these plans and programmes (Article 2(2)). The "public" is defined as "one or more natural or legal persons and . . . their associations, organizations or groups". The definition does not include an interest the public must have in order to be eligible for public participation concerning plans and programmes. More precisely:

- the public has to be informed (by public notices, electronic media or other appropriate means) of proposals for plans and programmes, as well as their modification or review and relevant information must be given about how these are made available to the public including inter alia information about the right to participate in decision making and about the competent authority to which comments or questions may be submitted (Article 2(2)(a));
- the public is entitled to express comments and opinions when all options are open before decisions on the plans and programmes are made (Article 2(2)(b));
- due account has to be taken of the results of public participation. Having examined the comments and opinions expressed by the

---

[28] The 1985 Directive, as amended, is now codified by Directive 2011/92 of 13 December 2011 on the assessment of the effects of certain public and private projects on the environment, [2012] OJ L 26/1.

[29] Now repealed by Directive 2010/75 on industrial emissions with effect from 7 January 2014.

public, the competent authority has to make reasonable efforts to inform the public about the decisions taken and the reasons and considerations upon which those decisions are based, including information about the public participation process (Article 2(2) (c) and (d)).

To enable the public to prepare and participate effectively, reasonable time frames for every step of the participation process and detailed arrangements have to be given (Article 2(3)).

Exceptions for public participation requirements are listed in paragraph 4. For "plans and programmes designed for the sole purpose of serving national defence or taken in case of civil emergencies", public consultation is not required. Further, excluded from the scope of the provisions of this Directive are plans and programmes which are subject to a public participation procedure under the EIA Directive,[30] as well as under the Water Framework Directive.[31]

The Union has established several tools to facilitate and improve the public participation process in practice. One tool is the European platform "Your voice" which has been set up as part of the Commission's minimum standard consultation requirements[32] and the interactive policymaking initiative.[33] The online platform enables citizens, organisations and public authorities to actively contribute to and give an opinion on legislative proposals and policy documents.

C. Access to Justice

As established above, the regulation of general access to justice to Member States institutions is not within the competence of the Union but is in the competence of the Member States only.[34] Some exceptions

---

[30] Directive 2001/42 on the assessment of certain plans and programmes on the environment now recast by Directive 2011/92 on the assessment of the effects of certain public and private projects on the environment, [2012] OJ L 26/1.

[31] Directive 2000/60 establishing a framework for Community action in the field of water policy, [2000] OJ L 327/1.

[32] Commission Consultation, General principles and minimum standards for consultation of interested parties by the Commission, COM (2002) 704.

[33] European Commission, "Your voice in Europe", available at http://ec.europa.eu/yourvoice/ipm/index_en.htm, last consulted 20.11.2015.

[34] See G. Winter, "National Administrative Procedural Law Under EU requirements. With a Focus on Public Participation", in: J.H. Jans, R. Macrory, A.-M. Moreno Molina (eds), *National Courts and EU Environmental Law*, The Avosetta Series (10), Groningen: Europa Law Publishing, Groningen, 2013, 11–33 at 11; as

exist, for example regarding access to justice within an EIA (Article 11 EIA Directive), as discussed in Chapter 7 I, and provisions included in the Strategic Environmental Assessment (SEA) or Industrial Emissions (IE) Directive (Article 25). In this regard, in *Commission v Germany*,[35] the Court held that the transposition of Articles 11 EIA Directive and 25 IE Directive in the German legal system have restricted the scope of judicial review and are hence incompatible with EIA and IE Directives.

What has been discussed by the European Court is the issue of costs. In *Edwards*[36] the ECJ ruled for the first time on the concrete consequences of the prohibition of prohibitively expensive legal proceedings in regard to the UK. The House of Lords had affirmed a Court of Appeal's decision to dismiss the appeal of Ms Pallikaropoulos and, on 18 July 2008, ordered her to pay the respondents' (including the Environment Agency) costs of the appeal, the amount of which, in the event of disagreement between the parties, was to be fixed by the Clerk of the Parliaments. The respondents submitted two bills for recoverable costs in the amounts of GBP 55,810 and GBP 32,290. The jurisdiction of the House of Lords was transferred to the newly established Supreme Court and the detailed assessment of the costs was carried out by two costs officers appointed by the President of the Supreme Court. In that context, Ms Pallikaropoulos relied on Directives 85/337 and 96/61 to challenge the costs order that had been made against her. The Supreme Court asked the ECJ inter alia

- [the] question [of] whether the cost of the litigation is or is not "prohibitively expensive" within the meaning of Article 9(4) of the Aarhus Convention as implemented by the directives be decided on an objective basis (by reference, for example, to the ability of an "ordinary" member of the public to meet the potential liability for costs), or should it be decided on a subjective basis (by reference to the means of the particular claimant) or upon some combination of these two bases? [and whether]
- in considering whether proceedings are, or are not, "prohibitively expensive", is it relevant that the claimant has not in fact been deterred from bringing or continuing with the proceedings?

The ECJ held that the cost of proceedings must neither exceed the financial resources of the person concerned nor appear, in any event,

---

well as also the other contributions in this volume. For the analysis of the access to justice in Belgium, Denmark, France, Germany, Italy, the Netherlands, Portugal and the United Kingdom please refer to the contributions in N. de Sandeleer, G. Roller and M. Dross (eds), *Access to Justice in Environmental Matters and the Role of NGOs*, Groningen: Europa Law Publishing, The Avosetta Series 6, 2005.

[35] C-137/14 *Commission v Germany* ECLI:EU:C:2015:683.
[36] Case C-260/11 *Edwards and Pallikaropoulos* ECLI:EU:C:2013:221.

to be objectively unreasonable. As regards the analysis of the financial situation of the person concerned, the assessment which must be carried out by the national court cannot be based exclusively on the estimated financial resources of an "average" applicant, since such information may have little connection with the situation of the person concerned. The national court may also take into account the situation of the parties concerned, whether the claimant has a reasonable prospect of success, the importance of what is at stake for the claimant and for the protection of the environment, the complexity of the relevant law and procedure and the potentially frivolous nature of the claim at its various stages. That the claimant has not been deterred, in practice, from asserting his or her claim is not in itself sufficient to establish that the proceedings are not, as far as that claimant is concerned, prohibitively expensive.

Further, in *Commission v United Kingdom*,[37] the Court assessed whether the UK did not comply with its obligations under the access to justice provisions (derived from Articles 3(7) and 4(4) of Directive 2003/35), inasmuch as those provisions required judicial proceedings not to be prohibitively expensive. It held amongst others that the discretion available to the UK courts when applying the national costs regime in a specific case cannot in itself be considered incompatible with the requirement that proceedings not be prohibitively expensive. The possibility for the court hearing a case of granting a protective costs order ensured greater predictability as to the cost of the proceedings and contributed to compliance with that requirement. However, it was not apparent that national courts are obliged by a rule of law to ensure that the proceedings are not prohibitively expensive for the claimant.

II. APPLICATION OF THE AARHUS CONVENTION TO UNION INSTITUTIONS AND BODIES

Regulation 1367/2006 transposes all Aarhus pillars to the EU institutions.[38] The Regulation lays down the common objectives and definitions as applicable to all three Aarhus pillars.

Article 1 lists these objectives for access to environmental information

---

[37] C-530/11 *Commission v United Kingdom* ECLI:EU:C:2014:67.
[38] See also G. Van Calster, "Access to Justice against European Community Institutions – Using Environmental Litigation as a Focal Point", Conference on Environmental Rights in Europe after the UN/ECE Aarhus Convention, IMER, K.U. Leuven, 30 August 2003.

and public participation and "access to justice in environmental matters at Community level". The Regulation further aligns the definitions provided in Aarhus in order to enhance transparency and rational legislation and implementation (see also Recital 5 to Regulation 1367/2006). The definition of a "Community institution or body" thereby exceeds the one provided for in Aarhus: the latter provides for a possible exclusion of the scope of the Convention where this institution or body is acting in a judicial or legislative capacity. The Regulation, however, explicitly states that such a derogation is not applicable to public institutions, bodies, offices or agencies acting in a legislative capacity regarding access to information. This is also in line with Regulation 1049/2001 regarding public access to European Parliament, Council and Commission documents[39] laying down the principles, conditions and limits for access to these documents. Access has to be granted without discrimination as to citizenship, nationality or domicile of the applicant.

A. Access to Environmental Information

The general regime of Regulation 1049/2001
As established above, Regulation 1049/2001 regarding public access to European Parliament, Council and Commission documents establishes the principles, conditions and limits for access to these documents, whether or not they relate to environmental information. In general any citizen of the Union, and any natural or legal person residing or having its registered office in a Member State has a right of access to the institutions' documents. The institutions may further grant access to documents to any natural or legal person not residing or not having its registered office in a Member State (Article 2(1) and (2)). The Regulation is generally applicable to all documents held by an institution, including drawn up, received and any documents in its possession, in all areas of activity of the EU, with the exception of sensitive documents, which are subject to special treatment as outlined in Article 9 of the Regulation, as well as rights of public access to documents held by the institutions which might follow from instruments of international law or acts of the institutions implementing them (Article 2(3–6)).

Exceptions are outlined in Article 4 of the Regulation. The institutions can refuse access to a document where disclosure would undermine the protection of:

---

[39] Regulation 1049/2001 of 30 May 2001 regarding public access to European Parliament, Council and Commission documents, [2001] OJ L 145/43.

- "the public interest, such as public security, defence and military matters, international relations and the financial, monetary or economic policy of the Union or a Member State;
- privacy and the integrity of the individual, in particular in accordance with Union legislation regarding the protection of personal data".

Further, disclosure can be refused on the following grounds, unless there is an overriding public interest in disclosure:

- "commercial interests of a natural or legal person, including intellectual property
- court proceedings and legal advice
- the purpose of inspections, investigations and audits" (Articles 4(1) and (2)).

Moreover, access to a document, drawn up by an institution for internal use or received by an institution, which relates to a matter where the decision has not been taken by the institution, shall be refused if disclosure of the document would seriously undermine the institution's decision-making process, unless there is an overriding public interest in disclosure. Access to a document containing opinions for internal use as part of deliberations and preliminary consultations within the institution concerned shall be refused even after the decision has been taken if disclosure of the document would seriously undermine the institution's decision-making process, unless there is an overriding public interest in disclosure (Article 4(3)).

These exceptions are only applicable for the period during which protection is justified on the basis of the content of the document. The exceptions may apply for a maximum period of 30 years. In the case of documents covered by the exceptions relating to privacy or commercial interests and in the case of sensitive documents, the exceptions may, if necessary, continue to apply after this period (Article 4(7)).

Moreover, as regards third party documents, the institution shall consult the third party with a view to assessing whether an exception as described above is applicable, unless it is clear that the document shall or shall not be disclosed. A Member State may request the institution not to disclose a document originating from that Member State without its prior agreement (Article 4(4–5)).

If only parts of the requested document are covered by any of the exceptions, the remaining parts of the document shall be released (Article 4(6)).

The Regulation further outlines the application procedure for accessing a document (Article 6), the processing of internal information and of confirmatory applications (Articles 7 and 8), as well as the access following an application (Article 10), the use of registries and direct access to documents in electronic form or through a register (Articles 11 and 12), the publication in the *Official Journal* (Article 13), administrative practice in the institutions, and reproduction of documents and reports (Articles 15–17).

In Case C-612/13, ClientEarth tried to challenge the Regulation in order to obtain access to studies on compliance with EU environmental law which were commissioned in the context of infringement procedures. The Court, however, held the Aarhus Convention could not be relied upon because it "was manifestly designed with the national legal orders in mind".[40]

The *lex specialis* of Regulation 1367/2006

Further, Regulation 1367/2006, as a *lex specialis*, contains more detailed provisions on the collection and dissemination and quality of environmental information (Articles 4 and 5), the application of exceptions concerning requests for access to environmental information (Article 6) and requests for access to environmental information which is not held by a Union institution or body (Article 7), as well as on cooperation (Article 8). The latter is required in case of imminent threat to human health, life or the environment between Union institutions and public authorities in order to immediately disseminate environmental information which could enable it to take measures to prevent or mitigate harm arising from the threat to the public affected (Article 8).

The relation between these two Regulations

One case involving both Regulations is *Stichting Greenpeace Nederland and PAN Europe v Commission*.[41] This is a limiting call upon intellectual property to justify non-disclosure of environmental information. The case in fact also included application of the plant protection Directive.[42] Under the plant protection directive, Germany had been the Member State with responsibility to report on the acceptability of approving glyphosate. Greenpeace and Pesticide Action Network Europe had requested access to

---

[40] C-612/13 P *ClientEarth v Commission* ECLI:EU:C:2015:486. The case is subject to appeal by the General Court.

[41] Case T-545/11 *Stichting Greenpeace Nederland and PAN Europe v Commission*, not yet reported in ECR.

[42] Directive 91/414 concerning the placing of plant protection products on the market, [1991] OJ L 230/1.

- a copy of the draft assessment report issued by Germany, prior to the first inclusion of glyphosate in Annex I to Directive 91/414;
- a complete list of all tests submitted by the operators seeking the inclusion of glyphosate in Annex I;
- the full, complete and original test documents supplied by the operators seeking the inclusion of glyphosate in Annex I, in so far as concerns all long-term toxicity tests, all mutagenicity tests, carcinogenicity tests, neurotoxicity tests and all reproduction studies.

The Commission, with assistance from Germany, granted access to the draft report, with the exception of volume 4, which the German authorities refused to disclose and which includes the complete list of all tests submitted by the operators seeking the first inclusion of glyphosate in Annex I. Germany was of the opinion that the document at issue contained confidential information relating to the intellectual property rights of the operators which had sought the inclusion of glyphosate in Annex I to Directive 91/414, namely the detailed chemical composition of the active substance produced by each of them, detailed information concerning the process by which each of them produced the substance, information on the impurities, the composition of the finished products and the contractual relations between the various operators which had sought the inclusion of glyphosate.

The ECJ noted the important impact of Regulation 1367/2006 on the working of the basic Regulation, Regulation 1049/2001: the first sentence of Article 6(1) of Regulation No 1367/2006 lays down a legal presumption that an overriding public interest in disclosure (relevant for the application of exceptions written into Regulation 1049/2001) exists where the information requested relates to emissions into the environment, except where that information concerns an investigation, in particular one concerning possible infringements of EU law. The Court held that accordingly,

> the first sentence of Article 6(1) of Regulation 1367/2006 requires that if the institution concerned receives an application for access to a document, it must disclose it where the information requested relates to emissions into the environment, even if such disclosure is liable to undermine the protection of the commercial interests of a particular natural or legal person, including that person's intellectual property, within the meaning of Article 4(2), first indent, of Regulation 1049/2001.[43]

The Court rejected any attempt by the Commission to soften the impact of Article 6(1) of Regulation 1367/2006: in *claris non fit interpretatio* the provision has to be read on its prima facie meaning. Any other application

---

[43] Case T-545/11 note 41 above, at 38.

"would amount to disapplying a clear and unconditional provision of a European Union regulation, which is not even claimed to be contrary to a superior rule of law".[44]

In addition the Court subsequently considered the meaning of "environmental information" at length and gave this a wide interpretation. The case is a good illustration of the complex web of transparency requirements and the consistent approach of the ECJ in favour of disclosure.

B. Public Participation

Article 9 of Regulation 1367/2006 lays down the provisions regarding public participation concerning plans and programmes relating to the environment. It establishes that Union institutions and bodies shall provide for early and effective opportunities for the public to participate during the preparation, modification or review of plans or programmes relating to the environment when all options are still open. In particular, where the Commission prepares a proposal for such a plan or programme which is submitted to other Union institutions or bodies for decision, it shall provide for public participation at that preparatory stage.

Further, the Union institutions and bodies shall identify the public affected or likely to be affected by, or having an interest in such a plan or programme. The Regulation establishes further that the public which has an interest has to be informed of

- the draft proposal,
- the environmental information or assessment relevant to the plan or programme under preparation, and
- practical arrangements for participation, including the administrative entity from which the relevant information may be obtained, as well as the administrative entity to which comments, opinions or questions may be submitted, and reasonable time-frames allowing sufficient time for the public to be informed and to prepare and participate effectively in the environmental decision-making process.

The Article further specifies the individual time frames and deadlines, as well as outlines that the Union institutions and bodies have to take the outcome of the public participation process into account when deciding on a plan or programme. They further have to publish the decision, the reasons upon which it is based and information on the public participation procedure.

---

[44] Ibid., at 44.

C. Access to Justice

Rules on access to justice are laid down in Regulation 1367/2006, as well as in the Treaty provisions themselves. In addition, the European legislator, in 2003, aimed at introducing a directive on access to justice in environmental matters.[45] However, notwithstanding Parliament's first reading, the proposal, according to the Union's legislative observatory, is still awaiting its first reading in the Council.

Thus, the proposal seems to be stuck. It is not entirely clear whether it has become redundant, after the introduction of the Lisbon Treaty which also introduced changes to Article 263 TFEU (see below), as well as the adoption of Regulation 1367/2006. The *travaux préperatoires* to the Regulation actually suggests the contrary, stating that

> [t]he further requirement of Article 9(3), of access to justice [of the Aarhus Convention] to also cover acts and omissions by private persons, has to be seen together with the proposal for a Directive on access to justice in environmental matters. It is proposed to address this aspect in that Directive, as it is above all for Member States to ensure private persons to abide by environmental law. The proposed Directive stipulates the objective in line with Article 9(3) of the Aarhus Convention, leaving it to Member States to set up appropriate criteria for related access to justice under national law. The present proposal hence establishes access to justice provisions in relation to acts and omissions by Community bodies and institutions, which contravene environmental law.

Article 263 TFEU

In primary law, rules on access to justice for EU institutions are currently included in Article 263(2–5) TFEU which distinguishes between two groups of applicants. Firstly, so-called "privileged applicants" are included in paragraphs 2 and 3 of the Article. These include the Member States, the Council and the Commission, as well as the European Parliament, the Court of Auditors and the European Central Bank. The latter three institutions may bring an action "for the purpose of protecting their prerogatives".

Secondly, the fourth and fifth paragraphs deal with the so-called "non-privileged" applicants: "Any natural or legal person may, . . . institute proceedings against an act addressed to that person or which is of direct and individual concern to them, and against a regulatory act which is of direct concern to them and does not entail implementing measures." The paragraph thus contains two substantive conditions for individuals, or legal

---

[45] COM (2003) 624.

persons (such as trade associations and non-governmental organisations (NGOs)), to have *locus standi* vis-à-vis decisions (in the generic meaning of the word) not addressed to them: these are direct concern and individual concern (unless the act does not entail "implementing measures" in which case direct concern suffices).[46] The interpretation of these two conditions is generally strict throughout all areas of Union law; however, in environmental matters, an additional layer of complexity is added through the "tragedy of the commons" conundrum inherently attached to much environmental litigation.

The criteria for "direct concern" were firstly established in the 1978 *Simmenthal* judgment.[47] For a person to be directly concerned by a Union measure, the measure must directly affect the legal situation of the individual and leave no discretion to the addressees of that measure who are entrusted with the task of implementing it, such implementation being pure, automatic and resulting from Union rules without the application of other intermediate rules. This condition is commonly a hurdle for individuals seeking action, especially because of the tragedy of the commons, which renders the direct concern difficult to prove.

However, the condition of "individual concern" adds an additional, even bigger hurdle. The approach of the ECJ is known as the "*Plaumann*" test, after a 1963 case involving a German importer of clementines.[48]

The ECJ held in *Plaumann* that

> (p)ersons other than those to whom a decision is addressed, may only claim to be individually concerned if that decision affects them by reason of certain attributes which are peculiar to them, or by reason of circumstances in which they are differentiated from all other persons and by virtue of these factors distinguishes them individually just as in the case of the person addressed.

This test is difficult enough in itself. However, in practice it becomes even more stringent in that, for economic operators, the Court typically holds that these are affected by reason of a commercial activity which may at any time be practised by any person and is not therefore such as to distinguish the applicant in relation to the contested measure as in the case of the addressee.

The *Plaumann* test essentially amounts to a "closed shop" test: to be individually concerned by a decision addressed to another person

---

[46] See also M. Lee, "The Environmental Implications of the Lisbon Treaty", 10 *Environmental Law Review* 2 (2008), 131–138, at 135f.
[47] Case 92/78 *Simmenthal v Commission*, [1979] ECR 777, at 25 and 26.
[48] Case 25/62 *Plaumann & Co. v Commission*, [1963] ECR 95.

(including regulations and directives addressed to Member States), an applicant needs to show that he is part of a "closed circle of persons who were known at the time of its adoption".[49]

The consequences of this approach, in the environmental area, came to a head in *Greenpeace*,[50] where both the CFI (Court of First Instance; now known as the General Court) and the ECJ rejected standing in a case where the Commission had granted financial aid to Spain, for the construction of power stations on the Canary Islands. *Locus standi* was rejected both for Greenpeace and for local residents. For the local residents, this was done by application of the Plaumann test: indeed other residents could move in to the area, even if temporarily. For Greenpeace's standing, both the CFI and the ECJ rejected the case for extending *locus standi* in the specific case of non-economic considerations, such as environmental protection. In that respect, the *Greenpeace* case is the archetype of the paradox of *locus standi* under Article 263, fourth paragraph: the wider the group potentially affected, the less likely *locus standi* will be granted.

The Lisbon Treaty has changed the provisions in Article 263. The fourth paragraph of the Article now reads:

> Any natural or legal person may, under the conditions laid down in the first and second paragraphs, institute proceedings against an act addressed to that person or which is of direct and individual concern to them, *and against a regulatory act which is of direct concern to them and does not entail implementing measures*. (Emphasis added)

Through the introduction of the provision emphasised above, the EU legislator aimed at facilitating challenges to EU non-legislative legal acts. This perception has been underlined by the European Courts in the third of the seal product cases.[51] In this case, the Grand Chamber of the Court dismissed the appeal by the seal hunters to annul the basic regulation prohibiting the marketing of seal products on the EU internal market. It confirmed the earlier judgment that the seal hunters had no standing to challenge a *legislative* act. In its reasoning the Court refers to the *travaux préparatoires* of the provision, concluding that

---

[49] S. Weatherill and P. Beaumont, *EC Law*, 2nd Edition, London: Penguin, 1995, at 238.

[50] Case C-321/95P *Stichting Greenpeace v Commission*, [1998] ECR I-1651. See F. De Lange, "Beyond Greenpeace, Courtesy of the Aarhus Convention", 3 *Yearbook of European Environmental Law*, [2003] 227–248.

[51] Case C-583/11 P *Inuit Tapiriit Kanatami and Others v Parliament and Council*, ECLI:EU:C:2013:625.

while the alteration of the fourth paragraph of Article 230 EC [now 263 TFEU] was intended to extend the conditions of admissibility of actions for annulment in respect of natural and legal persons, the conditions of admissibility laid down in the fourth paragraph of Article 230 EC relating to legislative acts were not however to be altered. Accordingly, the use of the term "regulatory act" in the draft amendment of that provision made it possible to identify the category of acts which might thereafter be the subject of an action for annulment under conditions less stringent than previously, while maintaining "a restrictive approach in relation to actions by individuals against legislative acts (for which the "of direct and individual concern" condition remains applicable)".[52]

Regulation 1367/2006
Standing of the EU institutions is also addressed by Regulation 1367/2006[53] which implements the provisions of the Aarhus Directive for the EU institutions. Title IV establishes the provisions dealing with *internal* review and access to justice. Article 10 of the Regulation establishes that NGOs meeting certain criteria (see below) are eligible to request an internal review into the Union institution or body that has adopted an administrative act or should have adopted an act (administrative omission) within six weeks after the act was adopted, notified or published (where it is an administrative omission, six weeks after the date the act was required), stating the grounds of the review in written form.[54] The request has to specify the administrative act or alleged administrative omission, as well as the environmental law provisions that the act is considered not to be in compliance with. The request further has to contain the grounds, and relevant information and documentation to substantiate the grounds, as well as the contact details of the organisation and the evidence that the organisation is entitled to submit a request.[55]

In *Council v Vereniging Milieudefensie and Stichting Stop Luchtverontreiniging Utrecht*,[56] the issues at stake were the scope of judicial review (in the specific context of information requests), the EU's long and difficult

---

[52] See ibid., at 59.

[53] Regulation 1367/2006 on the application of the provisions of the Aarhus Convention on Access to Information, Public Participation in Decision-making and Access to Justice in Environmental Matters to Community institutions and bodies, [2006] OJ L 264/13.

[54] Article 10(1) of the Regulation as well as Decision 2008/50 laying down detailed rules for the application of Regulation 1367/2006 as regards requests for the internal review of administrative acts, [2008] OJ L 13/24, and Article 2 for further details on the submission of requests.

[55] See Decision 2008/50, Article 1.

[56] Case C-401/12 P *Council v Vereniging Milieudefensie and Stichting Stop Luchtverontreiniging Utrecht* ECLI:EU:C:2015:4.

relationship with *locus standi* in environmental matters (again though within the perhaps more narrow context of access to information), the correct implementation of the Aarhus Convention and the direct effect of said Convention.

The judgment underlines the need to review the direct effect of international law on a case-by-case and indeed article-by-article basis. While it is clear that the ECJ overall has great sympathy for the binding impact of the Aarhus Convention, in this case the relevant environmental organisations failed to convince the ECJ that Article 9 of the Convention has direct effect. Article 9 Aarhus provides a review procedure in the event requests for information have been refused. Regulation 1367/2006 implements the Aarhus Convention vis-à-vis the EU institutions. The case concerns Article 10 of that regulation, entitled "Request for internal review of administrative acts", which provides in paragraph 1 thereof: "Any non-governmental organisation which meets the criteria set out in Article 11 is entitled to make a request for internal review to the Community institution or body that has adopted an administrative act under environmental law or, in case of an alleged administrative omission, should have adopted such an act." Article 2(1)(g) of that Regulation defines "administrative act" as meaning: "any measure of individual scope under environmental law, taken by a Community institution or body, and having legally binding and external effects".

The Netherlands, in accordance with Article 22 of the Ambient Air Quality Directive, Directive 2008/50, had notified the Commission that it had postponed the deadline for attaining the annual limit values for nitrogen dioxide in nine zones and that it was availing itself of a specific exemption from the obligation to apply the daily and annual limit values for particulate matter. The Commission accepted that postponement. Vereniging Milieudefensie and Stichting Stop Luchtverontreiniging Utrecht submitted a request to the Commission for internal review of that decision pursuant to the aforementioned Article 10(1). The Commission refused internal review. It considered the request inadmissible as the concerned acts in their view were not "administrative acts" as defined in Article 2(1)(g), not being, the Commission argued, of "individual scope" but rather of general application. The General Court sided with applicants: because Article 10(1) of Regulation 1367/2006 limits the concept of "acts" that can be challenged by NGOs to "administrative acts" defined in Article 2(1)(g) of the Regulation as "measures of individual scope", it argued that the Regulation is not compatible with Article 9(3) Aarhus. The AG in the current case also sided with the applicants (albeit following a different reasoning from the General Court).

The ECJ itself disagreed. The provisions of an international agreement to which the EU is a party can be relied on in support of an action for annulment of an act of secondary EU legislation or an exception based on the illegality of such an act only where, firstly, the nature and the broad logic of that agreement do not preclude it and, secondly, those provisions appear, as regards their content, to be unconditional and sufficiently precise (*ex multi*, the ECJ quoted its judgment in the Emissions Trading Scheme case, C-366/10). Article 9(3) Aarhus, the Court held, does not contain any unconditional and sufficiently precise obligation capable of directly regulating the legal position of individuals and therefore does not meet those conditions: since only members of the public who "meet the criteria, if any, laid down in . . . national law" are entitled to exercise the rights provided for in Article 9(3), that provision is subject, in its implementation or effects, to the adoption of a subsequent measure at the national level. The Aarhus Contracting Parties have a broad margin of discretion when defining the rules for the implementation of the "administrative or judicial procedures". *Vereniging Milieudefensie* does show both that an empowering effect cannot be assumed for all of the Convention's provisions, and secondly, that at the level of the Convention itself, beefing up one or two articles would certainly assist its implementation. That in itself, of course, may become more difficult the more frequent the ECJ and national courts, both in the EU and elsewhere, employ Aarhus against unwilling State authorities.

The Union institution or body has to consider such a request and give a reasoned reply within 12 weeks after receipt or, in the case that it is not able to do so after exercising due diligence, notify the NGO of the reasons for the failure to act and its intention to do so, within the time frame (paragraphs 2 and 3). As a result of these requirements the Commission amended its rules of procedure establishing detailed time frames, responsibilities and decision-making powers to the appropriate bodies or persons within the Commission.[57]

The NGO which issued the request for internal review is entitled to institute proceedings before the Court of Justice (Article 12(1) of the Regulation). Further, the organization can institute proceedings where the institution or body fails to act in accordance with the internal review procedure (Article 12(2) of the Regulation).

---

[57] Commission Decision 2008/401 amending its Rules of Procedure as regards detailed rules for the application of Regulation 1367/2006 on the application of the provisions of the Aarhus Convention on Access to Information, Public Participation in Decision-making and Access to Justice in Environmental Matters to Community institution and bodies, [2008] OJ L 140/22.

Article 11 establishes the criteria a NGO has to comply with in order to be entitled to make a request for internal review. The organisation has

> (a) to be an independent non-profit-making legal person in accordance with a Member State's national law or practice; (b) the primary stated objective of promoting environmental protection in the context of environmental law; (c) existed for more than two years and is actively pursuing the objective referred to under (b); (d) the subject matter in respect of which the request for internal review is made is covered by its objective and activities. (Article 11(1))

The exact procedure, criteria and required documents for evidence for the entitlement of NGOs are contained in Decision 2008/50 and especially Annex I thereof and can consist of, for example, statutes, activity reports and documents of legal registration. Indeed Article 9(3) of the Convention, with respect to *locus standi* inter alia for NGOs, leaves a lot of discretion to national – in this case EU – law. The Article provides

> 1. In addition and without prejudice to the review procedures referred to in paragraphs 1 and 2 above, each Party shall ensure that, where they meet the criteria, if any, laid down in its national law, members of the public have access to administrative or judicial procedures to challenge acts and omissions by private persons and public authorities which contravene provisions of its national law relating to the environment.[58]

Unlike other Articles of the Convention, which either do not provide for national criteria delimitating certain rights, or which specify the nature of these criteria, Article 9(3) is striking in its deference to national law.

---

[58] Note that Article 9(1) relates to access to justice, namely requests for access to information, and namely public participation.

6. Additional tools in implementing European environmental law

I. ENVIRONMENTAL MANAGEMENT SYSTEMS

Environmental management systems (EMSs) exist worldwide as an instrument to measure and verify the environmental performance of an organisation in practice. A definition of an EMS is provided by the International Organization for Standardization (ISO): "that part of the overall management system which includes organizational structure, planning activities, responsibilities, practices, procedures, processes, and resources for developing, implementing, achieving, reviewing, and maintaining the environmental policy". This definition is also applied by the European legislator, adding "and managing the environmental aspects".[1] Accordingly EMSs generally aim at the management of environmental aspects within an organisation.[2]

The international ISO 14000 Environmental management standard series has been developed by the ISO and is one of the most popular and most widely used standards at the international level. ISO 14001:2004 is part of the ISO 14000 series with respect to environmental standards (management, audit, eco-labels, life-cycle assessment). Even though it does not contain specific environmental performance criteria, the standard is a framework for an EMS for organisations in order for them to develop an environmental policy and objectives, as well as taking into account legal requirements.

EMSs also exist at the national level, as for example the "1.2.3. Environnement" standard in France, the "Bayerisches Umweltsiegel" in Germany, the "BS 8555" standard in the UK and the "e+5" label in Spain.

Influenced by the ISO standard, the EU founded its own environmental management and auditing system, promoting a coherent approach and with the aim to create a single credible scheme and avoiding the

---

[1] See Regulation 1221/2009 on the voluntary participation by organisations in a Community eco-management and audit scheme (EMAS), ("EMAS III"), [2000] OJ L 342/1, Article 2(13).

[2] For a definition of an organisation see below.

establishment of different national regimes (see also Recital 29 of the EMAS III Regulation). The Environmental Management and Auditing Scheme (EMAS) was firstly established in 1995[3] for industry but has been open to all sectors, including the public and private sectors, since 2001.[4] It was reviewed in 2009 and is now codified in Regulation 1221/2009. As its name suggests, the system is voluntary and relies on consumer and peer pressure to expand its popularity. State intervention is present, since it is the Union legislator which has drafted the criteria leading to EMAS recognition. Member States are to set up the necessary certification bodies to verify compliance with the criteria. Initially, the EMAS was the result of the renewed emphasis on the search for "new instruments" in the Union's environmental policy in the Fifth Environmental Action Programme (EAP). The recent EMAS III is an instrument promoting and implementing the Sustainable Industrial Policy by the European Commission.[5] It is designed to realise a more active involvement of the public and private sectors, but especially industry in environmental conservation.

A. Main Provisions and Duties for Companies Registering under EMAS

EMAS aims to proliferate the use of EMSs and audits and to promote the environmental performance of organisations, as well as to evaluate their performance and promote open stakeholder dialogue.[6] "Organisations" are thereby defined broadly, including public and private companies, corporations, firms, enterprises and authorities or institutions.[7]

An organisation seeking to receive EMAS registration must comply

---

[3] Regulation 1836/93 of 29 June 1993 allowing voluntary participation by companies in the industrial sector in a Community eco-management and audit scheme, [1993] OJ L 168/1.

[4] For a detailed analysis of the history and development of EMAS see M.S. Wenk, *The European Union's Eco-Management and Audit Scheme (EMAS)*, The Netherlands: Springer, 2005, 9–32. For a case study on the social responsibility ISO 26000, see S. Bijlmakers and G. Van Calster, "You'd Be Surprised How Much It Costs to Look This Cheap! A Case Study of ISO 26000 on Social Responsibility", in: P. Delimatsis (ed.), *The Law, Economics and Politics of International Standardisation*, Cambridge: Cambridge University Press, 2015, 275–310.

[5] Commission Communication on the Sustainable Consumption and Production and Sustainable Industrial Policy Action Plan, COM (2008) 397. See also Article 1 of the EMAS III Regulation.

[6] See also Article 1(2) of the EMAS Regulation.

[7] Article 2(21) of the EMAS Regulation.

with the criteria established in Articles 4 and 5 of the Regulation. To qualify, an organisation has to:

- Carry out an environmental review of all environmental aspects of the organisation's activities. Criteria for this environmental review are included in Annex I and parts of Annex II and require, for example, the identification of the applicable legal requirements relating to the environment and provide evidence of compliance therewith; and the identification of all direct and indirect environmental aspects with a significant impact on the environment, qualified and quantified as appropriate and compile a register of those identified as significant. These aspects have, for example, the potential to cause environmental harm: the fragility of the local, regional or global environment and the size, number, frequency and reversibility of the aspect or impact.
- Develop and implement an EMS, based on the results of the review and, taking into account the best environmental management practice for the relevant sector. Criteria for the EMS are included in Annex II of the Regulation. The core criteria are the ones established by Section 4 of the international ISO 14001:2004 standard, which have been complemented by a number of additional requirements specific to EMAS. The organisation's top management, for example, has to define the organisation's environmental policy and objectives and targets appropriate to the nature, scale and environmental impacts of its activities, products and services and include a commitment to continual improvement and prevention of pollution and compliance with legal requirements. The objectives and targets must be measurable and consistent with the environmental policy.
- Carry out an internal audit assessing the management systems in place, and determine conformity with the organisation's policy and programme, which shall include compliance with relevant environmental regulatory requirements (Annex III of the Regulation) at intervals of no longer than three or four years, depending on the specific activity.
- Prepare an environmental statement in accordance with Annex IV of the Regulation, including a clear and unambiguous description of the organisation; the environmental policy, targets and objectives and a description of the established EMS; and a brief description of the EMS of the organisation and other data, as referred to in the previous listed documents.

In addition, Article 4 paragraph 5 of the Regulation requires the initial environmental review, the EMS, the audit procedure and its implementation, as well as the environmental statement to be verified by an accredited or licensed environmental verifier.

The application has to be submitted to the competent body in the Member State, or for an organisation applying from outside the EU to any competent body that provides registration of organisations from outside the Union (Article 3(3) and Article 11(1)). This has to be a neutral and independent authority on either a national, regional or local level (Article 11(2) and (3)).

The competent authority is responsible for the registration of organisations located in the individual Member States (or having headquarters therein, see Article 3(2)). The authority is also responsible for the control of the entry and maintenance of organisations' details on the register, including suspension and deletion.

EMAS registration has to be renewed at least on a three-yearly basis (Article 6(1) of the Regulation). Internal audits, of environmental performance and legal compliance amongst others, have to be carried out on an annual basis (Article 6(1) of the Regulation). A derogation exists, however, for small organisations,[8] establishing a four and two-year frequency, respectively, provided that no significant environmental risks are present, especially at the local level where the organisation contributes, and that the company has no substantive changes planned (Article 7(1)). Substantive changes relate to "any change in an organisation's operation, structure, administration, processes, activities, products or services that has or can have a significant impact on an organisation's environmental management system, the environment or human health" (Article 2 No. 15). These conditions have to be verified by an independent verifier for the amended frequencies to become applicable.

However, it is fair to say that, overall, the actual uptake of the EMAS is not that successful other than in one or two Member States (Germany in particular), with several potential scheme users opting for the ISO standards instead.[9]

---

[8] A definition for small organisations is provided in Article 2(28) of the Regulation and refers to micro-, small- and medium-sized enterprises (SMEs) as defined in Commission Recommendation 2003/361, local authorities governing less than 10,000 inhabitants or other public authorities employing fewer than 250 persons and having an annual budget not exceeding EUR 50 million, or an annual balance sheet not exceeding EUR 43 million.

[9] For a discussion and evaluation of the implementation of EMAS in the individual Member States please refer to M.S. Wenk, *The European Union's*

II. PERMITTING AND BEST AVAILABLE TECHNIQUES

The actual permitting and licensing procedure for individual projects is subject to the national legislation of the individual Member States. Permitting mostly happens at a regional or local level, with local authorities involved, and hence will not be discussed in this volume.

However, the EU sets out the framework for an "integrated pollution prevention and control" ("IPPC") approach with the IPPC Directive[10] which has now been recast together with seven other directives[11] into the Industrial Emissions Directive.[12] The underlying understanding of the creation of an integrated regime is that different approaches to controlling emissions into the air, water or soil separately may encourage the shifting of pollution between the various environmental media rather than protecting the environment as a whole.[13]

The Directive is designed to coordinate[14] the authorisation procedures and conditions for environmental permits between competent authorities. Such authorities may grant a permit only when integrated protection measures for air, water and land have been put in place. The Directive provides that emission limits, parameters and technical measures should be based on the "best available techniques", taking into consideration

---

Eco-Management and Audit Scheme (EMAS), The Netherlands: Springer, 2005, 137–174.

[10] Directive 96/61 concerning integrated pollution prevention and control, [1996] OJ L 257/26 as codified by Directive 2008/1 concerning integrated pollution prevention and control, [2008] OJ L 24/8.

[11] Directive 78/176 on titanium dioxide industrial waste; Directive 82/883 on the surveillance and monitoring of titanium dioxide waste; Directive 92/112 on the reduction of titanium dioxide industrial waste; Directive 1999/13 on reducing emissions of volatile organic compounds (VOCs); Directive 2000/76 on waste incineration; Directive 2008/1 concerning integrated pollution prevention and control; and Directive 2001/80 on the limitation of emissions of certain pollutants from large combustion plants.

[12] Directive 2010/75 of 24 November 2010 on industrial emissions (integrated pollution prevention and control), [2010] OJ L 334/17.

[13] For a discussion of the Directive please refer to B. Lange, "EU Directive on Industrial Emissions: Squaring the Circle of Integrated, Harmonised and Ambitious Technology Standards?", 13 *Environmental Law Review* 3 (2011), 199–204.

[14] See for example the Dutch Council of State (Raad van State) 11 June 2014, ECLI:NL:RVS:2014:2120 X v College van gedeputeerde staten van Overijssel: even though the Directive does not specify the coordination mechanism, the requirement for coordination in and of itself has direct effect.

the technical characteristics of the installation concerned, its geographical location and local environmental conditions. It is up to the Member States to set the emission norms for particular installations (Article 1 IED).

The Directive creates a more transparent environmental permit system in those Member States where a system does not yet exist. It leaves room for local authorities to take into account matters such as the population penetration rate. The emission limit values, parameters or equivalent technical measures have to be based on the best available techniques (see below), without prescribing the use of one specific technique or technology and taking into consideration the technical characteristics of the installation concerned, its geographical location and local environmental conditions.

The Directive sets common provisions applicable to the permitting of all forms of installations but also contains special provisions for the permitting of different activities, for example combustion plants, waste incineration plants and waste co-generation plants, installations and activities using organic solvents, as well as installations producing titanium dioxide.

A. Obligations of the Member States

The purpose of the Directive is to achieve integrated prevention and control for the pollution arising from the industrial activities referred to in Chapters II to VI. It lays down measures designed to prevent or, where that is not practicable, reduce emissions in the air, water and land from these activities, including measures concerning waste, in order to achieve a high level of protection of the environment.

A permit means "a written authorisation to operate all or part of an installation or combustion plant, waste incineration plant or waste co-incineration plant" (Article 3(7)). Substances are defined as "any chemical element and its compounds, with the exception of radioactive substances and genetically modified organisms" (Article 3(1)). Pollution means the

> direct or indirect introduction as a result of human activity, of substances, vibrations, heat or noise into the air, water or land which may be harmful to human health or the quality of the environment, result in damage to material property, or impair or interfere with amenities and other legitimate uses of the environment (Article 3(2)).
>
> An installation is a "stationary technical unit where one or more activities listed in Annex VII or Part I are carried out, and any other directly associated activities on the same site which have a technical connection with the activities

listed in those Annexes and which could have an effect on emissions and pollution." (Article 3(3))

Best available techniques are defined as:

> the most effective and advanced stage in the development of activities and their methods of operation which indicates the practical suitability of particular techniques for providing the basis for emission limit values and other permit conditions designed to prevent and, where that is not practicable, to reduce emissions and the impact on the environment as a whole. (Article 3(10))

As a general rule, Member States have to ensure that no installation or combustion plant, waste incineration plant or waste co-incineration plant are operated without a permit (Article 4(1)). That permit can cover two or more installations or parts of installations operated by the same operator on the same site; however, it has to be ensured that all parts of an installation comply with the requirements laid down in the Directive (Article 4(2)). For installations and activities using organic solvents Member States might set a procedure of registration, as a binding act which at least includes notification to the competent authority of the operator (Article 4(1)).

The requirements for the granting of permits for existing installations are less straightforward. The authorities of the Member States have to ensure that existing installations operate in accordance with the requirements of Article 11 (General principles governing the basic obligations of the operator), Article 14 (permit conditions), Article 18 (environmental quality standards), Article 21 (reconsideration and updating of permit conditions), Article 8 (non-compliance), and Articles 24 and 25 on access to information, public participation and access to justice, by introducing additional permits or by reconsidering and, where necessary, updating the conditions of the permit.

Applications for a permit must include a description of (Article 12): the installation and its activities; the raw and auxiliary materials, other substances and the energy used in or generated by the installation; the sources of emissions from the installation; the conditions of the site of the installation; where applicable a baseline report on the possibility of soil and groundwater contamination; the nature and quantities of foreseeable emissions from the installation into each medium as well as identification of significant effects of the emissions on the environment; the proposed technology and other techniques for preventing or, where this not possible, reducing emissions from the installation; further measures planned to comply with the general principles of the basic obligations of the operator (see Article 11); and of the measures planned to monitor emissions into the environment. Further, a non-technical summary of all these details has to be provided.

The very essence of the integrated approach has been included in Article 5(2), which states that Member States have to ensure that the conditions of, and the procedure for the granting of, the permit are fully coordinated where more than one competent authority is involved, in order to guarantee an effective integrated approach by all authorities competent for this procedure.

For reasons of administrative management, Article 6 allows Member States to prescribe certain requirements for certain categories of installations in general binding rules instead of including them in individual permit conditions, provided that an integrated approach and an equivalent high level of environmental protection as a whole are ensured.

All permits must include emission limit values for polluting substances, in particular those listed in Annex II, likely to be emitted from the installation concerned in significant quantities, having regard to their nature and their potential to transfer pollution from one medium to another (Article 14(1)(a)). Further, the permit must include appropriate requirements ensuring protection of the soil and groundwater and measures concerning the monitoring and management of waste generated by the installation. Emission limit values may be supplemented or replaced by equivalent parameters or technical measures ensuring an equivalent level of environmental protection (Article 14(2)). The emission limit values and the equivalent parameters and technical measures have to be based on the best available techniques (Article 14(3)), but the Member States' authorities may set stricter permit conditions (Article 14(4)).

The permit must contain suitable release monitoring requirements, specifying the measurement methodology and frequency, evaluation procedure and, where applicable, that results of emission monitoring are available for the same periods of time and reference conditions as for the emission levels associated with the best available technique (Article 14(1)(c)).

Further, the permit must contain an obligation to supply the competent authority regularly and at least annually with information on the basis of the results of emission monitoring and other required data that enables the competent authority to verify compliance with the permit conditions and, where applicable, a summary of the results of emission monitoring which allows a comparison with the emission levels associated with the best available techniques (Article 14(1)(d)).

In addition, appropriate requirements for the regular maintenance and surveillance of measures taken to prevent emissions to soil and groundwater and concerning the periodic monitoring of soil and groundwater in relation to relevant hazardous substances and groundwater contamination (Article 14(1)(e)) have to be included.

Furthermore, the permit must contain measures relating to conditions other than normal operating conditions, that is, for start-up and shut-down, leaks, malfunctions, and momentary stoppages and definitive cessation of operations (Article 14(1)(f)), as well as provisions on the minimisation of long-distance or transboundary pollution (Article 20(2)).

Any change planned in the operation of the installation has to be notified to the authorities (Article 20(1)). Where appropriate, the competent authorities have to update the permit or the conditions. No substantive change in the operation of the installation planned by the operator may be made without a permit being issued (Article 20(2)). The application for a permit and the decision by the authority must cover those parts of the installation and those aspects listed in Article 12 that may be affected by the substantive change (Article 20(2)).

The competent authorities have to periodically reconsider and, where necessary, update permit conditions (Article 21). When reconsidering permit conditions, the competent authority shall use any information resulting from monitoring or inspections (Article 21(2)). Within four years of publication of decisions on best available techniques, the competent authorities have to ensure that all the permit conditions for the installation concerned are reconsidered and, if necessary, updated to ensure compliance and that the installation complies with those permit conditions (Article 21(3)). Where an installation is not covered by any of the best available technique conclusions, the permit conditions shall be reconsidered and, if necessary, updated where developments in the best available techniques allow for the significant reduction of emissions (Article 21(4)).

The reconsideration has to be undertaken in any event where the pollution caused by the installation is of such significance that the existing emission limit values of the permit need to be revised or new values need to be included in the permit; where the operational safety of the process or activity requires other techniques to be used; and where it is necessary to comply with a new or revised environmental quality standard (Article 21(5)).

Article 16 obliges the authorities to ensure that compliance with the permit requirements is properly monitored.

Interestingly, Article 26 introduces a number of obligations with respect to those operations which may have transboundary effects. Where a Member State is aware that the operation of an installation is likely to have significant negative effects on the environment of another Member State, or where a Member State likely to be significantly affected so requests, the Member State in whose territory the application for a permit was submitted must forward the information provided pursuant to Article 4 or Article 20(2). This information will then serve as a basis for any consultations necessary in the framework of the bilateral relations between the two Member States on a reciprocal and equivalent basis.

Member States are further required to adopt measures regarding incidents and accidents. Accordingly, the operator has to inform the competent authority immediately in the case of an incident or accident and further has to immediately take measures to limit the environmental consequences and to prevent further possible incidents or accidents. The competent authority has to require the operator to take any appropriate complementary measures that the competent authority considers necessary to limit the environmental consequences and to prevent further possible incidents or accidents (Article 7).

Member States shall take the necessary measures to ensure that the permit conditions are complied with. However, in the event of a breach of the permit conditions, Member States have to ensure that the operator immediately informs the competent authority and takes the measures necessary to ensure that compliance is restored within the shortest possible time. Further, the competent authority has to require the operator to take any appropriate complementary measures that the competent authority considers necessary to restore compliance. Where the breach of the permit conditions poses an immediate danger to human health or threatens to cause an immediate significant adverse effect upon the environment, and until compliance is restored, the operation of the installation or activity has to be suspended (Article 8).

A system of environmental inspections further promotes compliance. The inspection of the installations addresses the full range of relevant environmental effects from the installations concerned. Authorities have to be enabled to carry out any site visits, to take samples and to gather any information necessary for the performance of their duties. Further, it has to be ensured that all installations are covered by an environmental inspection plan at national, regional or local level and that this plan is regularly reviewed and updated. Based on the inspection plans, the competent authority shall regularly draw up programmes for routine environmental inspections, including the frequency of site visits for different types of installations. The frequency shall be based on a systematic appraisal of the environmental risks of the installations concerned and shall not exceed one year for installations posing the highest risks and three years for installations posing the lowest risks (Article 23).

B. Best Available Techniques

As noted above, best available techniques (BATs) refer to the most effective and advanced stage in the development of activities. "Techniques" include both the technology used and the way in which the installation is designed, built, maintained, operated and decommissioned. "[A]vailable techniques" means those developed on a scale which allows implementation in the relevant industrial sector, under economically and technically viable conditions, taking into consideration the costs and advantages, whether or not the techniques are used or produced inside the Member State in question, as long as they are reasonably accessible to the operator. Lastly, "best" refers to the most effective technique for achieving a high general level of protection of the environment as a whole (Article 3(10) (a–c)).

The criteria for determining BATs are included in Annex III of the IED Directive:

1. the use of low-waste technology;
2. the use of less hazardous substances;
3. the furthering of recovery and recycling of substances generated and used in the process and of waste, where appropriate;
4. comparable processes, facilities or methods of operation which have been tried with success on an industrial scale;
5. technological advances and changes in scientific knowledge and understanding;
6. the nature, effects and volume of the emissions concerned;
7. the commissioning dates for new or existing installations;
8. the length of time needed to introduce the best available technique;
9. the consumption and nature of raw materials (including water) used in the process and energy efficiency;
10. the need to prevent or reduce to a minimum the overall impact of the emissions on the environment and the risks to it;
11. the need to prevent accidents and to minimise the consequences for the environment;
12. information published by public international organisations.

The competent authority has to follow and be informed of the developments in BATs and of the publication of any new or updated BAT conclusions and make that information available to the public concerned (Article 19).

"Emerging techniques" means a novel technique for an industrial activity that, if commercially developed, could provide either a higher general level of protection of the environment or at least the same level of protection of the environment and higher cost savings than existing BATs (Article 3(14)). Member States have to encourage the development and application of emerging techniques, in particular for those emerging techniques identified in BAT reference documents (Article 17).

Article 13 establishes the BAT exchange of information for Member States, the industry and NGOs concerned and the Commission. This supports the drawing up, reviewing and updating of BAT reference documents. The exchange of information addresses the following: the performance of installations and techniques, the techniques used, associated monitoring, cross-media effects, economic and technical viability and developments therein and BATs and emerging techniques identified (Article 13(2)). In addition, the Commission establishes and regularly convenes a forum composed of representatives of Member States, the industries concerned and NGOs promoting environmental protection in order to collect information and opinions regarding these measures and make the ones relating to the proposed content of the BAT reference documents publicly available (Article 13(3–4)).[15] The BAT reference documents are established through Best Available Techniques Reference document (BREFs) via the Sevilla Process, a meeting of experts which takes two to three years for each BREF.

III. EU LABELLING

Over the last decades, food and product labelling has become an important tool for consumer information and protection. The overarching problem regarding eco-labelling is that the average consumer is surrounded by a multitude of environmental claims, labels and logos which promise that products limit harm to the environment, reduce the ecological footprint, are beneficial for human health and without chemicals, pesticides, and so on. It becomes increasingly difficult for the average consumer to distinguish between labels or logos actually demonstrating an environmental or human health benefit, and those established for commercial and marketing purposes.

The EU has acted in this regard, not only by introducing legislation[16] and guidelines[17] regulating the correct usage and prohibiting the misleading

---

[15] For the changes within the BAT system in the new IED please refer to B. Lange, "EU Directive on Industrial Emissions: Squaring the Circle of Integrated, Harmonised and Ambitious Technology Standards?", 13 *Environmental Law Review* 3 (2011), 199–204, at 202.

[16] Directive 2005/29 concerning unfair business-to-consumer commercial practices in the internal market, [2005] OJ L 149/22.

[17] For example, Commission Guidance on the implementation/application of the Directive 2005/29/EC on Unfair Commercial Practices, Brussels, 3 December

use of a (environmental) claim, logo or label, but also by establishing specific European labels. Examples in the areas of general product quality and environmental impacts as well as for energy performance and efficiency are the EU Ecolabel and the Energy label. These schemes have been established by legislation. The use of the former is voluntary; the latter is compulsory.

A. EU Ecolabel

Up to 2015, the EU Ecolabel had been displayed on more than 44,711 products and services and more than 2031 licences had been awarded. Product groups range from tissue paper, cleaning products, floor covering and camping sites to TVs, soaps and shampoos. An online Ecolabel catalogue on the Commissions website[18] makes it easy and fast for the consumer to identify and research the certified products. The scheme is voluntary. Producers are not required to attach the eco-label to their products and therefore to ensure that their production meets the developed criteria; the scheme trusts that consumer pressure will make participation attractive.

Figure 6.1 shows the current layout of the Ecolabel

Regulatory framework
The EC eco-labelling scheme was first established through Regulation 880/92 on a Community eco-label award scheme[19] in 1992; this was amended by Regulation 66/2010 on the EU Ecolabel.[20] The scheme is designed to inform the consumer of the quality of a product as well as of the impact of the product on the environment. Generally its aim is to promote the design, production, marketing and use of products which have a reduced environmental impact during their entire life cycle; and to provide consumers with better information on the environmental impact of products.

Medical products for human and veterinary use as well as food products

---

2009, SEC (2009) 1666; as well as Juan R. Palerm, "Guidelines for Making and Assessing Environmental Claims", commissioned by the EC, 2000, available at http://ec.europa.eu/consumers/cons_safe/news/green/guidelines_en.pdf, last consulted 11.11.2015.

[18] Available at http://ec.europa.eu/ecat/, last consulted 11.11.2015.
[19] Regulation 880/92 on a Community eco-label award scheme, OJ L 99, 11.4.1992, pp. 1–7, as amended by Regulation 1980/2000 on a revised Community eco-label award scheme, [2000] OJ L 237/1.
[20] Regulation 66/2010 on the EU Ecolabel, [2010] OJ L 27/1.

Source: www.euecolabel.eu.

Figure 6.1   EU Ecolabel

are excluded from the Regulation's scope (Article 2), as are goods containing toxic and hazardous substances or preparations/mixtures (Article 6(6)).

EU eco-labels are defined per product group; a group consisting of products that serve similar purposes and are similar in terms of use, or have similar functional properties, and are similar in terms of consumer perception (Article 3(1)).

An important requirement of the EU labelling scheme is that the environmental friendliness of the product group is judged by taking into account the entire life cycle of the product, via the so-called "cradle-to-grave" approach. This means including the life cycle of a product from manufacturing, including the choice of raw materials, distribution, consumption and use to disposal after use (Article 6(3)).

Main provisions of the Regulation
The eco-label may only be awarded to those products which not only meet the criteria for the specific label, but also all Union health, safety and environmental requirements. More precisely, in accordance with Article 6(3) of the Regulation, the following has to be considered:

- most significant environmental impacts, in particular the impact on climate change, the impact on nature and biodiversity, energy and resource consumption, generation of waste, emissions to all environmental media, pollution through physical effects and use and release of hazardous substances;
- the substitution of hazardous substances by safer substances, as such or via the use of alternative materials or designs, wherever it is technically feasible;

- the potential to reduce environmental impacts due to durability and reusability of products;
- the net environmental balance between the environmental benefits and burdens, including health and safety aspects, at the various life stages of the products;
- social and ethical aspects, e.g. by making reference to related international conventions and agreements such as relevant ILO [International Labour Organization] standards and codes of conduct;
- criteria established for other environmental labels, particularly officially recognised, nationally or regionally, EN ISO 14024 type I environmental labels, where they exist for that product group so as to enhance synergies;
- the principle of reducing animal testing.

The specific ecological criteria for each product group are established using the cradle-to-grave approach based on scientific evidence and the parameters of Articles 7 and 8, as well as Annex I. The criteria must be precise, clear and objective to ensure uniformity of application by the competent bodies. They must ensure a high level of environmental protection, be based as far as possible on the use of clean technology and, where appropriate, reflect the desirability of maximising product life. The Commission, Member States, competent bodies and other stakeholders with expertise in the individual product area may initiate and lead the development or revision of EU Ecolabel criteria, after consulting the EU Ecolabelling Board which consists of the representatives of the competent bodies of all the Member States and of other interested parties.

Annex I outlines the procedures to be followed when drafting the criteria, depending on the individual type of criteria to be adopted. In general the standard procedure laid down in Part A is applicable. However, where criteria have already been developed under another ecolabel scheme complying with the requirements of EN ISO 14024 type I environmental labels for a product group for which no EU Ecolabel criteria have been established as yet, the shortened criteria development procedure laid down in Part B of Annex I applies provided that the proposed criteria have been developed in line with Part A of Annex I. Further, if a non-substantial revision of the criteria is necessary, the shortened revision procedure laid down in Part C of Annex I is applicable. All established Ecolabel criteria will be published in the *Official Journal of the European Union*.

The period of validity of product groups is about three to five years. The period of validity of a criterion may not exceed the period of validity of the product groups to which it relates. The label is awarded for a fixed production period which may under no circumstances exceed the period of validity of the criteria. Where the criteria relating to products are extended without change, the validity of the label may be extended for the same period.[21]

B. EU Energy Label

The EU Energy Label was established through Directive 2010/30.[22] Contrary to the EU Ecolabel, the Energy label is mandatory. The label covers all energy-related products which have a significant direct (consuming energy during use) or indirect (contributing to energy conservation during use) impact on the consumption of energy. Only second-hand products, means of transport for persons or goods, and rating plates or their equivalent affixed for safety purposes to products are excluded from the scope of the Directive (Article 1(3)).

Figure 6.2 shows the current layout of the Energy label

Regulatory framework
Through the EU Energy Label, the legislator aims to establish a framework for the harmonisation of national measures on end-user information, particularly by means of labelling and standard product information, on the consumption of energy and other essential resources during use, and supplementary information concerning energy-related products, thereby allowing end users to choose more efficient products (Article 1(1)).

The Commission, through the issuance of delegated acts, lays down details of the label and the fiche relating to each type of product. The provisions in delegated acts regarding information provided on the label and in the fiche on the consumption of energy and other essential resources during use enables end users to make better informed purchasing decisions and enables market surveillance authorities to verify whether products comply with the information provided (Article 10). The following criteria are to be taken into account in drafting the delegated acts:

- according to most recently available figures and considering the quantities placed on the Union market, the products shall have a significant potential for saving energy and, where relevant, other essential resources;

---

[21] See for example, Commission Decision of 19 December 2013 amending Decision 2007/506 in order to prolong the validity of the ecological criteria for the award of the EU Ecolabel to soaps, shampoos and hair conditioners, [2013] OJ L 349/14.

[22] Directive 2010/30 of 19 May 2010 on the indication by labelling and standard product information of the consumption of energy and other resources by energy-related products, [2010] OJ L 153/1.

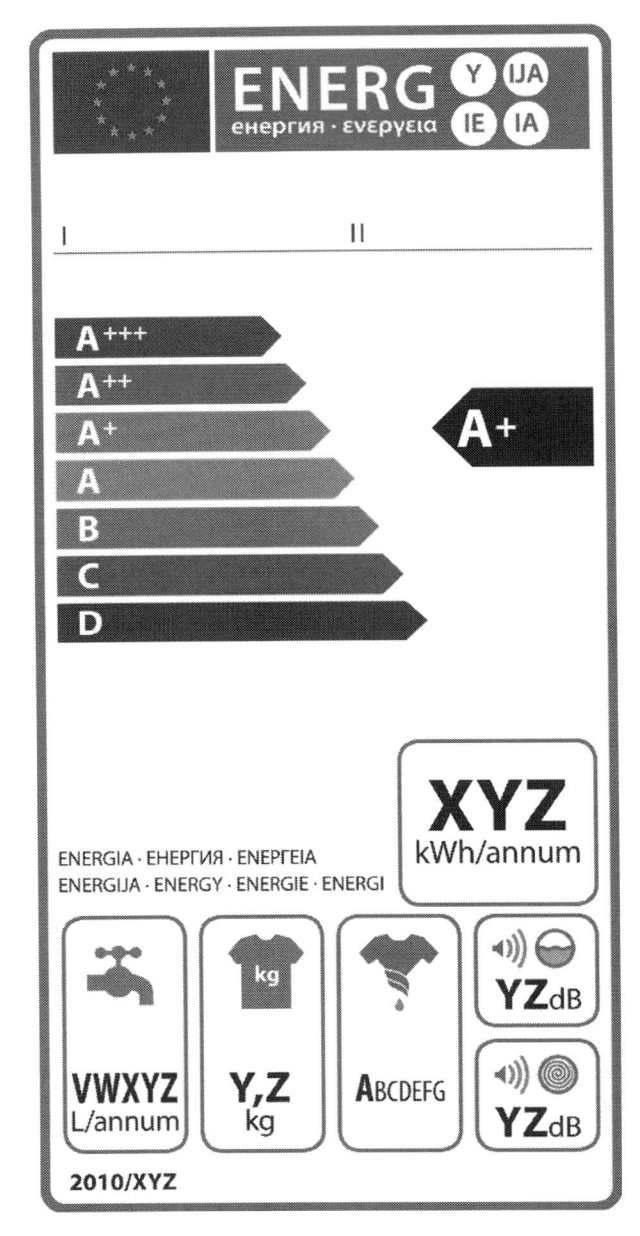

Source: EU Energy Label Directive 2010/30.

Figure 6.2   EU energy label

- products with equivalent functionality available on the market shall have a wide disparity in the relevant performance levels;
- relevant Union legislation and self-regulation shall be taken into account, such as voluntary agreements, which are expected to achieve the policy objectives more quickly or at lesser expense than mandatory requirements. (Article 10(2))

One example of such a voluntary agreement which has been implemented as unilateral commitments by industry is the Industry Self-Commitment to improve the energy performance of household consumer electronic products sold in the EU (July 2003).[23]

An example of a Commission Delegated Regulation is Regulation 811/2013.[24]

Energy-related products are all goods having an impact on energy consumption during use, which are placed on the market and/or put into service in the Union, including parts intended to be incorporated into energy-related products which are placed on the market and/or put into service as individual parts for end users and for which the environmental performance can be assessed independently.

Main provisions of the Directive
The Directive not only imposes responsibilities on the Member States, but also specifically addresses suppliers and dealers of the products. The latter are the retailers or other persons who sell, hire, offer for hire purchase or display products to end users, the former applying to manufacturers or their authorised representatives in the Union or the importers who place or put into service the product on the Union market. In their absence, any natural or legal person who places on the market or puts into service products covered by this Directive is considered a supplier (Article 2).

Accordingly, the suppliers are obliged to produce technical documentation including a general description of the product; the results of design calculations carried out, if applicable, and test reports, where available, including tests carried out by other organisations, as well as where values are used for similar models, the references allowing identification of those models. The technical documentation needs to

---

[23] Available at http://ec.europa.eu/energy/efficiency/labelling/doc/2003_eicta.pdf, last consulted 11.11.2015.
[24] Commission Delegated Regulation 811/2013 of 18 February 2013 supplementing Directive 2010/30 with regard to the energy labelling of space heaters, combination heaters, packages of space heater, temperature control and solar device and packages of combination heater, temperature control and solar device, [2013] OJ L 239/1.

be sufficient to verify the accuracy of the information contained on the label and the fiche. In addition, suppliers have to make the technical documentation available for inspection purposes for a period of five years (Article 5).

Retailers are obliged to display labels properly, in a visible and legible manner, and make the fiche available in the product brochure or other literature that accompanies products when sold to end users (Article 6).

The Directive further relates to distance selling. Where the potential end user cannot be expected to see the product displayed, for example if a product is offered by mail order, by catalogue, through the Internet or telemarketing, the end users have to be provided with the information specified on the label for the product and in the fiche before buying the product.

IV. GREEN PUBLIC PROCUREMENT

Including ecological considerations in procurement decisions is quite obviously viewed as a good means to drive environmental protection forward. Government sourcing of certain categories of goods may, in itself, be an important part of overall consumption of the goods concerned. This is an obvious incentive for companies to produce their goods in the preferred way. Moreover, when procuring ecologically, the government is seen as leading by example, encouraging national undertakings (and individual consumers) to take up the habit. Indeed, green procurement is so *en vogue* that the European Commission included environmental considerations in the review of EU procurement legislation.[25]

The 2008 Commission Communication on Public procurement for a better environment,[26] combined with a Commission Staff Working Document[27] established specific green public procurement (GGP) targets, inter alia: the establishment of a process and the setting of GPP criteria; the improvement on information on life cycle costing of products; and the drafting of legal and operational guidance.[28] It defines GPP as "a process

---

[25] For a detailed analysis see also European Commission, *Buying Green! A Handbook on Environmental Public Procurement*, Luxembourg: Office for Official Publications of the European Communities, 2011; as well as for practitioners' guidance L. Wozniacki, *Guidance to Foster Green Public Procurement*, Brussels: EEB, 2012.

[26] COM (2008) 400.

[27] SEC (2008) 2126.

[28] See COM (2008) 400, 4.

whereby public authorities seek to procure goods, services and works with a reduced environmental impact throughout their life cycle when compared to goods, services and works with the same primary function that would otherwise be procured".[29] Moreover, the Europe 2020 "strategy for smart, sustainable and inclusive growth"[30] promotes GPP as a key tool for innovation,[31] industry policy and for a resource efficient Europe,[32] and for smart budgetary consolidation for long-term growth.[33]

In 2010 a procedure for EU GPP criteria was put into place. More than 20 EU GPP criteria are now easily accessible for a wide range of products, for example copying and graphic paper, cleaning products and services, office IT equipment, furniture, and so on.[34]

The legal framework consists of Directive 2014/24[35] covering public works contracts, public supply contracts and public service contracts and Directive 2014/25[36] covering the procurement procedures of entities operating in the water, energy, transport and postal services sectors. These Directives repealed Directives 2004/18[37] and 2004/17,[38] respectively. The GPP Directives are supported by Directive 2009/81[39] establishing specific procurement rules in the area of defence and security and Directive 89/665[40] harmonising national legislation regarding the application of

---

[29] See COM (2008) 400, 4.
[30] COM (2010) 2020.
[31] Ibid., 12.
[32] Ibid., 15ff.
[33] Ibid., 26.
[34] See for the individual criteria and the technical background reports: http://ec.europa.eu/environment/gpp/eu_gpp_criteria_en.htm, last consulted 11.11.2015.
[35] Directive 2014/24 of 26 February 2014 on public procurement and repealing Directive 2004/18/EC, [2014] OJ L 94/65.
[36] Directive 2014/25 of 26 February 2014 on procurement by entities operating in the water, energy, transport and postal services sectors and repealing Directive 2004/17, [2014] OJ L 94/243.
[37] Directive 2004/18 on the coordination of procedures for the award of public works contracts, public supply contracts and public service contracts, [2004] OJ L 134/114.
[38] Directive 2004/17 coordinating the procurement procedures of entities operating in the water, energy, transport and postal services sectors, OJ [2004] L134/1.
[39] Directive 2009/81 on the coordination of procedures for the award of certain works contracts, supply contracts and service contracts by contracting authorities or entities in the fields of defence and security, and amending Directives 2004/17/EC and 2004/18/EC, [2009] OJ L 216/76.
[40] Directive 89/665 on the coordination of the laws, regulations and administrative provisions relating to the application of review procedures to the award of public supply and public works contracts, [1989] OJ L 395/33.

review procedures to the award of public supply and public works contracts.

The new Directives have simplified existing public procurement rules especially for SMEs. They further are to "allow(s) the procurers to make better use of public procurement in support of common societal goals such as protection of the environment, higher resource and energy efficiency, combating climate change, promoting innovation, employment and social inclusion and ensuring the best possible conditions for the provision of high quality social services".[41]

In terms of performance or functional requirements, Directive 2014/24 specifies that these may include environmental characteristics (Article 42(3)(a)). However, it also says that such parameters must be sufficiently precise to allow tenderers to determine the subject matter of the contract and to allow contracting authorities to award the contract. "Sufficiently precise" is a condition which applies of course to all tender criteria.[42] Article 43 of the Directive provides that, where contracting authorities intend to purchase works, supplies or services with specific environmental characteristics, a specific label can be required as proof that the characteristics are met, provided that:

- the label requirements only concern criteria which are linked to the subject matter of the contract and are appropriate to define characteristics of the works, supplies or services that are the subject matter of the contract;
- the label requirements are based on objectively verifiable and non-discriminatory criteria;
- the labels are established in an open and transparent procedure in which all relevant stakeholders, including government bodies, consumers, social partners, manufacturers, distributors and non-governmental organisations, may participate;
- the labels are accessible to all interested parties;
- the label requirements are set by a third party over which the economic operator applying for the label cannot exercise a decisive influence. (Article 43(1)(a–e))

Contracting authorities may indicate that the products and services bearing the label are presumed to comply with the technical specifications laid down in the contract documents. They must accept any other

---

[41] COM (2011) 896, at 2.
[42] For a recent example see *the UK Supreme Court in Healthcare at Home Limited (Appellant) v The Common Services Agency (Respondent) (Scotland)*, [2014] UKSC 49, and G. Van Calster, "The Clapham Omnibus, Objective Legal Standards and EU Procurement Law", 18 August 2014, www.gavclaw.com, last consulted 20.4.2015.

appropriate means of proof, such as a technical dossier of the manufacturer or a test report from a recognised body.

With respect to performance conditions, the Directive foresees that contracting authorities may lay down special conditions relating to the performance of a contract, provided that these are compatible with Union law and are indicated in the contract notice or in the specifications. The conditions governing the performance of a contract may, in particular, concern social and environmental considerations. The Court in *Dutch Coffee*[43] confirmed that requiring a specific eco-label, rather than using the detailed specifications defined by that eco-label, is incompatible with the Directive.

The Directive currently in force has effectively formalised the ECJ case law on the matter. *Helsinki Bus*[44] dealt with the extent environmental requirements could be taken into consideration at the award stage of a contract. The Court identified four conditions for assessing the most economically advantageous tender and environmental award criteria: these (a) need to be linked to the subject matter of the contract; (b) cannot give unrestricted freedom of choice on the contracting authority, meaning any environmental requirements must be specific and objectively quantifiable; (c) need to be expressly mentioned in the contract documents or in the tender notice; and (d) have to comply with the general EU principles, such as non-discrimination.

In addition, in *Wienstrom*,[45] the Court held that award criteria must be related to the subject matter of the contract. Further, in *Evropaïki Dynamiki*[46] the General Court clarified the approach to be taken by public authorities in assessing environmental management policies put forward by tenderers. It dismissed a challenge to a tender issued by the European Environment Agency (EEA), upholding the EEA's discretion on environmental criteria. It found that the EEA had made a "comparative assessment of the tenders, evaluating whether the environmental policies submitted by the tenderers were genuine, and that it found that only one of them had already put such a policy in place, whilst the others merely indicated good intentions in that respect".

---

[43] Case C-368/10 *Commission v Netherlands*, ECLI:EU:C:2012:284, at 70.
[44] Case C-513/99 *Concordia Bus Finland*, [2002] ECR I-7213.
[45] Case C-448/01 *EVN and Wienstrom*, [2003] ECR I-14527.
[46] Case T-331/06 *Evropaïki Dynamiki v EEA*, [2010] ECR II-136, at 76; the appeal to the ECJ, Case C-462/10 P *Evropaïki Dynamiki v EEA* was dismissed [2010] ECR II-136.

7. Environmental and Strategic Impact Assessments

I. ENVIRONMENTAL IMPACT ASSESSMENT

A. Basic Principles

The EIA Directive[1] is based on the principle that development consent for public and private projects which are likely to have significant effects on the environment should be granted only after an assessment of the likely significant environmental effects of those projects has been carried out (Recital 7 Directive 2011/92). While the Directives do not aim to harmonize all detail with respect to the procedure (among others because this would encroach upon Member States' reserved area for town planning), assessment of the environmental effects should be harmonised with reference to the projects which should be subject to assessment, the main obligations of the developers and the content of the assessment (Recital 3 Directive 2011/92).

The first EIA Directive came into force in 1985, meaning EU law has had an impact in this area for 30 years already. The criteria and procedure have been updated several times,[2] taking into account technical[3] and procedural developments, as well as international environmental law developments.[4] It is one way of transposing the principles of precaution

---

[1] Directive 2011/92 on the assessment of the effects of certain public and private projects on the environment, [2012] OJ L 26/1, repealing Directive 85/337, [1985] OJ L 175/40 as amended. Directive 2011/92 was last amended by Directive 2014/52, [2014] OJ L 124/1.

[2] Last in April 2014, Directive 2014/52 of 16 April 2014 amending Directive 2011/92 on the assessment of the effects of certain public and private projects on the environment, [2014], OJ L 124/1.

[3] For example the third amendment in 2009 included the technology of Carbon Capture Storage (CCS) into Annexes I and II to the Directive.

[4] For example, the first amendment of the Directive in 1997 brought the Directive in line with the requirements of the international 1991 Espoo Convention on EIA in a transboundary context, the second amendment in 2003 transposed some provisions of the Aarhus Convention, especially regarding public participation.

and prevention, as well as the principle of rectification at source and that the polluter should pay into practice (Recital 2 Directive 2011/92).

The general procedure can be outlined as shown in Figure 7.1.[5]

The Directive applies to the assessment of the environmental effects of those public and private projects which are likely to have significant effects on the environment (Article 1 EIA Directive). It thus has a wide scope of application and broad purpose:[6] the ECJ in *Leth* held that "the purpose of that directive is an assessment of the effects of public and private projects on the environment in order to attain one of the Community's objectives in the sphere of the protection of the environment and the quality of life".[7] Exceptions to the scope of the Directive are projects serving national defence purposes, and responses to civil emergencies have also recently been added, if the authorities consider that such application would have an adverse effect on those purposes.[8] This provision is to be interpreted restrictively. For example, an airport serving both civil and military purposes and whose main use is of a commercial nature does fall within the scope of the Directive.[9] The previous version of the Directive further exempted projects covered in detail by a specific national act, subject to the condition that the objectives of the Directive, including that of supplying information, were achieved through the national legislative process (Article 1(4) Directive 2011/92);[10] this, however, has been deleted in the 2014 version.

A "project" is the "execution of construction works or of other installations or schemes, [as well as] other interventions[11] in the natural surroundings and landscape including those involving the extraction of mineral resources" (Article 1 (2)(a)). The "public" means "one or more natural or legal persons and, in accordance with national legislation or

---

[5] Commission Staff Working Paper, Impact Assessment, Accompanying the document "Proposal for a Directive of the European Parliament and of the Council amending Directive 2011/92/EU on the assessment of the effects of certain public and private projects on the environment", SWD (2012) 355.

[6] See also cases ECJ, C-72/95 *Kraaijeveld and Others*, [1996] ECR I-5403, at 31 and 39; ECJ, C-435/97 *WWF and Others* [1999] ECR I-5613, at 40; ECJ, C-2/07 *Abraham and Others*, [2008] ECR I-1197, at 32; C-275/09 *Brussels Hoofdstedelijk Gewest and Others*, [2011] ECR I-1753, at 29.

[7] ECJ, C-420/11 *Jutta Leth*, ECLI:EU:C:2013:166, at 28.

[8] Article 1(1)(b) Directive 2014/52.

[9] ECJ, C-435/97 *WWF and Others*, note 6 above, at 65–67.

[10] ECJ, Case C-287/98 *Linster*, [2000] ECR I-6917, at 49–59; C-128/09 *Boxus and Others*, [2011] ECR I-9711, at 39–43 regarding the required degree of precision of the legislative act.

[11] C-2/07 *Abraham and Others*, note 6 above, C-275/09, *Brussels Hoofdstedelijk Gewest and Others*, note 6 above, at 20.

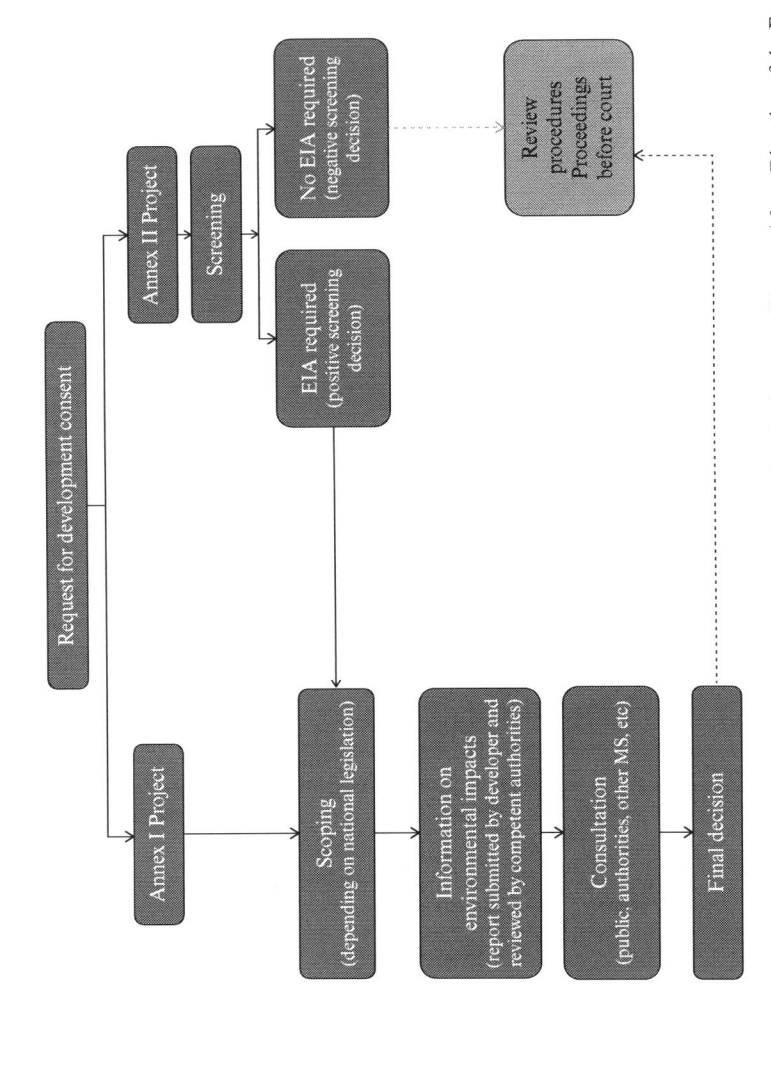

Source: Commission Staff Working Paper, Impact Assessment, Accompanying the document "Proposal for a Directive of the European Parliament and of the Council amending Directive 2011/92/EU on the assessment of the effects of certain public and private projects on the environment", SWD (2012) 355, p.3.

Figure 7.1 The EIA procedure

practice, their associations, organisations or groups" (Article 1 (2)(d)). The "public concerned" in this regard is "the public affected or likely to be affected by, or having an interest in, the environmental decision-making procedures referred to in Article 2(2). For the purposes of this definition, "non-governmental organisations promoting environmental protection and meeting any requirements under national law shall be deemed to have an interest" (Article 1 (2)(e)). The new Directive added a definition of an EIA. It refers to the process of

> (i) the preparation of an environmental impact assessment report by the developer, . . . (ii) the carrying out of consultations as referred to in Article 6 and, where relevant, Article 7; (iii) the examination by the competent authority of the information presented in the environmental impact assessment report and any supplementary information provided, where necessary, by the developer . . . and any relevant information received through the consultations under Articles 6 and 7; (iv) the reasoned conclusion by the competent authority on the significant effects of the project on the environment, taking into account the results of the examination referred to in point (iii) and, where appropriate, its own supplementary examination; and (v) the integration of the competent authority's reasoned conclusion into any of the decisions referred to in Article 8a.

Under the Directive, Member States are required to adopt measures necessary to ensure that, prior to giving consent, all projects likely to have significant effects on the environment regarding their nature, size or location are made subject to an EIA assessment with regard to their effects.[12] The results of the consultations and the information gathered is taken into consideration in the development consent procedure (Article 8).

The newly introduced Article 8a further specifies which information has to be incorporated in the decision to grant development consent. When a decision to grant or refuse development consent of a project has been taken, the public has to be informed, and relevant information published.[13] The Court considers these requirements as an attempt to involve the public concerned in supervising the implementation of the environmental principles included in Article 191 TFEU.[14] The Court specifies that Article 6(9) Aarhus and Article 9(1) EIA Directive must

---

[12] Article 2 EIA Directive, see also ECJ, C-72/95 *Kraaijeveld and Others*, note 6 above, at 50; C-2/07 *Abraham and Others*, note 6 above, at 37; C-75/08 *Mellor*, [2009] ECR I-3799, at 50; C-427/07 *Commission v Ireland*, [2009] I-627, at 4.

[13] The content of the decision and any conditions attached thereto; the main reasons and considerations on which the decision is based, including information about the public participation process (Article 9(1)).

[14] Case C-332/04 *Commission v Spain*, [2006] ECR I-40, at 55–59.

be interpreted as not requiring that the decision should itself contain the reasons for the competent authority's decision that an EIA was necessary. However, if an interested party so requests, the competent authority is obliged to communicate to it the reasons for that decision or the relevant information and documents in response to the request made.[15]

An applicant cannot initiate the work or activity relating to the project unless it obtained development consent (Article 2(1) and Recital 5 of Directive 2011/92, as applied in *Commission v Ireland*).[16]

Member States may integrate the assessment into existing procedures for project consent, for example into the integrated pollution prevention control procedure under the EID (Article 2(1–3) EIA Directive). Further, in exceptional cases, subject to the conditions listed in Article 2(4) of this Directive, projects might be exempt from the procedure established by this Directive. However, this alternative procedure must still satisfy the requirements of Articles 3 and 5–10 of the Directive, including the public participation requirements established in Article 6.[17]

B. Splitting of Projects, Incremental Projects, Cumulative Assessment

Projects may not be split to circumvent the purpose of the Directive[18] and the cumulative effects and impacts of several projects.[19] Regarding this issue, with respect to corresponding obligations, the ECJ has unequivocally rejected *inter alia* in *Ecologistas en Acción*,[20] the artificial splitting of projects to circumvent EIA requirements:

> as the Court has already noted with regard to Directive 85/337, the purpose of the amended directive cannot be circumvented by the splitting of projects

---

[15] Case C-182/10, *Solvay and Others*, not yet published in ECR, at 64.

[16] Case C-215/06 *Commission v Ireland*, [2008] ECR I-4911, at 51–53.

[17] Case C-435/97 *WWF and Others*, note 6 above, at 50–54; Case C-435/09 *Commission v Belgium*, [2011] ECR 36, at 62.

[18] Case C-392/96 *Commission v Ireland*, [1999] ECR I-5901, at 76 and 82; Case C-142/07 *Ecologistas en Acción-CODA v Ayuntamiento de Madrid*, [2008] ECR I-6097, at 44; Case C-205/08 *Umweltanwalt von Kärnten*, [2009] ECR I-11525, at 53; Case C-2/07 *Abraham and Others*, note 6 above, at 27; Case C-275/09 *Brussels Hoofdstedelijk Gewest and Others*, note 6 above, at 36.

[19] For a detailed analysis and a case study on this issue see G. Van Calster, "European Bank for Reconstruction and Development, Project Complaint Mechanism, Compliance Review Report", Complaint: Rivne Kyiv High Voltage Line Project, Request Number: 2012/02., available at http://www.ebrd.com/down loads/integrity/rivne_kyiv_cr.pdf, last consulted 13.10.2016

[20] Case C-142/07 *Ecologistas en Acción-CODA v Ayuntamiento de Madrid*, note 18 above.

and the failure to take account of the cumulative effect of several projects must not mean in practice that they all escape the obligation to carry out an assessment when, taken together, they are likely to have significant effects on the environment within the meaning of Article 2(1) of the amended directive (see, as regards Directive 85/337, Case C-392/96 Commission v Ireland [1999] ECR I-5901, paragraph 76, and Abraham and Others, paragraph 27).[21]

This strict approach of the Court prevents "salami" projects, that is, artificial splitting up in order to remain under relevant thresholds. The Court of Justice also held in *Ecologistas en Acción* that where individual projects carried out or planned to be carried out are part of a larger project, the authorities giving the go-ahead (and the national courts reviewing compliance with the Directive), must judge "whether they must be dealt with together by virtue, in particular, of their geographical proximity, their similarities and their interactions".[22]

Relevant case law with respect to incremental projects, also known as "cumulative assessment" may also be found in the application of Article 1(2)'s "development consent".[23] With reference to the concept of development consent in Article 1(2) of the EIA Directive, the term was found by the ECJ to refer to a single type of consent, that is, the authority's decision on whether a project can be proceeded with or not.[24]

However, as established in *Wells*, for multiple staged projects, the

> effects which the project may have on the environment must be identified and assessed at the time of the procedure relating to the principal decision. It is only if those effects are not identifiable until the time of the procedure relating to the implementing decision that the assessment should be carried out in the course of that procedure.

Further, in *Barker* the ECJ ruled that

> Articles 2(1) and 4(2) of Directive 85/337 are to be interpreted as requiring an environmental impact assessment to be carried out if, in the case of grant of consent comprising more than one stage, it becomes apparent, in the course of the second stage, that the project is likely to have significant effects on the environment by virtue inter alia of its nature, size or location.[25]

---

[21] Ibid., at 44.
[22] Ibid., at 45.
[23] Defined as "the decision of the competent authority or authorities which entitles the developer to proceed with the project" (Article 1(2)(c) of the Directive).
[24] Case C-332/04 *Commission v Spain*, at 53.
[25] Case C-290/03 *Diane Barker v London Borough of Bromley*, [2006] ECR I-3949, at 49.

In *Barker*, the local authority when issuing outline planning permission ruled that the first stages of the project would not have any significant effects on the environment and that only at a stage when reserved matters (part of the rolling-out of the planned project) were dealt with, might there be such effects and hence the need for an EIA.

In *Salzburger Flughafen*,[26] the Court rebuked Austria for operating a threshold for projects made subject to an EIA, which effectively meant that whole classes of projects (in particular gradual extensions of small airports) are in advance exempt from EIAs. It noted that "it can be necessary to take account of the cumulative effect of projects in order to avoid a circumvention of the objective of the European Union legislation by the splitting of projects which, taken together, are likely to have significant effects on the environment".

In *Marktgemeinde Straßwalchen*,[27] the ECJ insisted on a strict cumulation test. AG Rohöl-Aufsuchungs had obtained authorisation to undertake exploratory drilling within the territory of the Marktgemeinde Straßwalchen (Austria) up to a depth of 4150 metres, without an EIA. The Marktgemeinde Straßwalchen and 59 other persons challenged that decision before the Verwaltungsgerichtshof (Administrative Court).

"Extraction of petroleum and natural gas for commercial purposes where the amount extracted exceeds 500 tonnes/day in the case of petroleum and 500 000 cubic metres/day in the case of gas" is included in Annex I No. 14. However, the Court held that exploratory drilling, even if by nature "commercial" (unless it is carried out purely for research purposes), does not meet the conditions of Annex I No. 14, for that provision links the obligation to conduct an EIA to the quantities of petroleum and natural gas earmarked for extraction. Prior to an exploratory drilling operation, the actual presence of hydrocarbons cannot be determined with certainty. An exploratory drilling operation is carried out in order to establish the presence of hydrocarbons and, where they are found, to determine the quantity and ascertain, through a trial production, whether or not a commercial operation is feasible. Thus, it is only on the basis of an exploratory drilling operation that the quantity of hydrocarbons that can be extracted per day can be determined. Moreover, the quantity of hydrocarbons earmarked for extraction in such a trial, as well as its duration, are restricted to the technical needs arising from the objective of establishing the feasibility of a deposit.

EIAs are therefore not mandatory on the basis of Annex I. However,

---

[26] Case C-244/12 *Salzburger Flughafen*, [2013] ECLI:EU:C:2013:203, at 37.
[27] C-531/13 *Marktgemeinde Straßwalchen and Others*, ECLI:EU:C:2015:79.

Annex II No. 2d), includes "Deep drillings, in particular: (i) geothermal drilling; ii) drilling for the storage of nuclear waste material; (iii) drilling for water supplies; with the exception of drillings for investigating the stability of the soil." Exploratory drilling falls under that entry. With reference to previous case law, the ECJ emphasised that notwithstanding the discretion enjoyed by national authorities vis-à-vis projects included in Annex II, the characteristics of a project must be assessed, inter alia, in relation to its cumulative effects with other projects. Failure to take account of the cumulative effect of one project with other projects must not mean in practice that they all escape the obligation to carry out an assessment when, taken together, they are likely to have significant effects on the environment. With this approach the ECJ has countered the salami effect: the artificial splitting up of projects which do not individually meet EIA thresholds but which do so on a cumulative basis.

C. Obligations of the Directive

Article 3 of the Directive contains the fundamental provision and assessment obligation of the Directive.[28] However, it does not lay down the substantive rules in relation to the balancing of the environmental effects with other factors or prohibit the completion of projects which are liable to have negative effects on the environment.[29] It contains the substantive obligation, whereas Article 4 to 12 contain the procedural ones. The assessment shall identify, describe and assess on a case-by-case basis the direct and indirect effects of the project on (a) population and human health; (b) biodiversity, with particular attention to species and habitats; (c) land, soil, water, air and climate; (d) material assets, cultural heritage and the landscape; and the cultural heritage and the interaction between these factors.[30] The amended Directive introduces the focus on biodiversity.

Regarding the interpretation of "material assets",[31] the ECJ held in *Leth* that only those effects on material assets have to be taken into account which, by their very nature, are also likely to have an impact on the environment. This includes the direct and indirect effects of noise on human beings in the event of use of a property affected by a project, but does not include the assessment of the effects which the project under

---

[28] Case C-50/09 *Commission v Ireland*, [2011] ECR I-873, at, at 35.
[29] Case C-420/11 *Jutta Leth*, note 7 above, at 46.
[30] Article 3 EIA Directive.
[31] Article 3(1)(b) EIA Directive.

examination has on the value of material assets.[32] In addition, the court held that an assessment of the effects on one or more of the factors mentioned in Article 3 of the Directive other than that of material assets, does not entitle an individual to any compensation for pecuniary damage which is attributable to a decrease in the value of his material assets.[33]

Article 3 requires an

> examination of the substance of the information gathered as well as a consideration of the expediency of supplementing it, if appropriate, with additional data. That competent environmental authority must thus undertake both an investigation and an analysis to reach as complete an assessment as possible of the direct and indirect effects of the project concerned on the factors set out in the first three indents of Article 3 and the interaction between those factors.[34]

The Directive thus adopts an overall assessment framework of effects, taking into account the direct and indirect impacts of the project.[35]

Article 6 contains provisions regarding access to information, notice and consultation by the public. The public concerned shall be given early and effective opportunities to participate in the environmental decision-making procedures and shall be entitled to express comments and opinions when all options are open to the competent authority or authorities before the decision on the request for development consent is taken.

The newly introduced Article 8a paragraph 4 widens the scope of the EIA to also cover the project realisation phase, to the post-project monitoring stage. Member States need to determine monitoring procedures of significant adverse environmental effects. Annex IV paragraph 7 further specifies that an EIA needs to contain

> [a] description of the measures envisaged to avoid, prevent, reduce or, if possible, offset any identified significant adverse effects on the environment and, where appropriate, of any proposed monitoring arrangements (for example the

---

[32] Case C-420/11 *Jutta Leth*, note 7 above, at 29 and 30. Mrs Leth owns a house near Vienna-Schwechat airport (Austria) which got subsequently extended without EIAs, even though the Directive was in force. Mrs Leth claimed damages for the loss of value of her property resulting from aircraft noise, on the ground that the environmental effects of the expansion projects ought to have been assessed pursuant to the directive.

[33] Case C-420/11 *Jutta Leth*, note 7 above, at 31.

[34] Case C-50/09 *Commission v Ireland*, note 28 above, at 35, 37–41.

[35] Case C-322/04 *Commission v Spain*, note 24 above, at 33; Case C-2/07 *Abraham and Others*, note 6 above, at 43–45; Case C-142/07, C-142/07, *Ecologistas en Acción-CODA v Ayuntamiento de Madrid*, note 18 above, at 39; Case C-560/08 *Commission v Spain*, ECR [2011] I-199, at 98.

preparation of a post-project analysis). That description should explain the extent, to which significant adverse effects on the environment are avoided, prevented, reduced or offset, and should cover both the construction and operational phases.

Screening and scoping, and information to be provided
The key element of the Directive is that not all projects are subject to a mandatory impact assessment, only those listed in Annex I of the Directive. Annex I lists, for example, crude-oil refineries, thermal and nuclear power stations which fulfil certain production or output activities as subject to a mandatory EIA. The projects listed in Annex II of the Directive are subject to a screening procedure by the Member States.

Screening is commonly referred to as the process by which a decision is taken on whether or not an EIA is required for a particular project.[36] The competent authority in the Member State can make this decision either based on a case-by-case examination or by establishing thresholds or criteria, or both, and has to publish the decisions.

A newly introduced Annex II.A contains information which needs to be provided by the developer at the moment of the screening. The relevant selection criteria are set out in Annex III of the Directive. They refer to the characteristics of the project, such as size, use of natural resources and production of waste; the location of the project, the environmental sensitivity of geographical areas likely to be affected, such as existing land use, the relative abundance, quality and regenerative capacity of natural resources in the area and the absorption capacity of the natural environment, particularly regarding, for example wetlands and coastal zones; as well as characteristics of the potential impact, having regard to the extent of the impact (geographical area and size of the affected population), the transfrontier nature of the impact, its magnitude and complexity, as well as probability and duration, frequency and reversibility of the impact.

A Member State which has established thresholds and/or criteria at a level such that, in practice, all projects of a certain type would be exempted in advance from the requirement of an impact assessment exceeds the limits of that discretion, unless all the projects excluded could, when viewed as a whole, be regarded as not likely to have significant effects on the environment.[37] In addition, all selection criteria listed in Annex III

---

[36] European Commission, "Guidance on EIA – Screening", 2001, at 7. Available at http://ec.europa.eu/environment/archives/eia/eia-guidelines/g-screening-full-text.pdf, last consulted 12.11.2015.
[37] Case C- 392/96 *Commission v Ireland*, note 18 above, at 53 and 75; Case C-72/95 *Kraaijeveldand Others*, note 6 above, at 53; Case C-435/97 *WWF and*

have to be taken into account[38] and a Member State which has established thresholds and/or criteria taking account only of the size of projects exceeds the limits of its discretion under Articles 2(1) and 4(2) of the EIA Directive.[39] The use of other methods to determine if a project has to be subject to an EIA is possible as well, as long as this method does not undermine the objective of the Directive.[40]

For all projects subject to an EIA (mandatory ones or as a result of the screening procedure), the developer (the applicant for authorisation for a private project or the public authority which initiates a project (Article 1(2)(b)) has to supply the information specified in Annex IV of the Directive where the Member States consider that the information is relevant to a given stage of the consent procedure and to the specific characteristics of a particular project or type of project and of the environmental features likely to be affected and that they consider that a developer may reasonably be required to compile this information having regard, inter alia, to current knowledge and methods of assessment (Article 5(1)). This process is also referred to as scoping, meaning the process of identifying the content and extent of the environmental information to be submitted to the competent authority under the EIA procedure.

The competent authority shall give an opinion on the information to be supplied by the developer, after having consulted the developer and authorities likely to be concerned by the project according to Article 6(1) (Article 5(2)). Such an opinion is part of the consent process and thus preparatory in nature and not generally subject to appeal.[41]

Reasonable alternatives
Article 5 on the study of reasonable alternatives has been subject to review under the new Directive in order to improve the quality of the overall EIA assessment process. The minimum information the developer has to provide in the EIA report refers to

---

Others, note 6 above, at 38; Case C-66/06 *Commission v Ireland*, [2008] ECR I-158, at 65; Case C-427/07 *Commission v Ireland*, note 12 above, at 42.

[38] Case C-66/06 *Commission v Ireland*, note 18 above, at 62; Case C-255/08 *Commission v Netherlands*, [2009] ECR I-167, at 33; Case C-435/09 *Commission v Belgium*, note 17 above, at 53.

[39] Case C-392/96 *Commission v Ireland*, note 18 above, at 65 and 72; Case C-66/06 *Commission v Ireland*, note 37 above, at 64; Case C-255/08 *Commission v Netherlands*, note 38 above, at 32–39; Case C-435/09 *Commission v Belgium*, note 17 above, at 52, 55.

[40] C-435/97 *WWF and Others*, note 6 above, at 42, 43, 45; and C-87/02 *Commission v Italy*, [2004] ECR I-5975, at 41, 42, 44.

[41] C-332/04 *Commission v Spain*, note 24 above, at 54.

a description of the project including information on site, design, size and other relevant features of the project; a description of the likely significant effects of the project on the environment, measures envisaged in order to avoid, reduce and, if possible, offset likely significant adverse effects, a description of the reasonable alternatives studied by the developer, which are relevant to the project and its specific characteristics, and an indication of the main reasons for the option chosen, taking into account the effects of the project on the environment, as well as a non-technical summary of these points and finally, any additional information specified in Annex IV relevant to the specific characteristics of the project.

According to Annex IV, paragraph 2, alternatives refer to "project design, technology, location, size and scale"; the amendment thus establishes which alternatives should be studied. The fact that the wording "main alternatives" (used in the old Directive) has been replaced by "reasonable alternatives" further indicates that developers might be obliged to study extra alternatives, relating to the parameters outlined in Annex IV, paragraph 2.

Annex IV lists further requirements subject to the scoping procedure. Accordingly, the developer might also be required to submit amongst others a description of the aspects of the environment likely to be significantly affected by the proposed project, including, in particular, population, human health, biodiversity (for example fauna and flora), land (for example land take), soil (for example organic matter, erosion, compaction, sealing), water (for example hydromorphological changes, quantity and quality), air, climate (for example greenhouse gas emissions, impacts relevant to adaptation), material assets, cultural heritage, including architectural and archaeological aspects, and landscape. (Annex IV No. 4); as well as inter alia a description of the direct effects and any indirect, secondary, cumulative, short, medium and long-term, permanent and temporary, positive and negative effects of the project (Annex IV No. 5) and a description of the forecasting methods or evidence, used to identify and assess the significant effects on the environment, including details of difficulties (for example technical deficiencies or lack of knowledge) encountered compiling the required information and the main uncertainties involved (Annex IV No. 6).

D. Transboundary Projects

Article 7 includes the procedure of an EIA where a Member State is likely to be significantly affected by a project in the territory of another Member State. The implementation details are left open to the Member State. The Directive only sets the broader framework, outlining the overall consultation procedure and indicating that a reasonable time frame should be given within the process.

Article 7 EIA Directive only applies to intra-EU transboundary projects. Where a project is likely to significantly affect a third country outside the Union, the EIA additionally becomes subject to the provisions of the international 1991 Espoo Convention on EIA in a transboundary context.

The Commission published a guidance document[42] to further explain the individual steps of an EIA regarding these kinds of large-scale transboundary projects. These are defined as projects which are implemented in at least two Member States or having at least two parties of origin, and which are likely to cause significant effects on the environment or a significant adverse transboundary impact (Article 2(3) and (5) Espoo Convention). The guidance document identifies and provides a detailed explanation of the following seven steps of a transboundary EIA procedure:[43]

1. Notification and transmittal of information (Articles 7.1 and 7.2 of the EIA Directive; Article 3 Espoo);
2. Determination of the content and extent of the matters of the EIA information – scoping (Article 5.2 of the EIAD);
3. Preparation of the EIA information/report by the developer (Articles 5.1, 5.3 and Annex IV of the EIAD; Article 4 and Appendix II Espoo);
4. Public participation, dissemination of information and consultation (Articles 6, 7.3 EIAD, Article 3.8, 2.2, 2.6 and 4.2 Espoo);
5. Consultation between concerned Parties (Article 7.4 EIAD, Article 5 Espoo);
6. Examination of the information gathered and final decision (Article 8 EIAD, Article 6.1 Espoo);
7. Dissemination of information on the final decision (Article 9 EIAD, Article 6.2 Espoo).

The Commission published a guidance document on integrating climate change and biodiversity into EIA.[44] The guidance gives advice on how to identify and incorporate climate change and biodiversity into an EIA, as

---

[42] European Commission, "Guidance on the Application of the Environmental Impact Assessment Procedure for Large-scale Transboundary Projects", 2013, available at http://ec.europa.eu/environment/eia/pdf/Transboundry%20EIA%20Guide.pdf, last consulted 12.11.2015.

[43] Ibid., p. 4.

[44] European Commission, "Guidance on Integrating Climate Change and Biodiversity into Environmental Impact Assessment", 2013, available at http://

well as how to assess related effects and critical challenges.[45] Key steps to include these issues in an EIA are to:

- identify climate change and biodiversity concerns in EIA (useful for screening and scoping);
- analyze evolving baseline trends;
- identify alternatives and mitigation measures;
- assess effects (cumulative effects and uncertainty); and
- monitoring and adaptive management.[46]

E. The Relationship between the EIA Directive and the Aarhus Convention

Article 11 EIA Directive regulates access to justice for the public concerned, stating that the public needs to have a sufficient interest or, alternatively, maintaining the impairment of a right in order to have access to a review procedure before a court of law or another independent and impartial body established by law to challenge the substantive or procedural legality of decisions, acts or omissions subject to the public participation provisions of the Directive. What constitutes a sufficient interest and impairment of a right is determined by the Member States, consistent with the objective of giving the public concerned wide access to justice (Article 11(1–3)).[47]

Regarding the procedure, the Directive only states that such procedure must be, "fair, equitable, timely and not prohibitively expensive".

To interpret "not prohibitively expensive" in the EIA Directive, in *Edwards*,[48] as noted above (under the review of the Aarhus Convention in the Member States in Chapter 5), the ECJ turned to Aarhus and held that the cost of proceedings must neither exceed the financial resources of the person concerned nor appear, in any event, to be objectively unreasonable. As regards the analysis of the financial situation of the person concerned, the assessment, which must be carried out by the national court, cannot be based exclusively on the estimated financial resources of an "average" applicant, since such information may have little connection with the situation of the person concerned. The national court may also take into

---

ec.europa.eu/environment/eia/pdf/EIA%20Guidance.pdf, last consulted 12.11.2015.
[45] Ibid., at 9ff
[46] Ibid., at 26ff.
[47] See also Case C-263/08 *Djurgården – Lilla Värtans Miljöskyddsförening*, [2009] ECR I-9967, at 42–52.
[48] Case C-260/11 *Edwards and Pallikaropoulos*, not yet published in ECR.

account the situation of the parties concerned, whether the claimant has a reasonable prospect of success, the importance of what is at stake for the claimant and for the protection of the environment, the complexity of the relevant law and procedure and the potentially frivolous nature of the claim at its various stages. That the claimant has not been deterred, in practice, from asserting his or her claim is not in itself sufficient to establish that the proceedings are not, as far as that claimant is concerned, prohibitively expensive.

The impact of the EIA Directive and the Aarhus Convention regarding cost recovery has been recently dealt with by the UK High Court. In *Alyson Austin*[49] the Court had to consider the impact of the EIA Directive on cost orders. Ms Austin lived close to an opencast mining and reclamation site in Wales. She complained of noise from heavy machinery and dust, affecting her home and preventing her family from sleeping. Planning consent had been granted in 2005. Ms Austin's action was based on private nuisance proceedings, inter alia the allegation that some of the conditions attached to the consent have not been complied with. The claim therefore is related to post-EIA compliance and the order sought by Ms Austin was one to limit her costs.

The Court held that direct applicability of Aarhus in the UK is limited to those parts which have been incorporated in the EU's EIA Directive ("'otherwise, it remains a matter to be taken into account . . . in resolving ambiguities or in exercising discretions' – a narrow view perhaps, albeit supported by UK precedent, on the impact of the Convention in the UK's legal order") and that the Directive itself, as far as its impact on costs is concerned, relates to judicial review proceedings in the process of EIA-based consent only, not an action in private nuisance after such consent.

II. STRATEGIC ENVIRONMENTAL ASSESSMENT

A Strategic Environmental Assessment[50] or "SEA" is aimed at ensuring that environmental impacts are identified upstream, by ensuring that programmes and plans which will lead to EIA-bound projects are themselves checked.

Environmental and strategic impact assessments, the latter regulated

---

[49] *Alyson Austin v Miller Argent (South Wales) Ltd*, [2013] EWHC 2622.
[50] Directive 2001/42 on the assessment of the effects of certain plans and programmes on the environment, [2001] OJ L 197/30.

by Directive 2001/42,[51] to a large extent go hand in hand and complement each other. The procedures can be coordinated or joint (Article 11(2)). Whereas an EIA applies to individual projects, an SEA is carried out for plans and programmes, thus to the broader strategic framework.[52]

A. The Relationship between the EIA and SEA Directives

The overview in Figure 7.2 explains the interplay between both Directives.[53]

An SEA contributes to the integration of environmental considerations into the preparation and adoption of plans and programmes with a view to promoting sustainable development, by ensuring that an environmental assessment is carried out on certain plans and programmes which are likely to have significant effects on the environment (Article 1). The fundamental objective of the Directive is to ensure that plans and programmes which are likely to have significant effects on the environment are subject to an environmental assessment when they are prepared and prior to their adoption.[54]

A definition of these plans and programmes is contained in Article 2 as meaning plans and programmes, including those co-financed by the EU, as well as any modifications to them which are subject to preparation and/or adoption by an authority at national, regional or local level or which are prepared by an authority for adoption, through a legislative procedure by parliament or government, and which are required by legislative, regulatory or administrative provisions. This includes specific land development plans.[55]

These generally include all plans and programmes (not policies) prepared for agriculture, forestry, fisheries, energy, industry, transport, waste management, water management, telecommunications, tourism, town

---

[51] Regulated by Directive 2001/42 on the assessment of the effects of certain plans and programmes on the environment, [2001] OJ L 197/30.

[52] For a detailed discussion of the Directive and its relationship with the EIA Directive please refer to S. Marsden, *Strategic Environmental Assessment in International and European Law: A Practitioner's Guide*, Abingdon: Routledge, 2012.

[53] Imperial College London, "The Relationship between the EIA and SEA Directives", August 2005, available at http://ec.europa.eu/environment/eia/pdf/final_report_0508.pdf, last consulted 12.11.2015.

[54] Case C-295/10 *Valčiukienė and Others* [2011] ECR I-8819, at 37; and Case C-41/11 *Inter-Environnement Wallonie and Terre Wallonne* ECLI:EU:C:2012:103, at 40.

[55] Case C-567/10 *Inter-Environnement Bruxelles and Others*, ECLI:EU:C:2012:159.

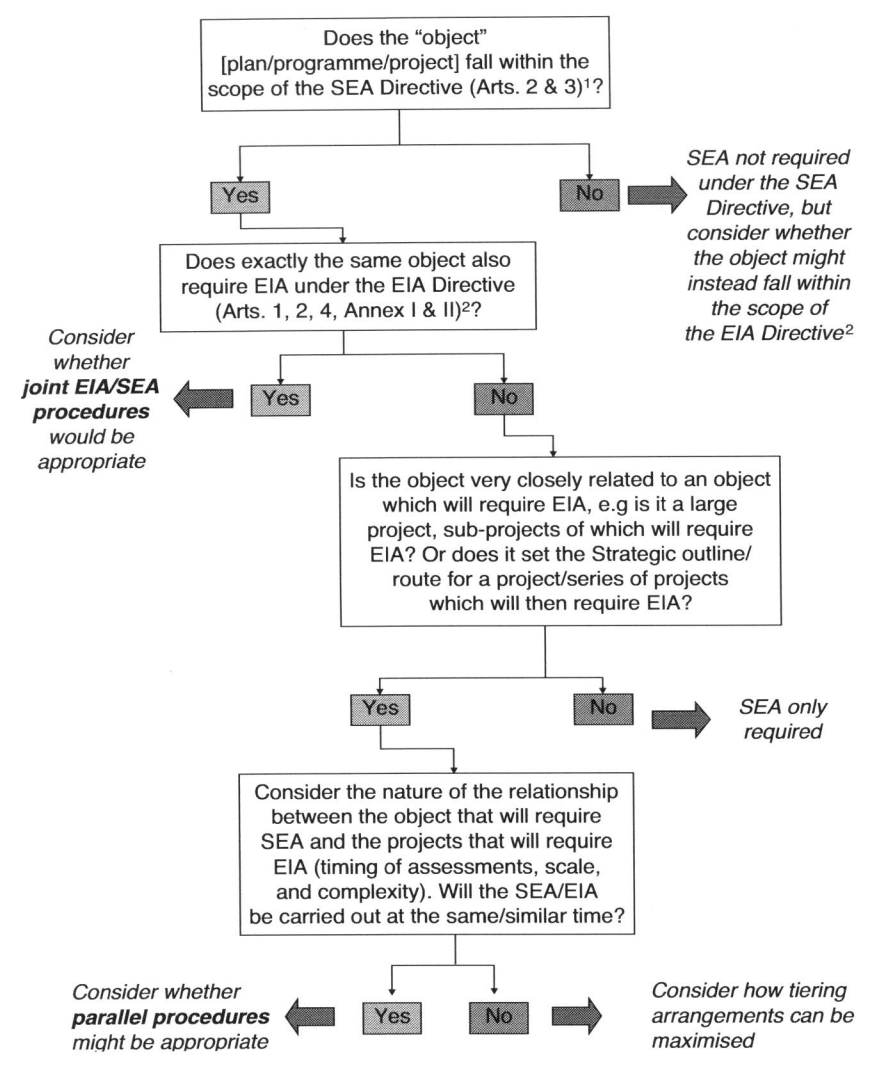

146   *EU environmental law*

```
                    ┌─────────────────────────────────┐
                    │ Does the "object"               │
                    │ [plan/programme/project] fall   │
                    │ within the scope of the SEA     │
                    │ Directive (Arts. 2 & 3)¹?       │
                    └─────────────────────────────────┘
                         │                    │
                        Yes                  No ──►  SEA not required
                         │                                under the SEA
                         ▼                                Directive, but
         ┌─────────────────────────────────┐              consider whether
         │ Does exactly the same object    │              the object might
         │ also require EIA under the EIA  │              instead fall within
         │ Directive (Arts. 1, 2, 4,       │              the scope of
         │ Annex I & II)²?                 │              the EIA Directive²
         └─────────────────────────────────┘
              │                    │
             Yes                  No
              │                    │
              ▼                    ▼
  Consider    ┌─────────────────────────────────┐
  whether     │ Is the object very closely      │
  joint       │ related to an object which will │
  EIA/SEA ◄── │ require EIA, e.g is it a large  │
  procedures  │ project, sub-projects of which  │
  would be    │ will require EIA? Or does it set│
  appropriate │ the Strategic outline/route for │
              │ a project/series of projects    │
              │ which will then require EIA?    │
              └─────────────────────────────────┘
                    │              │
                   Yes            No ──►  SEA only required
                    │
                    ▼
         ┌─────────────────────────────────┐
         │ Consider the nature of the      │
         │ relationship between the object │
         │ that will require SEA and the   │
         │ projects that will require EIA  │
         │ (timing of assessments, scale,  │
         │ and complexity). Will the       │
         │ SEA/EIA be carried out at the   │
         │ same/similar time?              │
         └─────────────────────────────────┘
                 │              │
                Yes            No
                 │              │
  Consider whether              Consider how tiering
  parallel procedures ◄──       arrangements can be
  might be appropriate          maximised
```

Notes:
1 Or within the scope of MS legislation on SEA if this is broader than the SEA Directive.
2 Or within the scope of MS legislation on EIA if this is broader than the EIA Directive.

Source: http://ec.europa.eu/environment/archives/eia/pdf/final_report_0508.pdf.

Figure 7.2 The relationship between the EIA and SEA Directive

and country planning or land use *and* which set the framework for future development consent of projects listed in Annexes I and II to the EIA Directive, as well as those which require an assessment under the Habitats Directive in view of the likely effect on sites (Article 3(2) SEA Directive).

Excluded are plans and programmes with the sole purpose of serving national defence or civil emergency, as well as financial or budget plans and programmes and those co-financed under Regulations 1260/1999[56] and 1257/1999[57] (Articles 3(8) and (9)). Further, plans and programmes relating to the activities listed above which determine the use of small areas at local level and minor modifications only require an environmental assessment if they are likely to have significant environmental effects (Article 3(3)).

B. The Provisions of the Directive

Similar to the EIA procedure, all other plans and programmes are subject to a screening procedure carried out by the Member States in order to establish whether they are likely to have significant environmental effects, either through a case-by-case examination or by specifying types of plans and programmes or by combining both approaches (Articles 3(4) and (5)). The Court stated that where a plan should have been subject to an SEA prior to its adoption, the national courts hearing an action for annulment of such a plan are obliged to take all general or particular measures for remedying the failure to carry out such an assessment.[58] In *L v M*[59] the Court clarified that a failure to include the adoption of a particular type of building plan in an environmental assessment under the SEA Directive is irrelevant to the legal validity of that plan.

For this purpose Member States shall in all cases take into account relevant criteria set out in Annex II, to ensure that plans and programmes with likely significant effects on the environment are covered by the Directive. These criteria relate to the characteristics of plans and programmes, such as the degree to which the plan or programme sets a

---

[56] Regulation 1083/2006 of 11 July 2006 laying down general provisions on the European Regional Development Fund, the European Social Fund and the Cohesion Fund and repealing Regulation (EC) No 1260/1999, [2006], OJ L 210/25.

[57] Council Regulation (EC) No 1257/1999 of 17 May 1999 on support for rural development from the European Agricultural Guidance and Guarantee Fund (EAGGF) and amending and repealing certain Regulations, OJ L 160, 26.6.1999, pp. 80–102 (as amended and partially repealed).

[58] Case C-41/11, note 54 above, paras 44 to 46.

[59] Case C-463/11 *L v M.*, ECLI:EU:C:2013:247.

framework for projects and other activities and the degree to which it influences other plans and programmes including those in a hierarchy, as well as its relevance for environmental integration with a view to promoting sustainable development, and the relevant environmental problems. The effects on the area likely to be affected have to be characterised taking into account amongst others the probability, duration, frequency and reversibility of the effects, as well as their cumulative and transboundary nature and the risks to human health or the environment.

The SEA has to be carried out during the preparation of a plan or programme and before its adoption or submission to the legislative procedure. For a hierarchical planning order, the assessment is to be carried out at the different hierarchical levels. Duplication, however, should be avoided. The SEA may be integrated into existing procedures for the adoption of plans or programmes (Article 4).

The SEA requires the drafting of an environmental report which assesses the likely significant effects on the environment of the implementation of the plan or programme. It further has to contain the identification, description and evaluation of reasonable alternatives, taking into account the individual objectives and the geographical scope of the plan or programme (Article 5).

Annex I of the Directive contains more detailed requirements on the information to be provided.[60] Competent authorities in the Member States have to be consulted when deciding on the scope and level of detail of the information which must be included in the environmental report.

The draft environmental report subsequently has to be made available to the authorities responsible and public and relevant NGOs affected or likely to be affected by, or having an interest in, the plan or project.

The Directive further provides for transboundary consultations.

Final information on the decision has to include a statement summarising how environmental considerations have been integrated into the plan or programme, the opinions and the results of the consultation process

---

[60] The report has to include amongst others the main objectives of the plan or programme and information on the relationship with other relevant plans and programmes; the relevant aspects of the current state of the environment and the likely evolution thereof without implementation of the plan or programme; and the likely significant effects on the environment, including on issues such as biodiversity, population, human health, fauna, and so on. These effects should include secondary, cumulative, synergistic, short, medium and long-term permanent and temporary, positive and negative effects. The report also has to include the reasons for selecting the alternatives dealt with, and a description of how the assessment was undertaken including any difficulties (such as technical deficiencies or lack of know-how) encountered in compiling the required information.

and the reasons for choosing the plan or programme as adopted, in the light of the other reasonable alternatives, as well as monitoring provisions (Article 9).

Finally, Member States are obliged to monitor the effects of the implementation of the plan or programme in order to identify unforeseen adverse risks at an early stage and to take remedial action if necessary (Article 10).

A good illustration of the difficulties in applying SEAs and EIAs is the UK's High Speed Rail link, in particular *HS2 Action Alliance v Secretary of State for Transport*.[61]

C. Guidance

The Commission further published a guidance document on integrating climate change and biodiversity into the SEA.[62] The guidance document is aimed at giving competent authorities, as well as policymakers, planners and SEA practitioners guidance on how to better integrate climate change and biodiversity issues into the SEA procedure. It firstly explains the importance of the climate change and biodiversity criteria for the SEA process. The main challenges of these areas are suggested as being the long-term and cumulative nature of effects; the complexity of the issues and cause–effect relationships and uncertainties surrounding these issues. The document further describes the scope of the climate change and biodiversity issues, as well as action and policy at the EU level.

Secondly, it provides specific tools and methods to assess the impact on climate change and biodiversity throughout the process. These are structured along the SEA process, taking into account practical elements and procedural steps of special importance. These are the consideration of reasonable alternatives, assessment of significant effects and identification of monitoring measures. Tools include, for example, biodiversity offsetting, ecosystem service approaches and ecosystem valuation and vulnerability assessments.

---

[61] *HS2 Action Alliance Ltd, R (on the application of) v The Secretary of State for Transport & Anor* [2014] UKSC 3 (22 January 2014).

[62] Guidance on integrating climate change and biodiversity into SEA available at http://ec.europa.eu/environment/eia/pdf/SEA%20Guidance.pdf, pp. 18ff., last consulted 12.11.2015.

8. Environmental liability and environmental crime

I. ENVIRONMENTAL LIABILITY*

Directive 2004/35 on environmental liability with regard to the prevention and remedying of environmental damage[1] entered into force on 30 April 2004, more than 20 years after the first draft was proposed. The deadline for transposition in the Member States was 30 April 2007; however, to date there remain problems regarding its implementation.[2]

The purpose of the Environmental Liability Directive is not, as its title might suggest, to establish a civil liability regime and to enable direct civil claims by private parties against polluters. Rather, it establishes an administrative law regime requiring public authorities to ensure that the polluter pays for environmental damage. In substance, therefore, the Directive lies firmly in the realm of public law, rather than civil law. The general approach of the Directive is to establish strict liability for environmental damage resulting from dangerous or potentially dangerous activities (as under the Council of Europe's Lugano Convention[3]) and complementary fault-based liability for other activities. The overall aim is to strengthen prevention and remediation through internalising costs and making the polluter pay. Emphasising the ELD's administrative law character, traditional damage to private persons, such as damage to property and persons

---

* This section is based on G. Van Calster and L. Reins, "The Environmental Liability Directive's background", in: L. Bergkamp and B. Goldsmith (eds), *The EU Environmental Liability Directive – A Commentary*, Oxford: Oxford University Press, 2013, 9–30.

[1] Directive 2004/35 on environmental liability with regard to the prevention and remedying of environmental damage, [2004] OJ L 143/56 (the "Directive", "Environmental Liability Directive" or "ELD").

[2] See, for example, Report from the Commission under Article 14(2) of the ELD, COM (2010) 581; G. Winter et al., "Weighing up the EC Environmental Liability Directive", 20 *Journal of Environmental Law*, 2 (2008), 163–191.

[3] Convention on Civil Liability for Damage Resulting from Activities Dangerous to the Environment, signed at Lugano in 1993 (Council of Europe, 1993).

(including death, personal injury, and pain and suffering) and economical damage (lost profits), is not covered by the ELD (Article 3(3) as well as Recitals 11 and 14).

The definition of "damage" has been subject in case *R (Seiont, Gwyrfai and Llyfni Anglers' Society) v Natural Resources Wales*.[4] Article 2(2) of the Directive provides the following definition: "'damage' means a measurable adverse change in a natural resource or measurable impairment of a natural resource service which may occur directly or indirectly". "Environmental damage" is further defined in Article 2(1), providing a variety of layers which need "unpacking" in the words of Hickinbottom J. He concludes, after lengthy and instructive analysis, that "damage" as defined in Article 2(2) of the Directive is restricted to a deterioration in the environmental situation, and does not in addition include the prevention of an existing, already damaged environmental state from achieving a level which is acceptable in environmental terms – or a deceleration in such achievement. Since "environmental damage" is a subset of "damage"; "environmental damage" necessarily has that same restriction.

Operators are defined as

> any natural or legal, private or public person who operates or controls the occupational activity or, where this is provided for in national legislation, to whom decisive economic power over the technical functioning of such an activity has been delegated, including the holder of a permit or authorisation for such an activity or the person registering or notifying such an activity.

More than two decades passed from the starting point in 1989 with a proposal for a sectoral directive dealing only with liability for damage caused by waste[5] to the actual adoption of the Directive. The long and complicated legislative history of the Directive illustrates that environmental liability has been a critical issue for all the stakeholders involved. Member States feared further loss of sovereignty to the EU, industry was concerned about unpredictable and expensive over-regulation and adverse effects on international competitiveness, while environmental organisations claimed that the legislation did not go far enough and left too much discretion to the Member States and too many loopholes for industry.

During this long gestation process, several accidents had resulted in

---

[4] In *R (Seiont, Gwyrfai and Llyfni Anglers' Society) v Natural Resources Wales* [2016] EWCA Civ 797.

[5] Proposal for a Council Directive on civil liability for damage caused by waste, COM (89) 282, [1989] OJ C 251/3; amended by COM (91) 219, [1991] OJ C 192/4.

extensive, and in some cases, transboundary, environmental damage. These accidents included the Aznacollar spill in Spain in 1998, and the Baia Mare spill in 2000 in Romania – both of which were caused by mining operations – and the Erika tanker accident in 1999 in France. Due to these accidents, the discussion intensified as to whether EU action was needed to establish a liability and recovery regime for environmental damage, especially in transboundary situations. At the same time, pleas were made for a regime that provided incentives for the prevention of these kinds of accidents.[6]

The ELD is based on, and, in a way, implements, some of the EU's key environmental policy principles. The ELD itself refers several times to the polluter pays principle as its basis (Article 1 and Recitals 1 and 2 of the preamble). The implementation of the polluter pays principle through the ELD aims at encouraging the adoption of preventive measures, and, where no cost-effective prevention is possible, reducing the quantitative level of the polluting activity that is carried out and thus diminishing the risk of pollution.[7] According to the Commission, the implementation of these environmental policy principles will promote investment in research and development of knowledge and technologies relevant to the prevention and remediation of environmental damage.[8]

The policy rationale underlying the ELD is that the polluter will invest in prevention of environmental damage (e.g. by implementing preventive measures, or changing or cutting back its operations) in response to the threat of liability for environmental damage that may ensue. This is the concept of cost internalisation, as a consequence of which there would be less environmental damage.[9] Prima facie, this would appear to provide a strong policy rationale for the ELD. Upon further analysis, there are reasons to be sceptical. First, whether and, if so, to what extent, cost internalisation and the application of the polluter pays and preventive principles actually creates incentives for investment in prevention and

---

[6] Commission White Paper on Environmental Liability, COM (2000) 66, at 2. Explanatory Memorandum to the Proposal for a Directive on environmental liability with regard to the prevention and remedying of environmental damage, COM (2002) 17. For further discussion, E. Brans, *Liability for Damage to Public Natural Resources – Standing, Damage and Damage Assessment*, The Hague: Kluwer Law International, 2001, 178ff.

[7] L. Bergkamp, "The Proposed EC Environmental Liability Regime and EC Law Principles", in: J Hamer (ed.), *Environmental Liability in the EU*, Trier: Europaeische Rechtsakademie, 2002, at 26ff, and 34.

[8] White Paper on Environmental Liability, note 6 above, at 12.

[9] Ibid., 11ff.

research remains disputed.[10] Article 1 ELD, however, leaves no doubt and provides that its objective is to "establish a framework of environmental liability based on the polluter pays principle", which is referenced in Recitals 2 and 18 of the Directive. Even though the polluter pays principle may justify environmental liability, there is a further question of whether it necessarily requires strict liability. This question has been raised, for instance, in cases where the victim might be in a better position to prevent the damage.[11] Second, as a related matter, various conditions have to be met before liability is imposed. For instance, the ELD regime applies only if there is significant environmental damage, and its application to diffuse damage is doubtful at best.

The EU environmental policy principles, in particular the polluter pays principle, are also used to justify the polluter's obligation to restore environmental damage.[12] "Environmental damage" is defined in Article 2 of the ELD as damage to species and habitats, as well as to water and land. Damage to species and habitats is covered only if these resources are protected under the Habitats Directive[13] and Wild Birds Directive;[14] the natural resources protected pursuant to these Directives jointly make up the Natura 2000 programme (see further Chapter 10). Since these regimes already require that the Member States protect the relevant habitats and species, the question arises whether inclusion under the ELD may have been redundant.[15] The protection of species and habitats outside the Natura 2000 network would appear to be more relevant, but these resources are not regarded as being of EU-wide importance and therefore not susceptible to protection by the EU.

In case 534/13[16] the main issue that arose was whether national (Italian)

---

[10] See ibid. For a contrary position, N. De Sadeleer, *Environmental Principles: From Political Slogan to Legal Rules*, Oxford; Oxford University Press, 2002, at 51: "the polluter pays principle calls for the establishment of strict liability".

[11] M. Faure and D. Grimeaud, *Financial Assurance Issues in Environmental Liability*, Maastricht University and European Centre for Tort and Insurance Law, 2000, at 22, available at http://ec.europa.eu/environment/legal/liability/pdf/insurance_gen_finalrep.pdf, last consulted 12.11.2015.

[12] See Recitals 2 and 18 of the Directive and White Paper on Environmental Liability note 6 above, at 12.

[13] Directive 92/43 on the conservation of natural habitats and of wild fauna and flora, [1992] OJ L 206/7.

[14] Directive 2009/147 on the conservation of wild birds [2010] OJ L 20/7.

[15] For a counter-argument, see Explanatory Memorandum to the Proposal for a Directive on environmental liability with regard to the prevention and remedying of environmental damage, COM (2002) 17, note 6 above, at 5ff.

[16] Case C-534/13 *Fipa Group and Others*, ECLI:EU:C:2015:140.

legislation, under which no provision is made for the authorities to require owners of polluted land who have not contributed to that pollution to carry out preventive and remedial measures, and the sole obligation imposed concerns the reimbursement of the measures undertaken by those authorities, is compatible with the "polluter pays" principle, the precautionary principle and the principles that preventive action should be taken and that environmental damage should be rectified at source as a matter of priority.

The ECJ emphasises the role of Directive 2004/35 in this context. The Court held that the Directive does not hold against such absence. It further recalled in line with previous case law that the environmental principles of the Treaty:

> do no more than define the general environmental objectives of the European Union, since Article 192 TFEU confers on the European Parliament and the Council of the European Union, acting in accordance with the ordinary legislative procedure, responsibility for deciding what action is to be taken in order to attain those objectives .... Consequently, since Article 191(2) TFEU, which establishes the "polluter pays" principle, is directed at action at EU level, that provision cannot be relied on as such by individuals in order to exclude the application of national legislation – such as that at issue in the main proceedings – in an area covered by environmental policy for which there is no EU legislation adopted on the basis of Article 192 TFEU that specifically covers the situation in question ... Similarly, the competent environmental authorities cannot rely on Article 191(2) TFEU, in the absence of any national legal basis, for the purposes of imposing preventive and remedial measures ... (at 39–41)

As stated above, the aim of the application of the polluter pays principle within the context of environmental liability is to prevent damage and pollution in the first place. This is in line with the preventive principle laid down in the Treaty provision stating that "environmental damage should be prevented" (Article 191 TFEU). To what extent liability, in practice, has a preventive effect is an empirical issue; there is a tendency to assume that it will have this effect and to overestimate the extent to which it does. The concern expressed by industry that liability would pose unacceptable and unpredictable economic risks and obstacles to economic growth,[17] reflects scepticism about the preventive effects of environmental liability in practice.

The ELD does not impose generalised strict liability. Rather, it limits strict liability to operations covered by EU legislation listed in Annex III; fault-based liability only for natural resource damage applies to unlisted

---

[17] G. Roller, "Liability", in: R. Macrory (ed.), *Reflections on 30 Years of EU Environmental Law*, Groningen: Europa Law Publishing, 2006, 134.

activities (Article 3 ELD). The Directive, including Annex III, has been amended three times in the past; the Annex now also includes the management of extractive waste,[18] geological storage of carbon dioxide according to Directive 2009/31[19] and offshore oil and gas operations according to Directive 2013/30.[20]

In its White Paper, the Commission argued that strict liability would generate incentives for research where it is not yet possible to prevent damage by due care alone.[21] Because the liable person would have to pay for the damage, that person would have a financial incentive to figure out whether the damage can be efficiently prevented; hence, this person would engage in research into preventive measures. Whether, in practice, companies will engage in prevention research will depend on the cost of developing preventive measures compared to the cost of paying for damage caused. Further, prevention can often be more effectively achieved through direct regulatory tools, such as permitting and EIAs, and incentives for research can also be directly created through subsidies.[22] If that is true, environmental liability would play a secondary role at best.

In short, the preventive effect of environmental liability remains somewhat elusive. In its Explanatory Memorandum to the Directive, the Commission, referring to a "socially efficient prevention" approach, reasoned that "EUR 1 spent on prevention is likely to avoid damage whose restoration costs more than EUR 1" and that, as a consequence, potential polluters should invest "in prevention rather than pay for the higher restoration cost".[23] The study for the Commission that sought to support this argument,[24] however, reached the conclusion that the incentives for prevention generated by liability are rather ambiguous.[25]

---

[18] Directive 2006/21 on the management of waste from extractive industries and amending Directive 2004/35, [2006] OJ L 102/15.

[19] Directive 2009/31 on the geological storage of carbon dioxide, [2009] OJ L 140/114.

[20] Directive 2013/30 on safety of offshore oil and gas operations and amending Directive 2004/35/EC, [2013] OJ L 178/66.

[21] See above, as well White Paper on Environmental Liability note 6 above, at 12 and L. Bergkamp, note 7 above, at 31ff.

[22] L. Bergkamp, note 8 above, at 31ff.

[23] See White Paper on Environmental Liability note 7 above, at 6.

[24] D. Austin and A. Alberini, "An Analysis of the Preventive Effect of Environmental Liability", *Environmental Liability, Location and Emission Substitution: Evidence from the Toxic Release Inventory* (2001), available at http://ec.europa.eu/environment/legal/liability/pdf/preventive_final.pdf, last consulted 12.11.2015.

[25] See also L. Bergkamp, "The Proposed Environmental Liability Directive", 11 *European Environmental Law Review* 12 (2002), at 298.

Under international law, a state is not allowed to knowingly cause harm to other States (*sic utere tuo ut alienum non laedas*), and this principle also applies to environmental damage.[26] The ELD, however, does not establish, at least not directly, liability of the State, but provides for cooperation between the Member States in transboundary damage cases. In this context, Article 8(4) of the ELD may raise complex issues. Pursuant to this provision, Member States may exempt operators from the obligation to bear prevention and remediation costs where they complied with specific permit conditions or the "state-of-science" did not predict the risk (these are known as the "permit" and "state-of-the-art" defences).[27] If a Member State permits these defences and an operator that has caused transboundary damage invokes either of them, would the state be exposed to liability?

As the ELD is based on Article 192, however, it sets only minimum standards and Member States are allowed to adopt stricter standards, for example with regard to scope.[28] This is also acknowledged in Article 16 of the Directive. Consequently, the scope and details of the individual Member State regimes are likely to vary, and a level playing field may not exist in practice.[29]

The ELD can be considered an important milestone in EU environmental law-making. Nobody would disagree that the prevention and restoration of environmental damage can be a laudable objective. The ELD tries to accomplish this objective through cross-sectoral regulation based on a holistic approach to environmental regulation. Most of all, it is also the first EU legislative instrument that implements the polluter pays principle in practice.

---

[26] Trail Smelter Arbitrage, *United States v Canada*, Arbitral Tribunal, Montreal, 16 April 1938 and 11 March 1941, 3 United Nations Reports of International Arbitral Awards, 1905.3; ICJ, *The Corfu Channel Case (United Kingdom v Albania)*; Assessment of Compensation, 15 XII 49, International Court of Justice (ICJ), 15 December 1949.

[27] For an in-depth discussion, see N. Farnsworth, "Subsidiarity – A Conventional Industry Defence: Is the Directive on Environmental Liability with Regard to Prevention and Remedying of Environmental Damage Justified under the Subsidiarity Principle?", 13 *European Environmental Law Review* 6 (2004), at 178ff.

[28] J. Jans and H. Vedder, *European Environmental Law after Lisbon*, 4th Edition, Groningen: Europa Law Publishing, 2012, 384.

[29] L. Bergkamp, note 7 above, at 17.

II. ENVIRONMENTAL CRIME

Tackling environmental crime is one of the intractable issues in the EU. The impacts of these environmental offences are mostly transboundary in nature and thus subject to EU measures to harmonise these diverse national laws and create a level playing field. Another reason for Union action in this regard is certainly the attempt to increase effective implementation and enforcement of EU environmental law.

The birth of the Environmental Crime Directive as it currently stands was not an easy one.[30] A decade passed from the adoption of the Convention on the protection of the environment through criminal law[31] in 1998 by the Council of Europe, which never entered into force because it did not reach the threshold of three ratifications, until the adoption of the Environmental Crime Directive in 2008.[32]

One of the key reasons for the difficulties in adopting such a legislative act was the disagreement of the European institutions on the legal basis of the matter. The Council of Europe (Council of the EU) drafted a Framework Decision[33] – the equivalent of a Directive under the (old) third pillar – on the issue which was based on Articles 29, 31(e) and 34(2)(b) on cooperation in criminal matters of the old TEU,[34] as well as the Convention on the protection of the environment through criminal law, which it later adopted in 2003.[35] Parallel to this, in 2001, the Commission, not agreeing with the legal basis chosen by the Council of Europe, put forward a legislative proposal of a directive based on (now) Article 191 TFEU.[36] The proposal found general support by the Parliament; the Commission revised it to include the suggested changes and additions.

---

[30] For a detailed description of the process see H.E. Zeitler, "Strengthening Environmental Protection through European Criminal Law", 4 *Journal for European Environmental and Planning Law*, 3 (2007), 213–220.

[31] CETS (Council of Europe Treaty Series) No.: 172, available at http://conventions.coe.int/, last consulted 12.11.2015.

[32] Directive 2008/99/EC of 19 November 2008 on the protection of the environment through criminal law, [2008] OJ L 328, 6.12.2008, pp. 28–37.

[33] Initiative of the Kingdom of Denmark with a view to adopting a Council framework Decision on combating serious environmental crime, [2000] OJ C 39/4.

[34] The provisions of Title VI of the TEU, on police and judicial cooperation in criminal matters, are replaced by the provisions of Chapters 1, 4 and 5 of Title IV (renumbered V) of Part Three of the TFEU.

[35] Council Framework Decision 2003/80/JHA on the protection of the environment through criminal law, OJ [2003] L 29/55.

[36] Proposal for a Directive on the Protection of the Environment through Criminal Law, COM (2001) 139, pp. 238–243.

However, it was never discussed in the Council. The latter, in its 2003 decision, incorporated some of the Commission's suggestions; however, not the 2002 amendment of the proposal for a Directive.

As a reaction to the adoption of the Framework Decision, the Commission asked the ECJ to annul the Framework Decision on grounds of an incorrect legal basis and holding that the Council disregarded the Commission proposal for a directive, which would enhance better protection of the environment through criminal law than the Framework Decision.[37] In its judgment the Court annulled the Council Framework Decision on the protection of the environment through criminal law, reasoning amongst others that "as regards the aim of the framework decision, it is clear both from its title and from its first three recitals that its objective is the protection of the environment"[38] and that "as a general rule, neither criminal law nor the rules of criminal procedure fall within the Community's competence"[39] and thus

> the last-mentioned finding does not prevent the Community legislature, when the application of effective, proportionate and dissuasive criminal penalties by the competent national authorities is an essential measure for combating serious environmental offences, from taking measures which relate to the criminal law of the Member States which it considers necessary in order to ensure that the rules which it lays down on environmental protection are fully effective.[40]

The judgment clarified the distribution of powers between the then first and third pillars as regards provisions of criminal law. The Commission then put forward a Communication explaining the implications and the affected instruments,[41] and also asked the Court to annul the Council Framework Decision 2005/667 to strengthen the criminal-law framework for the enforcement of the law against ship-source pollution[42] as this, too, invaded the competencies of the Community (now Union) and should have been adopted under the EC Treaty and not the EU Treaty.[43] The

---

[37] Case C-176/03 *Commission v Council* [2005] ECR I-7879.
[38] Ibid., at 46.
[39] Ibid., at 47 and also Case 203/80 *Casati* [1981] ECR 2595, para. 27, and Case C-226/97 *Lemmens* [1998] ECR I-3711, at 19.
[40] Case C-176/03 *Commission v Council* [2005] ECR I-7879, at 48.
[41] Communication on the implications of the Court's judgment of 13 September 2005, COM (2005) 583.
[42] Council Framework Decision 2005/667/JHA to strengthen the criminal-law framework for the enforcement of the law against ship-source pollution, [2005] OJ L 255/164.
[43] Case C-440/05 *Commission v Council*, [2007] ECR I-9097.

Court obliged but stated that the Community's (now Union's) competence could not include the definition of types and levels of criminal penalties.[44]

In 2007, the Commission put forward a new proposal.[45] The proposal, and therefore also the current Directive, is to a large extent based on the Council Framework Decision.

In 2008 the Environmental Crime Directive was finally adopted with the aim of establishing measures relating to criminal law in order to protect the environment more effectively (Article 1).[46] Under the Directive nine environmental crimes are considered as criminal offences, when unlawful and committed intentionally or with at least serious negligence (Article 3). "Unlawful" relates to the infringement of legislation adopted pursuant to the EC Treaty (now TFEU) and listed in Annex A or pursuant to the Euratom Treaty and listed in Annex B, as well as a law, an administrative regulation of a Member State or a decision taken by a competent authority of a Member State that gives effect to the Union (Article 2).

The environmental crimes considered to be offences are (Article 3(a–i)):

- discharge, emission or introduction of a quantity of materials or ionising radiation into air, soil or water, which causes or is likely to cause death or serious injury to any person or substantial damage to the quality of air, the quality of soil or the quality of water, or to animals or plants;
- the collection, transport, recovery or disposal of waste, including the supervision of such operations and the after-care of disposal sites, and including action taken as a dealer or a broker (waste management), which causes or is likely to cause death or serious injury to any person or substantial damage to the quality of air, the quality of soil or the quality of water, or to animals or plants;
- the shipment of waste, where this activity falls within the scope of Article 2(35) of the Waste Shipment Regulation[47] and is undertaken in a non-negligible quantity, whether executed in a single shipment or in several shipments which appear to be linked;
- the operation of a plant in which a dangerous activity is carried out or in which dangerous substances or preparations are stored or used and which, outside the plant, causes or is likely to cause death or serious injury to any person or substantial damage to the quality of air, the quality of soil or the quality of water, or to animals or plants;

---

[44] Ibid., at 40.
[45] Proposal for a Directive of the European Parliament and of the Council on the protection of the environment through criminal law, COM (2007) 51.
[46] For a detailed discussion of the Directive see H.E. Zeitler and Helge Elisabeth, "Happy End of a Long Saga–Agreement on the Directive for the Protection of the Environment through Criminal Law", 5 *Journal for European Environmental and Planning Law*, 3 (2008), 281–291.
[47] Regulation 1013/2006 on shipments of waste, [2006] OJ L 190/1.

- the production, processing, handling, use, holding, storage, transport, import, export or disposal of nuclear materials or other radioactive substances which causes or is likely to cause death or serious injury to any person or substantial damage to the quality of air, the quality of soil or the quality of water, or to animals or plants;
- the killing, destruction, possession or taking of specimens of protected wild fauna or flora species, except for cases where the conduct concerns a negligible quantity of such specimens and has a negligible impact on the conservation status of the species;
- trading in specimens of protected wild fauna or flora species or parts or derivatives thereof, except for cases where the conduct concerns a negligible quantity of such specimens and has a negligible impact on the conservation status of the species;
- any conduct which causes the significant deterioration of a habitat within a protected site (defined in Article 2);
- the production, importation, exportation, placing on the market or use of ozone-depleting substances (Article 3).

Most of these environmental crimes include the condition of causing death or serious injury or harm to persons or the environment; in these cases, the (non-)action alone is not considered to be a criminal offence. However, the actions of illegal shipment of waste; killing, destruction, possession or taking of specimens of protected wild fauna or flora species; trading in specimens of protected wild fauna or flora species; and the causation of significant deterioration of a habitat within a protected site are considered to be offences, regardless of their impact or outcome.

In addition inciting, aiding and abetting intentional conduct of these activities is punishable as a criminal offence (Article 4). Criminal penalties have to be effective, proportionate and dissuasive; however, the exact amount for the individual offences is left open for the Member States to decide.

The Directive further introduces a system of liability of legal persons and requests the Member States to establish effective, proportionate and dissuasive penalties (Articles 6 and 7). Accordingly, companies can be held liable for acts committed by their employees: legal persons can be held liable for the abovementioned offences when such offences have been committed for their benefit by any person who has a leading position within the legal person, acting either individually or as part of an organ of the legal person (Article 6(1)); and further can be held liable where the lack of supervision or control resulted in the commission of an offence for the benefit of the legal person by a person under its authority (Article 6(2)). The Directive introduces a system of dual liability. Article 6(3) states that liability of legal persons does not exclude criminal proceedings against natural persons who are perpetrators, inciters or accessories in the offences.

9. State aid and competition law

Both State aid and competition rules are of course first and foremost part of EU economic law. However, much like the Treaty articles on free movement, it is important for those with an interest in environmental issues to appreciate the impact which articles outside the environmental title of the Treaty have on environmental policy. With respect to State aid, the Commission devised a set of guidelines (the current version has a 1994 pedigree) which aim to provide a clear manual to assess this type of aid. Review of the Commission practice reveals a swing, moving with the economic tide: whilst the early nineties indicated a dip in the use of direct State aid for environmental purposes, this type of aid was more *en vogue* in the late nineties, only to slip again in current times. It is often replaced with tax incentives.

I. STATE AID

A. Regulatory Framework

EU rules on State aid centre around Article 107 TFEU (previously Article 87 EC and before that Article 92 EC), which provides that

1. Save as otherwise provided in the Treaties, any aid granted by a Member State or through State resources in any form whatsoever which distorts or threatens to distort competition by favouring certain undertakings or the production of certain goods shall, in so far as it affects trade between Member States, be incompatible with the internal market.
2. The following shall be compatible with the internal market:
    (a) aid having a social character, granted to individual consumers, provided that such aid is without discrimination related to the origin of the products concerned;
    (b) aid to make good the damage caused by natural disasters or exceptional occurrences;
    (c) ... [authors' note: relating to the division of Germany]
3. The following may be considered to be compatible with the internal market:
    (a) aid to promote the economic development of areas where the standard of living is abnormally low or where there is serious underemployment, and [authors' note: the remainder relates to overseas areas]

(b) aid to promote the execution of an important project of common European interest or to remedy a serious disturbance in the economy of a Member State;
(c) aid to facilitate the development of certain economic activities or of certain economic areas, where such aid does not adversely affect trading conditions to an extent contrary to the common interest;
(d) aid to promote culture and heritage conservation . . .;
(e) such other categories of aid as may be specified by decision of the Council on a proposal from the Commission.

The Commission has been regularly publishing guidelines on State aid for environmental protection, initially as part of its Report on Competition Policy 1974,[1] effectively extended until 1994 when formal guidelines were adopted.[2] These expired in December 2007, and were succeeded by the 2008 Guidelines,[3] themselves now having been replaced with the current guidelines that apply until 2020.[4]

The current Guidelines for the first time directly also address State aid in the energy area. The specific inclusion of State aid in the energy area has made the guidelines on the whole more technical, with plenty of energy jargon.

There are also more specific guidelines for State aid measures in the context of the greenhouse gas emission allowance trading scheme post-2012,[5] and various other specific regimes exist for aid in the automobile sector, shipbuilding, agriculture, steel and coal. On the whole, this regulatory inflation obviously does not facilitate enforcement.

Aid or overall regulatory economic framework
A point of contention is sometimes whether a given national regime merely concerns the organisation of the national economy, or in fact represents State aid. This was the case for instance in the environment-related *Gasunie* case, where the Netherlands had introduced different tariffs for gas supplies. Preferential tariffs applied, for example for the horticulture sector, in an attempt to reduce greenhouse gas emissions through a switch from electricity to gas. The Commission repeatedly decided that the Dutch regime did qualify as State aid, since it was not justified on purely

---

[1] Commission Fourth Report on Competition Policy, 1974, pp. 101–106.
[2] [1994] OJ C 72/3.
[3] [2008] OJ C 82/1.
[4] Communication from the Commission – Guidelines on State aid for environmental protection and energy 2014–2020, [2014] OC C200/1.
[5] [2012] OJ C 154/4.

economic grounds.⁶ As a result, the Netherlands have had to modify the price structure.⁷

Compensation which is purely a remuneration for services provided by a company does not constitute aid.⁸

Threat to competition
Article 107 is triggered only where the aid concerned distorts, or threatens to distort, competition by favouring certain undertakings or the production of certain goods.⁹ Particularly where aid is given to former public enterprises, or semi-autonomous public enterprises, the aid is often designed either to ensure a public service which would otherwise be neglected, or to help the enterprise concerned in fulfilling social tasks, such as the employment of economically disadvantaged people. If market conditions are such as not to make the enterprise concerned a major player, the Commission often gives such aid the benefit of the doubt, by deciding that it does not have a direct influence on competition. However, in such cases it does reserve the right to reverse its decision where market conditions change. This will be the case, for instance, where the aid eventually helps the enterprise concerned to lower its prices.¹⁰

---

⁶ Commission Decision 82/73 of 15 December 1981 on the preferential tariff charged to greenhouse growers for natural gas in The Netherlands, [1982] OJ L 37/29; Judgment of the Court of 2 February 1988 in Joined Cases 67, 68, and 70/85, *Gebroeders Van Der Kooy et al. v Commission*, [1988] ECR 219; Commission Decision 85/215 of 13 February 1985 on the preferential tariff charged to greenhouse growers for natural gas in The Netherlands, [1985] OJ L 97/49; Judgment of the Court of 29 February 1996 in Case C-56/93 *Belgium v Commission*, [1996] ECR I-723.

⁷ See for example also Commission Decision 96/615 of 29 May 1996 on the renewal, for the period 1993 to 1997, of the charge levied on certain oil products for the benefit of the Institut Français du Pétrole (IFP), [1996] OJ L 272/53 (also in Commission Competition Policy Newsletter, 1997, No.1, p. 27), and the prolongation for the period 1998–2002: "Commission gives green light to financing of Institut Français du Pétrole through taxation of certain petroleum products", IP/97/949.

⁸ See for example "The Commission decides that the system for collection and disposal of used tyres in Denmark does not involve State Aid within the meaning of Art.92(1)", IP/94/981, and Commission Competition Policy Newsletter, 1995, No. 6, p. 46.

⁹ In particular where those "certain products" happen to be products of national origin only; see for example "Aid for promotion of agricultural products in Belgium (Flanders)", IP/98/845, concerning a scheme with particular emphasis on the Flemish origin of the products involved.

¹⁰ See for example Commission Decision 98/353 of 16 September 1997 on State Aid for Gemeinnützige Abfallverwertung GmbH, [1998] OJ L 159/58, and IP/97/793.

Does non-internalisation of environmental externalities qualify as State aid? A call to reverse *Deutsche Bahn*

Does non-internalisation of environmental externalities qualify as State aid? The CJEU's 2006 decision in *Deutsche Bahn* (DB)[11] declined to entertain the proposition. Reversal would move the EU towards better internalisation of negative environmental externalities of fossil fuels, and would be in line with the EU Treaty.

Relevant secondary EU law and the EC's State aid decision   In DB, the German national railway challenged the Commission's decision with respect to DB's complaint that the German exemption from excise duties of aviation fuel led to an unlawful distortion of competition between low-cost airlines and DB's high speed trains.

The German exemption was carried out in implementation of Directive 92/81 on the harmonisation of the structures of excise duties on mineral oils.[12] Under Article 8(1) of the Directive, Member States are to exempt from the harmonised excise duty inter alia "mineral oils supplied for use as fuels for the purpose of air navigation other than private pleasure flying".

The Directive was replaced by Directive 2003/96 restructuring the Union framework for the taxation of energy products and electricity,[13] which overall leads to a much better integration of environmental concerns in national energy taxation. It does, however, contain a similar proviso with respect to international aviation in Article 14(9)(b). Directive 92/81, in Article 8(7), signalled that the exemption may be unwarranted from an environmental point of view:

> No later than 31 December 1997 the Council shall review the exemptions provided for in paragraphs 1 (b) and 2 (b), on the basis of a report by the Commission and taking account of the external costs entailed in such means of transport and the implications for the environment and shall decide unanimously, on a proposal from the Commission, whether to abolish or modify those exemptions.

The exemption provision in the Directive is a direct response to Article 24 of the 1944 Chicago Convention on international civil aviation, which states:

---

[11]   Case T-351/02 *Deutsche Bahn AG v Commission of the European Communities*, [2006] ECR II-1047.
[12]   [1992] OJ L 316/12.
[13]   [2003] OJ L 283/51.

Fuel, lubricating oils, spare parts, regular equipment and aircraft stores on board an aircraft of a contracting State, on arrival in the territory of another contracting State and retained on board on leaving the territory of that State shall be exempt from customs duty, inspection fees or similar national or local duties and charges.

The International Civil Aviation Organization (ICAO) later[14] declared that the exemption also applies to fuel reloading, rather than just to fuel already on board. The exemption included in the Directive is a direct result of the Member States wanting to implement the ICAO provision, bearing in mind that were they not to, this would raise international competitiveness concerns (with third States exempting their airlines from duties while the EU might not).[15]

Sweden had earlier attempted to limit the implications of the Directive by suggesting that the Directive only harmonised taxation triggered by fuel *consumption*, as opposed to relevant Swedish environmental taxes which taxed the fuel's environmental externalities, in particular carbon dioxide (CO_2) and nitric oxide. The Court disagreed and confirmed Article 8(1)'s direct effect under the *Van Gend & Loos* criteria.[16] No doubt it was influenced by the very fact that the Directive's review clause appreciates the negative impact the Directive may have on environmental protection. In other words, environmental protection was on the radar of the Directive (even if it utterly ignored it), contrary to the Swedish argument that the environment was out of the Directive's scope and hence that the Member States could not be restricted in regulating the fuel's environmental impacts.

DB's State aid complaint was rejected by the Commission on the basis that Germany's exemption was a direct implementation of EU secondary law. The Court then rejected all of DB's grounds for judicial review and upheld the Commission's decision. There is not the space to review all of the arguments for rejection of DB's claim but the most relevant ones are reviewed below.

---

[14] Resolution of 14 December 1993 Doc 8632-C/968, available via http://www.icao.int/publications/Documents/8632_2ed_en.pdf or http://goo.gl/hKqi8E, last consulted 11.7.2015.

[15] Report from the Commission (on Article 8(1) of Directive 92/81), COM (96) 549, p. 9.

[16] Case C-347/97 *Braathens Sverige AB v Riksskatteverket*, [1999] ECR I-3419: "The obligation imposed by Article 8(1)(b) of Directive 92/81 to exempt from the harmonised excise duty mineral oils supplied for use as fuel for the purpose of air navigation other than private pleasure flying may be relied on by individuals in proceedings before national courts in order to contest national rules that are incompatible with that obligation."

Revisiting the issues: a brief outline of the arguments

International law and the EU Directive DB argued amongst other things that ICAO's 1944 provisions are lex prior under the rules of the Vienna Convention and were superseded by the subsequent EEC Treaty. And that at the very least for relations between the Member States, prior public international law ought not to have an impact. The Court dismissed the pleas brought on the basis of public international law. It held that the EC's State aid decision was not based on public international law. Rather, the EC had referred to ICAO's provisions as context, not as content.

With respect, however, judicial economy ought not to stand in the way of substantive legality. If there is serious argument as to the incompatibility of public international law with later, or indeed earlier, EU law, then the Court ought to entertain it. For otherwise one risks having illegal EU law being maintained simply on the basis of procedural considerations.

The principle of equal treatment – seen in the light of externalities DB argued that the tax exemption for aviation fuel based on Article 8(1)(b) leads to unequal treatment between it and the airlines operating on German domestic routes. Given that the applicant and the airlines offer, on German domestic routes, a service which, in the eyes of users, is substitutable, they are in a comparable situation. Difference in treatment is not objectively justified. The Court rejected comparability of situations on the basis that

> the situation of air transport undertakings is clearly different from that of rail transport undertakings. As regards their operational characteristics, their costs structure and the regulations to which they are subject, air and rail transport services are very different and are not comparable for the purpose of the principle of equal treatment.... In the light of the international practice of exempting aviation fuel from excise duties, which is enshrined in the Chicago Convention and in international agreements concluded between States, competition between Community air transport operators and operators in non-member countries would be distorted if the Community legislature unilaterally imposed excise duties on that fuel. Consequently, the exemption provided for by Article 8(1)(b) of the Directive was objectively justified. (at 138–139)

The CJEU therefore bases its findings that air and rail transport are not comparable mainly on the different regulatory contexts to which they are subject. This is, however, a circular argument. DB's position was precisely that at the very least some of those differences in regulation are illegal, and it requested the CJEU to discuss those alleged illegalities. A regulator (the EC) can hardly be allowed to get away with unjustified discrimination by making reference to the very regulatory context whose legality is being questioned.

Environmental principles, in particular "polluter pays" The Treaty binds the institutions, including the Commission, to a number of environmental principles which they are pledged to uphold. These principles do not always and in all circumstances grant individuals rights in accordance with the Van Gend & Loos criteria. However, in cases where application of the principles is clearly wanting, or utterly ignored, such as here, it is the CJEU's duty to uphold them, both vis-à-vis individual Commission decisions, and vis-à-vis the secondary law which underpins these decisions.

The Court has adopted groundbreaking judgments in many areas of EU institutional and economic law, as in *Les Verts*;[17] *Rewe (Cassis de Dijon)*;[18] *Wood Pulp*;[19] *Keck*;[20] and *Air Transport Association of America*.[21] The Court has repeatedly pushed the boat out and in doing so has triggered or strengthened regulatory responses by the European institutions. Were it to reverse its case law in the circumstances at issue, it would give impetus to the discussion on negative environmental externalities and make the EU a true front-runner in international responses to pressing environmental concerns: for the current Directive[22] may well provide more room for Member States' initiatives in environmentally relevant taxation of energy products. However, arguably under the polluter pays principle, it should be a Treaty obligation for the EU institutions to ensure proper integration of the negative externalities, not merely a possibility for the Member States.

The CJEU's judgment at any rate means that, for the moment, the vast amount of State aid effectively granted to fossil fuels entirely escapes any kind of State aid scrutiny.

---

[17] Case C-294/83 *Les Verts v Parliament*, [1986] ECR I-1339.
[18] Case C-120/78 *Rewe v Bundesmonopolverwaltung für Branntwein*, [1979] ECR I-649.
[19] Joined cases C-89/85, C-104/85, C-114/85, C-116/85, C-117/85, C-125/85, C-126/85, C-127/85, C-128/85 and C-129/85 *A. Ahlström Osakeyhtiö and others v Commission of the European Communities (Wood Pulp)*, [1994] ECR I-99.
[20] Joined cases C-267/91 and C-268/91 *Keck and Mithouard*, [1993] ECR I-6097.
[21] Case C-366/10, *Air Transport Association of America and Others*, [2011] ECR I 13755.
[22] Note 4 above.

B. Antecedents of the Commission's Guidelines – The Troublesome Introduction of the Polluter Pays Principle

The first policy instrument of the Commission on State Aid for environmental protection dates back to 6 November 1974.[23] Until 1994, the Community agenda on State aid for environmental protection was covered only in so-called "Environmental Frameworks", that is, Communications from the Commission to the Member States, which were not published in the *Official Journal* and can only be found in the Commission Reports on Competition policy.

The point addressed in these instruments is how to balance aid to industries to adapt their installations to new environmental requirements, with the "polluter pays principle".[24] This principle, as discussed elsewhere in this volume, requires all environmental costs to be "internalised", that is, absorbed in firms' production costs. Theoretically, full introduction of the principle would mean that environmental costs are reflected in companies' accounts as a mere cost (and, therefore, a decrease in these costs as a benefit). This, however, has turned out to be quite a challenge.

The standard EU source with respect to the polluter pays principle and the allocation of environmental costs remains a Council Recommendation of 3 March 1975.[25] This Recommendation followed the appeal to the Commission in the first EC environmental action programme (EAP), to present the Council with a Communication which was to guide the application of the polluter pays principle. The Commission Communication was attached to the Council Recommendation, and was thereby approved at policy level.

The principal EU approach to State aid and environmental protection, as confirmed by the Council in the 1975 Recommendation, was that environmental protection should not in principle depend on policies which

---

[23] See letter from the Commission to the Member States S/74/30807 from 7 November 1974, with the Communication from the Commission to the Member States from 6 November 1974 in the annex. For an extensive study of these antecedents, see T. Joris, *Nationale steunmaatregelen en het Europees gemeenschapsrecht*, Antwerpen/Apeldoorn: Maklu, 1994, p. 126 *et seq.*; see also Ph. Renaudiere, "Environnement, concurrence et transports: vers l'intégration?", 8 *Journal des Tribunaux – Droit Européen*, 1994, 7–10.

[24] The first policy paper on the "polluter pays" principle was a Communication of the Commission of 25 July 1975 ([1975] OJ L 194/2), approved by the Council ([1975] OJ L 194/1). The principle was already mentioned in the first environmental action programme ([1973] OJ C 112/1, at part I, title II, no. 5).

[25] Council Recommendation 75/436 of 3 March 1975 regarding cost allocation and action by public authorities on environmental matters, [1975] OJ L 194/75.

rely on grants of aid, and place the burden of combating pollution on society. The Recommendation further set out the principles which should be followed in assessing State aid under what is now Article 107 TFEU. These principles lacked sufficient detail to be applicable in practice. They nevertheless confirmed the Commission Guidelines and give these more political weight. In the Recommendation, the Council considered the following not to be contrary to the polluter pays principle:

(a) Financial contributions which might be granted to local authorities for the construction and operation of public installations for the protection of the environment, the cost of which could not be wholly covered in the short term from the charges paid by polluter using them;
(b) Financing designed to compensate for the particularly heavy costs which some polluters would be obliged to meet in order to achieve an exceptional degree of environmental cleanliness; and
(c) Contributions granted to foster activities concerning research and development with a view to implementing techniques, manufacturing processes and products causing less pollution.[26]

These conditions have since become more sophisticated.

The initial view of the Community more specifically with respect to State aid (Communication of November 1974) was that its use had to be a transitional stage, paving the way for the gradual introduction of the "polluter pays principle". State aid in this area was to disappear gradually, since it was seen as preventing an effective, long-term EU environmental policy. During a transitional period, the opportunity was given to existing firms to adapt, via State support, to EU and national environmental regulations where the latter imposed an extraordinary financial burden. The only measures which the 1974 policy envisaged to be acceptable were investment schemes. Article 87(3)(b) EC served as the ground of justification.

The transitional period was due to expire in 1980, which turned out to be too short. Consequently, the framework was extended by six years, albeit with some fundamental changes, which made conditions on the whole more specific.[27] The framework was extended for a second time for the period 1987–1992, this time without any changes.[28] The context of the EU's environmental policy, however, changed significantly with the introduction, in the 1986 Single European Act, of a new section on the

---

[26] Ibid., at 7.
[27] See the synopsis by Commissioner Sutherland, answering a Parliamentary question by MEP Roelants du Vivier, [1988] OJ C 140/14.
[28] [1987] OJ C 328/1.

environment in the then EC Treaty. The "polluter pays principle" was reaffirmed. The Single European Act also introduced the need to integrate the environmental agenda into the other policies of the EC, including competition policy. The same framework was again extended, for a period of six months, in 1992[29] and in 1993.[30]

Meanwhile, however, the Commission view on State aid for environmental protection had altered.[31] In the fifth EAP, the Commission acknowledged the role economic instruments can play in the protection of the environment. It stated that the use of both positive financial incentives and disincentives, namely taxes and levies, should be further explored. The Council endorsed the Commission view. In its Resolution encompassing the Commission Proposal for an EAP, the Council recommended the development of "efficient economic instruments, such as taxes, levies, State Aid, authorisation of negotiable rebates, with a view to implementing the Polluter Pays Principle, in accordance with Council Recommendation 75/436".[32]

In the 1993 guidelines, however, the Commission emphasised the "polluter pays" principle, and it consistently treated subsidies as a second-best solution. The Commission therefore doubted the role the EU should give to subsidies.[33] Interestingly, where the previous Guidelines centred upon (the then) Article 87(3)(b), the later Guidelines adopted Article 87(3)(c) as the main provision for exemption. The latter is not only more appropriate for the kind of State aid concerned, its conditions of application are also less stringent.[34]

Scholarship has reviewed the application of the Guidelines in detail over the years – reference is made to those sources for detailed analysis.[35]

---

[29] *Bull.EC*, 12–1992, 1.3.75.

[30] *Bull.EC*, 6–1993, 1.2.55.

[31] See also W. De Wit, *Nationale milieubelastingen en het EG-Verdrag*, Deventer: Kluwer, 1997, 345 *et seq.*, who shares this view.

[32] Resolution of the Council of the European Communities and the representatives of the Governments of the Member States, meeting within the Council of 19 October 1987 on the continuation and implementation of a European Community policy and action program on the environment (1987–1992), [1987] OJ C 328/1, at "s".

[33] See *infra*.

[34] See D. Chalmers, "Environmental Protection and the Single Market: An Unsustainable Development. Does the EC Treaty Need a Title on the Environment?", 22 *Legal Issues of European Integration*, 1 (1995), 65–98, at 81, who calls the switch to Article 92(3)(c) a circumvention of the stricter requirements with respect to important projects of common European interest.

[35] In more or less chronological order: L. Hancher, "European Law and Energy Production: The Internal Market and the Environmental Dimension", 1

C. "Indirect" Aid: Tax Relief, Reductions in Charges and Various Tax Benefits

The most obvious form of aid is of course direct financial contributions from a Member State (often a region within a Member State) to a (number of) enterprises. Such contributions may be either in the form of a grant, or through measures such as loans with a long-running payback period, interest-free loans, guarantees, and so on. "Indirect aid" are those types of aid which are not the result of an expense for the State, but rather consist of a loss or non-realisation of revenue.

The obvious sector for such measures is taxation. Tax relief, reductions in charges and various tax benefits are subject to the Guidelines in the same way as direct financial support. Likewise, how taxation is designed to address environmental considerations in practice often favours one product or production process over another.

Specifically in the area of promoting renewable energy with a view to addressing climate change, prior to EU harmonisation in this area, Member States had already rolled out a number of regulatory measures. The confrontation of these national measures with EU trade law arguably started with *Outokumpu Oy*.

Outokumpu Oy: a strict CJEU view on border (energy) tax adjustments

National environmental priorities, as well as international commitments to reduce the emission of greenhouse gases, have led to the increased use of "smart" energy taxation. In particular in OECD countries, States aim to

---

Review of European Community and International Environmental Law, 2 (1992), 141–153; J. Jans, "State Aid and Articles 92 and 93 of the EC Treaty: Does the Polluter Really Pay?" 4 *European Energy and Environmental Law Review*, 4 (1995), 108–113; G. Van Calster, "State Aid for Environmental Protection: Has the EC Shut the Door?", 2 *Environmental Taxation & Accounting*, 3 (1997), 38–51; G. Van Calster, "Greening the EC's State Aid and Tax Regimes", 21 *European Competition Law Review* (2000), 294–314; B. Delvaux, "The EC State Aid Regime Regarding Renewables: Opportunities and Pitfalls", 12 *European Energy and Environmental Law Review*, 4 (2003), 103–112; W. Vandenberghe and G. Van Calster, "The Rules on competition" // "State Aid" // "Energy Taxation", in: M. Roggenkamp et al. (eds.), *Energy Law in Europe*, 2nd Edition, Oxford: Oxford University Press, 2007, 249–282, 283–299, 321–330; B. Andersen, "Revision of Environmental Guidelines (2008)", 17 *European Energy and Environmental Law Review*, 1 (2008), 23–30; A. Crespo van der Kooij and S. Lavrijssen, "A Legal Assessment of the Producer Exemption from Transport Tariffs under EU Law", 22 *European Energy and Environmental Law Review*, 6 (2013), 245–262; R. Callaerts, "State Aid for the Production of Electricity from Renewable Energy Resources", 4 *European Energy and Environmental Law Review*, 1 (2015), 17–26.

encourage amongst others the use of renewable sources of energy, through a layered system of taxation. Such system targets less environmentally friendly forms of energy, with a higher rate of taxation.

Competitiveness concerns of such a green taxation regime would normally be offset by Border Tax Adjustments (BTAs). However, in the energy sector, BTA is complicated by the fact that one cannot distinguish the method of production from the final product. In trade law jargon this is known as "non-product-related production processes and methods" or "n-Pr PPMs": the way in which, in the case at issue, electricity is produced is not visible in the final product.

In *Outokumpu Oy*, the CJEU adopted a strict approach to Member States' use of tax instruments to distinguish between renewable or fossil and nuclear sources of electricity.[36] Under Finnish legislation on the taxation of energy, excise duty on electricity was levied on electrical energy produced domestically, the amount of the duty depending on the method of production.[37] On imported electricity, the excise duty charged, regardless of the method of production of the electricity, was a set duty, higher than the lowest excise duty chargeable on electricity produced in Finland, but lower than the highest excise duty chargeable on such electricity.

This called into question the application of Article 110 TFEU (at the time, Article 90 TEC):

> No Member State shall impose, directly or indirectly, on the products of other Member States any internal taxation of any kind in excess of that imposed directly or indirectly on similar domestic products.
>
> Furthermore, no Member State shall impose on the products of other Member States any internal taxation of such a nature as to afford indirect protection to other products.

The CJEU accepted the principle that the rate of an internal tax on electricity may vary according to the manner in which the electricity is produced and the raw materials used for its production, in so far as that differentiation is based on environmental considerations. However, it referred to earlier case law which states that Article 110 is infringed where the taxation on the imported product and that on the similar domestic

---

[36] C-213/96 *Outokumpu*, ECLI:EU:C:1998:155.

[37] The highest for electricity produced by nuclear power, lower for electricity produced by water power; for electricity produced by other methods, for example from coal, excise duty was charged on the basis of the amount of input materials used to produce the electricity; finally, for electrical energy produced by some methods, for example in a generator with an output below two megavolt-amperes, no excise duty at all was charged.

product are calculated in a different manner on the basis of different criteria which lead, even if only in certain cases, to higher taxation being imposed on the imported product.[38]

Practical difficulties in levying the same kind of tax, in particular because of the specific nature of electricity and the difficulty of determining the method of production of imported electricity, could not justify the infringement. The Court also seemed to attach particular weight to the fact that the Finnish legislation did not even give the importer the opportunity of demonstrating that the electricity imported by him had been produced by a particular method in order to qualify for the rate applicable to electricity of domestic origin produced by the same method.

In *Outokumpu Oy* the CJEU strictly applied the condition of non-discrimination. This was an approach not altogether absent from previous case law. *Haahr Petroleum*,[39] too, applied Article 110 TFEU strictly. Here, the Court held that national legislation can only be compatible with Article 110 if it excludes higher taxation of imported products in all instances. This strict approach was subsequently confirmed, for instance in *Grundig Italiana*.[40] It represents a firm belief in a de facto interpretation of the condition of non-discrimination, where the legislator's intent is irrelevant.

The Court's attitude was less absolute in other instances, where the nature of the tax regime was held to be more important than its actual consequences.[41] *Chemial Farmaceutici* (see further, below) is a case in point. Generally, the Court had not, prior to the *Outokumpu* line of cases, employed non-discrimination as a separate condition in the three-tier test under Article 110.[42] Rather it assessed this condition in conjunction with

---

[38] Among others Case C-152/89 *Commission v Luxembourg*, [1991] ECR I-3141, at 20.

[39] C-90/94 *Haahr Petroleum v Åbenrå Havn and Others*, ECLI:EU:C:1997:368.

[40] Case C-68/96 *Grundig Italiana SpA v Minestero delle Finanze*, [1997] ECR I-3797.

[41] See for example Case 106/84 *Commission v Denmark*, [1986] ECR 833 (where the products subject to the highest tax rate were, due to their nature, all imported); Case 277/83 *Commission v Italy*, [1985] ECR 2049 (where imported products were excluded from qualification for a number of fiscal advantages); and Joined Cases 142/80 and 143/80 *Amministrazione delle Finanze dello Stato v Essevi SpA and Carlo Salengo*, [1981] ECR 1413 (where tax advantages were dependent on the inspection of production processes, *in situ*, by the authorities of the importing State).

[42] The Court's general application of Article 110 holds that EU law does not restrict the freedom of each Member State to lay down tax arrangements which differentiate between certain products on the basis of objective criteria, such as

the other two. This bundling of the three elements of the test was severed by the judgments in *Haahr Petroleum*, *Grundig Italiana* and *Outokumpu Oy*.

More specifically with respect to environmental taxation, the AG and the Finnish Government had suggested leniency, in the light of the ecological objectives of the regulations, and of technical difficulties coinciding with the nature of electricity.[43] The Court dismissed practical and technical difficulties. Rather than imposing a tax, calculated as a national average, Finland should have imposed the lowest tax rate on imported products. (AG Jacobs had suggested an improved version of the Finnish technique, which would have imposed an average tax that was a better reflection of the true proportion of Finnish products subject to the various tax levels. It would have been amended on a regular basis, to reflect changing consumption patterns.)

The Court's clarification of the condition of non-discrimination and absence of protective effect is of particular relevance for a substantial part of environmental taxes. An important part of those taxes aims to eliminate or at least limit the national production of a particular type of product. In *Chemial Farmaceutici*[44] the Court accepted that there was no discrimination, even though domestic products only fell within the advantaged category of the Italian fiscal legislation at stake. It reasoned that the tax treatment did apply to domestic production of the disfavoured kind (production of denatured alcohol by means of the synthetic process), in that it had the effect of preventing such production from arising.

In other words the leeway offered by the Court would seem to guarantee that only the most brutal environmental taxes, those where national production is virtually eliminated (where that was the objective of the tax), do not stumble over EU law hurdles. However, *Chemial Farmaceutici* did not lead to a series of similar decisions, and its impact is therefore

---

the nature of the raw materials used or the production processes employed. Such differentiation is compatible with EU law

- if it is based on objective criteria, such as the nature of the raw materials used or the production processes employed; and
- if it pursues economic or social policy objectives which are themselves compatible with the requirements of the Treaty and secondary law, and
- if the detailed rules are such as to avoid any form of discrimination, direct or indirect, in regard to imports from other Member States or any form of protection of domestic products.

[43] Once produced, it is impossible for the authorities to deduct, from the very electricity presented, the production process that was used in manufacturing it.
[44] Case 140/79 *Chemial Farmaceutici SpA v DAF SpA.*, [1981] ECR 1.

unclear. The decision in *Outokumpu Oy*, in particular, points to a rather less open approach to environmental taxation. This is in contrast with the Court's effective promotion of environmental measures based on quantitative restrictions to trade, as exemplified by the rulings in Essent and PreussenElektra.

II. COMPETITION LAW AND THE ENVIRONMENT

EU competition law applies to the environment sector just as it does to all other sectors. The basic principle on competition requires the Union to promote a "highly competitive social market economy" (Article 3(3) TEU), and to "establishing of the competition rules necessary for the functioning of the Internal Market" (Article 3(2) TFEU). The main Treaty rules on competition, included in Articles 101–102 TFEU and related secondary legislation, are primarily addressed to undertakings.[45] They prohibit concerted action between undertakings to obstruct free competition and the abuse of dominant market power respectively.

Some competition rules are addressed to Member States, rather than to companies, namely exclusive rights and State aids (see above). Member States are also under a duty not to distort competition.[46] Article 106 TFEU provides rules regarding public enterprises and enterprises with exclusive or special rights. The State aid rules in Articles 106–108 TFEU as reviewed above also provide a level playing field for market participants. Finally, the EU merger system assesses mergers and acquisitions.

These rules have over the years all received specific application in individual cases with an environmental angle,[47] as they have done in the energy sector.[48] One particular area which has attracted a lot of attention is the waste sector, more specifically the collection of wastes by combined economic operators. It is to this that we now briefly turn our attention by

---

[45] In Case C-198/01 *Fiammiferi* [2003] ECR I-08055, the Court confirmed that Member States' obligations are distinct from the obligations of enterprises under Articles 81 and 82 EC (para. 51).

[46] *Ex multi* see for example Case 13/77 *Inno v Atab* [1977] ECR 2115; Case 267/86 *Van Eyke v Aspa* [1988] ECR 4769.

[47] See in particular S. Kingston, *Greening EU Competition Law and Policy*, Cambridge: Cambridge University Press, 2011; H. Vedder, *Competition Law and Environmental Protection in the EU*, Groningen: Europa Law Publishing, 2003.

[48] See W. Vandenberghe and G. Van Calster, "The Rules On Competition", in: M. Roggenkamp, C. Redgwell, A. Ronne and I. del Guayo (eds), *Energy Law in Europe*, 2nd Edition, Oxford: Oxford University Press, 2007, 249–282.

way of illustration of the challenges of reconciling the classic principles of competition law with environmental policy.

Following a number of decisions which passed through the standard application of EU competition law, the Commission has clarified the application of competition law in the waste management sector in (non-binding) guidelines issued by its Competition Directorate-General. In September 2005, the Guidelines were published,[49] and in April 2006, they were followed up by a brief strategy overview in the Directorate-General's internal newsletter.[50] The paper is not just relevant (and does not just look into) packaging and packaging waste. In other sectors, too, often driven by EU waste law (Waste Electrical and Electronic Equipment (WEEE): end of life vehicles), collective organisations have a big impact on the practical implementation of waste management duties.

A. Eco-Emballages

In 1993, Eco-Emballages set up a complex system for the selective collection and recovery of household packaging waste. This system aims to meet the obligations imposed on firms by the French implementing legislation of the packaging and packaging waste Directive. The notification concerned the great number of agreements running in parallel.

Eco-Emballages at the time of notification was by far the largest organisation in this sector in France. Its members pay a financial contribution in return for having their legal obligations in the area of the recycling of packaging discharged. Eco-Emballages redistributes the revenues it collects from them to the local authorities, which are responsible amongst others for collecting household waste in their local area. In 2000, Eco-Emballages had contracts with about two thirds of them. Its contributions are intended to compensate the local authorities for the extra cost of selectively collecting and sorting this type of waste. The local authorities sell the sorted materials to industrial firms which recover them. Apart from Eco-Emballages, Adelphe SA also offers a collective collection system.

Shortly after it was set up, Eco-Emballages notified its articles of association and contracts to the Commission for approval under competition law. (This is a procedure of "clearance" which now no longer exists in EU competition law.) Its notification in particular covered the contract for the

---

[49] DG Competition Paper concerning issues of competition in waste management systems, available at http://goo.gl/PwpG9c, last consulted 3.8.2014.

[50] P. Kienapfel and G. Miersch, "Competition issues in waste management systems", Competition Policy Newsletter, 2006, No.1, pp. 52–56, available at http://goo.gl/0RMFwE, last consulted 16.12.2016.

use of the "Green Dot" logo on packaging and the standard "producer", "local-authority" and "sectorial" (i.e. for industrial firms responsible for recovery) contracts.

Following a warning from the Commission in January 2000, Eco-Emballages amended some of the clauses of its contracts, including on the matter of their duration and scope and on the granting of sub-licences for the use of the "Green Dot". Eco-Emballages agreed to amend its contracts and enter into commitments in such a way as to ensure that the contracts' duration and scope no longer restricted competition. Producers may now leave the system after a year and at the end of every subsequent year, and may also conclude a contract for all or only some of their packaging. Local authorities may also immediately terminate their contract with the system and conclude a contract for all or only some of the packaging waste they collect. Eco-Emballages also offers the possibility of using the "Green Dot" logo to anybody who legitimately needs to use it to carry on business.

By its decision,[51] the Commission defines the principles of competition to be complied with by arrangements of this nature while taking account of environmental demands. For example, to guarantee expected environmental benefits, the EC has accepted that the collective body concerned should be able to ask its partners to ensure that they act without fault in recovering household packaging. However, exclusive, long-term contracts are viewed with suspicion for they can lead to market foreclosure. Moreover, producers should, if they wish, also be able to establish individual arrangements for some of their packaging while calling on the services of a collective system for the rest.

B. DSD

Until August 2003 DSD was the only company that ran a countrywide system for the collection and recycling of sales packaging in Germany. DSD itself does not collect the waste but uses local collecting companies. DSD has concluded so-called service agreements with these undertakings. The originally notified service agreement had raised serious competition concerns in particular vis-à-vis the exclusivity provisions in favour of the collectors.

According to the service agreement the collector has the exclusive task of collecting and sorting sales packaging in a designated district. The assessment of this exclusivity provision showed – taking into account the

---

[51] COMP/34.950 – Eco-Emballages [2001] OJ L 233/37.

market position of DSD and the duration time of the service agreement – that access to the relevant market by domestic and foreign collectors was greatly obstructed; this goes a considerable way towards partitioning off a substantial part of the common market.

Most of the service agreements initially notified were to run until the end of 2007, thereby having overall contractual duration times of up to 15 years. Consequently, the EC[52] scrutinised whether such long-term exclusive agreements were indeed necessary. The results suggested that if the service agreements were to run until the end of 2003 collectors would have sufficient time to achieve an economically satisfactory recovery of their investment. DSD then set a termination date of 31 December 2003 for the agreements. This allowed the Commission to exempt service agreements containing an exclusivity clause running no further than the end of 2003.[53] The exemption decision therefore was issued for the period 1 January 1996 to 31 December 2003. Afterwards these service agreements had to be put out for tender.

The Commission did find against DSD in an Article 102 TFEU case (abuse of dominant position).[54] The payment system operated by DSD represented an abuse of a dominant position within the meaning of Article 102 TFEU. DSD customers had to pay fees corresponding to the volume of packaging bearing the "Green Dot" trademark rather than fees corresponding to the volume of packaging for which DSD was actually providing a take-back and recycling service. Under the Commission's decision, DSD could therefore no longer charge a fee in Germany for that part of the sales packaging bearing the "Green Dot" for which it could be shown that the take-back and recovery obligation, as set out in the German packaging ordinance, had been properly fulfilled by another party, either a competing system or a self-management solution.

With this decision, the Commission imposed a necessary condition to allow competition in the area of collection and recovery of used sales packaging in Germany. It prohibited the aforementioned practices, without, however, imposing a fine – recognising that DSD's quest for clarity in a hitherto unprecedented case did not justify a fine.

DSD appealed the decision at the CJEU[55] which fully upheld the EC's decisions.

---

[52] COMP D3/34493 DSD, [2001] OJ L 166/1.
[53] Decision 2001/837, [2001] OJ L 319/1.
[54] [2001] OJ L 166/1.
[55] Case C-385/07 *Der Grüne Punkt – Duales System Deutschland GmbH v Commission*, [2009] ECR I-06155.

PART II

Substantive legislation

10. Biodiversity and nature conservation

Risks to natural resources, that is, biodiversity loss and degradation, have been an intense focus of the EU for quite some time. In the Commission's 2001 Sustainable Development Study,[1] it was recognised that biodiversity loss in the EU was one of the biggest environmental challenges[2] threatening the "future well-being of European society".[3] Further, in the EU biodiversity strategy for the period up to 2020,[4] the EU, having failed to attain the 2010 goal, aims at "reversing biodiversity loss and speeding up the EU's transition towards a resource efficient and green economy".[5] Major threats to biodiversity are believed to be alien species, pollution, climate change, population growth, and the non-inclusion of the economic value of ecosystems into decision making.[6] Additional causes are habitat loss due to land use change and fragmentation, as well as overexploitation and unsustainable use of resources.[7] The EEA's report entitled "The EU 2010 biodiversity baseline"[8] provides information on the status of biodiversity in the EU, as well as trends. According to the report, 65 per cent of the European habitat types

---

[1] Sustainable Development Study, Communication from the Commission, "A sustainable Europe for a better world: a European Union strategy for sustainable development", COM (2001) 264.
[2] Ibid., 4.
[3] Ibid., 5.
[4] Commission, "Our life insurance, our natural capital: an EU biodiversity strategy to 2020", COM (2011) 244, adopted by European Parliament Resolution on Friday 20 April 2012. The EU biodiversity strategy, which was first adopted in 1998, was revised several times, for example in 2003 and 2006.
[5] Ibid., 1.
[6] Ibid., 4.
[7] A. Slingenberg et al., "Study on understanding the causes of biodiversity loss and the policy assessment framework", ECORYS Research and Consulting, 2009, 13ff., available at http://ec.europa.eu/environment/enveco/biodiversity/pdf/causes_biodiv_loss.pdf, last consulted 12.11.2015; as well as on the global scale, for example, Millennium Ecosystem Assessment, *Ecosystems and Human Well-being: Biodiversity Synthesis*, Washington, DC: World Resources Institute, 2005, at 8ff.
[8] EEA, "EU 2010 biodiversity baseline", 2010, available at http://www.eea.europa.eu/publications/eu-2010-biodiversity-baseline, last consulted 12.11.2015.

of Union interest whose conservation requires the designation of special conservation areas are of an "unfavourable" status; 37 per cent are in a "bad" position.[9] Only 17 per cent of the European habitats were considered "favourable", and the conservation status of 18 per cent of the habitats was stated as "unknown". The statistics for the conservation status of the species in the EU are not very different. An unfavourable status is held by 52 per cent; 22 per cent have a bad status. Likewise, 17 per cent of the species have a favourable status; the assessment of 31 per cent of the species is unknown.[10] These numbers are even more striking considering that European heads of State introduced the 2010 biodiversity target on halting the decline of biodiversity by the end of 2010 back in 2001 at the Göteborg European Council.[11] Realising that the Union failed in the achievement of the target, in March 2010 the Union's decision makers recognised the need for a long-term strategy building on the efforts already undertaken.

In its 2020 biodiversity strategy, the EU committed to the protection of biodiversity, and to stop biodiversity loss on the Union's territory by 2020, as well as to restore the degraded ecosystems. The EU biodiversity strategy, "Our life insurance, our natural capital: an EU biodiversity strategy to 2020,"[12] outlines the biodiversity policy and its focus until 2020. It further includes a 2050 vision: "By 2050, European Union biodiversity and the ecosystem services it provides – its natural capital – are protected, valued and appropriately restored for biodiversity's intrinsic value and for their essential contribution to human wellbeing and economic prosperity, and so that catastrophic changes caused by the loss of biodiversity are avoided." The 2050 vision aims at including the economic value of the natural resources and assets into decision making, thus including the externalities into the accounting and reporting systems.[13] In order to achieve this long-term goal, the EU has set four strategic objectives: (1) increasing a resource efficient economy, (2) employing a climate-resilient, low-carbon economy, (3) leading research and innovation, and lastly (4) creating new skills, jobs and business opportunities.[14]

Key to the 2020 strategy is the formulation of six "mutually supportive and inter-dependent" targets which all contribute to the overall target of

---

[9] See EEA, *EU 2010 biodiversity baseline*, EEA Technical report No 12/2010, 19.
[10] Ibid., 21.
[11] See Presidency Conclusions, Göteborg European Council, 15 and 16 June 2001, available at http://goo.gl/b9vxgi, last consulted 16.12.2016.
[12] 2020 biodiversity strategy, COM (2011) 244.
[13] Ibid., 2ff.
[14] Ibid., 3.

stopping biodiversity loss and the degradation of ecosystem services. Each target is further broken down into specific actions which are specified in the Annex of the strategy. Each action addresses a specific challenge of the overall target.

The targets relate to the conservation and restoration of biodiversity and the maintenance of ecosystems and the associated services; the stability of agriculture, forestry and fishery policy; the fight against invasive alien species; and the contribution of the Union to the global biodiversity targets agreed under the Convention of Biological Diversity (CBD).

I. NATURA 2000 NETWORK AND THE WILD BIRDS AND HABITATS DIRECTIVES

The Wild Birds and Habitats Directives, the key legislation establishing the Union's internal biodiversity and nature protection policy, establish the Natura 2000 network. The European network of nature protection for birds and habitats sites, as well as the marine environment includes 26,000 protected areas, which form 18 per cent or 750,000 km^2 of the Union territory.

A. The Wild Birds Directive

The Wild Birds Directive[15] is one of the oldest pieces of legislation in the European environmental area and certainly the oldest nature protection legislation. The Directive is applicable to the conservation of all species of naturally occurring birds in the wild state in the European territory of the Member States as well as to their eggs, nests and habitats (Article 1). The CJEU clarified in this regard that "the general system of protection which the directive seeks to establish concerns all bird species, including those with chromatic aberrations, even if such species are rare", including birds which are passing through or only living in the territory for a limited period, as well as "naturally occurring birds in the wild state in the European territory of another Member State which are not naturally or usually to be found in the territory of [a Member State] but which are transported there, kept there or marketed there, whether alive or dead".[16]

Article 4 of the Directive is key to the protection regime for birds,

---

[15] Directive 79/409 on the conservation of wild birds, [1979] OJ L 103/1, as amended.
[16] Case C-247/85 *Commission v Belgium*, ECR [1987] 3029, at 52, 21 and 22.

namely the protection of species' habitats in Special Protection Areas or "SPAs".

> Article 4(1) and (2) of the Wild Birds Directive requires the Member States to provide SPAs with a legal protection regime that is capable, in particular, of ensuring both the survival and reproduction of the bird species listed in Annex I to the directive and the breeding, moulting and wintering of migratory species not listed in Annex I which are, nevertheless, regular visitors.[17]

The designation and definition criteria for the establishment of SPAs are ornithological.[18] That means that a Member State cannot take account of the economic requirements as included in Article 2 of the Directive when designating a SPA and defining its boundaries.[19]

The Directive regulates species' protection, management and control, as well as exploitation. It generally prohibits (Article 5)

> (a) the deliberate killing or capture of birds, (b) the deliberate destruction, damage or removal of their eggs and deliberate significant disturbance of birds during breeding and rearing periods, (c) taking their eggs in the wild and keeping these eggs even if empty; (d) deliberate disturbance of these birds particularly during the period of breeding and rearing, in so far as disturbance would be significant having regard to the objectives of this Directive; (e) keeping birds of species the hunting and capture of which is prohibited.

The provisions in Article 5(b) and (c) apply without any limitation in time.[20] The sale and associated practices of live or dead birds and any recognisable parts or derivatives is further prohibited (Article 6) apart from a few exceptions for the species listed in Annex III of the Directive.

Hunting of the species listed in Annex II is subject to national legislation and depends on the population level, the geographical distribution and reproduction rate (Article 7). Member States are not allowed to extend the list contained in Annex II.[21] The use of hunting material listed in Annex IV (a) is generally prohibited (Article 8).[22]

---

[17] Case C-166/97 *Commission v France*, [1999] ECR I-1719, at 21; as well as Case C-355/90 *Commission v Spain*, [1993] ECR I-4221, at 28 to 32.

[18] Case C-355/90 *Commission v Spain – Santoña Marshes*, [1993] ECR I-4221.

[19] Case C-44/95 *R v Secretary of State for the Environment, ex parte RSPB*, [1996] I-3805, at 26 and 27.

[20] Case C-252/85 *Commission v France*, [1988] ECR I -2243, at 9.

[21] Case C-262/85 *Commission v Italy*, [1987] ECR I-3073, at p. 12.

[22] See also European Commission, Guidance document on hunting under Council Directive 79/409/EEC on the conservation of wild birds, DOC/ORN. 04/02, available at http://www.unece.org/fileadmin/DAM/env/pp/compliance/

Derogation from the abovementioned provisions is generally only possible on grounds of public health and safety, air safety, prevention of serious damage to crops, livestock, forests, fisheries and water; as well as for the protection of flora and fauna; and under the threshold that no satisfactory solution is conceivable (Article 9). The Court introduced three conditions in this regard:

> first, the Member State must restrict the derogation to cases in which there is no other satisfactory solution; secondly, the derogation must be based on at least one of the reasons listed exhaustively in Article 9 (1) (a), (b) and (c); thirdly, the derogation must comply with the precise formal conditions set out in Article 9(2), which are intended to limit derogations to what is strictly necessary and to enable the Commission to supervise them. Although Article 9 therefore authorizes wide derogations from the general system of protection, it must be applied appropriately in order to deal with precise requirements and specific situations.[23]

The Directive obliges the Member States to preserve, maintain and re-establish biotopes and habitats, especially through the creation and ecological management of protected areas and biotopes (Article 3). The Directive further establishes special conservation measures for certain endangered species which are listed in the Annex I to the Directive. The Annex covers species in danger of extinction, species vulnerable to specific changes in their habitat, rare species (in terms of small populations or restricted local distribution) and other species which require specific measures due to the specific nature of their habitat. The special measures are aimed to ensure the survival and reproduction of the species concerned (Article 4).

There is extensive case law on the exact requirements for the listing of SPAs, and their impact on local planning applications.

B. The Habitats Directive

The Habitats Directive is the equivalent to the Wild Birds Directive for natural habitats and wild flora and fauna.[24] More precisely, the Directive

---

C2007-18/Communication/SupportingDocumentation2006.12.04/EUKommissionenGuidance_birdsdirect_en.pdf, last consulted 12.11.2015.

[23] Case C-247/85 *Commission v Belgium,* [1987] ECR 3029, at para. 7.

[24] For a detailed analysis of the Directive please refer to the contributions in G. Jones (ed.), *The Habitats Directive. A Developer's Obstacle Course?*, Oxford: Hart Publishing, 2012; as well as C.H. Born, A. Cliquet, H. Schoukens, D. Misonne and G. Van Hoorick (eds), *The Habitats Directive in its EU Environmental Law Context - European Nature's Best Hope?*, London and New York: Routledge, 2015.

aims at maintaining or restoring natural habitats and species of wild fauna and flora of Union interest to a favourable conservation status (Article 2). Article 3 establishes the Natura 2000 system as a key tool to achieve these aims. Each Member State has to designate an area in proportion to the representation within its territory of the natural habitat types and the habitats of species listed in Annex I (natural habitats of a Union interest) and II (animal and plant species of a Union interest) to the Directive (Article 3). According to the EEA baseline report, around 200 habitats and 1000 species of animals and plants are included in the list requiring a favourable conservation status.[25] For each of the EU's biogeographical regions, the EC adopts a list of "Sites of Community Importance" or "SCIs". (The correct jargon would now be site of Union importance (SUI); however, this terminology so far has not been formally or informally adopted.) SCIs are then designated at the national level as Special Areas of Conservation or "SACs".

In SACs, the deterioration and significant disturbance of natural habitats and species has to be avoided. In *Grüne Liga Sachsen*[26] the Court dealt with the question of whether Article 6(2) of the Habitats Directive must be interpreted as meaning that

> a plan or project not directly connected with or necessary to the management of a site, and authorised, following a study that did not meet the requirements of Article 6(3), before the site in question was included in the list of SCIs must be the subject of a subsequent review, by the competent authorities, of its implications for that site if that review constitutes the only appropriate step for avoiding that the implementation of the plan or project referred to results in deterioration or disturbance that could be significant in view of the objectives of that directive. (at 46)

Both Directives require an assessment of the impacts of all plans and programmes which are likely to have a significant effect on the sites, even if they are not directly connected with the sites (Article 6). If a plan or project has a significant effect on a site, it cannot be carried out, unless it is necessary for what are called imperative reasons of overriding public interest (Article 6(4)). Being the very heart of the Natura 2000 system and the general policy objectives, the next section explains in detail the procedure of Articles 6(3) and 6(4) of the Habitats Directive, as well as the relation between the Habitats Directive and the EIA Directive.

---

[25] EEA, "EU 2010 biodiversity baseline", EEA Technical report No 12/2010, 19, available at http://www.eea.europa.eu/publications/eu-2010-biodiversity-baseline, last consulted 12.11.2015.
[26] C-399/14 *Grüne Liga Sachsen and Others*, ECLI:EU:C:2016:10.

The procedure of Articles 6(3) and 6(4) of the Habitats Directive[27]

Articles 6(3) and 6(4) of the Habitats Directive contain the procedure and the substantial requirements to be taken into account when assessing whether a proposed project can be authorised within a Natura 2000 site. These provisions read:

3. Any plan or project not directly connected with or necessary to the management of the site but likely to have a significant effect thereon, either individually or in combination with other plans or projects, shall be subject to appropriate assessment of its implications for the site in view of the site's conservation objectives. In the light of the conclusions of the assessment of the implications for the site and subject to the provisions of paragraph 4, the competent national authorities shall agree to the plan or project only after having ascertained that it will not adversely affect the integrity of the site concerned and, if appropriate, after having obtained the opinion of the general public.
4. If, in spite of a negative assessment of the implications for the site and in the absence of alternative solutions, a plan or project must nevertheless be carried out for imperative reasons of overriding public interest, including those of a social or economic nature, the Member State shall take all compensatory measures necessary to ensure that the overall coherence of Natura 2000 is protected. It shall inform the Commission of the compensatory measures adopted.

   Where the site concerned hosts a priority natural habitat type and/or a priority species, the only considerations which may be raised are those relating to human health or public safety, to beneficial consequences of primary importance for the environment or, further to an opinion from the Commission, to other imperative reasons of overriding public interest.

Article 6(3) Habitats Directive establishes an assessment procedure intended to ensure, by means of a prior examination, that a plan or project not directly connected with or necessary to the management of the site concerned but likely to have a significant effect on it is authorised only to the extent that it will not adversely affect the integrity of that site.[28]

The application of Article 6(3) comprises two different stages. The first stage, *the screening stage*, relates to whether an appropriate assessment concerning the impact of a plan or project has to be drawn up. The second stage, *the assessment stage*, relates to the drawing up of an appropriate assessment and the impact on the decision-making process.

---

[27] This section was co-authored with Christoph Schelfaut and Alec van Vaerenbergh.
[28] Case C-182/10 *Solvay*, ECLI:EU:C:2012:82 at 66.

Article 6(4) provides for an exception, the so-called IROPI exception, to authorise a plan or project, in spite of a negative outcome of the appropriate assessment. Even if the project may adversely affect the integrity of the site, it may go ahead for "imperative reasons of overriding public interest" (IROPI). This requires, firstly, that there are no alternative solutions for the plan or project and, secondly, that all compensatory measures are taken to safeguard the overall coherence of the Natura 2000 network. As with Article 6(3), Article 6(4) can be considered to comprise two different stages. Prior to invoking the IROPI exception, it will have to be assessed whether alternative solutions are available to implement the project without adverse impact on the integrity of the site. If the answer is positive, one should revert to this alternative solution rather than invoking the IROPI exception. If the answer is negative, one can effectively continue to invoke the IROPI exception.

The screening stage, the assessment stage, the alternative solutions test, and the IROPI exception are all reviewed below.

The screening stage The screening stage corresponds to the first sentence of Article 6(3) of the Habitats Directive, that is:

> Any plan or project not directly connected with or necessary to the management of the site but likely to have a significant effect thereon, either individually or in combination with other plans or projects, shall be subject to appropriate assessment of its implications for the site in view of the site's conservation objectives.

The crucial question at this stage is whether the proposed project is likely to have a "significant effect" on the site, either alone or in combination with other plans or projects.

The application of the screening stage requires prior clarification of the different constitutive elements of the first sentence of Article 6(3) of the Habitats Directive: (1) what is to be understood by the "likely" nature of the effects; (2) what is covered by the requirement to make the analysis "in combination with other plans or projects"; and (3) when is an effect to be considered "significant".

THE LIKELIHOOD OF THE EFFECTS For Article 6(3) of the Habitats Directive to kick in, it is not required that there be certainty of significant effects on the site. Likelihood is sufficient to trigger the requirement to draw up an appropriate assessment.

While the words "likely to have an effect" seem to suggest that a certain degree of probability has to be present, the Court dismissed this interpretation in *Waddenvereniging and Vogelbeschermingsvereniging*.[29] According to the Court these words have to be interpreted as the mere presence of the probability or risk that there might be a significant effect. This judgment is of particular importance, since it establishes a lower threshold to invoke an adequate assessment. Since then, this interpretation has become settled case law in the Court.[30]

The discussion on the interpretation of the word "likely" was addressed again by AG Sharpston in her opinion in *Sweetman*.[31] The Advocate General pointed out that there is a difference between the expression "likely to have an effect" in the English language version of Article 6(3) of the Habitats Directive and the expressions used in other languages, which all use a lower threshold (e.g. in the French and German versions the expressions "*susceptible d'affecter*" and "*beeinträchtigen könnte*" are used). Based on these findings, the Advocate General equally concluded that the mere possibility that a project has significant effects on the site is sufficient to trigger the drawing up of an appropriate assessment.

To determine whether a project might cause significant effects to the site, one has to rely on objective information. Objective information can be drawn from the Natura 2000 Standard Data Forms for the site, existing and historical maps, land use and other relevant plans, existing site survey material, existing data on hydrogeology, existing data on key species, state of the environment reports, geographical information systems, site history files and so on.[32]

The Court ruled in *Waddenvereniging* that this information must be assessed in the light of inter alia the characteristics and specific environmental conditions of the site concerned by that plan or project.[33]

Note that this initial screening does not require the type of comprehensive, in-depth assessment required in the appropriate assessment stage (see below). It only requires that sufficient information be gathered to

---

[29] Case C-127/02 *Waddenvereniging and Vogelbeschermingsvereniging*, [2004] ECR I-7405, at 42–43.
[30] See for example Case C-508/09 *Commission v Belgium*, ECLI:EU:C:2011:115 at 39; Case C-418/04 *Commission v Ireland*, ECLI:EU:C:2007:780, at 226.
[31] Sharpston AG in Case C-258/11 *Sweetman v An Bord Pleanala* ECLI:EU:C:2012:743.
[32] European Commission, "Assessment of plans and projects significantly affecting Natura 2000 sites. Methodological guidance on the provisions of Article 6(3) and (4) of the Habitats Directive", November 2001, 20, available at http://ec.europa.eu/environment/nature/natura2000/management/docs/art6/natura_2000_assess_en.pdf, last consulted 23.4.2015.
[33] *Waddenvereniging*, note 29 above, para. 49.

decide whether there is likely to be a significant effect[34] (or rather, as per the interpretation of the Court, whether it is reasonably possible that such a significant effect would occur).

INDIVIDUALLY OR IN COMBINATION WITH OTHER PLANS OR PROJECTS The interpretation of the provision in Article 6(3) Habitats Directive providing that significant effects could be caused "individually or in combination with other plans or projects" has so far barely been touched upon by the Court. In contrast, the Commission has provided extensive guidance on the interpretation of these words.

In its guidance on "Managing Natura 2000 sites", published in 2000, the Commission has taken the approach that the underlying aim of this combination provision is to take account of cumulative impacts of various plans and projects on the integrity of the site.[35] According to the Commission, the scope of the combination provision is threefold. It requires that plans or projects that have been: (1) completed; (2) approved but uncompleted; and (3) actually have been proposed have to be taken into account when assessing the combined impact on the integrity of the site. As a consequence of this combination provision, some plans or projects which on their own would not cause significant effects might be subject to the drawing up of an appropriate assessment, if their cumulative effects are considered to be significant. Plans or projects which have not yet been proposed have been excluded for reasons of legal certainty.

THE SIGNIFICANCE OF THE EFFECT The Court has also provided guidance on the interpretation of when effects are considered to be significant. In Waddenvereniging, it clarified that the significance of the effects is linked to the conservation objectives of the site.[36] Therefore, a plan or project will have to be regarded as having significant effects where it is likely "to undermine the site's conservation objectives". This means that all other projects or plans have to be taken into account which have or can have a negative impact on the presence of the natural habitat types or species which gave rise to the qualification as a protected site. If the plan or project is not likely to undermine the site's

---

[34] European Commission, "Non-energy mineral extraction and Natura 2000", Guidance Document, July 2010, 50, available at http://ec.europa.eu/environment/nature/natura2000/management/docs/neei_n2000_guidance.pdf, last consulted 23.4.2015.
[35] Note 32 above, 35.
[36] *Waddenvereniging and Vogelbeschermingsvereniging*, note 29 above, at 46ff.

conservation objectives, it has to be considered not to have any significant effect.[37]

The appropriate assessment stage Where the screening stage has found that a project might cause significant effects to the site, an appropriate assessment will have to be drawn up. Typically the applicant will be asked to draw up the appropriate assessment, which will then be approved and adopted as part of the file by the permitting authority.

The appropriate assessment stage corresponds to the second sentence of Article 6(3) of the Habitats Directive, that is,

> In the light of the conclusions of the assessment of the implications for the site and subject to the provisions of paragraph 4, the competent national authorities shall agree to the plan or project only after having ascertained that it will not adversely affect the integrity of the site concerned and, if appropriate, after having obtained the opinion of the general public.

The crucial question in this stage is whether an activity will have an "adverse effect on the integrity of the site" if one were to proceed with the project.

The aim of the appropriate assessment is to provide an answer to this question, since the protection regime under the Habitats Directive only allows a project to be authorised on condition that it will not adversely affect the integrity of the site concerned, unless the provisions of Article 6(4) are applied.

ADVERSELY AFFECT THE INTEGRITY OF THE SITE Central to the application of the second stage is the criterion of "adversely affecting the integrity of the site". The discussion of the interpretation of this criterion has been at the core of the Court's Sweetman judgment[38] in which the Court held that the interpretation of this criterion has to be construed in the light of the conservation objectives pursued by the Habitats Directive. The integrity of the site is not adversely affected if it can be preserved at its favourable conservation status. This entails the lasting preservation of the constitutive characteristics of the site concerned that are connected to the presence of the natural habitat type or the species whose preservation was the objective justifying the designation of the site in the list of SCIs.[39]

Based on this reasoning, the Court concluded that competent national

---

[37] Ibid.
[38] Case C-258/11 *Sweetman v An Bord Pleanala*, ECLI:EU:C:2013:220.
[39] Ibid., at 39.

authorities cannot authorise interventions in a site protected under the Habitats Directive where there is a risk of lasting harm to the ecological requirements of sites which host priority natural habitat types. According to the Court, that would particularly be so where there is a risk that an intervention of a particular kind will bring about the disappearance or the partial and irreparable destruction of a priority natural habitat type present on the site concerned.[40]

Previously, the Court had already taken a similar approach with regard to the disappearance of priority species in *Commission v Spain*.[41]

The aforementioned jurisprudence is also in line with the view taken by the Commission in its guidance on the application of Article 6 of the Habitats Directive.[42]

In *Briels*, the Dutch Raad van State queried whether there can be an adverse effect on the integrity of the site when the same natural habitat type of similar size is created within the site concerned and if affirmative, whether the creation of this similar area of the same habitat type has to be considered a compensatory measure within the meaning of Article 6(4) Habitats Directive.[43] The case had the potential to reduce the amount of negative appropriate assessments, had the Court held that the creation of the same natural habitat type of a similar size has to be considered a mitigating measure rather than a compensatory measure within the meaning of Article 6(4) of the Habitats Directive. Instead, it tightened requirements.

The widening of the A2 motorway towards Eindhoven impacted on the Natura 2000 site Vlijmens Ven, Moerputten & Bossche Broek ("the Natura 2000 site"). That site was designated by the Netherlands authorities as a SAC for, in particular, the natural habitat type molinia meadows, which is a non-priority habitat type. The Minister provided for

---

[40] Ibid., at 43.
[41] Case C-404/09 *Commission v Spain*, ECR [2011] I-11853 at 163. In this paragraph the Court ruled that: "Under the Habitats Directive, Member States must take appropriate protective measures to preserve the characteristics of sites which host priority natural habitat types and/or priority species and which have been identified by Member States with a view to their inclusion on the Community list. *Member States cannot therefore authorise intervention where there is a risk that the ecological characteristics of those sites will be seriously compromised as a result. That is particularly so where there is a risk that intervention of a particular kind will bring about the extinction of priority species present on the sites concerned*" (emphasis added).
[42] European Commission, "Managing Natura 2000 Sites. The provisions of Article 6 of the 'Habitats' Directive 92/43/EEC", 2000, 40, available at http://ec.europa.eu/environment/nature/natura2000/management/docs/art6/provision_of_art6_en.pdf, last consulted 23.4.2015.
[43] Case C-521/12 *Briels*, ECLI:EU:C:2014:330.

a certain number of measures aimed at lessening the environmental impact of the A2 motorway project.

Assessment concluded that the A2 motorway project would have negative implications for the existing area comprising the habitat type molinia meadows. The assessment also stated that sustainable conservation and development of the molinia meadows be achieved if the hydrological system was completed. In that regard the A2 motorway project provides for improvements to the hydrological situation in Vlijmens Ven, which will allow the molinia meadows to expand on the site. The Minister states that this will allow the development of a larger area of molinia meadows of higher quality, thereby ensuring that the conservation objectives for this habitat type are maintained through the creation of new molinia meadows.

Briels and Others brought an action against the two ministerial orders before the referring court. They took the view that the Minister could not lawfully adopt the orders for the A2 motorway project, given the negative implications of the widening of the A2 motorway for the Natura 2000 site in question. They argued that the development of new molinia meadows on the site, as provided for by the ministerial orders at issue in the main proceedings, could not be taken into account in the determination of whether the site's integrity was affected. They submitted that such a measure cannot be categorised as a "mitigating measure", a concept which is, moreover, absent from the Habitats Directive.

The Netherlands Raad van State suggested that the criteria for determining whether the integrity of the site concerned is affected are not to be found either in the Habitats Directive or the Court's case law, whence the question

> whether the expression "will not adversely affect the integrity of the site" in Article 6(3) of [the Habitats Directive is] to be interpreted in such a way that, where the project affects the area of a protected natural habitat type within [a Natura 2000 site], the integrity of the site is not adversely affected if in the framework of the project an area of that natural habitat type of equal or greater size [to the existing area] is created within that site?

and "[If not], is the creation of a new area of a natural habitat type then to be regarded in that case as a 'compensatory measure' within the meaning of Article 6(4) of the [Habitats Directive]?"

The Court held (at 28) that the application of the precautionary principle in the context of the implementation of Article 6(3) of the Habitats Directive requires the competent national authority to assess the implications of the project for the Natura 2000 site concerned in view of the site's conservation objectives and taking into account the protective measures forming part of that project aimed at avoiding or reducing any direct adverse effects for the site, in order to ensure that it does not adversely affect the integrity of the site.

However (at 29), protective measures provided for in a project which are aimed at compensating for the negative effects of the project on a Natura 2000 site cannot be taken into account in the assessment of the implications of the project provided for in Article 6(3).

As a supporting argument (at 32), the Court suggested that, as a rule, any positive effects of a future creation of a new habitat which is aimed at compensating for the loss of area and quality of that same habitat type on a protected site, even where the new area will be bigger and of higher quality, are highly difficult to forecast with any degree of certainty and, in any event, will be visible only several years into the future. Consequently, they cannot be taken into account at the procedural stage provided for in Article 6(3) of the Habitats Directive.

Authorisation for the project therefore needs to be given in accordance with the procedure for compensation measures, provided for in Article 6(4). This does not make the project impossible. It just makes the outcome less certain and at the least more lengthy.

Many developers (and authorities with them) had hoped that a different answer from the CJEU would have had the potential to reduce the amount of negative appropriate assessments. *Quod certe non.*

CONTENT OF THE APPROPRIATE ASSESSMENT To verify whether a project will adversely affect the integrity of a site an appropriate assessment has to be drawn up.

The appropriate assessment requires that all aspects of a project which can, by themselves or in combination with other plans or projects, affect the site's conservation objectives, be identified in the light of the best scientific knowledge in the field.

The purpose of the appropriate assessment is to remove all reasonable scientific doubt as to the effects of the works proposed on a site. An assessment cannot be regarded as appropriate if it contains gaps and lacks complete, precise and definitive findings and conclusions capable of removing all reasonable scientific doubt as to the effects of the works proposed.[44]

Scientific information will have to be collected to exclude potential risks of the projects. Where no existing information is available, this information will have to be generated by conducting further scientific investigations.[45]

---

[44] Case C-404/09 *Commission v Spain*, ECLI:EU:C:2011:768, at 100.
[45] Note 32 above.

Based on the acquired or generated information, the effects of the project individually or in combination with other projects and plans should be predicted and assessed against the conservation objectives of the site.

Where no exact prediction is possible, it is recommended to apply the precautionary principle and take into accounts the effects of the *worst-case scenario*.[46]

Finally, attention will have to be paid to mitigating measures. Mitigating measures are aimed at minimising or even cancelling the negative impact of a plan or project, during or after its completion[47] (e.g. no operation during the breeding season). They can be proposed either by applicant of the authorisation or imposed by the competent authorities. Mitigating measures can help to make a project acceptable to the competent authorities which, without these measures, individually or in combination with other projects or plans, would adversely affect the integrity of the site. Usually – although not strictly required for the application of Article 6(3) – alternative solutions are also considered in the appropriate assessment.

Taking into account the elements above, the appropriate assessment will have a duly justified conclusion on the impact of the project on a site, taking into account the mitigating measures. There are two possibilities: (1) a positive assessment (i.e. no adverse effects on the integrity of the site); or (2) a negative assessment (i.e. there will be adverse effects or it cannot be excluded that there will be adverse effects on the integrity of the site).

PUBLIC CONSULTATION   Article 6(3) Habitats Directive provides the possibility for the authorities to take a decision on the project after having obtained the opinion of the general public, if deemed appropriate. The

---

[46] This approach is consistent with the interpretation of the precautionary principle given by the European Commission in its Communication of 2 February 2000 on the precautionary principle, COM (2000) 1, 28. "Risk characterisation corresponds to the qualitative and/or quantitative estimation, taking account of inherent uncertainties, of the probability, of the frequency and severity of the known or potential adverse environmental or health effects liable to occur. It is established on the basis of the three preceding and closely depends on the uncertainties, variations, working hypotheses and conjectures made at each stage of the process. *When the available data are inadequate or non-conclusive, a prudent and cautious approach to environmental protection, health or safety could be to opt for the worst-case hypothesis. When such hypotheses are accumulated, this will lead to an exaggeration of the real risk but gives a certain assurance that it will not be underestimated*" (emphasis added).

[47] Note 42 above.

Wild Birds and Habitats Directives do not include a legal obligation to obtain the opinion of the general public.

AG Sharpston in *Sweetman* pointed out that invoking the view of stakeholders may often provide valuable practical insights based on their local knowledge of the site in question as well as other relevant background information that might otherwise be unavailable for conducting such assessment.[48]

On the other hand, from a developer's point of view, obtaining the opinion of the general public can imply multiple disadvantages. Firstly, the opinion of the general public will generally be asked after the appropriate assessment has been drawn up. This means that the late input of the general public could lead to unwelcome requirements from the competent authorities to carry out additional research, or, in a worst case, contradict the premises and outcomes of the appropriate assessment. Furthermore, public consultations generally slow down permitting procedures.

Alternative solutions test The third stage of the authorisation procedure corresponds to the first part of the first sentence of Article 6(4). Similar to the screening stage, it sets a threshold which has to be met prior to being able to invoke the actual IROPI exception. The first part of the first sentence of Article 6(4) reads: "If, in spite of a negative assessment of the implications for the site and in the absence of alternative solutions ..." (emphasis added). Thus, where one would seek to invoke the exception of Article 6(4), it will have to be demonstrated that there are no alternative solutions available for the carrying out of a project.

The alternative solutions test requires the competent authorities to examine whether the project put forward for authorisation is the least damaging solution for habitats, for species and for the integrity of the Natura 2000 site and that no other feasible alternative exists that would not affect the integrity of the site.[49] This examination could, for example, include alternative locations, different scales or designs of development, alternative processes or a withdrawal of the plan (the "zero-option").[50]

According to the settled case law of the Court, this examination of the existence of less harmful alternatives requires a weighing up against the damage caused to the site by the plan or project under consideration.[51]

---

[48] Opinion Sharpston AG in Case C-258/11 *Sweetman v. An Bord Pleanala*, ECLI:EU:C:2013:220, at 49.
[49] EC, note 42 above, 4.
[50] Ibid., 43.
[51] See for example Case C-182/10 *Solvay*, ECLI:EU:C:2012:82, at 73–74; and Case C-304/05 *Commission v Italy*, ECLI:EU:C:2007:532, at 83.

The case law of the Court is clear: alternatives can be weighed only against their effect on the integrity of the site. As a consequence, other assessment criteria, such as economic criteria, cannot be seen as overruling this ecological criterion.[52] The mere fact that the least harmful solution would for example be twice as expensive, cannot be taken into account in the alternative solutions test.

ANTICIPATING THE ALTERNATIVE SOLUTIONS TEST   Although Article 6(3) Habitats Directive does not require looking beyond the plan or project proposed and addressing alternative solutions while drawing up an appropriate assessment, the alternative solutions test of Article 6(4) will often already be integrated in the appropriate assessment document drawn up in the "assessment phase".

Invoking the "imperative reasons of overriding public interest" – exception (IROPI)   Once it has been demonstrated that there are no alternative solutions to the project concerned, the actual IROPI exception ("imperative reasons of overriding public interest") can be invoked. According to the settled case law of the Court, Article 6(4) as an exception to the general rule of Article 6(3) Habitats Directive must be strictly interpreted.[53]

The IROPI exception allows a competent authority to authorise a project, in spite of a negative assessment, where it considers that there are IROPI present which justify the project being realised.[54] In *Solvay*, the Court ruled that an interest, capable of justifying within the meaning of Article 6(4) Habitats Directive, must be both "public" and "overriding", meaning that it must be of such an importance that it can be weighed against that Directive's objective of the conservation of natural habitats and wild fauna and flora.[55] Subsequent case law confirmed this (in particular *Nomarchiaki Aftodioikisi Aitoloakarnanias*[56]).

According to the Commission's Guidance this requires a long-term

---

[52]   European Commission, "Guidance document on article 6(4) of the 'Habitats Directive' 92/43/EEC", July 2012, available at http://ec.europa.eu/environment/nature/natura2000/management/docs/art6/new_guidance_art6_4_en.pdf, last consulted 23.4.2015.
[53]   *Solvay*, note 51 above, at 73; *Commission v Italy*, note 51 above, at 82.
[54]   R. Clotten and I. Tafur, "Are Imperative Reasons Imperiling the Habitats Directive? An Assessment of Article 6(4) and the IROPI Exception", in: G. Jones (ed.), *The Habitats Directive. A Developer's Obstacle Course?*, Oxford: Hart Publishing, 2012, 167.
[55]   *Solvay*, note 51 above, at 75.
[56]   Case C-43/10, *Nomarchiaki Aftodioikisi Aitoloakarnanias*, ECLI:EU:C:2011: 253 at 121.

interest.⁵⁷ Short-term economic interests or other short-term interests are not sufficient to outweigh the long-term conservation objectives of the Habitats Directive.

In *Solvay* the Court clarified that works intended for the location or expansion of a private undertaking can only in exceptional cases fall within the ambit of the IROPI exception if their very nature and economic and social context demonstrate the presence of an overriding public interest.⁵⁸

Article 6(4) provides guidance on the reasons which can be taken into account as IROPI for the purpose of applying Article 6(4):

> If, in spite of a negative assessment of the implications for the site and in the absence of alternative solutions, a plan or project must nevertheless be carried out for imperative reasons of overriding public interest, *including those of a social or economic nature*, the Member State shall take all compensatory measures necessary to ensure that the overall coherence of Natura 2000 is protected. It shall inform the Commission of the compensatory measures adopted.
>
> Where the site concerned hosts a priority natural habitat type and/or a priority species, *the only considerations which may be raised are those relating to human health or public safety, to beneficial consequences of primary importance for the environment or, further to an opinion from the Commission, to other imperative reasons of overriding public interest.* (Emphasis added)

As is apparent from the text of Article 6(4), the nature of the IROPI that may be taken into account will depend on whether or not the plan or project proposed adversely affects a site which hosts a priority natural habitat type and/or a priority species.

The IROPI which might be taken into account will be more restrictive where a priority natural habitat type or a priority species is available on the site. Furthermore, additional procedural requirements come into play where a priority natural habitat type and/or a priority species is at issue.

In all cases, Member States are required to take compensatory measures to ensure the overall coherence of Natura 2000 is protected. These measures have to be notified to the Commission.

ABSENCE OF A PRIORITY NATURAL HABITAT TYPE OR PRIORITY SPECIES   If no priority species and priority natural habitat types are present on the site, the national authorities may invoke a broad range of imperative reasons of overriding public interest to justify its authorisation of the project, including those of a social or economic nature.

The text of Article 6(4) clarifies that reasons relating to human health,

---

⁵⁷ EC, note 52 above, 7.
⁵⁸ *Solvay*, note 51 above, at 76–77.

public safety and beneficial consequences of primary importance for the environment can constitute IROPI. Nevertheless, due to the inclusion of reasons of a social or economic nature for instances where no priority habitats or species are involved, a broader range of reasons to justify a project adversely affecting the integrity of a protected site can come into play.

In the past two decades, the Court has rarely expressed itself about which reasons can be considered to fall within the ambit of the IROPI exception. The facts of *Commission v Italy* are a good example of the Court's reluctance to enter into this issue. Italy had decided to improve a skiing area and to provide associated facilities in a protected area with a view to holding the 2005 World Alpine Ski Championships.[59] Italy had justified its authorisation of the project on the basis that a failure to carry out such plans would result in "slow but unavoidable economic decline" and sought to justify its decision on the basis of their socio-economic value.[60] The Court, however, did not rule on this issue, since it found that no appropriate assessment had been carried out.

In more recent jurisprudence however, the Court has ruled on what reasons can be understood to fall within the IROPI exception, and in particular under reasons of a social or economic nature. In *Commission v Spain*, at stake was whether Spain was allowed to justify its decisions to authorise several (open cast) mining projects in protected sites on the basis of the importance of these projects for the local economy. While the Court again noted that no appropriate assessment had been carried out, it did provide an answer to the question of whether the importance of mining activities for the local economy could fall within the ambit of the IROPI exception, in particular reasons of a social or economic nature. The Court explicitly ruled that the importance of mining activities for the local economy is capable of constituting an imperative reason of overriding public interest within the meaning of Article 6(4) Habitats Directive.[61]

Other reasons which have been considered to fall within the ambit of the IROPI exception for non-priority natural habitats and species are improvement of irrigation and the supply of drinking water.[62]

Further guidance on the reasons which can be considered IROPI where there is the presence of non-priority natural habitat types and non-priority

---

[59] *Commission v Italy*, note 51 above.
[60] R. Clotten and I. Tafur, "Are Imperative Reasons Imperiling the Habitats Directive? An Assessment of Article 6(4) and the IROPI Exception", in: G. Jones (ed.), *The Habitats Directive. A Developer's Obstacle Course?*, Oxford: Hart Publishing, 2012, 173.
[61] *Commission v Spain*, note 41 above, at 109.
[62] *Nomarchiaki Aftodioikisi Aitoloakarnanias*, note 56 above, at 122.

species on the site, can be found in the Commission Guidance document on the application of Article 6(4) of the Habitats Directive of 2012,[63] which clarifies that the Commission considers a reason to fall within the ambit of IROPI in cases where the plan or project proves to be indispensable:

- within the framework of actions or policies aiming to protect fundamental values for the citizen's life (health, safety, environment);
- within the framework of actions or policies aiming to protect fundamental policies for the State and Society;
- within the framework of carrying out activities of economic or social nature, fulfilling specific obligations of public service.

Note that where an EU Member State invokes the IROPI exception in the absence of a priority natural habitat type or priority species, there is no obligation to request an advice of the Commission.

PRESENCE OF A PRIORITY NATURAL HABITAT TYPE AND/OR A PRIORITY SPECIES Where an EU Member State seeks to authorise a plan or project with an adverse impact on a site hosting a priority natural habitat type and/or a priority species, the requirements to justify the project are in principle more limited. Article 6(4) Habitats Directive only expressly mentions a justification of the project on the basis of IROPI based on human health or public safety, if there are beneficial consequences of primary importance for the environment. Other IROPI can, however, be invoked as well, upon the condition that the competent national authority first seeks the non-binding opinion of the Commission.

The Commission has, for example, accepted the justification of a planned motorway in a protected site on the basis that the two regions where the motorway was going to be built suffered from high unemployment, had a lower than average gross national product, and were subject to development funding by the Structural Fund of the EEC.[64] With regard to the extension of a Daimler Chrysler plant (where jumbo jets were produced) into a Natura 2000 site, the Commission accepted the justification of the German authorities that the project was of outstanding importance for the region of Hamburg and northern Germany, as well as for the European aerospace industry.[65]

---

[63] Note 52 above, 8.
[64] Opinion of the European Commission of 18 December 1995 on the intersection of the Peene Valley (Germany) by the planned A12 motorway.
[65] Opinion of the European Commission of 14 April 2000 concerning the extension of the site of Daimler Chrysler Aerospace Airbus Gmbh in Hamburg-Finkenwerder (Germany).

Other reasons which have been given favourable advice by the Commission include the necessity for a new water reservoir where the currently available basin did not provide enough water for human consumption, industrial uses and agriculture;[66] expansion of airports into a Natura 2000 site which are considered airports of common interest within the meaning of the relevant EU legislation;[67] the building of a new port on an island;[68] and even the expansion of an existing economic area and to allow development of a car manufacturing complex together with the necessary infrastructure such as roads and railway connections.[69] In the latter case, the Hungarian Government invoked reasons related to the creation of long-term employment and sustainable development of the region, the potential of the project to prevent the labour force from leaving the region in search for job opportunities, a contribution to the Hungarian gross national product by 1.8 per cent, as well as reference to the facilitation of repayment of loans by Hungary to the International Monetary Fund (IMF) and its effects on the Hungarian foreign trade balance.

TAKING ALL NECESSARY COMPENSATORY MEASURES Article 6(4) imposes the obligation on the competent authority to take all compensatory measures (or have the applicant take all compensatory measures) necessary to ensure that the overall coherence of Natura 2000 is protected.

To be able to verify compliance with this obligation, there will have to be clarification prior to adoption of its decision (in case it concerns a non-priority natural habitat type or non-priority species) or prior to its request of the Commission's opinion (in case it concerns a priority natural habitat type or species) of the compensatory measures proposed.

Compensatory measures are measures independent of the project and are intended to offset the negative effects of the project (e.g. recreation of the habitat type concerned on another site). They have to be additional to the measures already taken or proposed by a Member State.

In addition, the compensatory measures have to be sufficient to ensure

---

[66] Opinion of the European Commission of 7 May 2005 concerning the request by the Kingdom of Spain in relation to the La Brena II Reservoir Project.

[67] Opinion of the Commission of 6 June 2005 delivered at the request of Germany on the planning approval procedure launched under aviation law for the expansion of Karlsruhe/Baden-Baden Airport.

[68] Opinion of the Commission concerning the request by the Kingdom of Spain in relation to the construction project of the new port in Granadilla (Tenerife).

[69] Opinion of the Commission of 25 January 2011 concerning the modification of the development plan of the Gyor town (Hungary). Note that in this case the Hungary Government invoked reasons relating to creation of long-term employment.

the overall coherence of Natura 2000. The meaning of this requirement is twofold.

- On the one hand, it has to be measured against the overall conservation objectives of the site and in particular the presence of habitats and species triggering its protection regime. This means that compensation measures should be considered and established with regard to restoring the negative effects towards those habitats and species. This implies that the habitat types or species concerned have to be restored at the level existing before the realisation of the project.
- On the other hand, the term "overall" implies reference to the broader region wherein the adverse effects take place. In this regard, it has to be recalled that the Habitats Directive has divided the EU into nine biogeographical regions, each of which has its own typical natural characteristics. Within the same biogeographical region, there is thus an assumption of similar natural characteristics. Reference to the word "overall" has to be interpreted as a reference to the wider biogeographical region wherein the site which is adversely affected is located.[70] Compensatory measures therefore do not necessarily have to be implemented on the same site, but they do have to pertain to the same biogeographical region.

Based on the above elements, in order to ensure the overall coherence of Natura 2000, a compensatory measure proposed for a project has to: (a) address, in comparable proportions, the habitats and species negatively affected; and (b) provide functions comparable to those which had justified the selection criteria of the original site within the biogeographical region concerned.[71] Both conditions have to be met at the same time.

As a general principle, the compensatory measures should have been implemented by the time the adverse effects to the site become effective.

It will normally be the polluter – that is, the person causing the adverse effects to the protected site – who will bear the costs for the implementation of these compensating measures. On a case-by-case basis arrangements can, however, be made about co-financing by the competent national authorities or the application of alternative funding mechanisms (e.g. subsidies).[72]

The Commission has provided further guidance on what to include in a

---

[70] Note 52 above.
[71] Ibid., 13.
[72] Such funding by the State may, however, raise issues of State aid, which depending on the scheme may warrant further investigation.

programme of compensatory measures as well as criteria to be taken into account for designing compensatory measures.[73]

Declassification of sites under the Habitats Directive
In *Cascina Tre Pini*,[74] the Court dealt with a case that concerned the possibility of declassification of a site as a SAC, and the rights of owners of the site concerned in same. Classification as a SAC evidently brings with it a variety of restrictions on the use of the land. Owners' interest in declassification therefore may understandably be very high. The fourth sentence of Article 4(1) Habitats Directive provides that "Where appropriate, Member States shall propose adaptation of the list in the light of the results of the surveillance referred to in Article 11."

Article 9 Habitats Directive refers to the possibility of withdrawing the protected status of certain areas:

> The Commission, acting in accordance with the procedure laid down in Article 21, shall periodically review the contribution of Natura 2000 towards achievement of the objectives set out in Article 2 and 3. In this context, a special area of conservation may be considered for declassification where this is warranted by natural developments noted as a result of the surveillance provided for in Article 11.

AG Kokott in her opinion,[75] even without using the expression, effectively resorted to the *nemo auditur* principle: the Directive does not limit the reasons for declassification to loss of suitability due to purely natural phenomena. However, it would be inappropriate to reward a sloppy Member State, or one which purposely neglects a SAC, with subsequent declassification of the site. Whence the AG suggested to answer one of the core questions of the preliminary review as follows:

> pursuant to the fourth sentence of Article 4(1) of the Habitats Directive, the competent national authorities must consider, on a request from an owner of land which forms part of an SCI, whether it should be proposed to the Commission that that land should be excluded from the SCI, provided that the request is based on substantiated reasoning that, *despite compliance with Article 6(2) to (4) of the directive*, the land cannot make a contribution to the conservation of natural habitats and wild fauna and flora or to the setting up of the Natura 2000 network. (Emphasis added: Article 6(2–4) lists the obligations of Member States vis-à-vis the areas.)

---

[73] Note 52 above, 23.
[74] Case C-301/12 *Cascina Tre Pini*, ECLI:EU:C:2014:214.
[75] Opinion Kokott AG in Case C-301/12 *Cascina Tre Pini s.s.*, ECLI:EU:C:2013:420, at 55.

The AG also suggested, in line with general principles of EU law, that owners of the land concerned must be given an opportunity to submit observations when Member States are considering whether to propose to the Commission that the list of SCIs should be adapted in respect of that land.

The Court, in its judgement,[76] agreed, albeit with emphasis on the more than just passing degradation of the site:

> It must, however, be pointed out that a mere allegation of environmental degradation of an SCI, made by the owner of land included in that site, cannot suffice of itself to bring about such an adaptation of the list of SCIs. It is essential that that degradation should make the site irretrievably unsuitable to ensure the conservation of natural habitats and of the wild fauna and flora or the setting up of the Natura 2000 network, so that that site can definitively no longer contribute to the achievement of the objectives of the directive set out in Articles 2 and 3 thereof. Thus, not all degradation of a site on the list of SCIs justifies its declassification.

The judgment makes common sense to owners (and in view of the right to property), as it emphasises authorities' duties under the Habitats Directive.

C. Relation between the Habitats Directive and the EIA Directive

As demonstrated above, Article 6 of the Habitats Directive requires an *appropriate assessment* to be drawn up for a project; the EIA Directive requires the drawing up of an EIA to identify the likely significant effects of the project. The procedures of the environmental assessment and the appropriate assessment are closely linked. Both procedures start off from the same definition of "project". Although this notion has not been defined in the Habitats Directive, it has become settled case law of the Court that the definition of project as mentioned in Article 1(2) of the EIA Directive (see further Chapter 7 I) is relevant to defining the concept of plan under the Habitats Directive.[77] Furthermore, both procedures use the concept of "likely to cause significant effects" to trigger the requirement to draw up an EIA and an appropriate assessment. It should be noted that the EIA Directive allows EU Member States to expressly provide for a single procedure in order integrate the EIA with the requirements

---

[76] Case C-301/12, note 74 above, at 30f.
[77] See for example ECJ 14 January 2010, C-226/08 *Stadt Papenburg*, para. 38; CJEU 27 September 2004, C-127-02 *Waddenvereniging and Vogelbeschermingsvereniging*, at 46.

of other directives, such as the appropriate assessment under the Habitats Directive (Article 2(2) EIA Directive). Both documents – either in an integrated form or individually – have to be drawn up prior to the permitting decision by the competent authorities.

However, while the appropriate assessment and the EIA requirements can be integrated into one single report, this does not prejudice the fact that the requirements of both Directives have to be met. Despite their similarity, there remain a number of important distinctions to be taken into account.

The most important distinction between the EIA and the appropriate assessment can be found in the application of the word "significant", as well as in their possible impact on the decision-making process. The application of "significant" within the framework of the EIA Directive will be much broader in scope than "significant" under the Habitats Directive. Significant effects under the EIA Directive can consist of direct and indirect secondary, cumulative, short, medium and long-term, permanent and temporary, positive and negative significant effects on human beings, fauna and flora; soil, water, air, climate and the landscape; material assets and cultural heritage; as well as on the interaction between the aforementioned elements.[78] The assessment of significant effects under the Habitats Directive is more targeted and, thus, more limited in scope. Only effects which relate to the site's conservation objectives, that is, which relate to the species or natural habitat types for which the site concerned has been designated as an SCI or SPA, are to be taken into account. This will require a different methodology to be applied for an appropriate assessment. Therefore, the Commission recommends in its methodological guidance on Articles 6(3) and 6(4) of the Habitats Directive that the appropriate assessment should be clearly distinguishable and identified within the EIA (where integrated in the EIA) or reported separately.[79]

The second major distinction between both assessments is their possible impact on the outcome of the decision-making process. An EIA only has to be taken into account by the competent national authority in the

---

[78] European Commission, "Non-energy mineral extraction and Natura 2000", Guidance Document, July 2010, 25, available on http://ec.europa.eu/environment/nature/natura2000/management/docs/neei_n2000_guidance.pdf, last consulted 16.12.16.

[79] European Commission, "Assessment of plans and projects significantly affecting Natura 2000 sites. Methodological guidance on the provisions of Article 6(3) and (4) of the Habitats Directive", November 2001, 35, available on http://ec.europa.eu/environment/nature/natura2000/management/docs/art6/natura_2000_assess_en.pdf, last consulted 16.12.16.

decision-making process.[80] It does not in any way prevent the competent authority from granting a permit for the project. It is rather an instrument to allow the competent national authorities to take a decision with full knowledge of the effects of a proposed project on the environment. By contrast, the outcome of an appropriate assessment is binding for a competent authority where it is negative. Where there is a negative appropriate assessment, the competent national authority will not be able to authorise the project, unless it considers the conditions for application of Article 6(4) of the Habitats Directive are met.

At present, there thus remains a gap between both the methodological approach and the possible outcome of an EIA and of an appropriate assessment on the decision-making process. The 2014 amendment of the Directive adapted the EIA Directive to take into account modern challenges such as biodiversity, climate change, disaster risks and availability of natural resources, as well as to reduce administrative complexity and increase economic efficiency, where the obligation to carry out an EIA arises together with the obligation to carry out an appropriate assessment. In order to foster this coordinated or joint approach by EU Member States, Article 3(1)(b) of the EIA has been modified to include a specific reference that both direct and indirect significant effects on species and habitats protected under the Habitats and the Wild Birds Directives should be included in the EIA.

II. SOIL[81]

According to the database of the EEA on soil contamination and clean-up, it will take several decades to clean-up the nearly 300,000 (potentially) contaminated sites in the EU.[82]

The distribution of polluting activities and the clean-up commitments vary from Member State to Member State and from one industry sector to the next. The most common sources of soil pollution are industrial and commercial activities (36 per cent), oil activities (17 per cent) and the treatment and disposal of waste (15 per cent); the least risk of soil pollution is associated with mining (2 per cent) and military activities (1 per cent).[83] Further, the most frequently spilled and polluting materials in the EU are

---

[80] Article 8 EIA Directive.
[81] This section was co-authored with Colienne Linard.
[82] EEA, "Overview of progress in management of soil contamination in WCE and some SEE countries", 2010.
[83] EEA, "Contamination from local sources", 2009.

heavy metals (37.3 per cent) and mineral oil (33.7 per cent).[84] Other risks of soil pollution and site contamination are posed by inadequate disposal of waste and industrial emissions resulting from inadequate storage and leakage of dangerous chemicals.[85] Between 1990 and 2006, at least 275 hectares of soil per day were permanently lost through soil sealing (the permanent covering of land and its soil by impermeable, artificial material such as asphalt or concrete), amounting to 1000 km² per year or an area of the size of Cyprus every ten years. Soil is not a renewable natural resource as it takes millions of years to regenerate and impacts are mostly of a transboundary nature.[86] Soil degradation affects the soil's function to produce food, prevent drought and flooding, stop biodiversity loss, and tackle climate change.[87]

Thus, once damage has occurred it is permanent and irreversible;[88] prevention is consequently important in that regard. To date, there is no European legal instrument expressly dealing with soil threats and imposing measures to protect it; the issue is only addressed indirectly through legal instruments that were not created to tackle the issue of soil in the first place.[89] Further, international conventions, such as the World Soil Charter[90] and the European Soil Charter (ESC)[91] are also addressing soil protection issues. Moreover, several Member States have drafted policy on soil protection at a national level. However, their non-binding nature tends to severely limit their on-the-ground impact.[92]

---

[84] Ibid.
[85] EEA, "Management of contaminated sites in Western Europe", 2000, at 8.
[86] EEA, "The European environment – state and outlook 2010: urban environment", 2010, at 6.
[87] Commission Report, "The implementation of the Soil Thematic Strategy and ongoing activities", Brussels, 13.2.2012, COM (2012) 46.
[88] EEA, "The European environment – State and Outlook 2010: Soil", 2010, at 4; Commission Communication, "Our life insurance, our natural capital: an EU biodiversity strategy to 2020", COM (2011) 244, 3.5.2011; as well as R. Scarenghe and F. Marsan, "The anthropogenic sealing of soils in urban areas", 90 *Landscape and Urban Planning* 1–2 (2009), 1–10, at 2.
[89] See the instruments discussed below.
[90] World Soil Charter, FAO, Rome, 1982.
[91] European Soil Charter, Council of Europe, 1972, further discussed below.
[92] A. Wyatt, "The dirt on international environmental law regarding soils: Is the existing regime adequate?", 19 *Duke Environmental Law & Policy Forum*, 1 (2008), 165–208, at 187.

A. The Soil Thematic Strategy

The only measure directly addressing the issue is the 2006 Soil Thematic Strategy (STS),[93] which provides a common framework for soil protection across the EU. The strategy consists of a communication that establishes a ten-year work programme; an impact assessment analysing the economic, social and environmental impacts of the proposed measures; and a draft framework directive, which has not yet been adopted.

The STS's objective is to define a common and comprehensive approach to soil protection, focusing on the preservation of soil functions. Its main goal is to slow down and reverse the process of degradation, ensuring that EU soils stay healthy for future generations and remain capable of supporting ecosystems.[94] The draft of the 7th EAP further includes a call to consider legislation addressing soil quality in Europe, offering a framework for action.

The draft Directive[95] establishes preventive measures aiming to ensure the sustainable use of soil. It is built on three pillars. Firstly, where soil is used in ways that hampers its functions, mitigating actions must be undertaken. As a result of its comprehensive construction, the proposed Directive encompasses all threats to soil protection. Second, Member States need to identify soil problems by determining areas where the soil undergoes certain threats such as erosion, sealing, or salinisation. The involvement of all Member States is essential to ensure soil protection tailored to each situation as the threats vary from place to place. Finally, the third pillar of the Soil Framework Directive proposal outlines operational measures that Member States have to take to act upon the risks identified by adopting programmes of measures for risk areas, national remediation strategies for the contaminated sites, and measures to limit or mitigate soil degradation. Member States are free to set their own targets and to determine means and time frame. This is one of the compromises taken as an attempt to find a common European answer to soil protection. Article 8 of the draft Directive establishes a programme of measures to combat erosion, organic matter decline, compaction, salinisation and landslides, including "at least risk reduction targets, the appropriate measures for

---

[93] Commission Report, "The implementation of the Soil Thematic Strategy and ongoing activities", Brussels, 13.2.2012, COM (2012) 46.
[94] EEA, "The European environment – state and outlook 2010: soil", 2010, at 30.
[95] Proposal of 22 September 2006 for a Directive of the European Parliament and of the Council establishing a framework for the protection of soil and amending Directive 2004/35/EC, COM (2006) 232 final.

reaching those targets, a timetable for the implementation of those measures and an estimate of the allocation of private or public means for the funding of those measures."

The Soil Framework Directive proposal has been pending since 2006 and remains at the proposal stage as certain Member States are reluctant to take on additional policy obligations and mandatory requirements to identify and remediate areas of risk of soil degradation.[96] Amongst other reasons, private ownership of soil resources was pinpointed as a potential issue against European regulation, as well as subsidiarity grounds.[97] This argument is debatable, taking into account the transboundary nature of soil degradation. Arguably, action at the EU level would lead to better overall results because of its scale and effects compared with actions taken at Member State level.[98] In addition, the fact that Member States have a discretionary power to determine the extent of their soil policy implementing this Soil Framework Directive should set aside the argument of the subsidiarity principle.[99]

B. European Soil Charter and other European Legislation Indirectly Addressing Soil

The Council of Europe adopted the ESC with the objective to promote the protection of soils against damage from natural or human causes, and their rehabilitation. The Charter is also open for signature for non-European Member States. Europe is the only region in the world to use this form of a non-binding instrument to develop special regional rules for soil, as well as a comprehensive definition of the term "soil".[100] The Charter embodies the balance between modern society and nature's needs.

Significantly, at European level there are various directives and policies

---

[96] M. Petersen, "European soil protection law after the setback of December 2007 – existing law and outlook", 17 *European Energy and Environmental Law Review*, 3 (2008), 146–155, at 149.

[97] Ibid., as well as EEA, "The European environment – state and outlook 2010: soil", 2010, at 30.

[98] Ibid.

[99] For more explanation on the controversy about the relevance of the subsidiarity principle impeaching the adoption of the Soil Framework Directive, see ibid., as well as G. Van Calster, "Will the EC get a finger in each pie? EC law and policy developments in soil protection and brown fields redevelopment", 16 *Journal of Environmental Law*, 1 (2004), 3–17.

[100] I. Hannam and B. Boer, "Legal and institutional frameworks for sustainable soils", IUCN, 2002, at 60; Preamble and Articles 1–2 of the European Soil Charter (ESC), Council of Europe, 1972.

that relate to soil protection through mechanisms initially developed for the purpose of inter alia combating climate change, protection of biodiversity and agriculture policy.

For instance, the Habitats Directive, which aims at biodiversity protection by the conservation of wild fauna and flora, is based on a comprehensive approach for all the natural components of a natural habitat. Member States are required to take measures to maintain or restore natural habitats and to designate SACs. Soil protection is not only mentioned in Annex I but it is in fact an immanent and essential part of nature conservation as a whole. Since soil literally constitutes the foundation of all terrestrial ecosystems and habitats, an effective protection of flora and fauna and their habitat requires soil protection as well. This shows that soil protection must be seen as a fundamental part of the European nature conservation laws as a whole.

Moreover, the Habitats Directive provides the option for Member States to insert soil protection in their land use planning and development policies for the Natura 2000 network to encourage the management of landscape features, which are important for fauna and flora (Article 10).

Another tool regarding biodiversity protection through limiting soil sealing is the Biodiversity Thematic Strategy.[101] It has not yet been adopted, but both the Parliament[102] and the Commission[103] have released communications and resolutions on the matter indicating further steps.

As for climate change, the White Paper on adapting to climate change of 2009[104] recognised the interlinkage of climate change matters and soil. In its White Paper, the Commission recognises the role that soil can play in providing ecosystems with services such as carbon sequestration or flood protection that are directly linked to climate change. Soil also has an important potential in terms of mitigation.

Moreover, the EIA Directive and the SEA Directive reinforce soil protection as they are supporting instruments for the protection of soil from harmful developments: on the one hand, Article 3 of the EIA

---

[101] Commission Communication, "Our life insurance, our natural capital: an EU biodiversity strategy to 2020", COM (2011) 244, 3.5.2011.

[102] European Parliament, "Resolution of the European Parliament on our life insurance, our natural capital: an EU biodiversity strategy to 2020", 20.04.2012.

[103] Commission Communication, "Our life insurance, our natural capital: an EU biodiversity strategy to 2020", COM (2011) 244, 3.5.2011.

[104] European Commission, "White Paper – adapting to climate change: towards European framework for action", COM (2009) 147.

Directive states that in the planning phase of large construction projects, all impacts on the affected environmental resources have to be taken into account and limited as far as possible. According to the literature, soil functions are vital to other environmental services, so this should be assessed to avoid inappropriate sealing.[105] The EIA should analyse any direct and indirect environmental impact that a project could have on several elements of the environment, and soil is stated as one such element, along with water and air. Land use is also considered as a criterion to take into account when analysing whether or not the project will affect the surrounding environment. However, regarding Annex II of the Directive, soil is not treated like water and air: only where projects would degrade it chemically or biologically is there a binding obligation for the Member States to undertake an EIA, not for physical degradation.

The SEA Directive does not include a direct reference to soil as an element of the environment which needs to be considered and for which an assessment is needed.

The SEA Directive requires plans and programmes which concern "agriculture, forestry, transport, tourism, town and country planning or land use" (Article 3(2)(a)) to be assessed for their environmental impacts. This allows the moving of urban development away from high value soils in order to reuse already developed sites.[106] The Directive thus considers urbanisation in its land planning. For these plans and programmes, Member States need to write an environmental report describing the potential environmental impacts of the plan, notably its impact on soil (Article 5).

As for the Common Agricultural Policy (CAP), all aspects of soil protection are comprised through the good agricultural and environmental conditions since the introduction of cross compliance in 2003.[107] Cross compliance is a mechanism which links compliance by farmers to basic standards regarding the environment and direct payments. Consequently, since 2005, all farmers benefiting from direct payments must comply with cross compliance. This mechanism comprises two streams:

---

[105] G. Prokop, H. Jobstmann and A. Schoenbauer, "Report on overview of best practices for limiting soil sealing and mitigating its effects in EU-27", Environment Agency Austria, 2011, at 42.

[106] Ibid.

[107] Regulation 73/2009 of 19 January 2009 establishing common rules for direct support schemes for farmers under the common agricultural policy and establishing certain support schemes for farmers, amending Regulations 290/2005, 247/2006, 378/2007 and repealing Regulation 1782/2003.

- Farmers must comply with the *Statutory Management Requirements* listed in Annex II of the Regulation stating regulatory disposition dealing with environmental protection as well as biodiversity protection (Article 5 of Council Regulation 72/2009).
- Besides, farmers are required to keep their land in good agricultural and environmental condition, meaning to comply with various standards, listed in Annex III of Regulation, related to soil protection, maintenance of soil organic matter and structure, and so on (Article 6 of the Regulation).

Through its two elements, statutory management requirements and good agricultural and environmental conditions, the mechanism of cross compliance ensures quite a strong protection of soil quality in agricultural areas, as it refers to all European regulatory dispositions addressing soil protection.

In addition, the 2011 resource efficiency roadmap contains a milestone on land and soil:

> By 2020, EU policies take into account their direct and indirect impact on land use in the EU and globally, and the rate of land take is on track with an aim to achieve no net land take by 2050; soil erosion is reduced and the soil organic matter increased, with remedial work on contaminated sites well underway.[108]

In order to do so, the European Commission and Member States are bound to a number of measures to be taken in order to reach the targets. With this roadmap, the Commission shows its intention to raise awareness about soil protection and address the issue at European level.

All these tools (legally binding or not) have in common that soil is only addressed as an implicit objective and thus only benefits from secondary protection.[109] Moreover, the regulation addressing soil protection against different threats remains fragmented.[110] Consequently, soil protection remains incoherent and incomplete. The challenge of setting a European soil protection framework starts in fact by developing a comprehensive modelling and monitoring system of European land uses, land take and soil degradation at EU level.

---

[108] European Commission, "Resource Efficient Europe", COM (2011) 571, at 15.
[109] I. Heuser, "Milestones of soil protection in EU environmental law", 3 *Journal of European Environmental and Planning Law* 3 (2006), 190–203, at 193.
[110] Ibid., at 200.

III. INVASIVE ALIEN SPECIES

Invasive alien species (IAS) are described as "species that are initially transported through human action outside of their natural range across ecological barriers, and that then survive, reproduce and spread, and that have negative impacts on the ecology of their new location as well as serious economic and social consequences".[111]

The battle against IAS is described as one of the targets of the 2020 biodiversity strategy. The currently 1200 to 1800 IAS in the Union cause economic damage of more than EUR 12.5 billion each year in the Union.[112] According to the strategy, by 2020, IAS and their pathways have to be identified and prioritised. Further, priority species have to be controlled or eradicated, and pathways have to be managed to prevent the introduction and establishment of new IAS.[113] The strategy further announces a legislative instrument on the issue, as there is no general common measure on this as yet, besides legislation on the use of alien and locally absent species in aquaculture.[114] Further, other sector-specific legislation such as the Water Framework Directive, the Birds and Habitats Directives and the Marine Strategy Framework Directive refer to IAS in relation to the requirement to restore ecological conditions.

In 2008 the Commission published a Communication "Towards an EU strategy on invasive species"[115] presenting policy options for a common strategy on IAS and outlining the current state of play in the Union and the individual Member States. The Communication stresses the need for EU action and the impact of IAS on the ecology, economy and human health. It further presents the currently existing tools for tackling IAS. The policy options presented range from business as usual to maximising the use of existing legal instruments together with voluntary agreements; the adoption of existing legislation; and finally the creation of a comprehensive EU legal instrument. The Communication has been debated in the Environment Council, the Committee of the Regions as well as in the Economic and Social Committee. Finally, almost five years later, in September 2013, the Commission presented its proposal for a

---

[111] COM (2013) 620, Brussels, 9.9.2013, p. 2.
[112] COM (2011) 244, p. 6.
[113] COM (2011) 244, p. 6.
[114] Regulation (EU) No 304/2011 of the European Parliament and of the Council of 9 March 2011 concerning use of alien and locally absent species in aquaculture, OJ L 88, 4.4.2011, pp. 1–4.
[115] COM (2008) 789, Brussels, 3.12.2008.

Regulation[116] which entered into force in January 2015 as Regulation 1143/2014.[117] The Regulation builds on guiding principles: prioritisation of IAS of Union concern and the application of a gradual and phased-in approach in defining the priority species; prevention of the introduction of new alien species and their release into the environment; as well as making use of and building on existing systems to combat IAS in the Member States.

The prioritisation of alien species of Union concern aims at increasing the efficiency and effectiveness of Union (and Member State) action. The Regulation foresees the adoption of a list of a maximum of 50 IAS of Union concern which has to be updated on a regular basis (Article 4). The Regulation further focuses on prevention through an early warning system.[118] It includes measures for early detection of IAS in the environment and the Union borders and rapid eradication. Such measures constitute, for example, a ban on IAS of Union concern amongst others to be brought into or transited through Union territory; to be permitted to reproduce; or to be placed on the market and released into the environment (Article 7). Permits for research and *ex situ* conservation are regulated under Article 8 and emergency measures to ban species not contained in the priority list under Article 9. The Regulation additionally contains provisions on early detection and rapid eradication of IAS and envisages a surveillance system collecting and recording data on the occurrence of IAS and the requirement of early detection notifications (Article 14), as well as official controls of animals and plants at Union borders (Article 15). A separate chapter further introduces provisions on the management of IAS that are widely spread in the Union and restoration of damaged ecosystems (Articles 19 and 20).

---

[116] COM (2013) 620, Brussels, 9.9.2013.
[117] Regulation (EU) No 1143/2014 on the prevention and management of the introduction and spread of invasive alien species, OJ L 317, 4.11.2014, pp. 35–55.
[118] For more information on the early warning system for IAS please refer to EEA, "Towards an early warning and information system for invasive alien species (IAS) threatening biodiversity in Europe", EEA Technical report No 5/2010.

11. Water protection legislation and policy

The history of European water legislation and policy can roughly be divided into two parts. In the years from 1975 to 1980 the main focus of European action was on combating point source pollution, more precisely on prevention of pollution of fresh waters with dangerous substances and to establish an adequate level of protection. The overall aim of the policy at that time was the protection of human health rather than the environment. Legislation was enacted mostly on the basis of the internal market provisions and after its introduction also on the environmental basis. Directives establishing environmental quality standards (EQS) for specific types of water were, amongst others the Drinking Water Directive,[1] the Bathing Water Directive,[2] the Directives on water as a habitat for fish[3] and shellfish.[4] Emission limit values (ELVs) were established through the Dangerous Substances Directives[5] and the Groundwater Directive.[6] Most of these Directives are, in an amended version, still existing today.

Later, in the years 1980–2000, policy and legislation tried to tackle diffuse pollution; although a more programmatic approach was taken to address these specific sources of pollution, it was still aimed at the protection of public health rather than environmental protection. Whereas enforcement was not an issue regarding point-based pollution, enforcement in the area

---

[1] Directive 75/440 of 16 June 1975 concerning the quality required of surface water intended for the abstraction of drinking water in the Member States, [1976] OJ L 194/26.

[2] Directive 76/160 of 8 December 1975 concerning the quality of bathing water, [1975] OJ L 31/1.

[3] Directive 78/659 of 18 July 1978 on the quality of fresh waters needing protection or improvement in order to support fish life, [1987] OJ L 222/1.

[4] Directive 79/923 of 30 October 1979 on the quality required of shellfish waters, [1979] OJ L 281/47.

[5] Directive 76/464 of 4 May 1976 on pollution caused by certain dangerous substances discharged into the aquatic environment of the Community, [1976] OJ L 129/23.

[6] Directive 80/68 of 17 December 1979 on the protection of groundwater against pollution caused by certain dangerous substances, [1980] OJ L 20/43.

of diffuse pollution is a lot more problematic as the cause of and reason for the pollution and who the polluter is, is mostly not easy to identify. Thus the Nitrates Directive[7] was difficult to apply and enforce in practice because control was problematic. Other key Directives at that time were the Urban Waste Water Treatment Directive[8] and the IPPC Directive,[9] which, however, aimed at tackling point rather than diffuse pollution. The main instruments used were the application of EQS, plans and designated areas, as for example under the Urban Wastewater Directive, environmental licences (IPPC Directive) and emission standards. The legislation was top-down for specific sources of pollution: the functional EQS were set by the EU. The legislation tried to establish a clear level of protection, for example by setting sufficiently precise and clear EQS. The legislation granted rights to individuals, as the CJEU confirmed in the *TOS*[10] case.

The Member States were increasingly affected by the impacts of climate change, such as drought and flooding, issues which, together with the issue of fresh water supply, were not addressed by the legislation in force at that time. Also the past regime did not pay enough regard to transboundary issues, the protection of the marine environment or hydromorphology.

A major review of the legislation and policy in place resulted in a new approach and the creation of the Water Framework Directive. The Directive creates an integrated river basin management system setting the overall framework. Specific issues are still addressed by explicit legislation, for example in the area of ground, drinking and bathing water.

Further, the "Blueprint to Safeguard Europe's Water Resources" is a recent EU initiative aiming at better implementation of water policy at the EU level and evaluating the existing policy. The first pillar is the Blueprint Communication which outlines existing obstacles in the water policy and solutions regarding the achievement of the good water status, inter alia concerning land use, the chemical and ecological status in the EU, as well as pollution and vulnerability of EU waters and water efficiency.[11] The second pillar consists of the 3rd Implementation Report on the Water

---

[7] Directive 91/676 of 12 December 1991 concerning the protection of waters against pollution caused by nitrates from agricultural sources, [1991] OJ L 375/1.

[8] Council Directive 91/271 of 21 May 1991 concerning urban waste-water treatment, [1991] OJ L 135/40.

[9] Council Directive 96/61 of 24 September 1996 concerning integrated pollution prevention and control, [1996] OJ L 257/26.

[10] Case C-381/07 *Association nationale pour la protection des eaux et rivières*, EHR [2008] I-8281.

[11] European Commission, "A blueprint to safeguard Europe's water resources", Brussels, 14.11.2012, COM (2012) 673, at 4–19.

Framework Directive on the River Basin Management Plans[12] and the review of the Strategy on Water Scarcity and Droughts.[13]

In addition, the Water Information System for Europe (WISE) is a web-based information exchange platform on EU water policy and legislation (secondary legislation, implementation reports and action plans), data, modelling and research activities created by the European Commission (DG Environment, Joint Research Centre and Eurostat), and the European Environment Agency in 2007.[14]

I. THE WATER FRAMEWORK DIRECTIVE AND INTEGRATED RIVER BASIN MANAGEMENT

The Water Framework Directive (WFD) aims at establishing

> a framework for the protection of inland surface waters, transitional waters, coastal waters and groundwater which (a) prevents further deterioration and protects and enhances the status of aquatic ecosystems ... (b) promotes sustainable water use based on a long-term protection of available water resources; (c) aims at enhanced protection and improvement of the aquatic environment, inter alia, through specific measures for the progressive reduction of discharges, emissions and losses of priority substances and the cessation or phasing-out of discharges, emissions and losses of the priority hazardous substances; (d) ensures the progressive reduction of pollution of groundwater and prevents its further pollution, and (e) contributes to mitigating the effects of floods and droughts ... (Article 1)[15]

The system of river basin management was firstly established in the international Helsinki Treaty. The Member States' boundaries are ignored; the natural boundaries of the individual rivers serve as management units. This has the advantage that pollution sources and causes of floods or droughts can be addressed inside each river basin with an approach that fits the individual situation. Both up- and downstream users are

---

[12] European Commission, "Report on the implementation of the Water Framework Directive (2000/60/EC) River Basin Management Plans", Brussels, 14.11.2012, COM (2012) 670.

[13] European Commission, "Report on the review of the European water scarcity and droughts policy", Brussels, 14.11.2012, COM (2012) 672.

[14] The platform and further information is available at http://water.europa.eu/, last consulted 20.11.2015.

[15] For a detailed discussion of the WFD refer to European Commission, "Water is for life: how the Water Framework Directive helps safeguard Europe's resources", Luxembourg: Publications Office of the European Union, 2010.

represented within each river basin, which also facilitates the identification of water use and users. A river basin is defined as the "area of land from which all surface run-off flows through a sequence of streams, rivers and, possibly, lakes into the sea at a single river mouth, estuary or delta" (Article 2(13)).

Further key terms and concepts of the Directive, such as surface, transitional, coastal, inland and groundwater, as well as rivers and lakes are defined in the same Article.

According to Article 3 of the Directive, Member States have to identify the individual river basins lying within their national territory and assign them to individual river basin districts. Transboundary river basins are further assigned to an international river basin district. For each river basin a management plan has to be drafted (Article 13 in combination with Annex VII). Article 4, in combination with Annex V to the Directive, specifies the environmental objectives and standards which need to be achieved for surface waters, groundwater and protected areas. The Article further contains a number of exemptions that allow less strict objectives and derogations (Article 4(4–7)).[16] Articles 4(4) and 4(5) provide for an extension of timescales for the achievement of a specific objective and Article 4(6) for extensions for *force majeure* which could not reasonably have been foreseen. Lastly, Article 4(7) includes exemptions for circumstances where Member States have not achieved the Directive's objectives. The CJEU in *Nomarchiaki Aftodioikisi Aitoloakarnanias*[17] held that

> the conditions governing the project cannot be more rigorous than those pertaining if it had been adopted subsequent to Article 4 of Directive 2000/60 having become applicable to it. In the case of such a project, the criteria and conditions laid down in Article 4(7) of Directive 2000/60 may, in essence, be applied by analogy and, where necessary, *mutatis mutandis*, as setting the upper limit for restrictions on the project.

A programme of measures is designed for each river basin (Article 11 in combination with Annex VI) in order to achieve good ecological status. The programme has to include instruments based on an integrated approach of point and diffuse source pollution (Article 10).

Key to the integrated approach is therefore the achievement of a good

---

[16] For further explanation and guidance on the exceptions provided under Article 4 see Guidance Document No. 20 of the common implementation strategy of the WFD, available at http://ec.europa.eu/environment/water/water-framework/objectives/pdf/Guidance_document_20.pdf, last consulted 20.11.2015.

[17] C-43/10 *Nomarchiaki Aftodioikisi Aitoloakarnanias and Others*, ECLI:EU:C:2012:560, at 64 and 65.

water status, more precisely a good chemical and ecological status for surface waters and a good quantitative and chemical status for groundwater. In *Bund für Umwelt und Naturschutz Deutschland*,[18] the Court reinforces the Member States' obligation to prevent deterioration under the WFD, as well as the obligation to enhance the good environmental status and water quality.[19] The Court further stresses that these are not "solely basic obligations, but that this also concerns individual projects".[20] It follows from that that

> Member States are required – unless a derogation is granted – to refuse authorisation for an individual project where it may cause a deterioration of the status of a body of surface water or where it jeopardises the attainment of good surface water status or of good ecological potential and good surface water chemical status by the date laid down by the directive.[21]

The chemical environmental quality standards are implemented in the Daughter Directives such as the Groundwater Directive and the Dangerous Substances Directive, as well as in national legislation. The standards for emissions and chemicals are not difficult to establish, as opposed to the ecological objectives which are not necessarily as easily definable and concrete. The underlying idea of good ecological status is to leave the waters alone, thus to minimise human interference and disturbance. Even if this is practically not possible, the CJEU confirmed that the achievement of good ecological status is an obligation of result and not of best effort, which is in line with the chemical obligations.

The CJEU held in *Commission v Luxembourg*: "Article 2 of the directive, read in conjunction with, for example, Article 4, *imposes on Member States precise obligations to be implemented* within the prescribed timescales in order to prevent deterioration of the status of all bodies of surface water and groundwater" (emphasis added).[22]

Other general requirements for an integrated river basin management approach are the establishment of a competent authority for each river basin (Article 3), the assessment of the characteristics of the river basin

---

[18] Case C-461/13 *Bund für Umwelt und Naturschutz Deutschland*, ECLI:EU:C:2015:433.
[19] Ibid., at 39.
[20] Ibid., at 47.
[21] Ibid., at 51.
[22] Case C-32/05 *Commission v Luxembourg*, ECR [2006] I-11323, at 63. As also previously recognised in Case C-121-03 *Commission v Spain*, ECLI:EU:C:2005:512, regarding Directive 80/778 relating to the quality of water intended for human consumption.

district and the review of the environmental impact of human activity and economic analysis of water use (Article 5), the monitoring of the surface water status, groundwater status and protected areas (Article 8), the recovery of costs for water services (Article 9) as well as public information and consultation and reporting (Articles 14 and 15).

A. Common Implementation Strategy

In order to support the Member States in the implementation of the WFD the Commission and the EU Water Directors drafted a common implementation strategy.[23] The demanding timetable in the nine preparatory years, capacity building and the technical character of the directive are perceived as key problems.[24] The strategy focuses on the methodology of understanding the technical and scientific effects of the Directive[25] through the establishment of different guidance documents and thematic information sheets addressing inter alia river basin management, reporting, ecological status, groundwater, chemicals, flood risk management and hydromorphology.[26] The implementation of the Floods Directive (discussed below under "Flood"), which is closely connected to the WFD, is also addressed in the CIS, inter alia through the work programme and mandate "Promoting early action" for floods.[27]

---

[23] Common Strategy on the Implementation of the Water Framework Directive, as agreed by the water directors under Swedish Presidency, 2 May 2001, available at http://ec.europa.eu/environment/water/water-framework/objectives/pdf/strategy.pdf, last consulted 20.11.2015.

[24] Ibid., at 1.

[25] Ibid., at 2.

[26] These and other Common Implementation Strategy (CIS) information sheets are available at Communication and Information Resource Centre for Administrations, Businesses and Citizens (CIRCABC) under https://circabc.europa.eu/faces/jsp/extension/wai/navigation/container.jsp, last consulted 20.11.2015. The guidance documents are listed at http://ec.europa.eu/environment/water/water-framework/facts_figures/guidance_docs_en.htm, last consulted 20.11.2015.

[27] Work programme and mandate 2008–2009 "Promoting early action", Working group F on Floods, as agreed by the water directors, available at goo.gl/cwc2nf, last consulted 16.12.2016.

II. ADAPTATION TO CLIMATE CHANGE: FLOODS, DROUGHTS AND WATER SCARCITY

Over the last decade, climate change has resulted in increased natural disasters such as storms and floods at one extreme and great temperature events leading to droughts and water scarcity at the other.[28] These events do not only result in environmental and social, but also economic damage. According to figures from the EEA, the overall loss was EUR 52 billion for floods inside the EU and EUR 5 billion for droughts.[29]

A. Floods

The Floods Directive[30] establishes a framework for the assessment and management of flood risks, aimed at the reduction of the adverse consequences for human health, the environment, cultural heritage and economic activity associated with floods in the Union (Article 1). The Directive adds to the WFD. Some of the provisions have to be applied in coordination, particularly regarding flood risk management plans and river basin management plans (Article 7) and public participation procedures (Articles 9(3) and 10).

The Directive covers floods from rivers, mountain torrents, Mediterranean ephemeral water courses, and floods from the sea in coastal areas, but may exclude floods from sewerage systems (Article 2(1)). One of the key provisions of the Directive is the drawing up of preliminary flood risk assessments (Articles 4 and 5) and flood hazard maps and flood risk maps (Article 6). The deadline to report the preliminary flood risk assessment was in 2012. The assessment included amongst others maps of the river basin districts, a description of floods which had occurred in the past, including their impacts inter alia on the environment and human health as well as on their extent and conveyance routes. On the basis of these data,

---

[28] See also from an international perspective, J. Verschuuren, "Climate change adaptation and water law", in: J. Verschuuren, *Research Handbook on Climate Change Adaptation Law*, Cheltenham, UK and Northampton, MA, USA: Edward Elgar, 2013, 250–272; for more information on the impacts and a description and analysis of these events see EEA, "Mapping the impacts of natural hazards and technological accidents in Europe: an overview of the last decade", EEA Technical Report No 13/2010, 2010, at 54–62 and 64–73.

[29] EEA, "Disasters in Europe: more frequent and causing more damage", figures available at http://www.eea.europa.eu/highlights/natural-hazards-and-technological-accidents/table-es1-overview-of-the, last consulted 20.11.2015.

[30] Directive 2007/60 of 23 October 2007 on the assessment and management of flood risks, [2007] OJ L 288/27.

areas are identified for which a potential significant flood risk exists or might be considered likely to occur (Article 5).

For the areas identified under Article 5, flood hazard maps and flood risk maps had to be drafted by March 2014. The flood hazard maps cover the geographical areas which could be flooded with low probability or extreme event scenarios; with a medium probability (likely return period ≥ 100 years); and with a high probability. For all scenarios the flood extent, water level and depth, flow velocity, number of inhabitants and economic activities/installations affected had to be identified (Article 6).

As a last step, Member States have to draw up flood management plans for the river basin districts on the basis of these maps. The deadline for reporting them is March 2016. These will address all aspects of flood risk management focusing on prevention, protection and preparedness, including flood forecasts and early warning systems and taking into account the characteristics of the particular river basin or sub-basin (Article 7).

Before the entry into force of the Floods Directive in 2007, in 2004 the Commission published an action plan on flood risk management, prevention, protection and mitigation.[31]

The action programme introduced the elements for the development of flood risk management which were later included into the Directive: prevention, protection, preparedness, emergency response and recovery, and lessons learned. However, it also stresses that floods are natural phenomena which generally cannot be prevented. What the Union can do is mitigate the human impacts which result in increased floods and thus reduce the likelihood of extreme floods occurring in the future.

The action plan further listed initiatives to be carried out at European and Member State levels prior to the enactment of the Floods Directive and called for European action, which lead to the drafting of the EU Floods Directive. The action plan also included guidelines, principles and objectives for the development and implementation of flood risk management plans and maps, which are mostly reflected in the later Directive.

B. Droughts and Water Scarcity

Droughts are defined as the "temporary decrease in water availability due for instance to rainfall deficiency", while water scarcity means the "water demand exceeds the water resources exploitable under sustainable

---

[31] COM (2004) 472, 12.7.2004.

conditions".[32] The Commission Communication from 2007 marked a first milestone in addressing water scarcity and droughts in the Union, presenting an integrated policy actions approach. Key aspects of the action plan are the establishment of a price tag on water, the more efficient allocation of water and water-related funding through inter alia improving land use planning. Further initiatives relate to the improvement of drought risk management by amongst others developing drought risk management plans and an observatory and an early warning system on droughts. Additional water supply infrastructure, water efficient technologies and practices and education towards a water-saving culture are other strategies proposed in the action plan. In the area of knowledge and data collection, the establishment of a water scarcity and drought information system, as well as research and development opportunities are key strategies in order to address droughts and water scarcity.[33] Every issue/need for action is further developed by providing good practice examples and actions which need to be taken at European and national levels. The 2007 strategy was followed up by three reports in 2008 to 2010 which assessed the implementation of the policy options in the Member States and has been viewed as one pillar of the "A blueprint to safeguard Europe's water resources" strategy.[34] This strategy assesses the seven integrated policy actions and reviews the integration of water scarcity and drought measures in the river basin management plans under the WFD. It further identifies gaps in the current water scarcity and droughts policy, relating to conceptual, information and governance and implementation issues. Firstly, water scarcity and droughts are not sufficiently distinguished; new indicators and a coherent data set at Union level are needed to remedy this.[35] Secondly, data gaps on water demand and accessibility are missing and consequently a reliable assessment of effectiveness and socio-economic impacts is lacking.[36] Lastly, implementation measures such as metering, pricing/subsidies and restriction of water consumption is not systematically applied in all river basin management plans; coordination amongst planning and financial stakeholders is unclear and not satisfactory.[37] The strategy further establishes tools to improve water quantity management

---

[32] European Commission, "Addressing the challenge of water scarcity and droughts in the European Union", COM (2007) 414, Brussels, 18.7.2007, at 2.
[33] See COM (2007) 414, at 5–13.
[34] European Commission, "A blueprint to safeguard Europe's water resources", Brussels, 14.11.2012, COM (2012) 673.
[35] COM (2012) 673, at 7.
[36] COM (2012) 673, at 7.
[37] COM (2012) 673, at 8.

in the next river management plans, namely the definition and implementation of ecological flows and targets for water efficiency, as well as the promotion of incentives for efficient water use and resilience to climate change. The enhancement of general drought management through an early warning system, and guidance in land use are key tools in order to address water scarcity and droughts.[38]

III. DRINKING WATER

The European Directive on the quality of water intended for human consumption[39] (Drinking Water Directive) aims at protecting human health from adverse effects of any contamination of water intended for human consumption by ensuring that it is wholesome and clean (Article 1). The Directive is applicable to all water intended for human consumption, such as drinking water from taps, tanks and for the food production, as well as to distribution systems serving fewer than 50 persons or providing less than 10 m^3 a day. Natural mineral waters[40] and waters which are medicinal products[41] are excluded from the scope of the Directive (Articles 1 and 2).

The Directive establishes the general obligation that drinking water has to be free from any micro-organisms and parasites and from any substances which, in number or concentration, constitute a potential danger to human health, and that it has to meet the minimum requirements and quality standards set out in Annex I (Articles 4 and 5). These are only minimum requirements and Member States are free to set more stringent measures.

The Directive provides for temporary derogations from the values included in Annex I(B), if these do not pose a potential danger to human health and under the condition that the water supply cannot otherwise be

---

[38] COM (2012) 673, at 8–10.

[39] Directive 98/83 of 3 November 1998 on the quality of water intended for human consumption, [1998] OJ L 330/32.

[40] Covered by Directive 80/777 of 15 July 1980 on the approximation of the laws of the Member States relating to the exploitation and marketing of natural mineral waters, [1980] OJ L 229/1, as repealed by Directive 2009/54/EC of the European Parliament and of the Council of 18 June 2009 on the exploitation and marketing of natural mineral waters, [2009] OJ L 164/45.

[41] Directive 65/65 of 26 January 1965 on the approximation of provisions laid down by Law, Regulation or Administrative Action relating to proprietary medicinal products, [1965] OJ 22/369, as repealed by Directive 2001/83/EC of 6 November 2001 on the Community code relating to medicinal products for human use, [2001] OJ L 311/67.

maintained. The maximum time frame for such a derogation is three years and is generally limited to two derogations. Only in exceptional circumstances can a third derogation can be granted. Derogations are not possible for drinking water offered for sale in bottles and containers (Article 9).

Member States are required to draft programmes to ensure the regular monitoring of the water quality (Article 7 in combination with Annex II on monitoring and Annex III on specifications for the analysis of parameters). Member States are further required to ensure remedial action and restrictions in use if the drinking water does not comply with the quality standards (Article 8) and quality assurance of treatment, equipment and materials (Article 10).

After a broad consultation on the review of the Directive, in 2011, the institutions decided that a complete review was not necessary and that a revision of the technical annexes through the Committee (comitology procedure, Article 12 of the Directive) was sufficient to update the requirements to the technological process.[42] The institutions further decided to focus on the implementation of the Directive in the Member States, which is also supported by the proposal of the 7th Environmental Action Programme.[43]

IV. BATHING WATER

The Bathing Water Directive[44] establishes the legal framework for the management, monitoring and classification of bathing water quality and regarding information to the public. It is aimed at the preservation, protection and improvement of environmental quality and human health and complements the WFD. The Directive applies to surface water where a large number of people is expected to bath and where no permanent bathing prohibition is imposed. The Directive does not apply to swimming pools and spas, treatment and therapeutic water and artificial waters, which are separate from surface and groundwater (Article 1).

---

[42] See also European Commission, "Future implementation of the Drinking Water Directive? Revision?", available at http://ec.europa.eu/environment/water/water-drink/pdf/explanation.pdf, last consulted 20.11.2015.
[43] "Increasing efforts to implement the Water Framework Directive, the Bathing Water Directive and the Drinking Water Directive, in particular for small drinking water supplies", Draft decision of 20 November 2013 on a General Union Environment Action Programme to 2020 "Living well, within the limits of our planet", at 48.
[44] Directive 2006/7/EC of 15 February 2006 concerning the management of bathing water quality and repealing Directive 76/160/EEC, [2006] OJ L 64/37.

Annually Member States are required to identify bathing waters and define the length of the bathing season and monitor in accordance with the requirements established in Annex IV the intestinal enterococci and *Escherichia coli* parameters for inland, coastal and transitional waters. Other parameters such as macro-algae and/or marine phytoplankton and pollution are to be included when the individual bathing water profile indicates (Article 9). A monitoring calendar has to be established for each bathing season (Article 3) and bathing water quality data are to be compiled through monitoring. Assessments are to be carried out in accordance with Annex II in relation to each bathing water after the end of each bathing season on the basis of the set of bathing water quality data compiled in the current and the three preceding bathing seasons (Article 4). Further, a bathing water profile has to be established in accordance with the requirements of Annex III (Article 6).

The Directive further establishes a classification system and quality status of bathing waters. As a result of the bathing water quality assessment bathing waters are to be classified as "poor", "sufficient", "good" or "excellent". The individual criterion for the assessment are laid down in Annex II of the Directive (Article 5). In May 2011 the Commission adopted a decision to establish symbols for public information on bathing water classification and bathing prohibition or advice against bathing.[45] Member States have to ensure that by the end of the 2015 bathing season all bathing waters are at least "sufficient" in quality. The Directive further promotes the active participation of the public and exchange of information (Articles 11 and 12).

The Commission publishes on an annual basis a summary report on the quality of bathing water, based on the information provided by Member States. Interactive maps and tables on the quality of bathing water are available on WISE. The 2014 bathing season was characterised by a general improvement in bathing water quality. The minimum standards are met in 95 per cent of the European bathing waters; 83 per cent of sites are of excellent quality. More than 21,000 sites in 28 Member States were examined.[46]

---

[45] Commission Implementing Decision of 27 May 2011 establishing, pursuant to Directive 2006/7/EC of the European Parliament and of the Council, a symbol for information to the public on bathing water classification and any bathing prohibition or advice against bathing, [2011] OJ L 143/38.

[46] EEA, "European bathing water quality in 2014", EEA Report No 1/2015, at 4.

V. GROUNDWATER

The legislative framework applicable to groundwater consists of the WFD, the Groundwater Directive[47] and several other directives applicable to specific substances or activities such as the Nitrates Directive, the Urban Wastewater Treatment Directive, the Biocides Directive and the Industrial Emissions.

Article 17 of the WFD provides for the establishment of strategies to prevent and control the pollution of groundwater taking into account the characteristics of the river basin districts, the environmental and human impacts and Annex II. The result of this is the Groundwater Directive outlining criteria for the assessment of good groundwater chemical status, for the identification and reversal of significant and sustained upward trends, and for the definition of starting points for trend reversals (Article 1). The criteria for groundwater quality standards are included in Annex I to the Directive, the procedure for establishing the threshold values in Annex II (Article 3). Particular attention has to be paid to impacts on and interrelation with associated surface waters and directly dependent terrestrial ecosystems and wetlands, and human toxicology and ecotoxicology knowledge. The values can be established at the national, the river basin district or international river basin district level, or at the level of a body or a group of bodies of groundwater (Article 3).

Article 4 of the Directive further lays down the procedure for assessing groundwater chemical status, Article 5 the procedure for the identification of significant and sustained upward trends and the definition of starting points for trend reversals, and Article 6 the measures to prevent or limit inputs of pollutants into groundwater.

Annexes I and II are currently under review; Article 10 provides for such a review every six years.

---

[47] Directive 2006/118/EC of the European Parliament and of the Council of 12 December 2006 on the protection of groundwater against pollution and deterioration, [2006] OJ L 372/19.

VI. WATER POLLUTION

The main legislation addressing water pollution at a European level are the Industrial Emission Directive (IED),[48] the Urban Waste Water Directive[49] and the Nitrates Directive.[50] The IED aims at ensuring, that

> the operation of an installation does not lead to a deterioration of the quality of soil and groundwater. . . . In order to detect possible soil and groundwater pollution at an early stage and, therefore, to take appropriate corrective measures before the pollution spreads, the monitoring of soil and groundwater for relevant hazardous substances is also necessary. (Recital 23, Preamble to the IED)

The Urban Waste Water Directive dates from 1991 and has been amended three times. The Directive regulates the "collection, treatment and discharge of urban waste water and the treatment and discharge of waste water from certain industrial sectors. The objective of the Directive is to protect the environment from the adverse effects of the abovementioned waste water discharges" (Article 1). Urban waste water is defined as "domestic waste water or the mixture of domestic waste water with industrial waste water and/or run-off rain water" (Article 2(1)). The Directive requires the establishment of collecting systems for urban waste water for all agglomerations regardless of size by 2005 at the latest. Further, they have to ensure that urban waste water that enters the collecting systems undergoes a secondary treatment before being discharged (Articles 3 and 4).

Member States are further required to designate "sensitive areas" (Article 5) and "less sensitive areas" (Article 6) in which special, more stringent treatment conditions for sensitive areas and less stringent conditions for less sensitive areas than the ones outlined in Article 4 apply, taking into account the criteria in Annex II.

For reasons of completeness, the Nitrates Directive concerning the protection of waters against pollution caused by nitrates from agricultural sources aims at pollution reduction and prevention through encouraging good agricultural practices. The Directive required the Member States to draw up an action programme cutting nitrate pollution. The Nitrates Directive is an integral part of the WFD.

---

[48] Directive 2010/75 of 24 November 2010 on industrial emissions, [2010] OJ L 334/17.
[49] Directive 91/271 of 21 May 1991 concerning urban waste-water treatment, [1991] OJ L 135/40.
[50] Directive 91/676 of 12 December 1991 concerning the protection of waters against pollution caused by nitrates from agricultural sources, [1991] OJ L 375/1.

VII. PROTECTION OF THE MARINE ENVIRONMENT

The Marine Strategy Directive[51] forms the environmental pillar of the European marine policy. Marine waters consist of

> waters, the seabed and subsoil on the seaward side of the baseline from which the extent of territorial waters is measured extending to the outmost reach of the area where a Member State has and/or exercises jurisdictional rights . . . and coastal waters as defined by [the WFD], their seabed and their subsoil . . . (Article 3)

The Directive applies to all these waters, except if the activities carried out are for the purposes of defence or national security (Article 2). The marine regions covered by the Directive are the Baltic Sea, the North-east Atlantic Ocean, the Mediterranean Sea and the Black Sea, which are further subdivided in sub-regions.

The Directive employs the ecosystem approach, aiming at the achievement of or maintaining good environmental status in the marine environment by the year 2020 at the latest (Article 1). Therefore, the Directive prescribes the development of marine strategies to "protect and preserve the marine environment, prevent its deterioration or, where practicable, restore marine ecosystems in areas where they have been adversely affected" and to "prevent and reduce inputs in the marine environment, with a view to phasing out pollution . . . so as to ensure that there are no significant impacts on or risks to marine biodiversity, marine ecosystems, human health or legitimate uses of the sea" (Article 1(2)). The Directive implements and specifically refers to the integration and sustainable development principle (Articles 1(3) and (4)).

The structure of the Directive is similar to the WFD: according to Article 5, the instruments used by Member States to establish a marine strategy and a programme of measures range from an initial assessment (Article 8) and the determination of good environmental status (Article 9), environmental targets (Article 10) and indicators by 2012 and a monitoring programme by 2014 (Article 11). The actual programme of measures is required by 2015 and has to enter into operation in 2016 at the latest (Article 13). The Directive further stresses the need for regional practical and institutional cooperation amongst the Regional Sea Conventions (Article 6).

---

[51] Directive 2008/56 of 17 June 2008 establishing a framework for community action in the field of marine environmental policy, [2008] OJ L 164/19.

Exceptions to derogate from environmental targets or good environmental status are granted in cases of action or inaction for which the Member State concerned is not responsible: natural causes; *force majeure*; and for modifications or alterations to the physical characteristics of marine waters brought about by actions taken for reasons of overriding public interest which outweigh the negative impact on the environment, including any transboundary impact. Further, exceptions can be granted if the natural conditions do not allow timely improvement in the status of the marine waters concerned (Article 14).

Annex I of the Directive contains qualitative descriptors for the determination of good environmental status. The descriptors relate to amongst others biodiversity, invasive species, commercially exploited fish and shellfish populations, marine food webs, eutrophication, hydrographical conditions and contamination. All the descriptors listed in the Annex have to be taken into account when determining good environmental status according to Article 9. The other annexes include inter alia an indicative list of characteristics, pressures and impacts (Annex III); an indicative list of characteristics to be taken into account for the setting of environmental targets (Annex IV); as well as further details on the monitoring programme (Annex V) and the programme of measures (Annex VI).

12. Noise pollution legislation and policy

In the EU, in the past, intervention in the area of noise pollution has focused on safeguarding the internal market rather than dealing with the environmental and health and safety impacts. This changed with the enactment of the 2002 Environmental Noise Directive, which marks the cornerstone in the Union's noise policy. In addition, an important part of noise pollution is addressed by imposing product standards on individual noise emitters. This chapter discusses both the Environmental Noise Directive and the sector specific regulation to noise. They all have in common that tackling noise pollution is best attained, to a large extent at least, by preventing pollution at source. Economic instruments are very rarely used in this sector. Taxing the emission of noise is only really done in the air transport sector. Subsidies and fiscal incentives for using less noisy techniques and/or tools are in fact completely absent in the Member States.

I. THE ENVIRONMENTAL NOISE DIRECTIVE

The Environmental Noise Directive[1] is the key European noise policy and introduces a management system for all environmental noise in Member States. The way to its entry into force in 2002 was not a straightforward one. The Commission's Green Paper, published in 1996,[2] was the start of the ambitious renewal of the Union's noise policy; however, this ambition seemed firstly to be frustrated by the principle of subsidiarity. The central idea throughout the paper was the principle of shared responsibility. The Commission was firmly convinced that because of the local impact of noise pollution, local authorities should play a predominant role in combating it. It would be up to the Union to fill the gaps caused by poor coherence

---

[1] Directive 2002/49 of 25 June 2002 relating to the assessment and management of environmental noise – Declaration by the Commission in the Conciliation Committee on the Directive relating to the assessment and management of environmental noise, [2002] OJ L 189/12.
[2] Commission Green Paper on the future EC noise policy, COM (96) 540.

and coordination. Initially, the Commission provided an overview of the existing scientific data of noise exposure in the Union's territory.

It favoured the introduction of a Directive which would include first of all a common Union noise exposure index, to ensure that data on environmental noise exposure would be made available using the same noise units.

The Directive as it stands includes some but not all of the aspects of the Green Paper. It introduces a common approach to avoid, prevent or reduce harmful effects and annoyance, due to exposure to environmental noise (Article 1). It provides a basis for the development of Union measures to reduce noise emitted by the major sources, in particular road and rail vehicles and infrastructure, aircraft, outdoor and industrial equipment and mobile machinery (Article 1(2)).

Environmental noise is generally defined as "unwanted or harmful outdoor sound created by human activities, including noise emitted by means of transport, road traffic, rail traffic, air traffic, and from sites of industrial activity . . . " (Article 2(a)).

The Directive is applicable to environmental noise to which humans are exposed, in particular in built-up areas, in public parks or other quiet areas in an agglomeration, in quiet areas in open country, near schools, hospitals and other noise-sensitive buildings and areas. Noise caused by the exposed individual, noise from domestic activities, noise created by neighbours, noise in workplaces and noise inside transport or due to military activities in military areas are not covered by the Directive (Article 2).

Strategic noise mapping is one of the key tools of the Directive. Member States are required to implement a set of actions: (1) determine exposure to environmental noise, through noise mapping and a common noise assessment; (2) ensure that information on environmental noise and its effects is made available to the public; (3) adopt action plans by Member States, with a view to preventing and reducing environmental noise (Article 1(1)).

Article 5 of the Directive introduces noise indicators for reporting and assessment; however, the setting of the individual noise limit values is up to Member States and they have to be reported on a regular basis to the Commission. Further, Member States are required to submit strategic noise maps every five years for all agglomerations and major roads and railways within their territories (Article 7). Noise maps present ranges of noise exposure for a particular area, by using different colours. In addition, the competent authorities of the Member States had to have drawn up action plans designed to manage noise issues and effects, including noise reduction, by 2008. The measures within the plans were at the discretion of the competent authorities but had to be in line with the minimum requirements set in Annex V of the Directive (Article 8). In 2011, only 20 Member States had correctly implemented the action plans.[3]

Furthermore, the Directive specifies that the strategic noise maps are made available to the public and that the public is to be consulted regarding the action plans (Article 9). According to Article 10(3), the Commission had to set up a database of information on strategic noise maps in order to facilitate the compilation of the report referred to in Article 11 and other technical and informative work.

The implementation of the Directive has been delayed due to the lack of sufficient and comparable data and difficulties in the assessment relating to the use of different ways of data collection, quality and availability. The Commission therefore launched the "CNOSSOS-EU" (Common Noise Assessment Methods in Europe) initiative which provides the technical basis for a revision of Annex II on assessment methods for noise indicators.[4]

The Commission Report further inter alia promotes the development of EU implementation guidance on noise as well as the improvement of synergies between air and noise management and the facilitation of reporting as tools to increase implementation of the Directive.[5]

II. SECTOR SPECIFIC REGULATION AND HARMONISATION

Sector specific Union directives with respect to noise levels employ a system of "minimum harmonisation". These standards lay down the minimum requirements which a product has to meet in order to enjoy free movement. Where a product meets the standards, a Member State cannot refuse the entry of this product into its market. Whether the standards are met has to be assessed following a harmonised procedure. Member States may subject their nationals to stricter regulation. Minimum harmonisation centres around the following concepts:

- "EU type approval" means the procedure whereby a Member State establishes, following tests, and certifies that a type of equipment conforms to the requirements harmonised under the relevant Directives.

---

[3] See Report from the Commission on the implementation of the Environmental Noise Directive in accordance with Article 11 of Directive 2002/49/EC, COM/2011/0321.
[4] Ibid., 9.
[5] Ibid., 9f.

- "EU type examination" means the procedure whereby a body approved for that purpose by a Member State establishes, following tests, and certifies that a type of equipment conforms to the harmonised requirements under the relevant Directives.
- "EU verification" means the procedure whereby a Member State can affirm, following tests, that each item of equipment conforms to the harmonised requirements.
- "EU self-certification" means the procedure whereby the manufacturer, or the authorised representative established in the Union, certifies, on his own responsibility, that an item of equipment conforms to the harmonised requirements under the relevant Directives.[6]

A. Noise from Motors in Vehicles

Directive 70/157,[7] as lastly amended by Commission Directive 2007/34[8] applies to "motor vehicle intended for use on the road, with or without bodywork, having at least four wheels and a maximum design speed exceeding 25 kilometers per hour, with the exception of vehicles which run on rails and of agricultural and forestry tractors and all mobile machinery". No Member State may refuse EU type approval or national type approval of a vehicle on grounds relating to the permissible sound level or the exhaust system if these satisfy the requirements set out in Annexes I or II. The Annexes establish inter alia the permissible sound levels. The equipment which is used for measuring the sound has to meet the ISO standards on the matter. The Annexes also set out the method of measuring the noise levels.

Amendments to the original Directive were introduced by the

---

[6] Article 1 of Directive 84/532 of 17 September 1984 on the approximation of the laws of the Member States relating to common provisions for construction plant and equipment, [1984] OJ L 300/11.

[7] Directive 70/157 of 6 February 1970 on the approximation of the laws of the Member States relating to the permissible sound level and the exhaust system of motor vehicles, [1970] OJ L 42/16. This Directive is directly linked to Directive 70/156 on the approximation of the laws of the Member States relating to the type-approval of motor vehicles and their trailers, [1970] OJ L 42/1.

[8] Commission Directive 2007/34/EC of 14 June 2007 amending, for the purposes of its adaptation to technical progress, Council Directive 70/157/EEC concerning the permissible sound level and the exhaust system of motor vehicles, [2007] OJ L 155/49.

Council (Directive 77/212,[9] Directive 84/424[10] and Directive 92/97[11]), including stricter emission limits. Amendments were also introduced by the Commission, especially with respect to the testing conditions for the exhaust system (Directive 73/350[12] and Directive 1999/101[13]); the introduction of a new testing method and the requirements for the administrative models for EU type approval (Directive 81/334[14] and Directive 1999/101); some technical amendments were made by Directive 84/372;[15] and the test frequency was dealt with by Directive 96/20.[16] The last amendment in 2007 substantively reviewed the Annexes and inter alia introduced further limiting values for the sound level of moving vehicles.

---

[9] Council Directive 77/212/EEC of 8 March 1977 amending Directive 70/157/EEC relating to the permissible sound level and the exhaust system of motor vehicles, OJ L 66, 12.3.1977, pp. 33–34.

[10] Council Directive 84/424/EEC of 3 September 1984 amending Directive 70/157/EEC on the approximation of the laws of the Member States relating to the permissible sound level and the exhaust system of motor vehicles, OJ L 238, 6.9.1984, pp. 31–33.

[11] Council Directive 92/97/EEC of 10 November 1992 amending Directive 70/157/EEC on the approximation of the laws of the Member States relating to the permissible sound level and the exhaust system of motor vehicles, OJ L 371, 19.12.1992, pp. 1–31.

[12] Commission Directive 73/350/EEC of 7 November 1973 adapting to technical progress the Council Directive of 6 February 1970 on the approximation of the laws of the Member States relating to the permissible sound level and the exhaust system of motor vehicles, OJ L 321, 22.11.1973, pp. 33–36.

[13] Commission Directive 1999/101 of 15 December 1999 adapting to technical progress Council Directive 70/157/EEC relating to the permissible sound level and the exhaust system of motor vehicles, OJ L 334, 28.12.1999, pp. 41–42.

[14] Commission Directive 81/334/EEC of 13 April 1981 adapting to technical progress Council Directive 70/157/EEC on the approximation of the laws of the Member States relating to the permissible sound level and the exhaust system of motor vehicles, OJ L 131, 18.5.1981, pp. 6–27.

[15] Commission Directive 84/372/EEC of 3 July 1984 adapting to technical progress Council Directive 70/157/EEC on the approximation of the laws of the Member States relating to the permissible sound level and the exhaust system of motor vehicles, OJ L 196, 26.7.1984, pp. 47–49.

[16] Commission Directive 96/20/EC of 27 March 1996 adapting to technical progress Council Directive 70/157/EEC relating to the permissible sound level and the exhaust system of motor vehicles, OJ L 92, 13.4.1996, pp. 23–35.

B. Agricultural and Forestry Tractors

Directive 2009/63[17] introduces provisions on certain parts and characteristics of wheeled agricultural or forestry tractors. "Agricultural or forestry tractor" means

> any motor vehicle, fitted with wheels or endless tracks and having at least two axles, the main function of which lies in its tractive power and which is specially designed to tow, push, carry or power certain tools, machinery or trailers intended for agricultural or forestry use. It may be equipped to carry a load and passengers. (Article 1)

The Directive applies to tractors which are fitted with pneumatic tyres and which have two axles and a maximum design speed of between 6 and 40 km/h (Article 1(2)). The Annexes include the tractor testing conditions, as well as specifications with respect to the exhaust system. Annex V to the Directive deals with the audible warning device, and Annex VI determines the permissible sound levels.

In addition, Directive 2009/76[18] concerns the driver-perceived noise level of agricultural and forestry tractors.

C. Two- or Three-wheel Vehicles and Quadricycles

Regulation No. 168/2013[19] lays down relatively high emission norms. The Regulation is applicable to "two- or three-wheel vehicles and quadricycles that are intended to travel on public roads, including those designed

---

[17] Directive 2009/63 of 13 July 2009 on certain parts and characteristics of wheeled agricultural or forestry tractors, [2009] OJ L 214/23. The Directive repeals Directives 74/151 of 4 March 1974 on the approximation of the laws of the Member States relating to certain parts and characteristics of wheeled agricultural or forestry tractors, [1974] OJ L 84/10 and Directive 74/150 of 4 March 1974 on the approximation of the laws of the Member States relating to the type-approval of wheeled agricultural or forestry tractors, [1974] OJ L 84/10.

[18] Directive 2009/76 of 13 July 2009 relating to the driver-perceived noise level of wheeled agricultural or forestry tractors, [2009] OJ L 201/18. The Directive repeals Council Directive 77/311 of 29 March 1977 on the approximation of the laws of the Member States relating to the driver-perceived noise level of wheeled agricultural or forestry tractors, [1977] OJ L 105/1.

[19] Regulation No 168/2013 of 15 January 2013 on the approval and market surveillance of two- or three-wheel vehicles and quadricycles, [2013] OJ L 60/52. The Regulation repeals Directive 78/1015 of 23 November 1978 on the approximation of the laws of the Member States on the permissible sound level and exhaust system of motorcycles, [1978] OJ L 349/21.

and constructed in one or more stages, and to systems, components and separate technical units, as well as parts and equipment, designed and constructed for such vehicles". As part of the requirements for environmental performance (Article 23) manufacturers have to undertake a sound test in order to receive the EU vehicle type approval (Annex II). In addition, Annex VI includes specifications regarding inter alia pollutant emission and sound-level limit values for type approval and conformity of production.

D. Protection of Workers from Exposure to Noise at Work

Directive 2003/10[20] is based on Article 153 TFEU (ex-137 TEC on social policy). The Directive is part of a set of measures on the introduction of actions to encourage improvements in the safety and health of workers at work.[21] The Directive foresees that for all agents, which it specifies, Union Directives may be enacted in order to protect workers.

Directive 2003/10 lays down minimum requirements for the protection of workers from risks to their health and safety arising from exposure to noise and in particular the risk to hearing (Article 1). It establishes exposure limit values and exposure action values in respect to the daily noise exposure levels and peak sound pressure (Article 3).

Employers have to undertake a risk assessment on the level of noise to which workers are exposed (Article 4). The assessment has to take into account inter alia the level, type and duration of exposure, the exposure limit values and action values, any effects concerning the health and safety of workers belonging to particularly sensitive risk groups; and any indirect effects on workers' health and safety resulting from interactions between noise and warning signals or other sounds that need to be observed in order to reduce the risk of accidents. The assessment further has to include the existence of alternative work equipment designed to reduce noise emission and extension of exposure to noise

---

[20] Directive 2003/10 of 6 February 2003 on the minimum health and safety requirements regarding the exposure of workers to the risks arising from physical agents (noise) (Seventeenth individual Directive within the meaning of Article 16(1) of Directive 89/391/EEC), [2003] OJ L 42/38 and repealing Directive 86/188 of 12 May 1986 on the protection of workers from the risks related to exposure to noise at work, [1986] OJ L 137/28.

[21] The system is put in place by Directive 89/391/EEC of 12 June 1989 on the introduction of measures to encourage improvements in the safety and health of workers at work, [1989] OJ L 183/1.

beyond normal working hours under the employer's responsibility (Article 4(6)).

Article 5 determines in a more general way that the risks resulting from exposure to noise must be reduced to the lowest level reasonably practicable, taking account of technical progress and of the availability of measures to control the noise, in particular at source. It determines that the most effective way of reducing noise levels at work is to incorporate noise prevention measures into the design of installations and to choose materials, procedures, equipment and working methods and organisation which produce less noise. The priority aim is to achieve reduction at source. Only if there are no reasonable means available to reduce the noise at source and by other means is the use of personal ear protectors required (Article 6). The Directive thus establishes a hierarchy between the obligations of the employer; priority is given to reducing the risks at source and collective protection measures have priority over individual protection measures.[22]

The Directive further contains provisions regarding the training and information for workers relating to risks resulting from exposure to noise (Article 8), consultation and participation (Article 9) and health surveillance.

E. Outdoor Use Equipment

Directive 2000/14[23] harmonises the method of determining noise emission standards, conformity assessment procedures, marking, technical documentation and collection of data concerning the noise emission in the environment of equipment for use outdoors (Article 1). It is applicable to equipment for use outdoors as defined in Annex I. The Directive is not applicable to equipment that is primarily intended for the transport of goods or persons by road, rail, air or on waterways and to equipment specially designed and constructed for military and police purposes and for emergency services (Article 2). The Directive differentiates between equipment which is subject to noise limits (Article 12) and equipment

---

[22] Case C-256/10 *Barcenilla Fernández and Macedo Lozano*, ECR [2011] I-4083, at 28 and 33.

[23] Directive 2000/14 of 8 May 2000 on the approximation of the laws of the Member States relating to the noise emission in the environment by equipment for use outdoors, [2000] OJ L 162/1, and repealing Directive 79/113 of 19 December 1978 on the approximation of the laws of the Member States relating to the determination of the noise emission of construction plants and equipment, [1979] OJ L 33/15.

subject to noise marking (i.e. the maximum noise level; Article 13). For the former category, limit values are set for the guaranteed sound power level; for the latter category, the guaranteed sound power level of the equipment is subject to noise marking only. In addition, Annex III establishes the method of measurement of airborne noise emitted by equipment for outdoor use.

Directive 2000/14 is the result of a replacement of a set of directives containing emission limits with respect to noise emission for different categories. This "mega Directive", which integrates all previous legislation and extends its scope of application, was announced in the 1996 Green Paper on future noise policy.[24] It inter alia replaced Directive 84/532 and the legislation adopted by the Council in amongst others the following categories: compressors (Council Directive 84/533[25] adapted by Commission Directive 85/406[26]); tower cranes (Council Directive 84/534,[27] amended by Council Directive 87/405[28]); welding generators (Council Directive 84/535[29]); power generators (Council Directive 84/536[30] amended by Commission Directive 85/408[31]); and hydraulic excavators, rope-operated excavators, dozers,

---

[24] Commission Green Paper on the future EC noise policy, COM (96) 540.

[25] Council Directive 84/533/EEC of 17 September 1984 on the approximation of the laws of the Member States relating to the permissible sound power level of compressors, OJ L 300, 19.11.1984, pp. 123–129.

[26] Commission Directive 85/406/EEC of 11 July 1985 adapting to technical progress Council Directive 84/533/EEC on the approximation of the laws of the Member States relating to the permissible sound power level of compressors, OJ L 233, 30.8.1985, pp. 11–15.

[27] Council Directive 84/534/EEC of 17 September 1984 on the approximation of the laws of the Member States relating to the permissible sound power level of tower cranes, OJ L 300, 19.11.1984, pp. 130–141.

[28] Council Directive 87/405/EEC of 25 June 1987 amending Directive 84/534/EEC on the approximation of the laws of the Member States relating to the permissible sound power level of tower cranes, OJ L 220, 8.8.1987, pp. 60–64.

[29] Council Directive 84/535/EEC of 17 September 1984 on the approximation of the laws of the Member States relating to the permissible sound power level of welding generators, OJ L 300, 19.11.1984, pp. 142–148.

[30] Council Directive 84/536/EEC of 17 September 1984 on the approximation of the laws of the Member States relating to the permissible sound power level of power generators, OJ L 300, 19.11.1984, pp. 149–155.

[31] Commission Directive 85/408/EEC of 11 July 1985 adapting to technical progress Council Directive 84/536/EEC on the approximation of the laws of the Member States relating to the permissible sound power level of power generators, OJ L 233, 30.8.1985, pp. 18–19.

loaders and excavator-loaders (Council Directive 86/662,[32] amended by Council Directive 89/514[33] and by Council Directive 95/27[34]).

F. Noise Emission by Aircraft

The regulation of noise emission by aircraft at source has to a great extent been dealt with at the international level. A lot of work in this field has been done by the 1944 Chicago Convention on International Civil Aviation, specifically by Annex 16 on Environmental Protection to this Treaty, and by the International Civil Aviation Organization. The Annex deals with inter alia the technical procedure which needs to be followed in order to obtain a "noise certificate", and it defines the emission norms. Regulation No 216/2008 on common rules in the field of civil aviation and establishing a European Aviation Safety Agency[35] provides binding authority in the Union to the emission standards of Annex 16 (Article 6).

Further, Regulation No 598/2014[36] establishes rules and procedures with regard to the introduction of noise-related operating restrictions at Union airports. The Regulation inter alia establishes rules regarding noise-related operating on an airport-by-airport basis. It aims at improving the noise climate and to limit or reduce the number of people significantly affected by the potentially harmful effects of aircraft noise and tries to establish a balanced approach (Article 1). Therefore it establishes some general rules on aircraft noise management, including economic incentives as a noise management measure and performance-based operating

---

[32] Council Directive 86/662/EEC of 22 December 1986 on the limitation of noise emitted by hydraulic excavators, rope-operated excavators, dozers, loaders and excavator-loaders, OJ L 384, 31.12.1986, pp. 1–11.

[33] Commission Directive 89/514/EEC of 2 August 1989 adapting to technical progress Council Directive 86/662/EEC on the limitation of noise emitted by hydraulic excavators, rope-operated excavators, dozers, loaders and excavator-loaders, OJ L 253, 30.8.1989, pp. 35–43.

[34] European Parliament and Council Directive 95/27/EC of 29 June 1995 amending Council Directive 86/662/EEC on the limitation of noise emitted by hydraulic excavators, rope-operated excavators, dozers, loaders and excavator-loaders, OJ L 168, 18.7.1995, pp. 14–17.

[35] Regulation No 216/2008 of 20 February 2008 on common rules in the field of civil aviation and establishing a European Aviation Safety Agency, and repealing Council Directive 91/670, Regulation No 1592/2002 and Directive 2004/36/EC, [2008] OJ L 79/1.

[36] Regulation No 598/2014 of 16 April 2014 on the establishment of rules and procedures with regard to the introduction of noise-related operating restrictions at Union airports within a Balanced Approach and repealing Directive 2002/30/EC, [2014] OJ L 173/65.

restrictions (Articles 5 and 8). It inter alia specifies the objectives and stresses the link with other elements of a balanced approach and other instruments to manage air traffic noise, as well as specifies the allocation of responsibilities and lists general requirements to manage noise.

Finally, Directive 2006/93[37] regulates the operation of civil subsonic jet aeroplanes. The Directive is applicable to all aeroplanes with a maximum take-off mass of 34,000 kg or more or with a certified maximum internal accommodation for the aeroplane type in question consisting of more than 19 passenger seats, excluding any seats for crew only (Article 1). Member States must ensure that all civil subsonic jet aeroplanes operating from airports situated in their territory comply with the standards specified in Part II, Chapter 3, Volume 1 of Annex 16 to the Convention on International Civil Aviation.

---

[37] Directive 2006/93 of 12 December 2006 on the regulation of the operation of aeroplanes covered by Part II, Chapter 3, Volume 1 of Annex 16 to the Convention on International Civil Aviation, second edition (1988), [2006] OJ L 374/1.

13. Air pollution legislation and policy

Air pollution has been on the European environmental agenda for several decades. The 2005 Thematic Strategy on air pollution assessed the situation and provided interim objectives and suggested inter alia to promote integration of air pollution and environmental concerns into other policy areas, as well as to modernise legislation and focus on the most serious pollutants. In its 2005 strategy, the Commission promoted the restructuring of existing provisions into a single directive and the introduction of new air quality standards for fine particulate matter, as well as the revision of national emissions ceilings as key to a successful implementation.[1] This chapter discusses air policy and its changes in the last decade, firstly looking at general legislative tools on air quality, then discussing air emissions and sector specific regulation and harmonisation applicable to air pollution.

I. AIR QUALITY

A. The Air Quality Directive

The new 2008 Air Quality Directive[2] recast the Framework Directive[3] and its three Daughter Directives[4] to one single instrument on ambient air

---

[1] COM (2005) 446, p. 5.

[2] Directive 2008/50 of 21 May 2008 on ambient air quality and cleaner air for Europe, [2008] OJ L 152/1.

[3] Council Directive 96/62 of 27 September 1996 on ambient air quality assessment and management, [1996] OJ L 296/55.

[4] Directive 1999/30 of 22 April 1999 relating to limit values for sulphur dioxide, nitrogen dioxide and oxides of nitrogen, particulate matter and lead in ambient air, [1999] OJ L 163/41, Directive 2000/69 of 16 November 2000 relating to limit values for benzene and carbon monoxide in ambient air, [2000] OJ L 313/12 and Directive 2002/3 of 12 February 2002 relating to ozone in ambient air, [2002] OJ L 67/14, as well as Decision 97/101 establishing a reciprocal exchange of information and data from networks and individual stations measuring ambient air pollution within the Member States, [1997] OJ L 35/14.

quality and cleaner air for Europe. Only the fourth Daughter Directive 2004/107[5] is still a stand-alone instrument.

The Directive defines and establishes objectives for ambient air quality designed to avoid, prevent or reduce harmful effects on human health and the environment. It introduces common methods and criteria to assess the ambient air quality in Member States. It further aims at obtaining information on ambient air quality in order to help combat air pollution and nuisance and to monitor long-term trends and improvements resulting from national and Union measures, as well as promoting cooperation between the Member States in reducing air pollution. In addition, the Directive establishes that information on ambient air quality is made available to the public and that good air quality is maintained or that it is improved in other cases (Article 1). Member States have to establish zones and agglomerations throughout their territory in which the air quality assessment and management is carried out (Article 4).

The air quality assessment itself relates to firstly sulphur dioxide, nitrogen dioxide (NO_2) and oxides of nitrogen, particulate matter (PM), lead, benzene and carbon monoxide. For these compounds upper and lower assessment thresholds are specified in Section A of Annex II and the assessment criteria are contained in Annex III (Article 5). In all zones and agglomerations where the level of pollutants *exceeds* the *upper* assessment threshold established for those pollutants, fixed measurements are to be used to assess the ambient air quality. Those fixed measurements may be supplemented by modelling techniques and/or indicative measurements to provide adequate information on the spatial distribution of the ambient air quality. In areas where the pollution level is *below* the upper assessment threshold established, a combination of fixed measurements and modelling techniques and/or indicative measurements have to be used to assess the ambient air quality. And lastly in cases where the level is *below* the *lower* assessment threshold, modelling techniques or objective-estimation techniques or both are sufficient for the assessment of the ambient air quality (Article 6). In addition, sampling points for the measurement of these compounds have to be set up in locations determined using the criteria set forth in Annex III of the Directive. In each zone or agglomeration where fixed measurements are the sole source of information for assessing air quality, the number of sampling points

---

[5] Directive 2004/107 of 15 December 2004 relating to arsenic, cadmium, mercury, nickel and polycyclic aromatic hydrocarbons in ambient air, [2005] OJ L 23/3.

for each relevant pollutant shall not be less than the minimum number of sampling points specified in Section A of Annex V (Article 7). The reference measurement methods and criteria are specified in Section A and Section C of Annex VI.

Secondly, in a zone or agglomeration where concentrations of ozone have exceeded the long-term objectives specified in Section C of Annex VII during any of the previous five years of measurement, fixed measurements need to be taken (Article 9). The siting of sampling points for the measurement of ozone need to be determined using the criteria set out in Annex VIII (Article 10) and the reference method for measurement of ozone is set out in point 8 of Section A of Annex VI (Article 11).

The Directive further includes provisions relating to the management of ambient air quality. It states that, for the case where the levels of sulphur dioxide, NO_2, PM10, PM2.5, lead, benzene and carbon monoxide in ambient air are below the respective limit values specified in Annexes XI and XIV, the levels of those pollutants below the limit values have to be maintained and the air quality has to be preserved. In general, the air quality objectives, as originally set in the Daughter Directives, remain unchanged and are now included in Annex I to the Directive. The new instrument adds to the existing quality objectives new ones for fine particles (PM2.5) including the obligation on the Member States to establish national PM2.5 exposure reduction targets, a PM2.5 target value and limit values for the protection of human health (Articles 15 and 16). In this regard, the Directive also foresees the possibility for time extensions of three years (PM10) or up to five years (NO_2, benzene) for complying with limit values, based on conditions and the assessment by the European Commission (Article 22); the Directive also includes the possibility of discounting natural sources of pollution when assessing compliance against limit values (Article 20).

The Directive sets requirements in zones and agglomerations where ozone concentrations exceed the target values and long-term objectives (Article 17) and where ozone concentrations meet these objectives (Article 18), as well as measures in the event that information or alert thresholds are being exceeded (Article 19).

The establishment of air quality plans is required for zones or agglomerations where the levels of pollutants in ambient air exceed any limit value or target value and a margin of tolerance (Article 23). Further, in areas where there is a risk that the levels of pollutants will exceed the alert thresholds specified in Annex XII, Member States have to draw up action plans indicating the short-term measures to be taken to reduce the risk or duration of the exceedance (Article 24). The drawing up of such action plans was the subject matter in *Janecek*[6] which dealt with Article 7(3) of the Air Quality Framework Directive. The CJEU held that

> where there is a risk that the limit values or alert thresholds may be exceeded, persons directly concerned must be in a position to require the competent national authorities to draw up an action plan, even though, under national law, those persons may have other courses of action available to them for requiring those authorities to take measures to combat atmospheric pollution. The Member States are obliged, subject to judicial review by the national courts, only to take such measures – in the context of an action plan and in the short term – as are capable of reducing to a minimum the risk that the limit values or alert thresholds may be exceeded and of ensuring a gradual return to a level below those values or thresholds, taking into account the factual circumstances and all opposing interests.

The Directive further addresses transboundary air pollution (Article 25) and includes provisions on information and reporting (Articles 26–28).

The CJEU, in *ClientEarth*[7] had to deal with questions relating to Articles 13, 22 and 23 of the Air Quality Directive, inter alia regarding the Member States' obligation to apply for postponement of the limit value deadline and related exceptions, as well as whether an air quality plan was sufficient to comply with obligations under the Directive. The court confirmed, regarding the postponement of compliance by a maximum of five years, that where a Member State cannot comply within the deadline and seeks for such an postponement, the Member State concerned is obliged to make an application and to establish for that purpose a plan, and that it follows both from the context of that provision and the aim pursued by the EU legislature, even though the wording of Article 22(1) does not expressively state so (para. 27). Article 22 of Directive 2008/50 does not contain any exception to the obligation flowing from Article 22(1) (para. 34). The court further specifies that

> it is incompatible with the binding effect that Article 288 TFEU ascribes to Directive 2008/50 to exclude, in principle, the possibility of the obligation imposed by that directive being relied on by the persons concerned. That consideration applies particularly in respect of a directive whose objective is to control and reduce atmospheric pollution and which is designed, therefore, to protect public health (see, to that effect, judgment in *Janecek*, EU:C:2008:447, paragraph 37). (Para. 54)

---

[6] Case C-237/07 *Janecek*, ECR [2008] I-6221.
[7] Case C-404/13 *ClientEarth*, ECLI:EU:C:2013:805.

B. The Fourth Daughter Directive

As established above, the new Directive on Air Quality repeals the Air Quality Framework Directive and all Daughter Directives, except the fourth Daughter Directive 2004/107 relating to arsenic, cadmium, mercury, nickel and polycyclic aromatic hydrocarbons in ambient air.[8]

The Directive completes the list of pollutants initially described in the Framework Directive. The aims of the Directive are the same as the ones established for the Air Quality Directive with the difference that it is applicable to the above-cited compounds in the air. The Directive contains similar provisions to the Air Quality Directive on target values (Article 3), assessment of ambient air concentrations and deposition rates (Article 4) and transmission of (public) information and reporting (Articles 5 and 7).

II. NATIONAL EMISSION CEILINGS

The National Emission Ceilings Directive[9] aims at limiting the emissions of acidifying and eutrophying pollutants and ozone precursors. It intends to improve the environmental and human health protection against risks of adverse effects from acidification, soil eutrophication and ground-level ozone. The pollutants responsible for these causes are sulphur dioxide, nitrogen oxides, volatile organic compounds and ammonia. The Directive is a means to move towards the long-term objectives of not exceeding critical levels and loads and of not increasing health risks from air pollution (Article 1). It is therefore aimed at protecting the public from emissions. The Directive establishes national emission ceilings, taking the years 2010 and 2020 as benchmarks, but leaves the exact measures on how to reach the emission ceilings up to the Member States. The ceilings are laid down in Annex I to the Directive.

The Directive generally covers all emissions of the Member States and all sources of pollutants, excluding inter alia emissions from international maritime traffic and aircraft emissions beyond the landing and take-off cycle (Article 2).

The Directive further establishes interim environmental objectives which had to be reached by 2010 relating to acidification and health- and

---

[8] Directive 2004/107 of 15 December 2004 relating to arsenic, cadmium, mercury, nickel and polycyclic aromatic hydrocarbons in ambient air, [2005] OJ L 23/3.

[9] Directive 2001/813 October 2001 on national emission ceilings for certain atmospheric pollutants, [2001] OJ L 309/22.

vegetation-related ground-level ozone exposure (Article 5). In order to achieve these objectives the Member States had to pass national programmes for the progressive reduction of the pollutants (Article 6). In addition, they have to annually update the national emission inventories and projections with the methodologies specified in Annex III (Article 7).

The Directive is currently under review and a proposal for a follow-up Directive establishing new national reduction commitments until 2030 has been published but is still awaiting its first reading in Parliament. The proposal does not only include targets for the substances already addressed but also for fine particulate matter and methane emissions.[10]

III. SECTOR SPECIFIC REGULATION AND HARMONISATION

The impact of human actions on the air is not only regulated by specific air quality and similar legislative tools but also through the legislation applicable to other sectors, such as transport, fuels and industry installations.[11] This section describes the sector specific regulation applicable to air pollution in the transportation sector, as well as the Paints Directive as an example from the industry sector.

A. Transport Emissions

Transport emissions are regulated by a vast amount of mostly very technical directives and regulations applicable to inter alia motor vehicles, ships, locomotives and the quality of petrol and diesel fuels,[12] as well as non-road mobile machinery.[13] This section will discuss the most important pieces of legislation but will not provide a complete overview.

---

[10] Proposal for a Directive on the reduction of national emissions of certain atmospheric pollutants and amending Directive 2003/35/EC, Brussels, COM (2013) 920, 18.12.2013, COD 2013/443.

[11] Directive 2010/75 of 24 November 2010 on industrial emissions, [2010] OJ L 334/17.

[12] Directive 98/70 of 13 October 1998 relating to the quality of petrol and diesel fuels and amending Directive 93/12, [1998] OJ L 350/58, as lastly amended by Directive 2011/63 of 1 June 2011 amending, for the purpose of its adaptation to technical progress, Directive 98/70 relating to the quality of petrol and diesel fuels, [2011] OJ L 147/15.

[13] Directive 97/68 of 16 December 1997 on the approximation of the laws of the Member States relating to measures against the emission of gaseous and

Road vehicles

In the past motor vehicle emissions have been regulated by Directive 70/220[14] for light-duty vehicles and 88/77/EC for heavy-duty vehicles. In order to keep up with technical progress in the industry, both Directives have been amended to strengthen the emission limit values of inter alia carbon monoxide (CO), volatile organic compounds (VOC) and nitrogen oxides (NOx).

Regulation 443/2009 sets emission performance standards for new passenger cars.[15] In addition, Regulation 333/2014[16] includes the emission target from 2020 onwards. The Regulations set out mandatory reductions of emissions of CO_2 with a view to attaining the objective of 120 g CO_2/km, and 95 g CO_2/km as of 2020. This will be achieved by two means: a reduction to 130 g CO_2/km through motor technology improvement, and a further reduction of 10 g CO_2/km via more efficient car features such as, for instance, mandatory fitting of gear shift indicators and tyre pressure monitoring systems, improved air conditioners in cars, lower rolling resistance of tyres, and in an increase in the use of biofuels.

These objectives do not apply individually to every new vehicle but to the average fleet of new cars of a particular manufacturer. Following discussions in the European Parliament and the Council of Transport Ministers, the text of the Regulation also contains a softening of the requirement put on the industry by varying the average to be met, as follows:

- 65 per cent in 2012,
- 75 per cent in 2013,
- 80 per cent in 2014,
- 90 per cent from 2015 to 2019,
- 95 per cent in 2020,
- 100 per cent by the end of 2020 onwards.

The Council of Transport Ministers justified such a progressive phase-in by the "length of industrial planning and production cycles" and by the

---

particulate pollutants from internal combustion engines to be installed in non-road mobile machinery, [1998] OJ L 59/1, as amended.

[14] Directive 70/220 of 20 March 1970 on the approximation of the laws of the Member States relating to measures to be taken against air pollution by gases from positive-ignition engines of motor vehicles, [1970] OJ L 76/1.

[15] Regulation No 443/2009 of 23 April 2009 setting emission performance standards for new passenger cars as part of the Community's integrated approach to reduce CO 2 emissions from light-duty vehicles, [2009] OJ L 140/1.

[16] Regulation 333/2014 of 11 March 2014 amending Regulation (EC) No 443/2009 to define the modalities for reaching the 2020 target to reduce CO 2 emissions from new passenger cars, [2014] OJ L 103/15.

necessity to give the industry time to adjust. Regulation 333/2014 further establishes the system of super-credits for reaching the 95 g CO_2/km target. Accordingly,

> in calculating the average specific emissions of CO 2, each new passenger car with specific emissions of CO 2 of less than 50 g CO 2 /km shall be counted as:
> - 2 passenger cars in 2020,
> - 1,67 passenger cars in 2021,
> - 1,33 passenger cars in 2022,
> - 1 passenger car from 2023,
>
> for the year in which it is registered in the period from 2020 to 2022, subject to a cap of 7,5 g CO 2 /km over that period for each manufacturer. (Article 1(5) Regulation 333/2014).

Manufacturers that do not meet the objectives will have to pay the following penalties:

- From 2012 until 2018, where the average emission of a manufacturer's fleet of new cars exceeds the target, a penalty for every new car of:
  - EUR 5 for the 1st gram,
  - EUR 15 for the 2nd gram,
  - EUR 25 for the 3rd gram,
  - EUR 95 for every gram above 3 grams of excess.
- From 2019, where a new car exceeds the target, a penalty of:
  - EUR 95 for every gram.

It will be possible for certain manufacturers that produce small volumes of cars to apply for a derogation to the Regulation for a period not exceeding five years. Manufacturers will also be able to apply for a derogation taking into consideration their CO_2 savings achieved through the use of innovative technologies.

Regulation 715/2007[17] on type approval of motor vehicles with respect to emissions from light passenger and commercial vehicles and on access to vehicle repair and maintenance information repeals Directive 70/220. The Regulation establishes common technical requirements on emissions for the type approval of motor vehicles and replacement parts, such as replacement pollution control devices. These devices are components

---

[17] Regulation No 715/2007 of 20 June 2007 on type approval of motor vehicles with respect to emissions from light passenger and commercial vehicles (Euro 5 and Euro 6) and on access to vehicle repair and maintenance information, [2007] OJ L 171/1.

of a vehicle that control and/or limit tailpipe and evaporative emissions (Article 3(11)). In addition, it lays down rules for in-service conformity, durability of pollution control devices, on-board diagnostic (OBD)[18] systems, measurement of fuel consumption and accessibility of vehicle repair and maintenance information (Article 1). It is applicable to vehicles of categories M1, M2, N1 and N2 as defined in Annex II to Directive 70/156 with a reference mass not exceeding 2610 kg, and, at the manufacturer's request 2840 kg (Article 2). Reference mass is the mass of the vehicle in running order less the uniform mass of the driver of 75 kg and increased by a uniform mass of 100 kg (Article 3(3)).

The Regulation outlines the manufacturers' type approval obligations. Accordingly, he has to inter alia demonstrate that all new vehicles sold, registered or put into service in the Union and all new replacement pollution control devices requiring type approval are type approved. These obligations include meeting the emission limits set out in Annex I. Further, manufacturers have to ensure that type approval procedures for verifying conformity of production, durability of pollution control devices and in-service conformity are met (Article 4). Article 5 of the Regulation establishes further requirements and tests for type approval. Chapter III of the Regulation contains provisions regarding access to vehicle repair and maintenance information. The latest amendment is Regulation 459/2012[19] introducing the "Euro 6" norm for emissions from light passenger and commercial vehicles, thus tightening the emission values even further. As of January 2014 all new motor vehicles have to be equipped with a Euro 6 certified engine. Euro 6 is reducing the emissions of NOx from diesel cars from 180 mg/km to 80 mg/km.

Emissions from heavy-duty vehicles are currently regulated under Regulation 595/2009[20] which establishes the emissions limit values from heavy-duty vehicles (Euro VI).

---

[18] Defined as "a system for emission control which has the capability of identifying the likely area of malfunction by means of fault codes stored in a computer memory" (Article 3(9)).

[19] Regulation No 459/2012 of 29 May 2012 amending Regulation No 715/2007 of Regulation No 692/2008 as regards emissions from light passenger and commercial vehicles (Euro 6), [2012] OJ L 142/16.

[20] Regulation No 595/2009 of 18 June 2009 on type-approval of motor vehicles and engines with respect to emissions from heavy duty vehicles (Euro VI) and on access to vehicle repair and maintenance information and amending Regulation No 715/2007 and Directive 2007/46 and repealing Directives 80/1269, 2005/55 and 2005/78, [2009] OJ L 188/1.

Marine emissions

Efforts to regulate and control the emissions from ships are, besides on the European level, to a large extent also done at the international level by the International Maritime Organization (IMO) and the UNFCCC in order to reach a global agreement. In 2011, the IMO adopted mandatory measures to reduce emissions of greenhouse gases (GHGs) from international shipping through adding Chapter 4 to Annex VI of the MARPOL[21] agreement. More precisely, the chapter adds regulations on energy efficiency for ships: the mandatory "Energy Efficiency Design Index" (EEDI) for new ships and the "Ship Energy Efficiency Management Plan" (SEEMP) for all ships. The measures entered into force in January 2013. The EU has been supporting this approach in its strategy on "Integrating maritime transport emissions in the EU's greenhouse gas reduction policies"[22] and included the maritime emissions in the Union's reduction commitment.[23]

In addition, the Union put forward a legislative proposal on monitoring, reporting and verification of CO_2 emissions from maritime transport.[24] The draft Regulation would amend Regulation 525/2013.[25] The proposal establishes common principles and methods for monitoring and reporting of CO_2 emissions and other climate relevant information from ships. It aims at covering ships above 5000 gross tons in respect of emissions released during their voyages from the last port of call to a port under the jurisdiction of a Member State and from a port under the jurisdiction of a Member State to their next port of call, as well as within ports under the jurisdiction of a Member State. It further outlines requirements regarding the content and submission of monitoring plans and of emission reports, as well as introducing verification and accreditation requirements.

To date, Directive 2012/33,[26] the Sulphur Directive, amending Directive 1999/32, regulates sulphur emissions from ships by limiting the maximum sulphur content of marine fuel. According to the Directive, Member States have to ensure that marine fuels are not used within their territory if their sulphur content exceeds 3.50 per cent by mass, except for fuels supplied

---

[21] International Convention for the Prevention of Pollution from Ships, 1973.
[22] Brussels, 28.6.2013, COM (2013) 479.
[23] See COM (2013) 479, 4f.
[24] Brussels, 28.6.2013, COM (2013) 480, 2013/224 (COD).
[25] Regulation No 525/2013 of 21 May 2013 on a mechanism for monitoring and reporting greenhouse gas emissions and for reporting other information at national and Union level relevant to climate change and repealing Decision No 280/2004, [2013] OJ L 165/13.
[26] Directive 2012/33 of 21 November 2012 amending Council Directive 1999/32 as regards the sulphur content of marine fuels, [2012] OJ L 327/1.

to ships using emission abatement methods operating in closed mode (Article 3a). The Directive also regulates the maximum sulphur content of marine fuels used in territorial seas, exclusive economic zones and pollution control zones of Member States, including sulphur emission control areas (SECAs) and by passenger ships operating on regular services to or from Union ports. It designates the Baltic Sea, the North Sea and the English Channel as SECAs and limits the maximum sulphur content of the fuels used by ships operating in these sea areas to 1.5 per cent. (Article 4a).

B. The Paints Directive

The 2004 Directive on the limitation of emissions of VOCs due to the use of organic solvents in certain paints and varnishes and vehicle refinishing products[27] aims at limiting the total content of VOCs in order to prevent or reduce air pollution resulting from the contribution of these compounds to the formation of tropospheric ozone. Therefore, the Directive harmonises the technical specifications for products set out in Annex I (Article 1). Products may only be placed on the market if the VOC content does not exceed the limit values set out in Annex II and if they carry a label indicating the subcategory of the product and the relevant VOC limit values in g/l as referred to in Annex II and the maximum content of VOC in g/l of the product in a ready to use condition (Articles 3 and 4). The analytical methods to be used in order to determine compliance with the VOC content limit values are set out in Annex III. Member States are required to set up a monitoring programme for the purpose of verifying compliance with the Directive (Article 6).

---

[27] Directive 2004/42 of 21 April 2004 on the limitation of emissions of volatile organic compounds due to the use of organic solvents in certain paints and varnishes and vehicle refinishing products and amending Directive 1999/13, [2004] OJ L 143/87.

14. Climate change legislation and policy

In the light of the Community's commitment under the Kyoto Protocol of the UN Framework Convention on Climate Change, the 7th Environmental Action Programme aims at achieving the climate change targets the Union has committed to and identifies policy gaps where additional action is needed. The need for structural changes, especially in the transport and energy sectors, calls for stronger efforts in energy efficiency and energy saving, the establishment of an EU-wide emissions trading scheme, further research and technological development and awareness raising with citizens so that they can contribute to reducing emissions are some of these concerns.

The strong focus of the European agenda on climate change was also strengthened at a constitutional level through the inclusion of a reference to climate change in the environmental title in the Lisbon Treaty. Article 191 on the environmental objectives now reads: "... promoting measures at international level to deal with regional or worldwide environmental problems, *and in particular combating climate change*" (emphasis added). This explicit inclusion strengthens the EU's leading role in the international battle against climate change.[1]

The 2050 roadmap for moving to a low-carbon economy[2] introduces long-term policy plans in the areas of transport, energy and climate change. The document reconfirmed the European objective to keep climate change below 2 °C, and reducing GHG emissions by 80–95 per cent by 2050 compared to 1990. Long-term goals are inter alia the establishment

---

[1] For a detailed discussion of the Climate Change phenomenon from an international, European and comparative perspective please refer to the contributions in E. Hollo, K. Kulovesi and M. Mehling (eds), *Climate Change and the Law*, Dordrecht: Springer, 2013; as well as G. Van Calster, W. Vandenberghe and L. Reins (eds), *Research Handbook on Climate Change Mitigation Law*, Cheltenham, UK and Northampton, MA, USA: Edward Elgar, 2015; and J. Verschuuren (ed.), *Research Handbook on Climate Change Adaptation Law*, Cheltenham, UK and Northampton, MA, USA: Edward Elgar, 2013.

[2] Brussels, 8.3.2011, COM (2011) 112.

of a "secure, competitive and fully decarbonised power sector, sustainable mobility through fuel efficiency and electrification, addressing the industrial sectors, including energy intensive industries and raising land use productivity sustainably". It further foresees "a major increase in capital investment in low carbon capital markets and the reduction on dependency on fossil fuel imports into the Union, just as the creation of new jobs".

In March 2013 the Commission presented a green paper on a 2030 framework for climate and energy policies.[3] As its name suggests, the policy outlines the priorities until 2030 and thereby takes into account the changes since 2008, when the 2020 goals were established. There are inter alia the world- and European-wide economic crises, which are to some extent still ongoing; financial and budgetary problems of Member States and businesses regarding their ability to pursue long-term investments; the recent developments in the energy markets, affecting all sources from renewables, unconventional gas and oil as well as nuclear energy; and the variation of engagement, commitment and ambition of the international community regarding the reduction of GHG emissions.

The currently most important policy documents addressing the issue of climate change in the EU, as it addresses the immediate future, is the "2020 strategy", which introduced the "2020" goals of a reduction of GHG emissions by 20 per cent, increasing the share of renewables in the EU's energy mix to 20 per cent, and achieving the 20 per cent energy efficiency target, all by 2020.[4]

In order to meet these objectives, the European institutions have passed a vast amount of legislation and policy. This book limits the discussion to the most important tools. In addition, some legislation and policy addressing climate change is discussed in other chapters, for example regarding air pollution (Chapter 13) and eco-labelling (Chapter 6 III).

I. ADAPTATION

The main policy tool regarding climate change adaptation is the 2013 EU adaptation strategy.[5] The strategy "contribute[s] to a more climate-resilient Europe. This means enhancing the preparedness and capacity to respond to the impacts of climate change at local, regional,

---

[3] Brussels, 27.3.2013, COM (2013) 169.
[4] Brussels, 3.3.2010, COM (2010) 2020.
[5] Brussels, 16.4.2013, COM (2013) 216.

national and EU levels, developing a coherent approach and improving coordination."[6] The key to the strategy is to promote the creation of national adaptation strategies. Most Member States have adopted such a strategy;[7] its drafting is also recommended by the UNFCCC as a tool to prioritise action and investment.[8] In 2017, the Commission will assess if the voluntary commitment to draft a national strategy is enough to ensure adaptation actions in the Member States or if a legally binding instrument is necessary. Further, the Commission promotes the Programme for the Environment and Climate Action (LIFE) funding programme to support capacity building and speed up adaptation action in Europe, especially for cross-border management of floods, transboundary coastal management, sustainable management of water and mainstreaming adaptation into urban land use planning, as well as supporting adaptation at the local level under the Covenant of Mayors initiative.[9]

The adaptation strategy further aims to improve informed decision-making by stakeholders by addressing knowledge gaps relating to amongst others, information on damage and adaptation costs and benefits as well as regional and local-level analyses and risk assessments. The Commission also seeks to further develop the Climate-ADAPT platform,[10] a Commission initiative serving as an information sharing and access platform. The platform currently contains information regarding the expected climate change in Europe; current and future vulnerability of regions and sectors; national and transnational adaptation strategies; adaptation case studies; and potential adaptation options and tools that support adaptation planning.[11] The adaptation strategy introduces the establishment of cost–benefit assessments of different policy experiences

---

[6] Brussels, 16.4.2013, COM (2013) 216, 5.

[7] See for an overview http://climate-adapt.eea.europa.eu/countries, last consulted 21.11.2015.

[8] For a detailed discussion on climate change adaptation in specific sectors from an international perspective please refer to J. Verschuuren (ed.) *Research Handbook on Climate Change Adaptation Law*, Cheltenham, UK and Northampton, MA, USA: Edward Elgar, 2013.

[9] "The Covenant of Mayors is the mainstream European movement involving local and regional authorities, voluntarily committing to increasing energy efficiency and use of renewable energy sources on their territories. By their commitment, Covenant signatories aim to meet and exceed the European Union 20% CO_2 reduction objective by 2020"; see also http://www.eumayors.eu/about/covenant-of-mayors_en.html, last consulted 21.11.2015.

[10] Available at http://climate-adapt.eea.europa.eu/, last consulted 21.11.2015.

[11] http://climate-adapt.eea.europa.eu/, last consulted 21.11.2015.

and an improvement in funding local and regional authorities, as well as the inclusion of the Copernicus service.[12]

The last set of actions outlined by the strategy relates to mainstreaming climate change adaptation into other policy sectors, called "climate-proofing" EU action. The strategy is therefore accompanied by several staff working documents for different areas. For example, in the area of agriculture and forestry, the document establishes principles and recommendations for integrating climate change adaptation considerations under the 2014–2020 rural development programmes[13] and EU Forest Strategy;[14] the document in the area of infrastructure is on adaptation of infrastructure to climate change[15] and provides guidance in conjunction with the Cohesion Policy.[16] Further staff documents addressing adaptation in coastal and marine issues exist;[17] as well as ones relating to climate change adaptation in the Maritime and Fisheries Fund operational programmes[18] and human, animal and plant health.[19]

However, as climate impacts differ in different regions, most adaptation initiatives are still taken at the local or national level.

II. MITIGATION

The EU has passed several legislative tools aimed at climate change mitigation, such as the Renewable Energy Directive,[20] the Energy Efficiency Directive,[21] the Buildings Directive[22] and a strategy on low-carbon technical

---

[12] The European Earth Observation Programme, more information available at http://ec.europa.eu/enterprise/policies/space/copernicus/, last consulted 21.11.2015.
[13] Brussels, 16.4.2013, SWD (2013) 139.
[14] Brussels, 20.9.2013, COM (2013) 659.
[15] Brussels, 16.4.2013, SWD (2013) 137.
[16] Brussels, 16.4.2013, SWD (2013) 135.
[17] Brussels, 16.4.2013, SWD (2013) 133.
[18] Brussels, 30.7.2013, SWD (2013) 299.
[19] Brussels, 16.4.2013, SWD (2013) 136.
[20] Directive 2009/28 of 23 April 2009 on the promotion of the use of energy from renewable sources and amending and subsequently repealing Directives 2001/77 and 2003/30, [2009] OJ L 140/16.
[21] Directive 2012/27 of 25 October 2012 on energy efficiency, amending Directives 2009/125 and 2010/30 and repealing Directives 2004/8 and 2006/32, [2012] OJ L 315/1.
[22] Directive 2010/31 of 19 May 2010 on the energy performance of buildings, [2010] OJ L 153/13.

development.[23] Not all these (mostly energy related) instruments will be discussed here.[24] The focus is on the EU Emission Trading System (EU ETS) which is a key tool for climate change mitigation, because industry activities are perceived as one of the main GHG emitters, alongside emissions from transport. These which will subsequently be assessed as well.

A. The European Emissions Trading System

In 2003, Directive 2003/87[25] established a scheme for GHG emission allowance trading within the Union in order to promote reductions of GHG emissions in a cost-effective and economically efficient manner. The EU ETS is the first and biggest international system for trading GHG emission allowances, covering 11,000 installations in 31 countries, as well as airlines.[26] It is applicable to the activities listed in Annex I to the Directive and includes the GHGs CO_2, methane (CH_4), nitrous oxide (N_2O), hydrofluorocarbons (HFCs), perfluorocarbons (PFCs) and sulphur hexafluoride (SF_6). The EU ETS has been developed in phases; allowances are valid for emissions during the trading period for which they are issued. The first trading period ranging from 2005 to 2007, and was characterised as the learning by doing phase; the second period from 2008 to 2012 reduced the number of available allowances by 6.5 per cent; however, the economic crises cut demand and thus emissions so that the phase ended with a surplus of unused allowances on the carbon market. This lead to calls for a structural reform of the EU ETS in order to address the growing surplus of emissions.[27]

The third trading period started in 2013 and is scheduled until 2020. The

---

[23] Communication from the Commission, A European strategic energy technology plan (SET plan) – "Towards a low carbon future", COM (2007) 723.

[24] For a discussion on climate change mitigation tools in the different sectors in the EU, the United States and the Asian Pacific Region, please refer to G. Van Calster, W. Vandenberghe and L. Reins (eds), *Research Handbook on Climate Change Mitigation Law*, Cheltenham, UK and Northampton, MA, USA: Edward Elgar, 2015.

[25] Directive 2003/87 of 13 October 2003 establishing a scheme for greenhouse gas emission allowance trading within the Community and amending Directive 96/61, [2003] OJ L 275/32.

[26] For an in-depth discussion see D. Ellerman, F.J. Convey and C. de Perthuis, *Pricing Carbon: The European Union Emissions Trading Scheme*, Cambridge: Cambridge University Press, 2010; as well as S. Weishaar, *Towards Auctioning: The Transformation of the European Greenhouse Gas Emissions Trading System – Present and Future Challenges to Competition Law*, Climate Change Law, Policy and Practice Series, Alphen aan den Rijn: Kluwer International Law, 2009.

[27] Proposal for a Decision amending Directive 2003/87 clarifying provisions

phase introduced an EU-wide cap on emissions, which is subsequently reduced by 1.74 per cent each year.[28] It is aimed at reducing the emissions from the activities covered by the Directive by 21 per cent compared to 2005. Further, in the past, the majority of the emission allowances were issued for free; however, from 2013 auctioning is the main method of allocation. Free allocation is aimed to be phased out in its entirety by 2027. The fourth period is scheduled from 2021 to 2028; each subsequent trading period will be seven years.

By 30 April each year at the latest, the operator of each installation has to surrender a number of allowances equal to the total emissions from that installation during the preceding calendar year. These allowances are subsequently cancelled. If the operator does not surrender enough allowances, penalties are issued. These must be effective, proportionate and dissuasive; however, the exact rules are left open to the individual Member States. In order to ensure the accurate accounting of the issue, holding, transfer and cancellation of allowances, Directive 2003/87 required the Member States to establish and maintain registries which are open to the public and contain separate accounts to record the allowances held by each person to whom and from whom allowances are issued or transferred. The 2009 amendment to the ETS Directive replaced the national registries by one Union registry which is also recording national implementation measures.

Commission Regulation 601/2012 establishes the monitoring and reporting provisions pursuant to Directive 2003/87,[29] laying down inter alia general principles for monitoring and reporting. Accordingly, monitoring and reporting has to be complete and cover all process and combustion emissions from all emission sources and source streams belonging to activities listed in Annex I to Directive 2003/87. Further, monitoring and reporting has to be consistent and comparable over time. To that end, operators and aircraft operators are required to use the same monitoring methodologies and data sets, subject to changes and derogations approved by the competent authority. Operators and aircraft operators have to ensure that emission determination is neither systematically nor knowingly inaccurate; they additionally are required to ensure the integrity of

---

on the timing of auctions of greenhouse gas allowances, Brussels, 25.7.2012, COM (2012) 416, 2012/0202 (COD).

[28] See Directive 2009/29 of 23 April 2009 amending Directive 2003/87 so as to improve and extend the greenhouse gas emission allowance trading scheme of the Community, [2009] OJ L 140/63.

[29] Commission Regulation No 601/2012 of 21 June 2012 on the monitoring and reporting of greenhouse gas emissions pursuant to Directive 2003/87, [2012] OJ L 181/30.

reported emission data and have to take account of the recommendations included in the verification reports issued by the European institutions.

Inclusion of the aviation sector

Given the growing emissions and the significant impact which the Commission argues aviation has in the EU and on global emissions, it outlined in its Communication of 27 September 2005, "Reducing the climate change impact of aviation", a strategy to reduce the climate change impact of aviation. One of the most important proposals in a comprehensive package of measures was the inclusion of aviation in EU ETS. Since then, many discussions and stakeholder consultations have been held. This consultation process resulted in Directive 2008/101[30] amending Directive 2003/87 so as to include aviation activities in the scheme for GHG emission trading within the Union. The Directive is aiming to reduce the climate change impact attributable to aviation by including emissions from aviation activities in the Union scheme. It applies to the allocation and issue of allowances in respect of "aviation activities" as specified in Annex I. The quantity of allowances is represented in a percentage based on the "historical aviation emissions", meaning the average of annual emissions in the calendar years 2004, 2005 and 2009 from aircraft performing an aviation activity, listed in Annex I. Respective percentages are as follows:

- From 1 January 2012 to 31 December 2012: total quantity of allowances to be allocated to aircraft operators shall be equivalent to 97 per cent of the historical aviation emissions.
- From 1 January 2013 onwards, in principle, unless amendments: total quantity of allowances to be allocated to aircraft operators shall be equivalent to 95 per cent of the historical aviation emissions multiplied by the number of years in the period.

From 1 January 2012 to 31 December 2012, 15 per cent of the allowances were auctioned. This percentage will remain the same in principle; however, it may be reviewed as part of a general review of the Directive. The revenues generated by Member States as a result of auctioning should be used to tackle climate change in the EU and third countries. For each trading period, aircraft operators can apply for an allocation of allowances free of charge. Therefore the tonne-kilometre data of the previous

---

[30] Directive 2008/101 of 19 November 2008 amending Directive 2003/87 so as to include aviation activities in the scheme for greenhouse gas emission allowance trading within the Community, [2009] OJ L 8/3.

year have to be submitted to the competent authority in the administering Member State. For this purpose, monitoring and reporting plans have to be handed over to this authority and it has to approve these plans.

Directive 2008/101 is a highly political Directive, strongly opposed (not only) by airlines. In November 2012, the Commission "stopped the clock" for flights into and out of Europe, meaning it temporarily deferred the enforcement of the Directive regarding these flights. The "stopping of the clock" was carried out against the background of negotiations by the ICAO which aimed to find a global solution for the problem of emissions from aviation activities. However, after considerable debate, the ICAO adopted a Resolution on 4 October 2013, holding inter alia that the EU must not extend its emissions trading scheme to flights covering non-EU territory, unless and until bilateral deals are concluded with the States concerned (see in particular point 16 of Resolution 17.2).[31] This eventual position is considerably stricter for the EU than previous drafts. The ICAO did forecast work to start on an international scheme by 2016, with a view to resulting in a regime that will start in 2020. This delay is unlikely to be palatable to the European Parliament, especially in light of the ECJ's support for the extension.[32] The EU therefore had the following options: to up the stakes and lift its deferment of the ETS extension; leave the deferment in place and engage fully with the ICAO's search for multilateral action (as it had been trying to do in the past); pursue bilateral agreements with third countries; or amend its ETS.

The Commission chose the option to limit the EU ETS to the European regional airspace and, in October 2013, put forward a proposal to adjust the legislation so that the new regulations do apply from January 2014 until a global market-based mechanism is established by 2020. The revised version still covers all emissions from flights between airports within the EEA, but flights, and thus emissions outside the EEA, as well as overflights are exempted. In addition, flights to and from third countries which are not developed countries and which emit less than 1 per cent of global aviation emissions are exempted as well.[33]

---

[31] Available at http://www.icao.int/Meetings/a38/Documents/WP/wp430_en.pdf, last consulted 21.11.2015.

[32] Case C-366/10 *Air Transport Association of America and Others*, ECLI:EU:C:2011:864.

[33] Proposal for a Directive amending Directive 2003/87 establishing a scheme for greenhouse gas emission allowance trading within the Community, in view of the implementation by 2020 of an international agreement applying a single global market-based measure to international aviation emissions, Brussels, 16.10.2013.

B. Emissions from Land Transport

Transport remains the worst performing sector under the UN's Kyoto Protocol and threatens to undermine the global agreement's reduction targets. Emissions from the transport sector in the EU, US and China increased continuously between 1990 and 2006 (+27.3 per cent), due primarily to high growth in both passenger and freight transport by road. This compares with a reduction of 3 per cent in emissions across all sectors. The share of transport in CO_2 emissions in the EU-27 was 18.9 per cent in 1990, but by 2006 it had grown to 24.6 per cent, with emissions from so-called light-duty vehicles (passenger cars and vans) being responsible for approximately half of this figure. Policy instruments to reduce emissions from land transport thus mainly focus on light-duty vehicles, but a fully fledged mitigation solution should also take into account heavy-duty vehicles as well as off-road vehicles such as locomotives. A detailed discussion of the individual law and policy documents relating to climate change and air pollution in the transport sector is provided in Chapter 13 III.

Light-duty vehicles

In 2007, the Commission reviewed its 1995 strategy to reduce CO_2 emissions from passenger cars and light-commercial vehicles.[34] The strategy was based on three pillars: voluntary commitments from the car industry to cut emissions, improvements in consumer information and the promotion of fuel efficient cars through fiscal measures. Although agreements with car makers to reduce CO_2 emissions from light-duty vehicles were concluded, it appeared that additional measures were necessary to meet the Community objective of average emissions from the new car fleet of 120 g CO_2/km by 2012 and 95 g CO_2/km by 2020. The Commission then pleaded for an integrated approach. On this basis, it proposed various measures aiming to reduce CO_2 from either the supply side or the demand side.

On the supply side, mandatory reduction of CO_2 emissions are introduced through inter alia Regulation 443/2009 setting emission performance standards for new passenger cars.[35] Further measures on the supply side are type approvals: the vehicle type approval organises the phasing-out of light passenger and commercial vehicles that do not comply with

---

[34] Brussels, 7.2.2007, COM (2007) 19.
[35] Regulation No 443/2009 of 23 April 2009 setting emission performance standards for new passenger cars as part of the Community's integrated approach to reduce CO 2 emissions from light-duty vehicles, [2009] OJ L 140/1.

"Euro" emission standards (Regulation No 715/2007). These standards lay down common EU rules on the construction of motor vehicles with regard to their emissions of atmospheric pollutants. As of 2014, the Euro 6 standard – which is the follow-up to the Euro 5 standard, which has been applied since 1 September 2009 – is adhered to when selling cars in the EU market. This imposes stricter emissions limits on both diesel and petrol cars than currently applicable. It limits in particular nitrogen oxides and particulates which are responsible for serious health problems.

Further, demand behavioural-oriented measures focus on consumer information and taxation. To help consumers choose vehicles with low fuel consumption, the Car Labelling Directive requires dealers in new passenger cars to provide potential buyers with useful information on these vehicles' fuel consumption and CO_2 emissions (Directive 1999/94[36]). This information must be displayed on the car's label, on posters and other promotional material, and in specific guides.

As tyres account for 20–30 per cent of vehicles' total fuel consumption, the institutions adopted a regulation on the labelling of tyres which aims to ensure that standardised information, notably on fuel efficiency, is provided to consumers and end users.[37]

Although taxation is not a competence of the EU, the Commission insists on the necessity of adopting fiscal incentives for greener cars at Union level. So far, Member States have been reluctant to approve the 2005 proposal on passenger taxation, allowing tax differentiation to support the market introduction of fuel efficient and low CO_2 emitting cars.[38]

Heavy-duty vehicles
Heavy-duty vehicles are to be type approved in order to be allowed to circulate in the EU, in the same way as light-duty vehicles. Where trucks do not comply with Union requirements (Euro standards) in terms of emissions of gaseous and particulate pollutants, as well as of opacity of smoke, the type approval is not granted.[39]

---

[36] Directive 1999/94 of 13 December 1999 relating to the availability of consumer information on fuel economy and CO 2 emissions in respect of the marketing of new passenger cars, [2000] OJ L 12/16.

[37] Regulation No 1222/2009 of 25 November 2009 on the labelling of tyres with respect to fuel efficiency and other essential parameters, [2009] OJ L 342/46.

[38] COM (2005) 261.

[39] Regulation No 595/2009 of 18 June 2009 on type-approval of motor vehicles and engines with respect to emissions from heavy duty vehicles (Euro VI) and on access to vehicle repair and maintenance information and amending Regulation

Road charges have traditionally been used mostly to raise funds to build new infrastructure. The "Eurovignette" Directive[40] is setting out a Union method of infrastructure charging for heavy-duty vehicles through a kilometrical tax, taking into account the external costs, on the basis of the polluter pays principle.

Locomotives

Railway locomotives are also subject to type approval, in same way as heavy- and light-duty vehicles. This acceptance procedure of locomotives takes into account gaseous emissions of railways, in particular nitrogen oxides and particulate matter. A new generation of standards, on average ten times more stringent than those currently in place, started in 2010 and will be fully effective in 2014 (Directive 2004/26[41]).

No 715/2007 and Directive 2007/46 and repealing Directives 80/1269, 2005/55 and 2005/78, [2009] OJ L 188/1.

[40] Directive 1999/62 of 17 June 1999 on the charging of heavy goods vehicles for the use of certain infrastructures, [1999] OJ L 187/42.

[41] Directive 2004/26 of 21 April 2004 amending Directive 97/68 on the approximation of the laws of the Member States relating to measures against the emission of gaseous and particulate pollutants from internal combustion engines to be installed in non-road mobile machinery, [2004] OJ L 146/1.

15. Waste legislation and policy

EU law on waste management is prolific, has an important business impact, and ranks historically among the earlier pieces of EU environmental law. It is also very regularly the subject of preliminary review procedures with the Court of Justice, has led to a string of infringement procedures by the European Commission, and is of course routinely applied in national courts by virtue of the primacy of EU law in national legal orders. It is impossible to give even a succinct overview in the space justified in a book of this nature.[1] Instead, we give an overview of the EU's overall waste policy (I) and we highlight the main issues surrounding the "definition" of waste, since it is only when a substance is defined as "waste" that the (many) waste laws apply (II).

I. EU WASTE POLICY

A. General Policy Orientation

Historically, the EU's waste management approach was inspired to a considerable degree by the Organisation for Economic Co-operation and Development (OECD). The bottom line of EU waste law as well as of OECD interest is to combine a healthy business interest in the sector with the need to ensure proper environmental protection. The EU is very much of the view that were business to lose interest in waste management, local authorities in particular would be overwhelmed by the logistic and financial strains involved.

This approach has led to a visible, if gradual, change in the economic operators active in the sector. In particular, most Member States have gradually moved away from a first-tier role of public authorities in waste processing – these typically retain responsibility for waste collection. Moreover, while in most Member States up until the 1990s, a wide variety of companies

---

[1] Some have written entire books devoted to the sector: see in particular G. Van Calster, *EU Waste Law*, Second edition, Oxford: Oxford University Press, 2015.

operated in the waste sector, this has now been substantially reduced to a more limited number of, inevitably larger, operators. This has made the sector on the whole more professional than was previously the case.

EU legislation on waste and waste management represents an important part of the Union's environmental legislation. Over the years, waste legislation has expanded drastically. Academics and practitioners alike are now faced with a considerable amount of EU law in this area – we have included a table (Table 15.1) at the end of this chapter. The vast amount of laws in this area has led to inconsistency.

The 2005 thematic strategy for prevention and recycling of waste crucially influenced current Commission thinking on waste management strategy. Despite it being a pivotal strategy document that had been long in the making, it nevertheless is interesting to note the change of focus vis-à-vis current "circular economy" and "sustainable materials management" thinking (see below).

The 6th Environmental Action Programme had emphasised the need for a number of framework decisions which should ensure that the use of resources is pursued with a view to ensuring sustainable development. The Action Programme clarified that this would amongst others entail a thematic strategy for waste recycling, as well as a number of initiatives in the field of waste prevention.

B. The 2003 Communication "Towards a Thematic Strategy on the Prevention and Recycling of Waste"

The Commission adopted a Communication in May 2003[2] which initiated the development of this thematic strategy. This initiative put EC thoughts to paper and also kicked off a wide consultation exercise. The Communication invited a very broad discussion, including on:

- identifying potentials for waste prevention;
- exchange of good practices and experience with a view to defining how the EU may contribute to these;
- the role of the future chemicals policy as regards qualitative prevention of waste;
- exploring how voluntary or mandatory waste prevention plans could contribute to waste prevention;
- assessing the waste prevention potential of the directive on Integrated Pollution Prevention and Control (IPPC).

---

[2] COM (2003) 301.

The Commission itself identified two core issues:[3]

- Fixing quantitative targets for waste prevention. The Communication asked for comments on several potential measures including:
    - waste prevention plans: the Commission could encourage the involvement of industry sectors and individual companies in the development of such plans, which would include concrete measures.
    - low-waste production techniques: the Commission could ensure that these are used by European industry.
    - diffusing best practice: the Commission could identify the most effective national strategies and broaden them to EU level.
    - Use market forces to recycle more. Potential measures included
    - setting recycling targets for materials. Currently, EU law requires the recycling of materials from certain wastes (e.g. packaging, cars, electronics), but does not require the recycling of these same materials when they are used in other products. For example, packaging cardboard has to be recycled, but office paper or newsprint does not, and the same goes for aluminium, plastics and other materials. A more coherent approach to recycling could result in greater environmental benefits.
    - getting the prices of the different waste treatment options right. Despite strict EU legislation, disposing of waste in landfills and incinerators at the time of the Communication continued to be cheaper than recycling. This, the EC suggested, could be corrected through tradable certificates, the coordination of national landfill taxes, promoting pay-as-you-throw (PAYT) schemes and making producers responsible for recycling.
    - ensuring recycling is both easy and clean. In some cases, implementation of EU waste law may have led to unnecessary burdens on the recycling industry. The EC wanted common approaches to be developed to ensure that recycling businesses apply the best available technology.

The 2003 Communication is a very extensive document, and it is not always easy to see the wood for the trees. A number of issues, however, were quite striking.

First, the emphasis on materials, rather than on specific types of waste. In general, comments expressed sympathy for this approach, which is

---

[3] IP/03/762, available at http://goo.gl/FXPUDg, last consulted 22.6.2016.

not that surprising in the light of the figures quoted. For instance, the EC argued that the packaging and packaging waste Directive applies to about 5 per cent of all waste in the EU, and the end-of-life vehicles Directive just 1 per cent. Focusing on the materials would therefore seem to be of some value. Conversely, however, the Commission itself indicated that a shift of focus towards materials rather than types of waste would endanger the concept of producer responsibility. Producer responsibility acts as a strong signal in the marketplace, by focusing on an identifiable group within the waste stream. This may be in danger should one leave this focus and opt for a more diffuse approach.

A further point to note is the Commission's taste for identifying recycling targets per material, to be set not at the national level but at the EU level.

This should enable the recycling industry to operate flexibly in a pan-European recycling area. This was a proposal which is very market focused and which led to a number of negative reactions. In particular, commentators feared that should the approach entail the EU as a whole to reach certain targets, rather than each Member State individually, this may tempt the environmentally weaker Member States to withdraw from the stricter obligations without fear of backlash. Moreover, it is argued by some that the approach would also lead to increased trade in waste, in particular to Member States with weaker standards for the recycling of waste.

The Commission also expressed a strong preference for economic instruments to reach the targets put forward.

The EC was thinking, for example, of tradable waste rights. An undisputed, inevitable consequence of the focus on economic instruments are higher charges for the landfill of waste. Comments received with respect to this route (focus on economic instruments) were overwhelmingly positive, suggesting the old chestnut (sadly still very much around) that waste processing techniques which do not entail the internalisation of environmental costs need to be addressed. The option of tradable waste rights, however, was generally received as being too radical. The option of economic instruments, even in 2003, of course could hardly be labelled "new", given that the Commission has been putting it forward for some years; the crucial question is how to translate it into practice.

In the 2003 Communication the EC also announced that it wanted to investigate how the IPPC Directive[4] may be employed to facilitate more harmonised recycling techniques throughout the EU.

---

[4] In the meantime replaced with the Industrial Emissions Directive, Directive 2010/75 on industrial emissions (integrated pollution prevention and control) (Recast), [2010] OJ L 334/17.

The instrument which the Commission was thinking of is that of BREFS – Best Available Techniques Reference guides, which are completed by the European IPPC bureau. Using BREFS, the EC suggested, would help create a "level playing field" in the European recycling market, and would avoid a "race to the bottom" in which environmentally less ambitious Member States would employ weak EU standards in order to attract recycling industries. Comments on this approach have been supportive overall, and the IPPC Bureau has indeed resorted to issuing a number of BREFs in the waste management area.[5]

The 2003 Communication was extremely pessimistic with respect to any substantial EU role in the prevention of waste. The Commission suggested that it was waiting for the results of a better collection of data by the Member States; however, it would seem that it simply was not quite certain how to advance an EU role in this area: Member States have always been very reluctant to accept much of an EU role in this area.

Finally, many commentators observed that the Communication pays very little attention to reuse, and that with respect to the definition of waste, disposal and so on, the Communication merely observes that there is an issue, without putting forward any direction as to how this should be solved. With respect to reuse, there are clearly a number of Member States (including, e.g. Germany) which argue that the Commission ought to play a much more proactive role in this area. With respect to the definitions, there was a growing sentiment that new definitions would not necessarily lead to better practice or increased legal certainty. (Which indeed may be clear from the overview in relevant sections below, too.)

C. 2011 Thematic Strategy and Beyond

Progress towards the objectives set out in the strategy was reviewed in 2011 when the Commission adopted a "Report on the Thematic Strategy"[6] and a staff working document.[7] The latter included a summary of the main actions taken by the Commission, the main available statistics on waste generation and management, a summary of the main forthcoming challenges and recommendations for future actions.

The Commission concluded that main objectives of the strategy still remained valid. It underlined that it has played an important role

---

[5] They may be consulted via http://eippcb.jrc.ec.europa.eu/reference/ last consulted 22.6.2016.
[6] COM (2011) 13.
[7] Available at goo.gl/Vm7Jj, last consulted 16.12.2016.

in guiding policy development and that significant progress has been achieved in the improvement and simplification of legislation, the establishment and diffusion of key concepts such as the waste hierarchy and life-cycle thinking, on setting focus on waste prevention, on coordination of efforts to improve knowledge, and on setting new European collection and recycling targets. These latter underwent a process of review and reassessment[8] which was finalised in June 2014 in the Circular Economy Communication (see below).

Looking ahead, the targets and goals of the EU in terms of resource efficiency and waste strategy are caught by a variety of high profile policy documents. These include the 7th Environmental Action Plan ("Living well, within the limits of our planet");[9] the Europe 2020 strategy;[10] the roadmap for resource efficiency;[11] and most recently, the June 2014 Communication "Towards a circular economy: a zero waste programme for Europe".[12] (This latter document additionally has led to proposed amendments to a variety of individual waste directives. Those, however, are at the very initial stages of discussion only.)

A common thread throughout these documents is recognising waste as a commodity and as an important source of energy. In line with the new waste framework Directive, these instruments aim at creating a more competitive EU market for recycling and recovery, using waste as a resource to relieve the pressure on finite raw materials. Waste prevention, too, ranks high in the policy priorities. This is an area where the EC is having difficulties with the introduction of binding targets.

The General Union Environment Action Programme to 2020[13] highlights as a second priority objective, the shift towards an economy that is resource efficient. Points 39ff. of the Programme set forth the following main Commission objectives in the field of waste regulation:

> There is also considerable potential for improving waste management in the EU to make better use of resources, open up new markets, create new jobs and reduce dependence on imports of raw materials, while having lower impacts on the environment. Each year in the EU, 2.7 billion tonnes of waste are produced, of which 98 million tonnes is hazardous. On average, only 40% of solid waste

---

[8] More information at http://goo.gl/KmmkAM, last consulted 30.7.2014.
[9] EP and Council Decision 1386/2013, [2013] OJ L 354/171.
[10] Communication from the Commission "Europe 2020: a strategy for smart, sustainable and inclusive growth", COM (2010) 2020.
[11] Communication from the Commission on a "Roadmap to a Resource Efficient Europe", COM (2011) 571.
[12] COM (2014) 398.
[13] Note 9 above.

is reused or recycled. The rest goes to landfill or incineration. In some Member States, more than 70% of waste is recycled, showing how waste could be used as one of the EU's key resources. At the same time, many Member States landfill over 75% of their municipal waste. Turning waste into a resource . . . requires the full implementation of EU waste legislation across the EU based on strict application of the waste hierarchy and covering different types of waste. Additional efforts are needed to reduce per capita waste generation in absolute terms, . . . limit . . . energy recovery to non-recyclable materials, phase out landfilling, ensure high quality recycling, and develop markets for secondary raw materials . . . To achieve that aim, market-based instruments and other measures that privilege prevention, recycling and re-use should be applied much more systematically throughout the Union, including extended producer responsibility, while the development of non-toxic material cycles should be supported. Barriers facing recycling activities in the Union internal market should be removed and existing prevention, re-use, recycling, recovery and landfill diversion targets reviewed so as to move towards a lifecycle-driven "circular" economy, with a cascading use of resources and residual waste that is close to zero.

Waste management is also firmly linked to sustainable materials management. Sustainable materials management (SMM) is "an approach to promote sustainable materials use, integrating actions targeted at reducing negative environmental impacts and preserving natural capital throughout the lifecycle of materials, taking into account economic efficiency and social equity".[14]

The EU Environment Council adopted SMM at its meeting of December 2010,[15] linking it to sustainable production and consumption. SMM has many aspects, which altogether represent almost the entire plethora of legal challenges associated with a successful EU environmental policy.

There is no shortage of studies reviewing all types of aspects of waste management.[16] Of particular note in this succinct overview is a Bio Intelligence et al. study[17] which maps the relationship between waste management and the use of economic instruments in the Member States. It highlights the importance of using smart economic instruments for creating a competitive market in waste management and recycled products, while

---

[14] OECD, Working Group on Waste Prevention and Recycling, Outcome of the first workshop on SMM, Seoul, 28–30 November 2005.
[15] Available at http://goo.gl/6DjR7t, last consulted 2.8.2014.
[16] See for an overview of those financed by the EC, http://goo.gl/FpngQf, last consulted 2.8.2014.
[17] Bio Intelligence service et al. study on the Use of Economic Instruments and Waste Management Performances, 10 April 2012, available at http://goo.gl/SLOkKz, last consulted 21.7.2014.

reducing the regulatory burdens on industry.[18] The study analysed the regime of charges for waste disposal and treatment (landfill taxes and restrictions), incineration taxes and restrictions, PAYT schemes, and harmonised producer responsibility for specific waste streams. Some suggested economic instruments were: (1) recycling partnerships with the countries that currently absorb most of the resources; (2) harmonisation of the methods for calculating a minimum tax level for landfills and incineration (taxes could be more strongly encouraged in the worst performing Member States); (3) introduction of responsibility schemes based on successful models already used in the EU;[19] and (4) recognising the importance of recycling under the EU ETS for the reduction of air emissions and the saving of primary resources.

A further study of note is the July 2014 study on extended producer responsibility,[20] an in-depth evaluation of 36 case studies focusing on six waste streams: packaging, waste electric and electronic equipment, end-of-life vehicles, batteries, paper and oils.

In conclusion, many of us with close contact to the waste management sector have had first-hand experience with the ability of the engineering profession to do wonderful things with waste. Many of those ideas did not receive the level of attention they deserved as long as waste was seen as just that: end of pipe, a nuisance, an unsightly outcome of society. Dealing with it in an "environmentally sound" (to borrow a phrase from the Basel Convention[21]) manner was seen as the most one could hope to achieve. This perception has now fundamentally changed.

This change was brought about *not* by a desire to push out the regulatory boat to what was technically achievable (environmental law continues to be subordinate to economic considerations in most instances). Rather, because waste has now been properly discovered as a resource and its suboptimal use, well, a waste.

As a result of this sea change in looking at waste resources, the current legal framework arguably needs to be revisited to review its suitability to regulate waste as a resource.

---

[18] For example, by introducing a catch-all permit for the operating plants that are likely to produce waste (e.g. a permit addressing obligations under the IPPC (now Industrial Emissions) Directive and waste legislation).
[19] Some countries implement economic instruments for stimulating a better waste management. For example, the UK has a system of tradable rights of recovery similar to the emissions trading scheme for greenhouse gas emissions.
[20] Available at http://epr.eu-smr.eu/, last consulted 2.8.2014.
[21] Basel Convention on the control of transboundary movements of hazardous wastes and their disposal, adopted on 22 March 1989, entered into force on 5 May 1992, available via http://goo.gl/WdzarD, last consulted 21.7.2014.

D. The "Circular Economy Package"

The circular economy in and of itself is not a dramatically innovative concept: if the EU is to make the most of the scarce resources available to it, it had better ensure an optimal regulatory management of the whole cycle: from resource mining via production and consumption to waste management and the market for secondary raw materials. What is new is the sense of urgency with which the EC has embraced it since 2014. A bump in the road was the fact that the initial proposal suffered under the regulatory optimisation drive of EC vice-president Frans Timmermans, following which a new package was adopted end of 2015. Key elements include:[22]

- A common EU target for recycling 65% of municipal waste by 2030;
- A common EU target for recycling 75% of packaging waste by 2030;
- A binding landfill target to reduce landfill to maximum of 10% of municipal waste by 2030;
- A ban on landfilling of separately collected waste;
- Promotion of economic instruments to discourage landfilling;
- Simplified and improved definitions and harmonised calculation methods for recycling rates throughout the EU;
- Concrete measures to promote re-use and stimulate industrial symbiosis - turning one industry's by-product into another industry's raw material;
- Economic incentives for producers to put greener products on the market and support recovery and recycling schemes (e.g. for packaging, batteries, electric and electronic equipment, vehicles).

The package implies the amendment of a wide range of the secondary legislation listed below, in particular the Waste Framework Directive; the packaging waste and landfill Directives; and the WEEE Directive. The Netherlands presidency of the EU in the first half of 2016 worked hard to make progress on the detailed discussion; however, at the time of writing it is too early to say how the proposals will develop.

II. THE DEFINITION OF WASTE

As noted, it is only when a substance meets with the definition of waste under the Waste Framework Directive that the whole range of EU waste

---

[22] European Commission, "Closing the loop: an EU action plan for the circular economy", http://ec.europa.eu/environment/circular-economy/index_en.htm, last consulted 22.6.2016.

law is triggered. The Directive defines "waste" as meaning "any substance or object which the holder discards or intends or is required to discard" (Article 3(1)). Following extensive case law concerning the definition of waste,[23] the following criteria have been employed by the CJEU for determining waste. The Court does emphasise that all these elements are mere indications and do not, in themselves, suffice to classify a given substance as "waste" (one simple criterion will not suffice):

- specifically, the consideration that the use of the substance concerned in lieu of primary resources indicates someone discarding the substance, thus leading to the substance being waste (*Arco Chemie*);[24]
- likewise, the Court held in *Arco Chemie*, recourse to a "common method" of "disposal" (in the sense of Dutch practice, i.e. both encompassing final disposal and recovery). But see *Saetti and Frediani*:[25] there this was not found to be relevant;
- the common perception of what is waste may be evidence that the substance is indeed being discarded (*Arco Chemie*);
- the fact that a substance used as a raw material is the residue of the manufacturing process of another substance (*Arco Chemie*);
- that no use for that substance other than disposal can be envisaged (*Arco Chemie*); and
- that the composition of the substance is not suitable for the use made of it, or that special environmental precautions must be taken when it is used (*Arco Chemie*)/the risk that the holder will discard that consignment in a way likely to harm the environment (*Shell*[26]). However, in *Palin Granit*[27] it was concluded that no risk to health or the environment and capability of immediate use are *not* conclusive elements in holding that the substance is not waste (but see *Saetti and Frediani*).

In *Arco Chemie* it was determined that whether substances may be recovered in an environmentally responsible manner and without substantial

---

[23] See in detail G. Van Calster, note 1 above.
[24] Joined Cases C-418/97 and C-419/97 *Arco Chemie v VROM* and *Vereniging Dorpsbelang Hees et al v provincie Gelderland*, ECLI:EU:C:2000:318.
[25] Case C-235/02 *Criminal proceedings against Saetti and Frediani*, ECLI:EU:C:2004:26.
[26] Joined Cases C-241/12 and C-242/12 *Criminal proceedings against Shell Nederland Verkoopmaatschappij BV* and *Belgian Shell NV*, ECLI:EU:C:2013:821.
[27] Case C-9/00 *Palin Granit Oy*, ECLI:EU:C:2002:232.

treatment is *not relevant* for the definition of waste. It is relevant for the definition of waste recovery, and for the issue as to whether such use of the waste should be authorised and/or encouraged, and under what degree of control.

It was established in *Palin Granit* that, specifically for by-products, the Waste Framework Directive does not apply to goods, materials or raw materials which have an economic value as products regardless of any form of processing (i.e. the degree of likelihood that that substance will be reused, without any further processing prior to its reuse). These products, as such, are subject to the applicable legislation. However, this is confined to situations in which the reuse of the goods, materials or raw materials is not a mere possibility but a certainty, without any further processing prior to reuse and as an integral part of the production process.

If, in addition to the mere possibility of reusing the substance, there is also a financial advantage to the holder in so doing, the likelihood of reuse is high.

In *Shell* it was established that, specifically for off-spec/reverse logistics:

- the possibility of selling the off-spec product to another buyer in its off-spec state;
- the fact that no waste operations (disposal or recovery) such as outlined in the Waste Framework Directive had to be carried out;
- the fact that the market value of the off-spec product sold corresponds almost one to one to the value of the on-spec product; and
- the client's acceptance of the product with a view to re-marketing it, even with a form of further processing (in *Shell* that process consisted of blending).

III. TABLE: RELEVANT EU WASTE LAW

Table 15.1   Relevant EU waste law

Directives	Regulations
75/439 Waste Oils Directive	259/93 Regulation concerning waste shipments
75/442 Waste Directive	1774/2002 Regulation concerning health rules for animal by-products
76/403 PCBs/PCTs Directive	
78/319 Toxic and Dangerous Waste Directive	
84/360 Air Pollution Control Directive	
84/631 Directive on shipments of hazardous waste	1013/2006 Regulation concerning waste shipment (WSR)
85/339 Containers of Liquids Directive	1907/2006 Regulation concerning the Registration, Evaluation, Authorisation and Restriction of Chemicals (REACH)
85/467 PCBs/PCTs Directive	
87/101 Directive amending Directive 75/439	
89/369 Air Pollution Prevention from Waste Incineration Plants Directive	
91/156 Waste Directive	
91/157 Batteries and Accumulators Directive	1418/2007 Export Waste Regulation
91/271 Urban Waste Treatment Directive	219/2009 Regulation on packaging waste
91/676 Water Protection Directive	
91/689 Hazardous Waste Directive	596/2009 Regulation amending PCB/PCT Directive
91/692 Directive amending Directive 75/439	
92/3 EURATOM Directive	
94/31 Directive repealing Directive 78/319	1103/2010 Regulation relating to batteries and accumulators
94/62 Packaging and Packaging Waste Directive	
94/67 Directive on incineration of hazardous waste	222/2011 Regulation on scrap waste
96/59 PCB/PCT Directive	1179/2012 Regulation on glass cullet waste
96/61 Pollution Prevention and Control Directive	715/2013 Regulation on copper scrap waste
96/82 Seveso II Directive	1257/2013 Regulation on ship recycling
1999/31 Landfill Waste Directive	660/2014 Regulation amending WSR
2000/53 End-of-life Vehicles Directive	
2000/59 Port Reception Facilities Directive	
2000/60 Water Framework Directive	
2000/76 Waste Incineration Directive	
2002/95 Directive on recovery targets for WEEE	
2002/96 WEEE Directive	
2004/12 Directive amending Directive 94/62	
2005/20 Directive amending Directive 94/62	
2006/12 Waste Directive	
2006/21 Management of Waste Directive	

Table 15.1 (continued)

Directives	Regulations
2006/66 Batteries Directive 2008/1 the IPPC Directive 2008/33 Directive amending the End-of-life Vehicles Directive 2008/98 Waste Framework Directive 2008/112 Directive amending the End-of-life Vehicles Directive 2010/75 Industrial Emissions Directive 2010/85 Industrial Emissions Directive 2011/65 Directive repealing the RoHS Directive 2012/19 Directive repealing the WEEE Directive 2013/56 Batteries Directive	

16. Chemicals legislation and policy*

I. REACH

The REACH Regulation[1] entered into force on 1 June 2007, although its key requirements on economic operators kicked in one year later, with several obligations rolling out in a phased fashion from then on.[2]

As its full title indicates, the REACH Regulation replaced the former legislative framework for chemical substances – a patchwork of many different directives and regulations which had developed historically. This framework was characterised by several flaws, which necessitated new EU chemicals legislation.[3]

In particular, the REACH Regulation was designed to ensure a better protection of human health and the environment from the risks created by chemicals, by generating more information on their effects and their use. It does so by starting from the key premise of industry responsibility, which assumes that industry is best placed to ensure that its products are safe. Accordingly, REACH places the burden of demonstrating the safety of chemicals on the companies that want to manufacture or market these chemicals in the EU.

The key premises underpinning REACH are given substance by a number of concrete mechanisms. Among the most important ones are the system for the registration of chemicals, the procedure for the prior authorisation for high risk chemicals, and the process allowing for the

---

* This chapter has been co-authored with Lieselot Marien.
[1] Regulation No 1907/2006 of 18 December 2006 concerning the Registration, Evaluation, Authorisation and Restriction of Chemicals (REACH), establishing a European Chemicals Agency, amending Directive 1999/45 and repealing Regulation No 793/93 and Regulation No 1488/94 as well as Directive 76/769/EEC and Directives 91/155, 93/67, 93/105 and 2002/21, [2006] OJ L 396/1.
[2] For a detailed analysis of the REACH Regulation please refer to D. Drohmann and M. Townsend (eds), *REACH – Best Practice Guide to Regulation (EC) No 1907/2006*, Baden-Baden: C.H. Beck, Hart, Nomos, 2013.
[3] European Commission, DG Environment, "REACH in brief", October 2007, available at http://ec.europa.eu/environment/chemicals/reach/pdf/publications/2007_02_reach_in_brief.pdf, last consulted 21.11.2015.

introduction of restrictions on the manufacture, marketing or use of chemical substances.

A. Registration

Pursuant to Articles 6(1) and 7(1) REACH, manufacturers or importers of a substance on its own, in a mixture or in an article need to submit a registration if that substance is manufactured or imported in the EU in quantities larger than one tonne.

Article 5 REACH provides a heavy sanction where this obligation is not complied with: "no data, no market". In other words: substances that were unlawfully not registered, cannot be manufactured or placed on the market in the Union.

Registration is required for all substances manufactured or imported in quantities of one tonne or more per year per manufacturer or importer unless these substances are exempted from the scope of registration.

Substances

The registration obligation (Article 6 REACH) applies to individual substances on their own or in mixtures as defined in Article 3(2), and to individual substances in articles, as defined in Article 3(3), when they are intended to be released under normal or reasonably foreseeable conditions of use (Article 7 REACH). A substance is defined in Article 3(1) REACH and means a chemical element and its compounds. The term substance also includes its additives and impurities where these are part of its manufacturing process. Therefore, these additives and impurities do not need a separate registration. By contrast, the term substance excludes any solvent which can be separated without affecting the stability of the substance or changing its composition. As a consequence, such solvents do need a separate registration.[4]

Quantitative threshold

The registration requirement is triggered by the volume of the substance manufactured or imported. When this volume equals one tonne or more per year, registration is needed. In principle the volume to be taken into account is the total volume of one substance that is manufactured or

---

[4] ECHA, "Guidance on registration", May 2012, available at http://echa.europa.eu/documents/10162/13632/registration_en.pdf, 13; ECHA, "Guidance on substance identification", March 2012, available at http://echa.europa.eu/documents/10162/13643/substance_id_en.pdf, last consulted 21.11.2015.

imported by a given potential registrant. However, if certain exemptions to registration apply, the potential registrant does not need to include those quantities in his calculation to determine the volume.[5]

Substances exempt from registration
A number of categories of substances do not need to be registered.

Firstly, there are substances exempted from the REACH Regulation.[6] Articles 2(1–3) REACH exclude from the scope of application *ratione materiae* of the REACH Regulation certain substances: radioactive substances,[7] substances under customs supervision,[8] non-isolated intermediates,[9] transported substances,[10] waste,[11] and substances used in the interest of defence and covered by national exemptions.[12] These substances are therefore also exempt from the registration obligation.

Secondly, substances that are adequately regulated under other legislation are also exempted from registration.[13] This category of substances includes substances in food or feeding stuffs (Article 2(5)(b) REACH)

---

[5] ECHA, "Guidance on registration", 43–47.
[6] Ibid., 27–29.
[7] Such radiating substances are already regulated by Directive 96/29/Euratom of 13 May 1996 laying down basic safety standards for the protection of the health of workers and the general public against the dangers arising from ionising radiation, [1996] OJ L 159/1.
[8] In order to benefit from this exemption, transiting substances must not undergo any form of treatment and processing on EU territory and must be kept under customs supervision at all times (Article 2(1)(b) REACH).
[9] Non-isolated intermediates are defined in Article 3(15)(a) REACH.
[10] The rationale for this exemption lies in the fact that the safety conditions of dangerous substances' carriage are already regulated in various instruments of EU legislation. However, this exemption only covers transport activities. It does not relieve importers and manufacturers of their obligations under the REACH Regulation.
[11] For a definition of waste, the REACH Regulation refers to Directive 2006/12 of 5 April 2006 on waste, [2006] OJ L 114/1. This Directive was repealed by Directive 2008/98 of 19 November 2008 on waste and repealing certain Directives, [2008] OJ L 312/3. Article 3(1) of Directive 2008/98 defines waste as "any substance or object which the holder discards or intends or is required to discard". However, as soon as a substance, mixture or article is recovered, it no longer meets this definition and thus falls, in principle, back within the scope of the REACH Regulation. See: ECHA, "Guidance on waste and recovered substances", May 2010.
[12] ECHA, "Guidance on registration", 27–28; information on the situation in the different EU Member States, as well as on national procedures, can be found on the REACH portal of the European Defence Agency at http://www.eda.europa.eu/reach/, last consulted 21.11.2015.
[13] For a full list of references, as well as for examples, see ECHA, "Guidance on registration", 29–31.

and substances in medicinal products (Article 2(5)(a) REACH) which fall under the relevant legislation.

Thirdly, substances that present minimum risk because of their intrinsic properties[14] also do not fall within the provision. These substances are exempted from registration pursuant to Article 2(7)(a) REACH and are listed in Annex IV of REACH. Examples are water and nitrogen.

Fourth, substances for which registration is deemed inappropriate or unnecessary[15] are pursuant to Article 2(7)(b) REACH, covered by Annex V to REACH. Annex V lists 13 broad categories of substances, to which the registration exemption applies, provided that they meet the conditions for the exemption which are given with the particular categories in Annex V.

Fifth, polymers,[16] as defined in Article 3(5) REACH, are exempted from registration in accordance with Article 2(9) REACH. However, manufacturers and importers of polymers must register the monomer substance(s) or other substance(s) used for the manufacture of the polymers if the conditions mentioned in Article 6(3) REACH are fulfilled. The concept of "monomer substances" thereby relates only to reacted monomers which are integrated in polymers.[17]

Sixth, substances used for the purpose of research and development:[18] REACH distinguishes scientific research and development (Article 3(23) REACH) and product and process orientated research and development (PPORD; Article 3(22) REACH). Since the former is carried out by definition with substances in quantities less than 1 tonne per year, a substance being used solely for scientific research and development does not need to be registered. As to the latter, Article 9 REACH provides an exemption from registration for five years for substances used for PPORD in quantities of one tonne or more per year, on the condition that they are notified to the European Chemicals Agency (ECHA).

Seventh, substances already registered, thus substances exported and re-imported into the Union:[19] pursuant to Article 2(7)(c) REACH,

---

[14] ECHA, "Guidance on registration", 31.
[15] Ibid., 31–33; ECHA, "Guidance for Annex V", November 2012, available at http://echa.europa.eu/documents/10162/13632/annex_v_en.pdf, last consulted 21.11.2015.
[16] ECHA, "Guidance on registration", 37–38; ECHA, "Guidance for polymers", April 2012, available at http://echa.europa.eu/documents/10162/13632/polymers_en.pdf, last consulted 21.11.2015.
[17] C-558/07 *S.P.C.M. and Others*, ECR [2009] I-5783.
[18] ECHA, "Guidance on registration", 38–39; ECHA, "Guidance on PPORD", February 2008, available at https://echa.europa.eu/documents/10162/13632/ppord_en.pdf, last consulted 21.11.2015.
[19] ECHA, "Guidance on registration", 35.

substances which are registered and subsequently exported from the Union by an actor in the supply chain are exempt from registration when they are re-imported into the Union by the same or another actor in the same supply chain. This exemption is subject to the conditions of Article 2(7)(c)(i) and (ii).

Eighth, substances recovered through a recovery process in the Union[20] are covered by Article 2(7)(d) REACH. The provision exempts from registration substances which are recovered in the EU, provided a number of conditions are met. A non-exhaustive list of recovery processes is provided in Annex II of the Waste Framework Directive 2008/98/EC. One example is recycling.

Lastly, substances considered as being registered are exempted as well, that is, active substances for use in plant protection products and active substances for use in biocidal products (see also Section III).

Substances are considered as registered under the REACH Regulation if they are included in one of the EU decisions, directives or regulations mentioned in Article 15 REACH.[21]

Substances notified in accordance with Directive 67/548/EEC[22] are regarded as registrations (Article 24 REACH).[23]

Who has to register?

The obligation to register a substance applies only to three types of actors established in the EU.

It firstly relates to EU manufacturers and importers of substances on their own or in mixtures.[24]

Pursuant to Article 6(1) REACH, any manufacturer or importer of a substance, either on its own or in one or more mixture(s), in quantities of one tonne or more per year needs to submit a registration to the ECHA.

Article 3(9) REACH defines the term manufacturer. Accordingly, in order to be considered as a manufacturer under REACH, a natural or legal person must meet the double requirement of establishment within the Union and manufacturing within the Union. The registration obligation for manufacturers also applies where the substance is not marketed in the EU but exported outside the EU after manufacturing.

---

[20] Ibid., 33–34; ECHA, "Guidance on waste and recovered substances".
[21] ECHS, "Guidance on registration", 39–41.
[22] Directive 67/548 of 6 November 1967 on the approximation of laws, regulations and administrative provisions relating to the classification, packaging and labelling of dangerous substances, [1967] OJ 196/1, see also Section II.
[23] ECHA, "Guidance on registration", 41–42.
[24] Ibid., 16–20.

Pursuant to Articles 3(10) and 3(11) REACH, an importer is a natural or legal person established within the Union who is responsible for the physical introduction of the substance into the customs territory of the Union. REACH applies to the EEA, that is, the 28 EU Member States and Iceland, Liechtenstein and Norway.[25] This means that imports from Iceland, Liechtenstein and Norway are not considered imports for the purposes of REACH.

The second group are EU producers and importers of articles. Pursuant to Article 7(1) REACH, any producer or importer of articles shall submit a registration to the ECHA for any substance contained in those articles, if the substance is present in those articles in quantities totalling over one tonne per producer or importer per year and the substance is intended to be released under normal or reasonably foreseeable conditions of use.

According to Article 3(4) REACH, the producer of an article is any natural or legal person who makes or assembles an article within the EU.

In order to verify whether a producer or importer of a certain object needs to register, it first needs to be assessed whether the object fits the definition of an article in Article 3(3) REACH. It also needs to be determined whether the relevant substance is intended to be released under normal or reasonably foreseeable conditions of use. Further guidance on both issues, which involve complex and technical questions, is provided by the ECHA.[26]

In addition, as a general rule[27] the importer or producer of articles needs to notify the ECHA where a substance in those articles is a substance of very high concern (SVHC), if the substance present in those articles totals one tonne or more per year per producer or importer, and if the substance is present in those articles above a concentration of 0.1 per cent weight by weight (w/w) (Article 7(2) REACH). The ECHA can then require the registration.

The third group are only representatives established in the EU: in principle, substances imported into the EU need to be registered by their EU importers. Non-EU manufacturers cannot be registrants. However, if they do not want to depend on importers' registrations, natural or legal persons established outside the EU can appoint an only representative to

---

[25] Decision of the EEA Joint Committee No 25/2008 of 14 March 2008 amending Annex II (Technical regulations, standards, testing and certification) to the EEA Agreement, [2008] OJ L 182/11.

[26] ECHA, "Guidance on requirements for substances in articles", April 2011, available at http://echa.europa.eu/documents/10162/13632/articles_en.pdf, last consulted 21.11.2015.

[27] Article 7(3) REACH provides exceptions.

carry out the required registration of the substance that is imported (in a mixture or in an article) into the EU (Article 8(1) REACH). This relieves the EU importers within the same supply chain from their registration obligations.[28]

Information submitted in registration
The registration provisions require EU manufacturers and importers of substances and only representatives established in the EU to collect or generate data on the substances manufactured or imported in order to compose a technical dossier. They can also be required to assess the risks related to these substances and to develop and recommend appropriate risk management measures to control these risks.

To ensure that they actually meet these obligations, as well as for transparency reasons, manufacturers, importers and third party representatives are required to prepare a registration dossier and submit it to the ECHA.[29]

Technical dossier[30] For every substance that requires registration, a technical dossier needs to be compiled, which contains the elements listed in Article 10(a) REACH. For each of these elements, Annexes VI to XI to the REACH Regulation further specify the information to be submitted.

Article 12 REACH establishes a waterfall system with regard to the information requirements, pursuant to which the quantity of information to be submitted depends on the tonnage level of manufactures or imports. Accordingly, Annex VII defines the minimum information that the registrant has to provide on the intrinsic properties of substances manufactured or imported in quantities of one tonne or more. For substances manufactured or imported in the next tonnage band (>ten tonnes), the requirements of Annex VIII need to be added. The same system applies for the Annexes IX and X: every time a new tonnage level is reached (>100 tonnes, >1000 tonnes), the requirements of the corresponding Annex need to be added.

As a rule, manufacturers and importers have to collect all available existing information on the properties of the substance for registration purposes. This information subsequently needs to be compared with the standard information requirements set up by the REACH Regulation. Where available data are not adequate to meet the minimum requirements of REACH, additional information needs to be gathered. Article 13

---

[28] ECHA, "Guidance on registration", 20–23.
[29] Ibid., 13.
[30] Ibid., 52–57.

REACH lays down important requirements for the generation of such information. Title III of the REACH Regulation also lays down rules concerning data sharing[31] and avoidance of unnecessary testing (especially on vertebrate animals).

Chemical safety assessment and risk management measures[32] Pursuant to Article 10(b) REACH, read in conjunction with Article 14(1) REACH, a chemical safety assessment is generally[33] required when a substance is manufactured or imported at ten tonnes or more per year. The purpose of such a chemical safety assessment is to ensure that the risks arising from the manufacture and use of a substance are under control.

To this aim, a hazard assessment needs to be carried out, which addresses, pursuant to Article 14(3) REACH, potential human health hazards, physicochemical hazards and environmental hazards related to the manufacture and use of the substance at issue. The physicochemical hazards assessment needs to verify in particular the substance is persistent, bioaccumulative and toxic (PBT)[34] or very persistent and very bioaccumulative (vPvB).[35]

Where the substance is found to be PBT or vPvB, Article 14(4) REACH stipulates that the chemical safety assessment will have to include two additional steps, aside from the hazard assessment. These steps are the generation of an exposure scenario and a risk characterisation. The same obligation applies where the substance fulfils the criteria for any of the hazard classes or categories set out in Article 14(4) REACH.

An exposure scenario consists of determining quantitatively or qualitatively the dose/concentration of the substance to which humans and the environmental are or may be exposed. The assessment must consider all stages of the life cycle of the substance resulting from the manufacture and use of the substance. The exposure scenario should indicate how exposure of humans and the environment to the substance is or can be controlled, and should refer to appropriate risk management measures.

---

[31] Ibid., 64 *et seq.*
[32] Further guidance can be found in Annex I to the REACH Regulation, as well as in ECHA, "Guidance on registration", 77 *et seq.* and ECHA, "Guidance on information requirements and chemical safety assessment", December 2011, available via http://echa.europa.eu/web/guest/guidance-documents/guidance-on-information-requirements-and-chemical-safety-assessment, last consulted 21.11.2015.
[33] Except for the situations listed in Article 14(2) REACH.
[34] For further information on the term PBT, see http://echa.cdt.europa.eu/SearchByQuery.do, last consulted 21.11.2015.
[35] For further information on the term vPvB, see http://echa.cdt.europa.eu/SearchByQuery.do?method=searchDetailCr&lilId=7547&sourceLanguage=en&targetLanguages=DEF, last consulted 21.11.2015.

In a risk characterisation, the exposure levels calculated in the exposure scenario are compared to the derived no-effect level (DNL) (for humans) and to the predicated no effect concentration (PNEC) (for the environment). The DNL and PNEC represent the doses/concentration values below which no detrimental effect to humans or the environment is anticipated. The risk characterisation also consists of the assessment of the likelihood and severity of an event occurring due to physicochemical properties of the substance.

The registration process

With regards to the registration process, a number of aspects need to be highlighted. First, the registration requirements entered into force on 1 June 2008. Nonetheless, potential registrants who need to register can benefit from certain transitional regimes (Article 23 REACH). Potential registrants who qualified for these transitional regimes and who wished to benefit from these regimes were obliged, pursuant to Article 28 REACH, to submit a pre-registration to the ECHA before 2 December 2008.

Second, although each registrant is obliged in principle to submit his own registration dossier for each of his substances to the ECHA, where a substance is manufactured or imported or intended to be manufactured or imported by more than one company, the REACH Regulation requires that certain data must be shared and submitted jointly. In order to increase the efficiency of the registration system, save costs and reduce testing on vertebrate animals, Articles 29 and 30 of the REACH Regulation created the mechanism of the Substance Information Exchange Forums (SIEFs). While participation in a SIEF is compulsory, a registrant may opt-out from some information requirements and submit the information separately to ECHA in certain specified cases.[36]

Evaluation

The registration of substances is subject to two types of evaluation.

Dossier evaluation by the ECHA Dossier evaluations are performed by the ECHA. They consist of a completeness check (for each registration), a compliance check (for at least 5 per cent of the registrations within each tonnage band) and an examination of testing proposals.

For each registration, the ECHA undertakes, within three weeks of

---

[36] ECHA, "Guidance on registration", 61; ECHA, "Guidance on data sharing", April 2012, available at http://echa.europa.eu/documents/10162/13631/guidance_on_data_sharing_en.pdf, last consulted 21.11.2015.

the submission date of a registration, a completeness check (Article 20(2) REACH). The completeness check does not include an assessment of the quality or the adequacy of any data or justifications submitted.

In addition, the ECHA also checks the compliance of a registration dossier with all the requirements of the REACH Regulation (Article 41 REACH). A compliance check does verify the quality of dossiers.

Pursuant to Article 40 REACH, the ECHA also examines testing proposals, in order to ensure that unnecessary animal tests and costs are avoided and that test results are relevant for the chemical safety process.

Substance evaluation by Member State Substance evaluation is performed by the Member States' authorities, in cooperation with the ECHA. The ECHA will prioritise the substances for evaluation on a risk-based approach, on the basis of the criteria set forth in Article 44(1) REACH. These criteria are the point of departure for the ECHA in drafting a Community rolling actions plan (CoRAP) (Article 44(2) REACH). The CoRAP is a list of substances to be evaluated. A Member State may choose one or more substances from the CoRAP to perform the substance evaluation and, if necessary, to prepare a draft decision within one year of the publication of the CoRAP (Article 45(2) REACH). The ECHA will coordinate the substance evaluation processes carried out in the Member States (Article 45(1) REACH).

B. Authorisation

Certain substances of very high concern (SVHC) can only be used or marketed in the EU on the condition that the ECHA has granted them a permit, a so-called authorisation. The substances at issue are listed in Annex XIV to the REACH Regulation. Article 56 REACH prohibits manufacturers, importers and downstream users (as defined in Article 3(13) to place a substance on the market or to use it if that substance is included in Annex XIV, unless an authorisation is granted for their specific use, or the use is exempted from authorisation; it is referred to as the "no authorisation, no market and no use" principle.

Inclusion of substances in the authorisation list
Presently, the list in Annex XIV to REACH contains 14 substances. Pursuant to Article 57 REACH, additional substances can be added to this annex if they qualify as SVHCs. Substances can be identified as SVHCs if they display one of the hazard properties listed in Article 57, namely carcinogenicity, mutagenicity and toxicity for reproduction. Substances also qualify as SVHCs if they are PBT or vPvB, or if there is

scientific evidence of their probable serious effects to human health or the environment.

Articles 58 and 59 REACH provide for a two-step regulatory procedure for the inclusion of additional substances in the authorisation list.[37] First,[38] the SVHC needs to be included in the candidate list. This process is started by the generation of an Annex XV dossier by a Member State (Article 59(3) REACH) or, on request from the Commission, by the ECHA (Article 59(2) REACH). This dossier proposes the inclusion of the substance in the candidate list by outlining the scientific evidence for identifying the substance as a SVHC. Comments on the Annex XV dossier are then invited from the Member States, the ECHA and stakeholders (Article 59(4) REACH). Once an agreement has been reached that the substance meets one or more of the hazard properties outlined in Article 57, the substance will be placed on the candidate list. The inclusion of a substance on this list can only be challenged once it has been published on the ECHA website and not from the date of the ECHA's decision to include a substance on the list.[39] Further, irregularities occurring in the procedure to include a substance on the candidate list does not render the decision to list the procedure void.[40]

Second, the substances on the candidate list need to be included in the authorisation list. The ECHA, taking into account the opinion of the Member State Committee, recommends priority substances to be included on Annex XIV to the Commission. Priority will normally be given to substances with PBT or vPvB properties, or wide dispersive uses or high volumes (Article 58(3) REACH). Before the ECHA sends a recommendation to the Commission, the recommendation is made public via the ECHA's website, and all interested parties are invited to comment. In particular, comments on uses which should be exempted from the authorisation requirement are requested. The recommendation may then be updated to take account of the comments received (Article 58(4) REACH). Pursuant to Article 58(1) REACH, the Commission

---

[37] ECHA, "Guidance on the preparation of an application for authorisation", January 2011, available at http://echa.europa.eu/documents/10162/13637/authorisation_application_en.pdf, last consulted 21.11.2015, 18 *et seq.*

[38] ECHA, "Guidance for the preparation of an Annex XV dossier on the identification of substances of very high concern", June 2007, available at http://echa.europa.eu/documents/10162/13638/svhc_en.pdf, last consulted 21.11.2015.

[39] T-1/10 RENV *PPG and SNF v ECHA*, ECLI:EU:T:2014:616.

[40] T-94/10 *Rütgers Germany and Others v ECHA*, ECLI:EU:T:2013:107, at 75f.; T-95/10 *Cindu Chemicals and Others v ECHA*, ECLI:EU:T:2013:108, at 82f., as well as T-96/10 *Rütgers Germany and Others v ECHA* ECLI:EU:T:2013:109, at 76f.

eventually takes the decision on the inclusion of substances in Annex XIV in accordance with the Regulatory procedure with scrutiny referred to in Article 133(4) REACH.

In *Bilbaina de Alquitranes*,[41] the ECJ (General Court) held that producers of chemical substances may challenge the legality of the decision by ECHA to put a substance on the candidate list of SVHCs under the REACH Regulation.

Authorisation procedure
An application for an authorisation has to be lodged with the ECHA for the use or the placing on the market for use of SVHCs (Article 62 REACH).[42]

Opinions on the applications will then be drafted by the ECHA Committee for Risk Assessment and the ECHA Committee for Socio-economic analysis, as appropriate (Article 64(1) REACH).[43] Once the draft opinions of the Committees are available there will be an opportunity for the applicant to comment on the opinions before these are finalised and sent to the Commission, the Member States and the applicant (Article 64(5) REACH). The Commission will ultimately be responsible for granting (or denying) an authorisation (Articles 60(1) and 64(8) REACH).

The Commission can grant authorisation on two bases, the so-called adequate control route and the socio-economic analysis route.[44] With regard to the first option, the Commission will grant authorisation if it is demonstrated that the risk to human health or the environment from the use of the substance arising from the intrinsic properties specified in Annex XIV is adequately controlled (Article 60(2) REACH). For substances to be authorised on this basis, the Commission's decision will be taken based on the evidence presented in the chemical safety report.[45] For some substances, however, the adequate control route cannot be a basis for authorisation (Article 60(3) REACH).

Under the socio-economic analysis route, the authorisation may be granted if it can be demonstrated that the risk to human health or the

---

[41] T-93/10 *Bilbaina de Alquitranes and Others v ECHA*, ECLI:EU:T:2013:106.
[42] ECHA, "Guidance on the preparation of an application for authorisation", 23–30.
[43] Section 1.5; ECHA, "Guidance on the preparation of an application for authorisation", 30–32.
[44] ECHA, "Guidance on the preparation of an application for authorisation", 32–35.
[45] ECHA, "Guidance on information requirements and chemical safety assessment", 36–38.

environment from the use of the substance is outweighed by the socio-economic benefits and if there are no suitable alternative substances or technologies (Articles 60(4) and (5) REACH).

Restrictions[46]

The restrictions procedure is a safety net to address unacceptable risks to human health or the environment, arising from the manufacture, use or placing on the market of substances, which need to be addressed on an EU-wide basis (cf. Article 68(1) REACH). Restriction means any condition for or prohibition of the manufacture, use or placing on the market of substances.

All final decisions on whether or not to restrict the manufacture, use or placing on the market of a substance are taken by the Commission (Article 73(2) REACH), upon advice of the ECHA (Article 70–71 REACH). Any adopted restrictions will be included in Annex XVII to the REACH Regulation, and will thereby form part of the REACH Regulation.

Pursuant to Article 67 REACH, a substance on its own, in a mixture or in an article, for which Annex XVII contains a restriction, shall not be manufactured, placed on the market or used, unless it complies with the conditions of that restriction.

Articles 67 and 68(1) REACH contain exceptions to the restrictions.

Information up and down the supply chain

The obligation to pass information down the supply chain is the general rule. Article 31 REACH requires the provision of safety data sheets[47] to recipients of hazardous substances or preparations. In other cases, there is a duty to communicate information down the supply chain comprising the registration number if available, details of any authorisation (if this is applicable), details of any applicable restrictions, and other risk management information as necessary (Article 32 REACH).

These obligations fall upon the suppliers of substances, which are defined in Article 3(32) REACH as the manufacturers, importers and downstream users or distributors placing on the market a substance, on its own or in a mixture. The supplier needs to provide the required information on the substance or the mixture to the recipient, defined in Article

---

[46] ECHA, "Guidance for the preparation of an Annex XV dossier for restrictions", June 2007, available at http://echa.europa.eu/documents/10162/13641/restriction_en.pdf, last consulted 21.11.2015, at 10.

[47] ECHA, "Guidance on the compilation of safety data sheets", December 2013, available via http://echa.europa.eu/documents/10162/13643/sds_en.pdf, last consulted 21.11.2015.

3(34) REACH as a downstream user or distributor being supplied with the substance or mixture.

The supplier of an article does not have an obligation to provide subsequent actors in the supply chain with a safety data sheet. However, he does not escape communication obligations in the supply chain, as Article 33 REACH contains special provisions for the duty to communicate information on substances in articles.

Finally, REACH also contains information obligations up the supply chain. Article 34 requires that all actors in the supply chain of a substance or mixture to communicate to the next actor up the supply chain new information on hazardous properties, as well as any other properties that might call into question the appropriateness of the risk management measures identified in a safety data sheet supplied to him. REACH does not contain any similar obligation for substances in articles.

The European Chemicals Agency[48]

Title X of the REACH Regulation establishes the ECHA. The ECHA is the driving force among regulatory authorities in implementing the EU's chemicals legislation. It plays a role, not only in the framework of the REACH Regulation, but also in the framework of the CLP Regulation (see Section II) and the Biocidal Products Regulation (see Section III).

II. REGULATION ON THE CLASSIFICATION, LABELLING AND PACKAGING OF SUBSTANCES AND MIXTURES ("CLP REGULATION")[49]

The CLP Regulation aligns the EU system for the classification, labelling and packaging of chemical substances and mixtures to the Globally Harmonized System (GHS) which was developed in the framework of the UN (Recitals 5–7 CLP Regulation). The CLP Regulation harmonises the criteria for the classification of substances and mixtures as "hazardous", as well as the rules on labelling and packaging for hazardous substances and

---

[48] The ECHA's website can be consulted via http://echa.europa.eu/home, last consulted 21.11.2015. It contains useful guidance on the chemicals legislation discussed in this chapter.

[49] Regulation No 1272/2008 of 16 December 2008 on classification, labelling and packaging of substances and mixtures, amending and repealing Directives 67/548 and 1999/45, and amending Regulation (EC) No 1907/2006, [2008] OJ L 353/1.

mixtures (Article 1(a) CLP Regulation). It also imposes obligations on different actors in the supply chain to classify, label and package substances and mixtures in accordance with these criteria (Article 1(b) CLP Regulation). Lastly, the CLP Regulation establishes a list of substances with harmonised classifications and labelling elements (Article 1(d) CLP Regulation).

The obligations of the CLP Regulation relate to substances and mixtures. According to Article 2(7) of the CLP Regulation, a substance means

> a chemical element and its compounds in the natural state or obtained by any manufacturing process, including any additive necessary to preserve its stability and any impurity deriving from the process used, but excluding any solvent which may be separated without affecting the stability of the substance or changing its composition.

According to Article 2(8) of the CLP Regulation, a mixture means "a mixture or solution composed of two or more substances".

Article 1(2) of the CLP Regulation excludes a number of substances and mixtures from the scope of the Regulation.

A. Harmonised Criteria

The CLP Regulation contains harmonised criteria for the classification of substances and mixtures as "hazardous". The hazard of a substance or mixture is the potential for that substance or mixture to cause harm. It depends on the intrinsic properties of the substance or mixture.[50]

More concretely, Article 3, first paragraph of the CLP Regulation provides that "[a] substance or a mixture fulfilling the criteria relating to physical hazards, health hazards or environmental hazards, laid down in Parts 2 to 5 of Annex I is hazardous and shall be classified in relation to the respective hazard classes provided for in that Annex."

Annex I distinguishes between three hazard classes (as defined in Article 2(1) CLP Regulation) – physical hazards, health hazards and environmental hazards – which are each further subdivided in different categories (as defined in Article 2(2) CLP Regulation). For each hazard category, Annex I provides a definition and classification criteria. It also specifies label elements for substances and mixtures meeting the criteria for classification in a specific subcategory.

For example, Section 2.2 of Annex I concerns flammable gases, which are a subsection of the physical hazards class. Section 2.2.2 lays down the

---

[50] ECHA, "Introductory guidance on the CLP Regulation", August 2009, available at http://echa.europa.eu/documents/10162/13562/clp_introductory_en.pdf, last consulted 21.11.2015, at 8.

Source: CLP Regulation.

Figure 16.1 Hazard pictogram

classification criteria for flammable gases, pursuant to which two categories are distinguished. Gases, which at 20 °C and a standard pressure of 101.3 kPa, are ignitable when in a mixture of 13 per cent or less by volume in air; or have a flammable range with air of at least 12 percentage points regardless of the lower flammable limit, are classified in the first category of flammable gases. Section 2.2.3 of Annex I states that flammable gases of category 1 should be labelled with the hazard pictogram shown in Figure 16.1.[51]

In addition, the label of category 1 flammable gases should contain the signal word "Danger" (as defined in Article 2(4) CLP Regulation), as well as the hazard statement (as defined in Article 2(5) CLP Regulation), "H2 20 Extremely flammable gas" and certain specific precautionary statements (as defined in Article 2(6) CLP Regulation) relating to prevention, response and storage.

B. Obligations to Classify, Label and Package[52]

Article 4 of the CLP Regulation lays down general obligations to classify, label and package. It requires suppliers in the supply chain to cooperate to meet the requirements for classification, labelling and packaging of the CLP Regulation (Article 4(9) CLP Regulation). Suppliers' specific obligations under the CLP Regulation depend upon their role in the supply chain.

---

[51] As defined in Article 2(3) CLP Regulation; ECHA, "Guidance on labelling and packaging in accordance with Regulation (EC) 1272/2008", April 2011, available via http://echa.europa.eu/documents/10162/13562/clp_labelling_en.pdf, last consulted 21.11.2015.

[52] ECHA, "Guidance on labelling and packaging in accordance with Regulation (EC) 1272/2008".

Where the requirements of the CLP Regulation are not met, Article 4(10) provides a considerable sanction, in the form of a prohibition to place non-compliant substances and mixtures on the market.

Obligation to classify
One of the main aims of the CLP Regulation is to determine whether a substance or mixture displays properties that lead to a classification as hazardous.

To this aim, Article 4(1) CLP Regulation requires manufacturers (defined in Article 2(15) CLP Regulation), importers (defined in Article 2(17) CLP Regulation) and downstream users (defined in Article 2(19) CLP Regulation) to classify substances or mixtures before placing them on the market. The same obligation applies, pursuant to Article 4(8) of the CLP Regulation, to producers of explosive articles.[53] In general, these actors need to comply with their classifying obligation by assigning, after careful evaluation of the information, to the substance or mixture one or more hazard categories, in accordance with Title II of the CLP Regulation.

However, in line with Article 4(6) CLP Regulation, downstream users only need to classify the substances or mixtures they place on the market if they change the composition of a substance or mixture. In all other cases, they are allowed to use the classification that was made earlier by another actor in the supply chain.

In addition to the classification triggered by the CLP Regulation, manufacturers, producers of articles (defined in Article 2(10) CLP Regulation) and importers are obliged, pursuant to Article 4(2) CLP Regulation, to classify substances not placed on the market that are subject to registration or notification in line with Articles 6, 9, 17 or 18 of REACH.[54]

Obligation to label
Once hazardous properties are identified and the substance or mixture is classified accordingly, the identified hazards need to be communicated to other actors in the supply chain, including to consumers. Hazard labelling allows the communication of hazard classification to the user of a substance or mixture, to alert the user to the presence of a hazard and the need to avoid exposures and the resulting risks. Another key element of hazard communication is the safety data sheet whose general format and

---

[53] As defined in Article 2(10) CLP Regulation, read in conjunction with Section 2.1 of Annex I to the CLP Regulation.
[54] ECHA, "Introductory guidance on the CLP Regulation", at 35.

content are set out in Article 31 and in Annex II to Regulation REACH (see Section I above).

Pursuant to Article 4(4) CLP Regulation, read in conjunction with Article 2(26) CLP Regulation, the obligation to label hazardous substances and mixtures in accordance with Title III of the CLP Regulation before placing them on the market applies to manufacturers, importers, downstream users and distributors (defined in Article 2(20) CLP Regulation). As a consequence of Article 4(5) and Article 4(6) of the CLP Regulation, distributors and downstream users who do not change the composition of a substance or mixture may take over the classification made by another actor in the supply chain.

In addition to substances and mixtures which have themselves been classified as hazardous, mixtures which also contain one or more substances classified as hazardous need to be labelled (Article 25(6) CLP Regulation). The same applies to explosive articles in the sense of Section 2.1 of Annex I to the CLP Regulation (Article 4(8) CLP Regulation).

Articles 19 to 22 of the CLP Regulation stipulate that the label needs to include the relevant hazard pictograms, signal words, hazard statements and precautionary statements.

Title III of the CLP Regulation contains further provisions with regard to hazard communication in the form of labelling.

Obligation to package

Pursuant to Article 4(4) CLP Regulation, read in conjunction with Article 2(26) CLP Regulation, the obligation to package hazardous substances and mixtures in accordance with Title IV of the CLP Regulation before placing them on the market applies to manufacturers, importers, downstream users and distributors. As a consequence of Article 4(5) and Article 4(6) of the CLP Regulation, distributors and downstream users who do not change the composition of a substance or mixture, may take over the classification made by another actor in the supply chain.

The requirements for packaging containing hazardous substances or mixtures are laid down in Article 35 CLP Regulation.

C. Harmonised Classification and Labelling

In line with Article 4(3), first subsection CLP Regulation, the classification and labelling of certain substances[55] does not take place in accordance

---

[55] Mixtures must always be self-classified by downstream users or importers of mixtures.

with the harmonised criteria as set out in Section 3.2 above. For these substances, which are listed in the tables in Part 3 of Annex VI to the CLP Regulation, harmonised classification and labelling have been established.

In other words, these substances are not subject to self-classification on the basis of harmonised criteria by the responsible actors in the supply chain. Rather, the decision on classification and labelling for a particular hazard of a substance is taken at EU level.[56] Where a harmonised classification is available for selected hazards only, Article 4(3), second subsection CLP Regulation, provides that for the hazard classes not included a self-classification in accordance with Title II of the CLP Regulation still needs to take place.

The use of a harmonised classification and labelling of a substance is mandatory.

Further provisions on harmonisation of classification and labelling of substances can be found in Title V of the CLP Regulation.

III. THE BIOCIDAL PRODUCTS REGULATION ("BPR")

The text of the BPR[57] was adopted in 2012 and is applicable as from September 2013, with a transitional period for certain provisions. It repeals the Biocidal Products Directive (Directive 98/8/EC).[58] The BPR lays down rules for the establishment of a list of active substances which may be used in biocidal products, for the authorisation of biocidal products and for the placing on the market of treated articles. In addition, the BPR provides for data protection and data sharing rules.

A. Active Substances[59]

The BPR applies to biocidal products which, in the form in which they are supplied to the user, consist of, contain or generate one or more active substances (Recital 9 BPR). Pursuant to Article 19(1)(a) BPR, biocidal products can only be used or marketed in the Union if the active substances therein are approved. However, biocidal products containing

---

[56] ECHA, "Introductory guidance on the CLP Regulation", at 8.
[57] Regulation No 528/2012 of 22 May 2012 concerning the making available on the market and use of biocidal products, [2012] OJ L 167/1.
[58] Directive 98/8/EC of 16 February 1998 concerning the placing of biocidal products on the market, [1998] OJ L 123/1.
[59] As defined in Article 3(1)(c) BPR.

one or more substances, which have been manufactured in a different location or according to a different process from a substance evaluated for approval pursuant to the BPR, can still be authorised. Such authorisation is subject to the establishment of technical equivalence.[60]

Approval
With regard to the approval of active substances, a distinction should be drawn between existing active substances which were on the market in biocidal products on 14 May 2000, and new active substances which were not yet on the market in biocidal products on that date (Recital 7 BPR).

New substances Article 4(1) BPR stipulates that a new active substance (defined in Article 3(1)(e) BPR) can be approved for an initial period of ten years, on the condition that at least one biocidal product containing that active substance fulfils the criteria laid down in Article 19(1)(b) BPR (i.e. the biocidal product must be sufficiently effective and it cannot have any unacceptable effects on the target organism, on the health of human and animals or on the environment). Active substances meeting the exclusion criteria laid down in Article 5(1) BPR (e.g. carcinogens, mutagens, endocrine disruptors, persistent, bioaccumulative and toxic substances) cannot be approved (except in accordance with Article 5(2) BPR).

Article 4(3) BPR states that the approval can specify conditions, relating to, for example, the minimum degree of purity of the active substance, the designation of categories of users or the expiry date of the approval. Persons wishing to market or use the biocidal product containing the active substance at issue need to comply with these conditions in order to obtain authorisation (Article 19(1)(a) BPR).

The approval of active substances takes place at Union level. In accordance with Article 7 BPR, applications need to be submitted to the ECHA. The application needs to indicate the name of the competent authority of the Member State that the applicant proposes should evaluate the application. Pursuant to Article 8 BPR, the competent authority will evaluate the applications, and subsequently the ECHA will prepare and submit to the Commission an opinion on the approval of the active substance having regard to the conclusions of the evaluating competent authority. Article 9 BPR stipulates that the Commission eventually decides on the approval of the active substance by means of an

---

[60] Recitals 2 and 3 of Commission Delegated Regulation No 837/2013 of 25 June 2013 amending Annex III to Regulation No 528/2012 as regards the information requirements for authorisation of biocidal products, [2013] OJ L 234/1.

implementing Regulation. Approved substances are included in a Union list of approved active substances.[61]

Active substances meeting the substitution criteria laid down in Article 10 BPR (i.e. substances of particular concern to public health or the environment) need to undergo a public consultation before they can be approved (Article 10(3) BPR). When a substance is identified as a candidate for substitution, products containing that active substance will have to be subject to a comparative assessment at the time of authorisation (Article 23 BPR) and will only be authorised if there are no better alternatives.

Existing substances[62]   Chapter III of the BPR lays down the conditions and the procedure for the renewal and review of approval of an active substance.

Technical equivalence

The BPR provides a centralised procedure for the assessment of technical equivalence (defined in Article 3(1)(w) BPR). The legal basis is Article 54 which sets out the procedure for the assessment of technical equivalence applications, under the responsibility of the ECHA.[63]

B.   Biocidal Products[64]

Pursuant to Article 17(1) BPR, all biocidal products must get an authorisation before they can be made available on the market. Companies can choose between several alternative authorisation procedures, depending on their product and the number of countries where they wish to sell it.

Companies planning to sell their products in one EU Member State must apply for product authorisation in that country. To do so, they submit an application for *national authorisation* to the competent authority of the Member State for which they want to obtain authorisation (Article 17(2) BPR). The Member State competent authority evaluates the application and makes a decision on the authorisation (Article 30 BPR).

If, after a national authorisation has been granted by a Member State,

---

[61]   The list can be consulted at http://echa.europa.eu/web/guest/information-on-chemicals/biocidal-active-substances, last consulted 21.11.2015.
[62]   As defined in Article 3(1)(d) BPR.
[63]   ECHA, "Guidance on applications for technical equivalence", August 2013, available at http://echa.europa.eu/documents/10162/15623299/guidance_applications_technical_equivalence_en.pdf, last consulted 21.11.2015, at. 7.
[64]   As defined in Article 3(1)(a) BPR.

a company subsequently wishes to extend the national authorisation to other markets, it can ask other Member States to recognise it. This procedure is called *mutual recognition in sequence*, and is described in detail in Article 33 BPR. Companies can also apply for the so-called *mutual recognition in parallel* (Article 32 BPR). This entails a company submitting an application for product authorisation in one reference Member State and simultaneously asking other countries to recognise the authorisation as soon as it is granted.

In some cases, a biocidal product may be made available on the market in other Member States without the need for mutual recognition. This is the so-called *simplified authorisation procedure* of Articles 25–28 BPR. This procedure is available for biocidal products which meet certain conditions, for example, do not contain any substances of concern or any nanomaterials (Article 25 BPR). Under the simplified procedure, the authorisation holder needs to notify each relevant Member State 30 days before placing the product on its territory (Article 27 BPR).

Lastly, the BPR provides for the possibility to have certain biocidal products authorised at Union level. The so-called *Union authorisation* of biocidal products is regulated by Chapter VIII of the BPR.

C. Treated Articles[65]

Pursuant to Article 58(2) BPR, articles can only be placed on the market if the biocidal products they were treated with have been approved in the EU for that purpose. In addition, Article 58(3) BPR requires manufacturers and importers of treated articles to label these when a claim is made that the treated article has biocidal properties or when the conditions of the approval of the active substance used to treat the article require specific labelling provisions to protect public health or the environment.

D. Data Protection and Data Sharing[66]

Chapter XIV of the BPR contains rules with regard to data protection and data sharing.

Article 62 BPR obliges existing data owners and prospective applicants to share certain data from tests and studies on biocidal active substances

---

[65] As defined in Article 3(1)(l) BPR.
[66] ECHA, "Q&A on data sharing", available at http://echa.europa.eu/qadisplay/-/qadisplay/5s1R/view/biocidalproductsregulation/datasharing, last consulted 21.11.2015.

and products submitted to EU authorities. Article 63 provides for compensation where data are shared.

IV. GENETICALLY MODIFIED ORGANISMS

The drafting of the regulations on genetically modified organisms (GMOs) in the EU has been a difficult and controversial task. EU regulators have been faced with the challenge of creating rules that address the possible risks to health and the environment from GMOs, in the face of scientific uncertainty regarding these risks. They have also had to ensure that the new rules will give consumers confidence in the safety of those GMOs that are approved for use in the EU. This is part of a general effort to address the erosion of consumer confidence in the EU regulatory system following several recent food-safety crises. With all these considerations in mind, the EU has been revising its legislative regime with regard to the approval and marketing of GMOs. European Community legislation on GMOs was enacted in early 1990, and has been progressively refined over the years. The regulation of GMOs in the Union is comprised of three main regulatory instruments. These are Regulation No 1830/2003 on traceability and labelling of genetically modified organisms[67] and Regulation No 1829/2003 on genetically modified food and feed,[68] together with the third instrument, the amended Directive 2001/18/EC; these Regulations form the regulatory framework for GMOs in the EU in order to address the concerns of Member States and restore consumer confidence in the regulatory regime for GMOs sufficiently, and to proceed with the approval of new varieties of GMOs. This legislation must be complied with not only by business operators within the EU, but also by foreign traders wishing to export GM products into the EU. The existing legislation regulates three main issues: authorisation for placing GMOs on the market, labelling of products containing GMOs and traceability of these products.

---

[67] Regulation No 1830/2003 Concerning the traceability and labelling of genetically modified organisms and the traceability of food and feed products produced from genetically modified organisms and amending Directive 2001/18/EC, [2003] OJ L 268/24.
[68] Regulation No 1829/2003 on genetically modified food and feed, [2003] OJ L 268/1.

A. The GMO Directive: Authorisation

The authorisation procedure for the approval of GM products in the EU is intended to ensure that the safety of these products is scientifically established before they are allowed on the market. Directive 2001/18/EC[69] (the Authorisation Directive or AD) sets out the authorisation procedure for the approval of products consisting of or containing GMOs, before they may be placed on the market or released into the environment. According to these rules, a company (whether local or foreign) must submit an application for the approval of the relevant GMO or GM product to the Member State where it intends to first place the product on the market, together with an environmental risk assessment. If the Member State gives a favourable opinion, it informs other Member States of this. If there are no objections, the Member State can authorise the marketing of the product, in which case it may be marketed *throughout* the EU, provided it meets any conditions attached to the approval. If other Member States do raise objections, a decision must be taken on the issue at the EU level, on the basis of advice from EU scientific committees composed of independent experts.

Products *produced from* GMOs, in other words products that are derived from GMOs but which no longer contain GM material (such as GM protein or DNA), are not covered by this Directive. For example, the process to make tomato sauce from GM tomatoes may eliminate all traces of GM protein or DNA from the final product. Such tomato sauce is not subject to the rules in this Directive.

The Directive defines a GMO as "an organism, with the exception of human beings, in which the genetic material has been altered in a way that does not occur naturally by mating and/or natural recombination" (Article 2(2) AD).

Pursuant to Article 4(1) of the AD, GMOs may only be released or placed on the market in conformity with the authorisation procedures provided by the AD and, if applicable, with the conditions imposed in the authorisation decision.

Articles 6 and 11 AD lay down the standard authorisation procedure for the introduction of GMOs (or combinations of GMOs) into the environment (e.g. cultivation) without the use of specific containment measures (deliberate release, as defined in Article 2(3) AD). Pursuantly, a

---

[69] Directive 2001/18 of 12 March 2001 on the deliberate release into the environment of genetically modified organisms and repealing Directive 90/220, [2001] OJ L 106/1, as amended.

person wishing to undertake such a deliberate release of GMOs into the environment must submit a notification to the competent authority of the Member State within whose territory the release is to take place.

Articles 13 to 15 AD and 18 to 19 AD lay down the standard authorisation procedure where a GMO (or a combination of GMOs) is placed on the market (as defined in Article 2(4) AD). Before a GMO is placed on the market for the first time, a notification needs to be submitted to the competent authority of the Member State where the GMO is to be placed on the market. The competent authority will subsequently make an assessment report, in which it indicates whether or not the GMO in question should be placed on the market. Competent authorities of other Member States or the Commission can make comments or present reasoned objections to the placing on the market of the GMO. If no reasoned objection is received within the specified time period, or if the outstanding issues raised by the other competent authorities or the Commission can be resolved within the specified time period, consent for the placing on the market should be granted within 30 days (Article 15(3) AD). If an objection is maintained, however, the competent authority which prepared the assessment report needs to decide within 120 days (Article 18(1) AD). The decision can be favourable or unfavourable.

Consent for the placing on the market is valid for a maximum period of ten years, but the decision can limit this period of validity (Article 19(3)(b) AD). The decision can also impose conditions for the placing on the market of the product, including any specific condition of use, handling and packaging of the GMO(s) as or in products (Article 19(3)(c) AD). In this respect, Article 21 AD provides that Member States need to take all necessary measures to ensure that the labelling and packaging of GMOs placed on the market as or in products comply with the requirements specified in the favourable decision at all stages of the placing on the market. In particular, Articles 4 and 6 of Regulation 1830/2003 are relevant in this respect.[70]

When consent for the placing on the market is granted, Member States need to respect the free circulation of GMOs as or in products, and cannot prohibit, restrict or impede their placing on the market, except in accordance with the safeguard clause of Article 23 AD. The AD further provides for compulsory monitoring after GMOs have been placed on the market.

---

[70] Regulation No 1830/2003 of 22 September 2003 concerning the traceability and labelling of genetically modified organisms and the traceability of food and feed products produced from genetically modified organisms and amending Directive 2001/18, [2003] OJ L 268/24.

Article 26a of the Directive allows Member States to take measures to avoid the unintended presence of GMOs in other products. The Court in *Pioneer Hi Bred Italia*[71] clarified that these do not "entitle a Member State to prohibit in a general manner the cultivation on its territory of such GMOs pending the adoption of co-existence measures to avoid the unintended presence of GMOs in other crops".

Directive 2000/18/EC contains a general obligation on Member States to ensure traceability at all stages of placing on the market of authorised products containing or consisting of GMOs. This requirement applies only to the notifier applying for authorisation for the GM product, not to later business operators in the marketing or distribution chains. This Directive does not define traceability or contain a coherent approach for its implementation.

B. Traceability and Labelling

The Regulation on Traceability and Labelling of GMOs establishes an EU system to ensure that all GM products (including food and feed) that have received EU authorisation to be placed on the market are traceable and labelled. This regulation applies not only to products consisting of or containing GMOs, but also to food and feed *produced from* GMOs (i.e. food/feed derived from GMOs but where DNA or protein of GM origin cannot be found in the final product). For example, highly refined soya oil produced from GM soya must meet the requirements of this Regulation, even if the final product bears no trace of the GM material. However, the Regulation does not apply to products *produced with* GMOs. In other words, where GMOs were used as processing aids but did not form part of the product itself, the rules on traceability and labelling do not apply. For example, beef or milk from cows fed with GM feed or treated with GM veterinary drugs are not subject to the rules on traceability and labelling in this Regulation since the beef or milk itself is not genetically modified, although GMOs were used in the production process. Similarly, bread or cheese produced with the help of a GM enzyme does not need to be labelled.

The labelling rules in this Regulation require that pre-packaged products, intended for sale to the ultimate consumer, consisting of or containing GMOs must be labelled as follows: "This product contains genetically modified organisms." Where bulk products consist of or contain GMOs, the business operator must transmit information regarding the GMO

---

[71] Case C-36/11 *Pioneer Hi Bred Italia*, ECLI:EU:C:2012:534, at 76.

content of the product to the operator receiving the product. These rules are intended to ensure that consumers' freedom of choice is protected.

The rules on traceability are there to ensure that a product can be tracked throughout the production and distribution chains. Traceability ensures that it is possible to verify and control labelling, facilitates monitoring the potential effects of GMOs on the environment and enables withdrawal of a GM product if an unforeseen risk to health or the environment materialises. According to this Regulation, at each stage of the placing on the market of GMOs, business operators that use or handle these GMOs are obliged to retain specified information regarding the identity of the GMO that the product contains and the identity of the operator from whom and to whom the GM product has been made available, for five years after the transaction. This is known as the "one step forward, one step back" system. Thus, for example, a seed company that develops a GMO would have to provide the purchaser of the seed with specified information allowing the GMO to be precisely identified and would have to retain information on the identity of all the purchasers of this seed for five years. The farmer that buys the seed would have to retain the information on the identity of the GMO and the seed producer for five years and pass the information regarding the GMO on to the food companies that buy his harvest. The farmer would also have to retain information on the buyers of the harvest. The food company that buys and processes the harvest would have to retain information on the identity of the GMO and the farmer from whom the harvest was bought, for five years and transmit the information regarding the GMO to the supermarket that sells the processed food. The supermarket would have to retain this information for five years, but does not have to retain information on the identity of the final consumers that purchase the processed food product.

The traceability requirements differ with respect to products consisting of or containing GMOs on the one hand and products produced from GMOs on the other hand. Where products consist of or contain GMOs, the individual GMOs in the product must be traceable on the basis of authorised transformation events (in other words, the event by which a conventional organism is transformed into a GMO by the introduction of modified DNA sequences). Where products are produced from GMOs, there is no requirement for the identification of the GMOs from which they are produced.

The European Commission established a system of assigning unique codes to GMOs, on the basis of the transformation event notified in the application for authorisation (called the "unique identifier"). It is the transformation event that ultimately determines the modified characteristics of the GMO. These codes therefore assist in operationalising the traceability requirements in the Regulation.[72]

C. Genetically Modified Food and Feed

There is specific EU legislation that covers GM food products. Regulation 1829/2003[73] on genetically modified food and feed (GMFF) strengthens the rules for the authorisation, marketing and labelling of GM food and extends the rules to GM feed. It replaces the Regulation on novel foods and food ingredients[74] with regard to GM food. It sets out a uniform authorisation procedure that applies to all food and feed consisting of, containing or produced from GMOs (Article 3(1) GMFF and Article 15(1) GMFF). Chapter II (Article 3 *et seq.* GMFF) addresses genetically modified food, Chapter III (Article 15 *et seq.* GMFF) addresses genetically modified feed, and Chapter IV (Article 27 *et seq.* GMFF) contains common provisions. It is important to note that no exception is made for "substantially equivalent" products. Just as is the case with the new Regulation on traceability and labelling of GMOs, the Regulation on GM food and feed does *not* apply to products *produced with* GMOs (i.e. where GMOs were used as processing aids but did not form part of the product itself), for example eggs from chickens fed GM corn.

Pursuant to Article 4(2) GMFF and Article 16(2) GMFF, products referred to in Article 3(1) GMFF and Article 15(1) GMFF cannot be placed on the market unless they comply with the provisions of the GMFF. The implementation of the zero-tolerance policy on non-authorised GM material in feed is harmonised by the Commission with Regulation EC 619/2011.[75] The authorisation procedure simplifies the procedure under Directive 2000/18/EC discussed above. The GMFF provides for a single authorisation procedure, which is regulated in Articles 5 to 7 GMFF for food and Articles 17 to 19 GMFF for feed. A single authorisation can be requested for both the release of a GMO into the environment and its use

---

[72] Regulation No 65/2004 of 14 January 2004 establishing a system for the development and assignment of unique identifiers for genetically modified organisms, [2004] OJ L 10/5.

[73] Regulation 1829/2003 of 22 September 2003 on genetically modified food and feed, [2003] OJ L 268/1.

[74] Regulation 258/97 concerning novel foods and novel food ingredients, [1997] OJ L 43/1.

[75] Commission Regulation 619/2011 of 24 June 2011 laying down the methods of sampling and analysis for the official control of feed as regards presence of genetically modified material for which an authorisation procedure is pending or the authorisation of which has expired, [2011] OJ L 166/9.

in food and/or feed. This is known as the "one door, one key" procedure. While the authorisation decision is ultimately taken by the Commission, thus on EU level, rather than divided between the Member States and the EU (Article 7(3) GMFF and Article 19(3) GMFF), the European Food Safety Authority, which is responsible for risk assessment in the food sector, fulfils an important role (Article 6 GMFF and Article 18 GMFF). The scientific assessment of risks to health or the environment will be carried out by the European Food Safety Authority and on this basis the Commission will propose the granting or refusal of authorisation. The Member States will decide on this proposal by a qualified majority vote. Products authorised under this Regulation will be entered into a register of GM food and feed which will contain information on studies demonstrating the safety of the product and detection methods, which will have to be provided by the business operator applying for authorisation. Authorisation will be granted for a ten-year period, which is renewable on application to the European Food Safety Authority.

With regard to labelling, this regulation requires that all food and feed consisting of, containing or produced from GMOs be labelled as such, regardless whether GM material can be identified in the final product. However, food or feed *produced with* GMO processing aids, such as eggs, milk or meat from animals fed with GM feed, need not be labelled. Food and feed products which contain a proportion of GMOs of less than 0.9 per cent of each ingredient are not labelled as GMO on the condition that the presence of the GMO is adventitious or technically avoidable (Article (2) GMFF and Article 24(2) GMFF). In addition to the labelling requirements laid down in the GMFF, GMO food and feed must also respect the labelling conditions of Articles 5 and 6 of Regulation 1830/2003.[76] The ECJ, in *Bablok*[77] held that honey with trace quantities of pollen from GM corn must be labelled as such and go through a full safety authorisation before it can be sold.

The Regulation introduced Article 26a and the concept of co-existence into the AD Directive. Co-existence refers to the ability of farmers to choose between growing conventional, organic and GM crops, in accordance with the relevant rules. The possibility of unintended admixture of crops could not only have great economic impact on producers but also affect consumer choice. In order for European consumers to have a real

---

[76] Regulation 1830/2003 of 22 September 2003 concerning the traceability and labelling of genetically modified organisms and the traceability of food and feed products produced from genetically modified organisms and amending Directive 2001/18, [2003] OJ L 268/24.
[77] Case C-442/09 *Bablok and Others*, ECR [2011] I-7419.

choice between organic, conventional and GM products, it is necessary to ensure the ability of the agricultural industry to choose between the different forms of agriculture by preventing unintended admixture of crops. For this reason, the new Regulation allows Member States to take measures to ensure co-existence. In addition, in 2003, the Commission issued a recommendation with guidelines for the development of national strategies and best practices to ensure co-existence.[78] This recommendation is non-binding, and naturally applies only to the EU agricultural industry, not to the agricultural industries of exporting countries.

Article 34 of the Regulation on emergency measures provides the Member States with the opportunity to provisionally suspend or prohibit the sale or use of GMO. The Court in *Monsanto*[79] amongst others held that bans under this clause are possible, provided that Member States establish, "in addition to urgency, the existence of a situation which is likely to constitute a clear and serious risk to human health, animal health or the environment".

D. Regulatory Developments[80]

In mid-2010, the Commission proposed new rules for the authorisation of GMOs.[81] EU countries are able to restrict or ban GMO cultivation on their territory. They are able to use any acceptable reason under the Treaty without undermining the EU risk assessment, which remains unchanged.

In June 2014, the Council published its first-reading position on a draft directive granting Member States more flexibility to decide whether or not they wish to cultivate GMOs on their territory. In the text, the possibility is provided for a Member State to request the Commission to present to the notifier/applicant its demand to adjust the geographical scope of its notification/application to the effect that all or part of the territory of that Member State be excluded from cultivation. The Commission will facilitate the procedure by presenting the request of the Member State

---

[78] Recommendation on guidelines for the development of national strategies and best practices to ensure the co-existence of genetically modified crops with conventional and organic farming, C(2003).

[79] Joined cases C-58/10 to C-68/10, *Monsanto and Others*, ECR [2011] I-7763.

[80] Legislative observatory, available via http://www.europarl.europa.eu/oeil/popups/ficheprocedure.do?reference=2010/0208(COD)&l=en, last consulted 21.11.2015.

[81] Proposal for a Regulation of the European Parliament and of the Council amending Directive 2001/18/EC as regards the possibility for the Member States to restrict or prohibit the cultivation of GMOs in their territory, 2010/0208 (COD), 13 COM (2010) 375.

to the notifier/applicant without delay and the notifier/applicant must respond to that request within an established time limit. In the event of refusal, the Member State may block cultivation on its territory for reasons other than the scientific assessment which will have been carried out by the relevant authorities. After refusal, the EC may also proceed to geographically adjust the request for authorisation for scientific reasons. The list of "compelling reasons" which may lead a Member State to refuse cultivation, is non-exhaustively listed as:

(a) environmental policy objectives distinct from the elements assessed according to the Directive and to Regulation 1829/2003 (since those environmental objectives will have been considered in the scientific assessment);
(b) town and country planning;
(c) land use;
(d) socio-economic impacts;
(e) cross-contamination with other products;
(f) agricultural policy objectives; and
(g) public policy.

Those grounds may be invoked individually or in combination, with the exception of the public policy exception (which needs to be coupled with one of the other grounds). An authorisation procedure will apply, however without the need to apply the transparency Directive, 98/34, concurrently. An important point to note is that the Directive only applies to growing ("cultivation") of GMOs *in situ*, not to the import, marketing and so on of GMO-containing products, food, feed and so on. The text eventually adopted is Directive 2015/412.[82]

---

[82] 07 [2015]L 68/1.

17. Trade and the environment

I. INTRODUCTION

"Trade and environment" now has a familiar sound to it. It refers to the need for, and the challenges of, reconciling ever freer international trade, with the prerequisites of environmental protection. The debate has its origins in the apparent contradiction between two premises.

Some argue that free international trade is a precondition for realising such aims as environmental protection and social progress. In this view, the fruits of the economic axiom of free trade, namely the doctrine of comparative advantages, will free up the necessary means to ensure "sustainable development".

The opposite view holds that unlimited free trade damages the environment, inter alia through a lack of internalisation of the environmental costs caused by manufacturing. In this view, corrective mechanisms are necessary if not to limit trade, then at least to ensure its environmental outlook. This view argues that environmental protection is a main task for humanity, which requires far-reaching cooperation in the international community, including the possible use of trade sanctions to encourage environmentally friendly behaviour.

For EU regulatory law, "trade and environment" essentially has two angles.

At the purely internal level, it deals with the question of whether the EU's internal market provisions are reconcilable with its environmental policies and those of its Member States.

Externally, the issue is the role of the EU in the international debate on the reconciliation of "domestic regulatory autonomy" with international trade law – including the potential illegality of EU regulatory law with international free trade agreements.[1]

The internal angle relates in the main to the Treaty Articles on the free movement of goods (Articles 28ff. TFEU), competition policy, especially

---

[1] See G. Van Calster and D. Prevost (eds), *Research Handbook on Environment, Health and the WTO*, Cheltenham, UK and Northampton, MA, USA: Edward Elgar, 2013.

on cooperation issues between companies (Articles 101–102 TFEU), State aid for environmental protection (Articles 106ff. TFEU) and tax distinctions made on the basis of environmental policy considerations (Article 110 TFEU).

In each of these debates, CJEU case law has emphasised two issues: exhaustion and proportionality.

Exhaustion refers to the "pre-emptive" effect which harmonisation directives often have on unilateral State action. Once a particular directive has exhaustively (i.e. completely, at least in the eyes of the Union legislator) harmonised the environmental angle to a particular challenge, Member States are prohibited from going it alone. There is an important exception to this mechanism in the case of directives adopted on the basis of Article 191 TFEU (the environmental title of the Treaty) or Article 114 TFEU (which leads to harmonisation in the context of the internal market). In both cases Member States retain freedom to move unilaterally even after harmonisation, subject to conditions. However, it is fair to say that Member States, even the traditionally more environmentally proactive "Northern" States, have not rushed to take advantage of that possibility.

Proportionality refers to the requirement that Member States may take action unilaterally to protect their environment (because there is no exhaustive secondary legislation on the matter or because the environmental guarantee applies). They need to apply what is commonly known as a least-trade-restrictiveness test. This means that among the measures which are reasonably available to them, they must choose the measure which is equally effective in protecting the environment, with the least impact on the internal market.

As for the external element of trade and environment, the Commission in particular has always been very active in the relevant committee at the World Trade Organization – albeit with mixed success. Some of the more entrenched issues of direct relevance between trade and environmental issues have been stalled in the Committee for years.

Of more immediate concern to the EU and its trading partners is the level of scrutiny which is often directed at the EU's regulatory policies. Amongst others because of its insistence on the cradle-to-grave approach, and the emphasis it lays on producer responsibility, the EU is often accused of defining perhaps well-intentioned regulatory developments in a way which has a disproportionate impact on its trading partners. US and Japanese criticism of earlier versions of the REACH regime is a case in point.

In the external area of trade and environment issues, one of the current hotbeds is undoubtedly European measures taken to combat climate change.

II. MUTUAL RECOGNITION, POSITIVE AND NEGATIVE HARMONISATION

The scope for harmonisation of national *environmental* standards in the EU is embedded in a much wider context of tensions between free movement of goods and protection of national interests.

A central theme of the EU is, of course, the establishment of the internal market. The internal market aims to achieve free movement of goods, services, persons and capital. Two means are employed to achieve this.

Positive harmonisation refers to the legislative programme of the Union institutions. Such legislation endeavours to introduce a varying degree of harmonisation in Member States' regulatory regimes. The degree of harmonisation depends on the sector concerned, and on the type of measures at issue (for instance whether they are of a fiscal nature, in which case Member States are not keen to sign away sovereignty to the Union). The greater the degree of harmonisation by Union legislation, the less important the regulatory varieties in the Member States and, as a result, the easier the free flow of goods.[2]

Negative harmonisation is reflected in the case law of the CJEU with respect to the Treaty Articles on the internal market. The Court's approach to these Articles has always been teleological. It employs the objectives of the founding fathers of the Treaty, as reflected in the Treaty's "mission statement" (the more general Articles at the beginning of the Treaty). A centrepiece of the Court's case law is, of course, the requirement of "mutual recognition" as set out in *Cassis de Dijon*.[3] The Court held that products which have been manufactured in accordance with the regulatory regime of the home Member State have to be allowed access to the free movement of goods between Member States. They may be freely marketed in other Member States, except where "mandatory requirements" require restrictions to intra-EU trade. Such requirements were held to include the effectiveness of fiscal controls, fair competition, consumer protection and, in a later stage, environmental protection. As the mandatory requirements rule is a judicial intervention, the list is not closed. The exceptions based on such mandatory requirements are commonly referred to as the "rule of reason" and are in addition to the exceptions foreseen in Article 36 TFEU.

---

[2] See P.J. Slot, "Harmonisation", 21 *European Law Review* (1996), 378–397.
[3] Case 120/78 *Rewe-Zentral AG v Bundesmonopolverwaltung für Branntwein*, [1979] ECR 649.

A. The New Approach – Including the Emphasis on "Minimum Harmonisation"

The Court's ruling in *Cassis* had an enormous impact. The Commission responded with an initiative dubbed the "New Approach" in Community harmonisation (subsequently adopted by the Council[4]).

The original harmonisation programme of the Community was far too ambitious. It aimed at creating one set of regulations throughout the Member States, in a variety of sectors (using the technique of so-called "total harmonisation"). Voting procedures, as they then stood, required unanimity for legislation to be adopted. The opposition of one single Member State in a given area effectively halted harmonisation efforts. As a result, quite a big chunk of the harmonisation programme led to nothing. *Cassis de Dijon* and its requirement of mutual recognition helped to focus minds on how to take the programme further. Moreover, the European Single Act introduced qualified majority voting for the great majority of harmonisation issues.

The New Approach programme of the Commission centres around a principal role for so-called "minimum harmonisation". This entails defining a standard at the European level which, if it is met by products in the sector concerned, guarantees free movement of goods for these products. Member States may subject national production to stricter standards, albeit in principle only within a purely national context.

The New Approach also entails a greater emphasis on manufacturers' self-assessment of inter alia safety standards. This is reflected in the widely known trademark, "CE", which, contrary to public perception, does not refer to *Communauté Européenne*, but rather to *Conformité Européenne*. The toy sector is a foremost example of reliance on manufacturers' self-inspection, rather than on lengthy and expensive procedures by national authorities (albeit that, of course, even in a New Approach context, national authorities perform sample testing).

B. Community Pre-emption – or the Exhaustive Effect of Community Legislation

As noted, it is established case law that recourse to the exceptions of Article 36 TFEU and/or of the rule of reason is no longer possible where Union law has harmonised the national legislation at issue. National measures

---

[4] Council Resolution of 7 May 1985 on a new approach to technical harmonization and standards, [1985] OJ C 136/1.

derogating from the harmonised regime are then said to be "pre-empted" by the Union initiative.

The underlying assumption is that the protection of the interests caught under Article 36 and under the rule of reason is guaranteed by Member States' approval (via the legislative procedure and voting requirements) of the measures concerned. It is noteworthy that the protection of these interests is often additionally guaranteed through a so-called "safeguard clause" in the harmonising legislation itself. Such a clause, often in Article 36-like language, grants Member States the (usually temporary, often subject to Commission review) right to derogate from the legislation to ensure the protection of a number of interests on their territory.

Needless to say, the assessment of whether secondary EU legislation is exhaustive with respect to any of the interests protected by Article 36 TFEU by the rule of reason is a defining moment[5] which is not expressed verbatim in the legislation itself: there is no standing formula for a recital declaring the legislation's exhaustive character.

It is also worthwhile re-emphasising that the underlying assumption mentioned above no longer holds where legislation is based upon Article 191, or Article 114 TFEU in the light of the (albeit conditional) room for Member States to introduce permanent deviations from the legislation at issue. Given that these Articles grant Member States the conditional right to introduce stricter measures, they serve as a permanent hurdle to pre-emption.

C. The Compassion Case – Taking Exhaustion Too Far

In the area of environmental protection, *Compassion*[6] addressed many sticky points of the application of Article 35 TFEU, and may well be best remembered for its approach to the pre-emption issue. It should be underlined that *Compassion*, just as *Lomas* (see below), is ranked as an "environmental" case by virtue of the animal interests at stake; however,

---

[5] *Ex multi*, see the Compassion case, Case C-1/96 *R v MAFF, ex parte Compassion in World Farming*, [1998] ECR I-1251, Case C-473/98 Toolex, ECLI:EU:C:2000:379. *Kemikalieninspektionen v Toolex Alpha A.B.*, or more recently, Case C-361/10 *Danske Svineproducenter*, [2011] ECR I-13721 (on the exhaustive harmonisation, or not, of the European Regulation of road transport of pigs held as pets) or Case C-112/15 *Kødbranchens Fællesråd*, ECLI:EU:C:2016:185, on whether the European Regulation on fees that may be charged for official controls of feed and food, covers costs in connection with the training of official auxiliaries. A good example is also Case C-422/05 *Commission v Belgium*, ECLI:EU:C:2007:342, on the Directive relating to airport management.

[6] Note 5 above.

in both cases, the Community legislation at issue was based on agricultural policy. Recourse to the environmental guarantee was therefore impossible.

Terminology is of the essence with respect to harmonisation.[7] There is a set of terms that describes the *technique* used in harmonisation legislation. This refers to such concepts as total (now "maximum"[8]), optional and minimum harmonisation.[9] The issue of "exhaustion" is completely separate from the consideration of the various harmonisation *techniques*. It addresses the question whether Union legislation occupies the area to pre-empt national action. The debate on exhaustion is often confused with harmonisation techniques; typically, one equates total harmonisation with exhaustion. In this respect, the Court is veracious in *Compassion*, where it states that directives providing for minimum harmonisation can still nevertheless exhaustively lay down Union rules in the sector concerned.[10]

The application of the concept of "exhaustive harmonisation" in *Compassion*, however, took the exhaustive character of minimum harmonisation to the extreme. As noted, Member States action is only excluded to the extent that Union legislation provides for the *complete* harmonisation of all measures necessary to ensure the protection of the interests enumerated in that Article.

Consider the judgment in *Van Bennekom*,[11] where the Court stated:

---

[7] See in particular Slot in 21 *European Law Review* (1996), 379–397.

[8] See European Parliamentary Research Service, "Methods for unifying private law in the EU", Briefing 23 January 2014, available at http://www.europarl.europa.eu/RegData/bibliotheque/briefing/2014/130628/LDM_BRI(2014)130628_REV1_EN.pdf or http://ow.ly/gO93301qFHD, last consulted 20.6.2016.

[9] Slot, note 2 above: *Total harmonisation* occurs where no derogation from the rules maintained in the legislation exist, except for those foreseen in the Directive itself ("safeguard measures"); In the case of *optional harmonisation*, manufacturers may follow either the national rules of the home state, or the harmonised rules. Should they wish to market their products in other Member States, however, the harmonised rules have to be followed (that is the essence of mutual recognition), or the rules of the country of destination; in the event of *minimum harmonisation*, minimum rules are set at the Community level, and have to be followed by all manufacturers, but States may individually or jointly provide for more stringent rules. Applying higher national standards to imported products is not allowed, *if* the Directive provides that products conforming with the minimum standard have to be accepted. If there is no such clause, higher national standards can be imposed, but have to be assessed under Articles 34ff.

[10] Always bearing in mind that for Directives adopted on the basis of Article 114 or 193, stricter national measures are always possible (subject to conditions).

[11] Case 227/82. Criminal proceedings against Leendert van Bennekom, [1983] ECR 3883.

It is only when Community Directives, in pursuance of Article 100 . . . , make provision for the full harmonisation of all the measures needed to ensure the protection of human and animal life *and* institute Community procedures to monitor compliance therewith that recourse to Article [30] ceases to be justified.[12]

Motte included similar phrasing.[13] These cases suggest that recourse to Article 36 TFEU becomes only *gradually* unnecessary, to the extent Union legislation has harmonised the interests at issue.

Motte is a good illustration of the need carefully to consider the scope of harmonising directives, and of the importance of keeping the debate on harmonisation techniques separate from that of exhaustion. The Directive at issue[14] was of the type "total harmonisation": by use of a positive list, only those foodstuffs that are included may be used as additives in foodstuffs throughout the Union. For the very acceptance of a colorant as an additive, this Directive is also exhaustive. However, the decision concerning the use of a specific colorant for a specific foodstuff was not subject to the harmonising efforts at all; that was entirely up to the Member States, with due regard to Articles 34ff. TFEU.

Likewise, in *Van Bennekom*, it is imperative to keep a close eye on the scope of the Directive, on its limited aims (limitation to procedural requirements) and therefore on the intact competence of the Member States for all that falls outside the Directive's objectives.

In *Lomas*, the Court had already indicated a trend, by holding that recourse to Article 36 is no longer possible where Union directives provide for harmonisation of the measure necessary to achieve the specific objective which would be furthered by reliance upon this provision.[15] This statement, which drops the qualification "complete", went largely unnoticed. Indeed, in that case, the UK sought recourse to Article 36 in order unilaterally to enforce the provisions of a directive which all parties agreed provided for full harmonisation of the standards. The UK in that case did not seek to introduce stricter standards. The point of contention was the enforcement procedure.

---

[12] This extract illustrates the confusion: the Court refers to "full" or "total" harmonisation, rather than to exhaustion.

[13] Case 247/84 *Criminal proceedings against Léon Motte*, [1985] ECR 3887 (colorants in feedstuffs), at 16.

[14] Council Directive of 23 October 1962 on the approximation of the rules of the Member States concerning the colouring matters authorized for use in foodstuffs intended for human consumption, OJ English special edition 1959–62, p. 279.

[15] Joined Cases C-38/90 and C-151/90 *Lomas and Others*, [1992] ECR I-1781, at 18.

The core of the Court's approach in *Compassion* is that even minimum standards exhaustively lay down common Union rules, therefore occupy the field and prevent Member States' action. This coincides with the Advocate General's (AG's) reasoning, that it is not because the standards laid down by the Union are weak from an animal welfare point of view, but it's that they prevent the harmonisation from being exhaustive.[16]

Even if one did agree that *weak* standards may occupy the field, the *absence* of standards arguably does not. This is the case for the diet requirements of calves intended for the production of white meat, which was at issue in *Compassion*. The exception for calves reared for "white veal" made a crucial requirement for the inclusion of solid feed in calves' diets completely nugatory. Moreover, what if, such as in the case at issue, there are effectively no standards for a substantial period of time, due to the operation of transitional provisions? Until the end of 2003, holdings built before 1994 could escape the standards applicable to those built after that date. Holdings built during the transitional period of four years only had to conform with the standards by 2008.[17]

The transitional provisions convinced the AG that recourse to Article 36 was still possible. AG Léger in this respect saw similarities with the case law that holds that a directive does not have the effect of removing recourse to Article 36, when the period the directive gives them for adopting the provisions necessary to comply with it has not expired.[18] The Court, however, did not adopt this reasoning.[19]

D. The Environmental Guarantees of Articles 114 and 193 TFEU

Arguably considerably more so than in the context of other EU policies, Member States seek to resort to unilateral measures to protect their environmental interests, or their ethical interests, such as in the case of animal welfare. This may be partially explained by the perceived "North–South" divide in environmental proactiveness (the reality of which is, however, uncertain). Almost by definition, the environmental standard reached in harmonising legislation does not meet with the expectations of the

---

[16] Opinion AG Léger in *Compassion*, at 56, *in fine*.
[17] Ibid., at 64.
[18] The AG decided against the invocation of (the then) Article 30 on "extraterritoriality" grounds; see also his view in *Lomas*, and the critique in G. Van Calster, "Hedley Lomas", 3 *Columbia Journal of European Law*, 1 (1996), 132–145.
[19] See, for example, Case 35/76 *Simmenthal*, [1976] ECR 1871; Case 251/78, *Denkavit*, [1979] ECR 3369.

"greenest" Member States. To achieve their environmental goals, these States can make recourse to the environmental safeguard clauses.

III. SECOND-GUESSING OF NATIONAL ENVIRONMENTAL PRIORITIES?

The conditions for application of the environmental guarantee imply that it is perfectly possible for the Commission to hold that whilst scientific evidence supports the environmental or public health claims of a particular Member State, market studies show a "disproportionate" impact on the internal market. Such a decision would amount to a direct condemnation of a State's policy choices, as it would tell them that the very level of protection which it seeks is too high, vis-à-vis the objectives of the internal market.

This role of the Commission "second-guessing" Member States' internal policy objectives arguably sits uneasily with the application of Article 30ff. TFEU by the Court of Justice. In a convincing number of cases, the CJEU[20]– has expressly held that the setting of the level of protection is up to the Member States themselves, in the absence of Union harmonisation.[21] The proportionality test to which the national measures are then subject condemns manifestly unreasonable measures only,[22] and obliges Member States to cooperate with the authorities in

---

[20] See, for example, Joined Cases C-1/90 and C-176/90 *Aragonesa de Publicidad Exterior SA and Publiva SAE v Departamento de Sanidad y Seguridad Social de la Generalitat de Cataluña*, [1991] ECR I-4151, at 16; Case C-347/89 *Freistaat Bayern v Eurim-Pharm GmbH*, [1991] ECR I-1747, at 26; Case 125/88 *Criminal proceedings against H.F.M. Nijman*, [1989] ECR 3533, at 14; Case C-131/93 *Commission v Germany*, [1994] ECR I-3303, at 16; Case 174/82 *Criminal proceedings against Sandoz BV*, [1983] ECR 2445, at 15 *et seq.* (in particular at 19, where the Court upholds a "wide discretion" for the Member States, in the absence of scientific certainty); Case 227/82 *Criminal proceedings against Leendert van Bennekom*, [1983] ECR 3883, at 36 *et seq.* (similar "wide discretion" for the Member States, in the absence of scientific certainty); Case C-293/94 *Criminal proceedings against Jacqueline Brandsma*, [1996] ECR I-3159, at 11; and in Case C-400/96 *Criminal proceedings against Jean Harpegnies*, [1998] ECR I-5121, at 33.

[21] The Commission reportedly takes the same view: see, for example, Opinion of AG Fennelly of 16 June 1998 in Case C-67/97 *Criminal proceedings against Ditlev Bluhme*, [1998] ECR I-8033, at 20.

[22] See Joined Cases C-1/90 and C-176/90 *Aragonesa de Publicidad Exterior SA and Publivía SAE v Departamento de Sanidad y Seguridad Social de la Generalitat de Cataluña*, ECLI:EU:C:1991:327.

other Member States, to avoid unnecessary delays in and obstacles to the free movement.[23]

However, the Court has left the door open for speculation, since it often adds to the recognition that it is up to the Member States themselves to set their desired level of protection, the leeway that they have in regard to "the requirements of the free movement of goods".[24] Moreover, the much-cited *Danish Bottles* case has caused confusion. The Court reviewed Danish legislation which limited the marketing of beers and soft drinks to those in containers which were returnable and which were sold in previously approved containers. The marketing of non-approved albeit returnable containers was limited to 3000 hl per producer per year. That the Danish system amounted to a quantitative restriction to trade was not contested. The CJEU found that the very obligation to use reusable containers and to organise a recovery system, including the use of mandatory deposits, was not *in se* contrary to the free movement of goods.[25] However, it did find against the obligation for foreign producers either to use approved containers, or to limit themselves to marketing 3000 hl only of reusable, non-approved containers. The Court found that even though the use of non-approved but reusable containers did not guarantee the same level of environmental protection as the use of approved containers, the former nevertheless also serve to protect the environment. This tilted the balance of proportionality, even though the use of non-approved containers is not just a less trade-restrictive means: it is also a less environmentally effective means. The Court did not assess in particular whether the Danish measures were indistinctly applicable, focusing instead solely on the issue of proportionality. This is remarkable, since the "indistinctly applicable test" is the standard first tier of the rule of reason.

IV. PREUSSENELEKTRA, ESSENT 1 AND ESSENT 2

Case law on the relationship between free movement and environmental protection is frequent. This volume is not the place to review it *in*

---

[23] This duty of cooperation refers for instance to the mutual recognition of scientific analysis and laboratory tests.
[24] For example in Case 174/82 *Sandoz*, ECLI:EU:C:1983:213, where the Court subsequently found the national blanket ban to market a product, unless the manufacturers supply proof that a particular additive was safe, to be unlawful; it held that national authorities are obliged to assess the merits of each case, taking into account all relevant information.
[25] Case 302/86 *Commission v Denmark*, [1988] ECR 4607, at 13.

extenso.²⁶ Instead, three recent cases illustrate the challenges associated with the debate.

A. PreussenElektra

*PreussenElektra*²⁷ showed the Court in a very lenient mood vis-à-vis German measures which prima facie did not seem passable under the Treaty's Articles on the free movement of goods. It concerned the German Feeding-in Act 1990 (Stromeinspeisungsgesetz). The Act intervened both in the demand side of the market and in the price paid for the electricity concerned. Electricity suppliers which operate a general supply network were obliged, within certain limits, to purchase the electricity produced in their area of supply from renewable sources of energy and to pay compensation for those inputs of electricity in accordance with a number of parameters. The minimum price varied between 65 and 90 per cent of the average sales price per kilowatt hour of electricity supplied to all final customers by electricity supply undertakings.

The regime did have an in-built safeguard ("hardship clause"): in so far as the kilowatt hours to be compensated for exceeded 5 per cent of the total kilowatt hours supplied by the electricity supplier through its network during a calendar year, the upstream network operator was obliged to reimburse the supplementary costs.

The Commission had regarded the system as being an acceptable form of State aid, among others in view of its relatively small impact (given the limited share of the energy concerned in the overall electricity market). However, in view of the increase in this share, the Commission was in the process of reviewing this decision.

Schleswag sourced almost its entire supply of electricity from PreussenElektra. From an original 0.77 per cent in 1991, the share of wind energy rose to 15 per cent in 1998. Schleswag consequently claimed a substantial amount from PreussenElektra, in accordance with the hardship clause. PreussenElektra, however, argued that the relevant part of the Act amounted to a change in the State aid regime, which had not been separately notified to the EC. We will not further review the State aid

---

[26] See most recently N. de Sadeleer, *EU Environmental Law and the Internal Market*, Oxford: Oxford University Press, 2014, and also idem, "Reconciling the Irreconcilable: Trade vs Environment in the EU", *The European Financial Review*, 28 February 2014; for case law prior to 2000 see G. Van Calster, *International and EC Trade Law – The Environmental Challenge*, London: Cameron May, 2000.

[27] Case C-379/98 *PreussenElektra*, ECLI:EU:C:2001:160.

element of the case here, given that it is less relevant for the purposes of comparison with Essent.

With respect to the internal market aspects of the case, given that distributors were obliged to purchase electricity produced within the territory in which they are active, there is no doubt that intra-EU trade was affected. However, the Court found these restrictions to be justified, in view of two parameters: the aim of the regime (environmental protection) as well as the specific characteristics of the EU electricity market at the time of the judgment.

The environmental credentials of the regulations, as identified by the Court, were indeed rather impressive: the increased use of renewable sources of energy is a central part of the EU's commitment to tackling climate change; this is obviously beneficial for the environment (one of the mandatory requirements of the Court's rule of reason) – it also fosters the life and health humans, animals and plants (one of the exceptions provided for in Article 36 TFEU). The Court also referred to the integration principle, to emphasise the importance of an "environmentally conscious" internal market. Finally, the Directive on the internal market in electricity applicable at the time[28] specified that Member States may give priority to the production of electricity from renewable sources of energy.

The recognition of the positive environmental impact of renewable energy was not surprising. What remains controversial, however, is whether such hindrance of the internal market is proportionate. The Court in *PreussenElektra* did not conduct a proportionality test, lest its references to the characteristics of the electricity market had to be understood in a proportionality context. In this respect the Court noted

- that the liberalisation of the electricity market was as yet in an intermediary phase only, and
- that the nature of electricity is such that, once it has been allowed into the transmission or distribution system, it is difficult to determine its origin and in particular the source of energy from which it was produced. It also referred to the Proposal at the time for a Directive on the promotion of electricity from renewable energy sources in the internal electricity market, that the implementation in each Member State of a system of certificates of origin for electricity produced from renewable sources, capable of being the subject of

---

[28] Directive 96/62/EC of the European Parliament and of the Council of 19 December 1996 concerning common rules for the internal market in electricity [1997] OJ L 27/20.

mutual recognition, was essential in order to make trade in that type of electricity both reliable and possible in practice.

In other words, the Court urged a solution to the technical challenge of presenting reliable certificates of origin.

PreussenElektra is especially noteworthy in that the Court's evaluation of the national measure within the context of Articles 34–36 TFEU is much milder than its similar considerations under Article 110 TFEU (*Outokumpu Oy* – reviewed in Chapter 9 on State aid).

PreussenElektra may have seemed like good case law only for as long as no reliable system of certificates of origin existed. However, *rien n'est absolu que le provisoire*: as *Vindkraft*[29] and *Essent*[30] show, PreussenElektra kick-started a more flexible approach with respect to non-tax restrictions to the free movement of goods – even if restrictions, such as in the case of *PreussenElektra*, are blunt and disproportionate.

B. Ålands Vindkraft and Essent 1: A Clear Preference For Market-based Renewable Energy Support

AG Bot opined in both Vindkraft and Essent, with Essent first, followed by Vindkraft. The Court itself held in Vindkraft first, followed by Essent.

AG Bot in Essent: call for an explicit reversal of *Cassis de Dijon*, nevertheless rejection of the Flemish scheme on the merits

In Essent, AG Bot rephrased the questions of the referring court to ask whether the Flemish support scheme for renewable energy, which grants renewable energy certificates to producers of such energy only if they are located in the Flemish Region, and which obliges electricity distributors to surrender a minimum amount of such certificates without being able to offer such certificates obtained in other EU Member States, is compatible with the free movement of goods and with the EU's non-discrimination principle. Directive 2001/77[31] regulates both renewable energy (or "green") certificates – which are used by a Member State to show it is meeting its obligations to produce a minimum amount of electricity from renewable sources – and certificates of origin, which allow an electricity distributor to prove that x amount of its electricity distributed originates from renewable energy.

---

[29] Case C-573/12 *Ålands Vindkraft*, ECLI:EU:C:2014:2037.
[30] Case C-204/12 *Essent Belgium*, ECLI:EU:C:2014:2192.
[31] Directive 2001/77/EC of the European Parliament and of the Council of 27 September 2001 on the promotion of electricity produced from renewable energy sources in the internal electricity market, OJ L 283, 27.10.2001, pp. 33–40.

The AG did not entertain at length the issue of whether renewable certificates in themselves qualify as "goods" under the Treaty. The Flemish system may definitely have an impact on the import of "green" electricity, with the latter undeniably having been held to be a "good" under the protection of the free movement of goods. If the certificates scheme unjustifiably restricts the free movement of goods, it would at any rate be illegal and in need of proper justification.

Unlike in PreussenElektra, distributors of electricity could still purchase renewable energy abroad – however, such electricity is often more expensive (for it does not receive Flemish government support), and even if distributors were to purchase abroad, they would still have to surrender, after purchase, the necessary Flemish certificates.

The AG notes that the Court in PreussenElektra allowed the German scheme despite it being discriminatory. This might have been an implicit reversal of the case law (*Cassis de Dijon*[32]) that infringements of the free movement of goods may only be based on the court-invented "mandatory requirements" (of which environmental protection is one, as opposed to those societal interests which are included in the explicit list of exceptions of Article 36 TFEU) where they do *not* discriminate.[33] That it might have been such a reversal leads the AG to suggest, finding support in the integration principle, that the Court in Essent should make that reversal explicit. Our alternative reading of PreussenElektra, above, suggested that the judgment was simply poor precedent, especially given that the court did not only ignore the discriminatory nature of the German measure, but omitted at the same time to assess its proportionality. The poor judgment in PreussenElektra, as noted, may be explained by the series of harmonising measures in the internal market for electricity, which were being prepared at the time of the judgment and which have since entered the statute books.

Despite the AG suggesting such a rare explicit reversal of the Court's case law on the free movement of goods, he did not suggest that, in the case at issue, the infringement is justified.

Among his arguments for rejecting the measure (which also features the argument that the Flemish Region violated a promise made at the time the relevant scheme was approved by the Commission under State aid rules) was also the "local production" requirement. Sadly, that relevant Union

---

[32] Case 120/78 *Rewe-Zentral AG v Bundesmonopolverwaltung für Branntwein*, note 3 above.

[33] More detail on the core issues in G. Van Calster, *International and EC Trade Law – The Environmental Challenge*, London: Cameron May, 2000.

law requires Member States to roll-out their own, national renewable energy capabilities has been seized upon by proponents of schemes such as the Flemish one, to argue that discriminative support may be required to assist industry to work towards that goal.

AG Bot in *Ålands Vindkraft*: turning on the heat

Vindkraft concerns the successor to Directive 2001/77 (at stake in Essent), that is, Directive 2009/28.[34] The AG essentially argued that the new Directive itself is contrary to EU primary law in allowing Member States to discriminate against foreign produced renewable electricity by limiting access to their national support scheme to electricity generated on their territory, and that such illegality is not backed by the environmental exceptions to the Treaty.

The Court does not follow Bot's lead in *Ålands Vindkraft*

The CJEU in *Vindkraft* first of all found that Directive 2009/28 is not exhaustive on the issue of territorial restrictions of support schemes, hence requiring assessment under primary EU law. Member States can continue to restrict access to their support schemes (in the strict sense of not rolling out financing to renewable energy of foreign origin): this constitutes an infringement to the free movement of goods but one which can be justified. As pointed out above, AG Bot had suggested, finding support in the integration principle, that the Court in Essent should make the PreussenElektra implicit reversal of *Cassis de Dijon* explicit. In the end the Court decided Vindkraft before Essent and simply refers (at 80) to its PreussenElektra case law: no explicit reversal.

The Court instead focuses on proportionality. In that assessment,[35] the CJEU emphasises the market-based elements of the Swedish scheme (the certificates can be sold separately from the underlying electricity and the market is operated in a transparent and liquid fashion). A less market-oriented approach may not have survived ECJ scrutiny.

---

[34] Directive 2009/28/EC of the European Parliament and of the Council of 23 April 2009 on the promotion of the use of energy from renewable sources and amending and subsequently repealing Directives 2001/77/EC and 2003/30/EC, OJ L 140, 5.6.2009, pp. 16–62.

[35] See also C. Banet's analysis available at http://www.ecohz.com/facts-news/news/aaland-case/, 3 July 2014, last consulted 16.12.2016.

The Court in Essent puts the ball back in the national court's camp: outcome far from clear

Deciding Vindkraft together with Essent would have been helpful. Instead, the Court ruled in Essent a couple of months later. Like in Vindkraft, it first of all does not rule on the qualification of certificates of origin as being "goods" or not: the legislation at any rate hinders the free movement of the electricity underlying the certificates.

It subsequently basically confirms the main findings of Vindkraft, including the absence of express reversal of the non-applicability of the rule of reason to discriminatory measures. Yes, the Flemish regime restricts trade. Yes, this can in principle be justified for environmental reasons. However, the Court does emphasise the proportionality test. In Vindkraft, the CJEU itself held the scheme to be compatible with the Treaty by virtue essentially of its highly transparent and market-driven character. In Essent, however and importantly, this final call is left to the national judge. The Court does hand the national court the markers along which this assessment needs to be made:

- For the Flemish scheme to meet the proportionality test, it is important that mechanisms be established which ensure the creation of a genuine market for certificates in which supply can match demand, reaching some kind of balance, so that it is actually possible for the relevant suppliers to obtain certificates under fair terms (at 112).
- Furthermore, the fine in the absence of quota fulfilment must not impose excessive penalties on the traders concerned (at 114).

The Swedish scheme, held to be compatible with EU economic law, does differ rather drastically from the Flemish scheme, which may not qualify as a genuine market operating under fair and transparent terms.

There is arguably quite an imbalance between foreign and domestic suppliers. Most of the larger suppliers in the Flemish Region also operate as producers. This makes the market and its prices subject to the overall strategy of these suppliers/producers. They choose whether their producers' certificates are kept for meeting their own obligation to surrender certificates, being a supplier, or whether these are sold on a bilateral basis (to competitor suppliers), via the energy stock exchange or via the grid operator guaranteeing a legal minimum price for certificates. Such variety of strategies in managing one's certificate stock is not open to suppliers producing outside the Flemish Region. These can only buy certificates as such, and have to do so to a considerable extent from competitors on the supply market.

Moreover, producer–suppliers are able to sell certificates along with electricity (as a package deal). They can also choose to sell them separately. Foreign producers do not have the package deal choice.

Alongside the observation that in the past the regulator concerned has refused any non-Flemish certificate, it is in our view quite doubtful that the Flemish regime actually functions as the open, transparent and effective market which the ECJ requires. In many ways the mechanism is very similar to a standard feed-in tariff scheme, arguably falling far short of the requirements of the ECJ.

Conclusion
The lack of explicit reversal of *Cassis de Dijon* is unfortunate.[36] We are now left to ponder whether PreussenElektra/Vindkraft/Essent needs distinguishing: do renewable energy/Kyoto/UNFCCC commitments stand out from other regulatory requirements in no longer insisting on non-discriminatory measures, or has this condition now been dropped for all "mandatory requirements"?

Further, in both Vindkraft and Essent the Court insists on market-based instruments being required to justify the market infringement. The final outcome of the Essent case is quite uncertain. We would have liked the CJEU itself to have highlighted the crucial differences between the Swedish and the Flemish schemes, and to have concluded disproportionality itself.

C. Essent 2[37]

To promote the generation of renewable energy, Flanders law makes transmission of electricity generated from renewable sources free of charge. However, this courtesy is limited to electricity generated in installations directly connected to the grid. Essent imports (a considerable part of) its green electricity from the Netherlands. It does not therefore enjoy free transmission. In his opinion[38] Bot's disapproval of trade restrictions like these is well established; see also his Opinion in Essent 1, above. Mr Bot continues to find the Court's case law unconvincing and makes no attempt to hide it. He repeatedly mentions that he is duty-bound to apply Essent/Vindkraft without believing they are good law. It is with obvious regret that he opines that, given the Court's stand in Essent/Vindkraft,

---

[36] On this issue see also F. Fontanelli, "The Essent Judgment: Another Revolution in the Case-law on Free Movement of Goods?", *EU Law Analysis*, S. Peers ed., www.eulawanalysis.blogspot.be, last consulted 21.9.2014.
[37] C-492/14 *Essent Belgium*, ECLI:EU:C:2016:732.
[38] 14 April 2016, ECLI:EU:C:2016:257.

he has no option but to propose that the Court finds the Flemish regime acceptable.

The AG does, however, leave open a future window for change: in particular, if and when the secondary law regime on renewable energy specifically, and energy as a whole, is amended, one may be able to distinguish Essent/Vindkraft.

Bot also reminds us of the unclear position of environmental exceptions under Article 36 TFEU and the rule of reason. He again calls upon the Court formally to acknowledge that the *Cassis de Dijon* distinction between the rule of reason and Article 36 (the former does not allow "distinctly applicable" national measures (read "discrimination") while the latter does) no longer exists.

We agree with the AG: we do not like judgment in *PreussenElektra* or in Essent. They discourage the creation of a true European energy market.

The Court itself has now distinguished its own case-law:[39] the EU has not harmonised the national support schemes for green electricity; this means that it is possible in principle for Member States to limit access to such schemes to green electricity production located in their territory. However, the Court's sympathy is now limited to schemes that support *producers* only. Green energy support schemes, whose production costs seem to be still quite high compared with the costs of electricity produced from non-renewable energy sources, are inherently designed in particular to foster, from a long-term perspective, investment in new installations, by giving producers certain guarantees about the future marketing of their green electricity (at 110, with reference to Vindkraft).

However, it is not the purpose of the Flemish scheme to give direct support to producers of green electricity. Rather, the free distribution of green electricity constitutes a financial advantage conferred primarily on the supplier of such electricity, which may, in certain circumstances, depending notably on the sale price which the consumer is charged by the supplier for his electricity, to a certain extent and indirectly also benefit the consumer (at 112).

Such a support mechanism offers no certainty that the economic advantage thus obtained for suppliers will ultimately actually and essentially be required to benefit producers of green electricity, particularly the smallest local generating installations which the Flemish Region claims to have wanted to support, which are not both producers and suppliers (at 113).

The Court is not game to assist the AG with his call for an explicit recognition of the potential to use discriminatory measures within the context

---

[39] C-492/14 *Essent Belgium*, note 37 above.

of mandatory requirements (the implications of *Cassis de Dijon*). That is a pity, but not a surprise.

Overall, the Court's judgment is a welcome safeguard to its more open-ended sympathy for renewable energy support schemes. Those who challenge such schemes in future know what to do. They need to show that there is no certainty that the economic advantage obtained for suppliers will ultimately actually and essentially be required to benefit producers of green electricity, as opposed to distributors or consumers.

V. RESTRICTIONS ON THE USE OF LAWFULLY MARKETED PRODUCTS AND THE EU'S INTERNAL MARKET

When reviewing restrictions of use for environmental purposes, it becomes immediately apparent that very little recourse is made to them, either by national or by European authorities. The *Mickelsson* case below is one of very few examples (restrictions on the lighting of bonfires in private gardens in some Member States, another).

In the case of European law, this is in no small measure due to subsidiarity considerations. The instrument of choice for European environmental law is directives which are either process-based or relate to product standards. Those that are process-based are all the so-called "procedural" or "horizontal" laws which aim to regulate (in the main) manufacturing processes likely to have an impact on the environment. The preference for product standards as a legal instrument is a legacy from the early stages of EC environmental law, when the Commission had to justify its interference in national environmental matters by reference to the internal market implications of divergent national environmental laws (this is prior to the introduction of an environmental title proper in the Treaty). Evidently, many of the product standards have an immediate impact on the question as to whether further, specific restrictions to use have any residual value. Consider, for example, the case of noise pollution. Where EC law already provides for a noise emission standard for mopeds, it sharply reduces the need for the introduction of local laws to deal with the nuisance caused by the revving engines.

Further restrictions to use for environmental purposes which are not an implied consequence of EU-defined product standards are considered to be apt only in the face of local circumstances, and therefore fall foul of the subsidiarity principle (which suggests or, indeed in the case of EU law, proscribes, that regulatory action be taken as close as possible to the level where it is going to have the maximum impact. In the case of the EU this has led to a general presumption against the EU being the appropriate level for action).

Indeed there are other areas of regulatory concern where restrictions of use have either taken flight some time ago or are being increasingly mooted, and which may well inspire more such examples in the environmental sector. As the examples below illustrate, public (and occupational) health and safety for the time being would seem to be the driving factor behind these initiatives:

- telecoms, health and use restrictions: see, for example, the tendency in a number of schools to scale back or completely remove the use of wireless Internet technology; government guidelines on the safe use of mobile phones; restrictions on the *installations* of mobile phone masts,
- public safety, human health and use restrictions: these relate in particular to road safety, and refer to, for example, the obligatory wearing of cycling helmets, and the prohibition of MP3 players in traffic,
- food and health: for example limiting sales options in fast food restaurants (mooted only so far, as far as the authors are aware); restrictions on the use of alcohol and tobacco products,
- infotainment and health: for example the widely publicised idea of the German federal government to prohibit paintball; or sales restrictions on computer games (in particular because of their violent or sexually explicit content),
- healthcare, and general welfare: for example restrictions on points of sales for medicines; restrictions on the use of nanotechnology in food processing.

As a result of there not being many examples of use restrictions for environmental purposes at the national level, inevitably of course there is not much CJEU case law on them either. In *Commission v Austria* (Tiroler lorry restrictions),[40] Austria was rapped for not having even considered less trade-restrictive alternatives to far-reaching use restrictions, other than a ban on specific types of transport during specific periods. This judgment underlines the need for sound and properly prepared science as a requirement for use restrictions with trade impact to be kosher. Whereas in the *Tiroler* case, though the trade impact of the measure was clear, this is different in those cases where restrictions of use are applied

---

[40] Case C-320/03 *Commission v Austria*, [2005] ECR I-9871.

indiscriminately and without even a hint of protectionism. It is in this context that calls have been made to simply regard such modalities or restrictions of use as not being covered by the prohibitions of Articles 34 and 35, much like in the case of "modalities of sale" in the *Keck* route.[41]

In *Commission v Italy* (motorcycle trailers),[42] the Court refused to rule on that question, opting instead for a market access test. If restrictions of use (in the case at issue, a prohibition) have a considerable influence on the behaviour of consumers, it affects the access of that product to the market of that Member State and falls foul of Article 34 EC. However, the Court granted Italy the right to introduce the ban on public interest/mandatory requirements grounds, in the process, however, giving Italy a very easy ride on the least-trade restrictiveness test (it would seem that the Commission could have pressed Italy more on the issue of proportionality).

Mickelsson[43] is the case which shed some light on the exact room for Member States to seek restrictions to use (as opposed to *Commission v Italy*[44] – moped trailers, which concerned a product prohibition). Swedish jet-ski regulations prohibit the use of personal watercraft other than on a general navigable waterway or waters in respect of which the local authority has issued rules permitting their use (on the basis of environmental considerations).

AG Kokott opined that restrictions of use, as long as they are not product-related, apply to all relevant traders operating within the Member State and affect in the same manner in law and in fact, the marketing of domestic and import products, do not qualify as quantitative restrictions to trade.

The CJEU disagreed: the prohibition *was* caught by Article 34, but can be justified under Article 36 TFEU.

The above analysis in summary shows that regulatory authorities both at the national and at the EU level enjoy a high level of discretion when putting in place product restrictions and/or restrictions of use; that, in doing so, they need to take due account of sound science; and that any such restrictions need to take account the principle of proportionality.

The test which Member States[45] ought to pursue when considering the legality of restrictions of use, should focus on the most objective elements of the exercise:

---

[41] Case C-267/91 *Keck und Mithouard*, ECLI:EU:C:1993:905.
[42] Case C-110/05 *Commission v Italy*, [2009] ECR I-519.
[43] Case C-142/05 *Aklagaren v Percy Mickelsson and Joakim Roos*, [2009] ECR I-4723.
[44] Case C-110/05 *Commission v Italy*, note 42 above.
[45] And eventually the CJEU if disputes arise.

- whether the decision is based on sound science; and
- whether the decision is proportionate, that is, whether based on that sound science, there is not a less trade or individual freedom-restrictive alternative which could equally effectively reach this result.

Index

Page numbers in **bold** indicate information in tables and page numbers in *italics* indicate information found in figures

Aarhus Convention 53–4, 81
  access to environmental information 83
    charging for access 90–92
    duty of information and transparency 86–7
    "environmental information" defined 83–4
    grounds for refusal of access 88–9
    lex specialis and 89
    limitations to public access 88–9
    power of member states 87–8
    "public administrative functions" defined 86
    "public authority" defined 84–8
  access to justice 79–80, 81–2, 93–4, 101
    Art. 263 TFEU 101–4
    direct concern 102
    individual concern 102
    non-privileged applicants 101–2
    Plaumann test 102–3
    privileged applicants 101
    Regulation 1367/2006, 104–7
  application of procedural principles 95–6
    access to environmental information 96–100
    access to justice 101–7
    public participation 100
  Environmental Impact Assessments
    access to justice 143
    costs 143–4
    direct applicability 144
    procedure 143
  implementation of procedural principles 82–3
    access to environmental information 83–92
    access to justice 93–5
    public participation 92–3
  procedural principles
    application 95–6
      access to environmental information 96–100
      access to justice 101–7
      public participation 100
    implementation 82–3
      access to environmental information 83–92
      access to justice 93–5
      public participation 92–3
  refusal of access to information
    appeals 91–2
    grounds for refusal 88–9
  secondary law and 81–2
access to information
  Aarhus Convention 83–92, 96–100
  charging for access 90–92
  duty of information and transparency 86–7
  Environmental Impact Assessments 138
  "environmental information" defined 83–4
  grounds for refusal of access 88–9
  lex specialis and 89
  limitations to public access 88–9
  power of member states 87–8
  "public administrative functions" defined 86
  "public authority" defined 84–8
access to justice 81–2
  Aarhus Convention 93–5, 101–7
  Art. 263 TFEU 101–4

331

direct concern 102
individual concern 102
member state duties 93
   exceptions 93–5
non-privileged applicants 101–2
Plaumann test 102–3
privileged applicants 101
Regulation 1367/2006, 104–7
agriculture and forestry
   climate-proofing of policies 256
   Common Agricultural Policy 211–12
   noise pollution 236
   Strategic Environmental Assessments 145–6, 211
   water pollution 228
   see also genetically modified organisms
air pollution 242
   Air Quality Directive 242–5
      daughter directives 246
      transboundary air pollution 245
   national emission ceilings 246–7
   sector specific regulation
      harmonisation 247–52
      marine emissions 251–2
      Paints Directive 252
      road vehicles 247–50
      transport emissions 247–52
Air Quality Directive 242–3
   air quality assessments 243
   air quality plans 244
   daughter directives 246
   management of ambient air quality 244
   objectives 243
   ozone concentrations 244
   transboundary air pollution 245
aircraft
   Chicago Convention 164–5
   emissions 246, 258–60
   noise pollution 240–241
Amsterdam Treaty (1997), 3–4
   Committee of the Regions 45
   Economic and Social Committee 47
   environmental guarantee 62–63
   proportionality principle 20
   subsidiarity principle 20
   sustainable development 9, 25

attributed powers principle 7, 55, 70
aviation *see* aircraft

best available techniques (BAT), 9, 114
   determination of 118
   "emerging techniques" 118–19
   emissions 115–16
   exchange of information for member states 119
   Integrated Pollution Prevention and Control Directive 112–13
   not entailing excessive costs 9
   reference guides (BREFS), 268
Biocidal Products Regulation (BPR), 295
   active substances 295–7
   biocidal products 297–8
   data protection and data sharing 298–9
   existing substances 297
   groundwater 227
   new substances 296–7
   treated articles 298
biodiversity 181–2
   2020 Biodiversity Strategy 182–3
   Environmental Impact Assessments 137, 142–3
   Habitats Directive 185–6
      Arts 6(3) and 6(4), 187–203
      declassification of sites 203–4
      Environmental Impact Assessment Directive and 204–6
   invasive alien species 213–14
   Natura 2000 network 183
      Habitats Directive 185–206
      Special Protection Areas 184
      Wild Birds Directive 183–5
soil 206–7
   Biodiversity Thematic Strategy 210
   Common Agricultural Policy 211–12
   Environmental Impact Assessment Directive 210–211
   European Soil Charter 209–10
   Habitats Directive and 210
   resource efficiency roadmap (2011), 212
   Soil Thematic Strategy 208–9

Strategic Impact Assessment
    Directive 210–211
special conservation areas 186
    status 182
Strategic Environmental
    Assessments 149
Wild Birds Directive 183–4
    derogation 185
    killing or capture 184
    member state responsibilities 185
    Special Protection Areas 184

charges and fees 38
    access to information 90–91
    collection disposal and treatment of
        waste 270–271
    landfill 267
    see also costs
Charter of Fundamental Rights of the
    European Union 4
    integration principle 24
chemicals
    Biocidal Products Regulation 295
        active substances 295–7
        biocidal products 297–8
        data protection and data sharing
            298–9
        existing substances 297
        new substances 296–7
        treated articles 298
    Classification Labelling and
        Packaging regulation 290–291
        classification 293
        harmonisation 291–2, 294–5
        labelling 293–4
        obligations 292–4
        packaging 294
        pictogram *292*
    European Chemicals Agency 290
    genetically modified organisms 299
        authorisation procedure 300–302
        food products 304–6
        labelling 302–3, 305
        regulatory developments 306–7
        traceability 303–4
    harmonisation
        Classification Labelling and
            Packaging regulation
            290–292
        REACH regulation 277–8
        authorisations 286–90
        exempted substances 279
        registration 278–86
        registration of substances under
            other legislation 279–80
        registration of substances under
            REACH 278
        actors/parties concerned 281–3
        chemical safety assessment and
            risk management measures
            284–5
        evaluation 285–6
        exempt substances 279–81
        importers 282
        information required 283–5
        manufacturers 281
        process 285
        producers 282
        quantities 278–9
        representatives 282–3
        substances concerned 278
        technical dossiers 283–4
    substances of very high concern
        authorisation procedure 288–9
        ECHA authorisation 286–8
        obligation to exchange
            information 289–90
        restrictions procedures 289
    Classification Labelling and Packaging
        (CLP) regulation 290–291
        classification 293
        harmonisation 291–2, 294–5
        labelling 293–4
        obligations 292–4
        packaging 294
        pictogram *292*
climate change 221
    2013 EU adaptation strategy 254–5
    "climate proofing" 256
    cost-benefit assessments 255–6
    adaptation
        2013 EU adaptation strategy
            254–6
        droughts and water security
            222–4
        floods 221–2
    European Emissions Trading System
        257–9
        aviation sector and 259–60
    Kyoto Protocol 253

legislation and policy 253–4
mitigation 256–7
   European Emissions Trading System 257–60
   heavy-duty vehicles 262–3
   land transport 261–3
   light-duty vehicles 261–2
   rail transport 263
Committee of the Regions 45
   decision-making commissions 46
   origins 45
   proportionality principle 46
   role 45–6
      cross-border cooperation 46
   structure 45
   subsidiarity principle and 46
common agricultural policy (CAP), 57, 211–12
competences
   division of competences 5–6
   "environmental guarantee" 7–8
   exclusive 6–7
   joint competence 5–6
   non-exclusive 7
   proportionality 7
   shared competence 6
   subsidiarity 7
   supportive 7
competition law 175
   DSD case 177–9
   Eco-Emballages case 176–7
   environmental application 175–6
   see also state aid
conferral principle *see* attributed powers principle
costs
   legal proceedings 94–5
   see also charges and fees; polluter pays principle
Council of Ministers *see* Council of the European Union
Council of the European Union
   role and responsibilities 42
Court of Justice of the European Union (CJEU)
   accessorium sequitur principale approach 55, 56
   actions for annulment 44
   actions for failure to act 44
   actions for failure to fulfil obligations 44
   lack of specialisation 44–5
   powers 44
   preliminary ruling requests 44
   structure 43
decision-making 66–7
   Committee of the Regions 45–6
   Council of the European Union 42
   Court of Justice of the European Union 43–5
   Economic and Social Committee 46–7
   European Chemicals Agency 49–50
   European Commission 42–3
   European Environment Agency 48–9
   European Investment Bank 47–8
   European Maritime Safety Agency 49
   European Parliament 40–42
   public participation 92–3
   qualified majority voting 2, 67–8
determination of legal basis 54–5
   accessorium sequitur principale approach 55, 56
   attributed powers principle 55
   civil protection humanitarian aid and solidarity 60–61
   common agricultural policy 57
   common commercial policy 60
   ECJ case law 55–7
   energy 60
   environment 61
   internal market provisions 58–9
   primacy principle 55, 56
   research and technological development 59–60
   social policy 59
   taxes and indirect taxation 58
   transport 58
Deutsche Bahn case
   equal treatment principle 166–7
   international law and 166
   polluter pays principle 167
   relevant secondary law 164–5
direct effect principle 4, 74
   primacy principle compared 74–5

Index

drinking water 224–5
  IROPI exception and 199

Economic and Social Committee
  45–7, 67–8
EEC Treaty 1–2
EIA Directive
  Aarhus Convention and 143–4
  basic principles 130–134
  cumulative assessment 134–7
  obligations 137–41
  scoping 138–9
  screening 139–40
  splitting of projects 134–7
  transboundary projects 141–3
  see also Environment Impact
    Assessments
emissions
  aircraft 246, 258–60
  best available techniques 115–16
  European Emissions Trading System
    257–60
  integrated pollution prevention and
    control 112–13
  marine emissions 251–2
  motor vehicles 247–50
  protection of human health 246
  transport emissions 247–52
enforcement procedures
  EU citizens
    role of 79–80
  IMPEL 71, 72
  fines 76, 77–9
  REACH 278
  trade sanctions 308
Environment Public Health and Food
  Safety Committee (European
  Parliament)
  powers and responsibilities 41
environmental crime
  causing death or serious injury 160
  criminal nature of offences 160
  dual liability 160
  Environmental Crime Directive
    complicated nature of 157–8
    distribution of powers 158
    origins 157
  types of offence 159–60
environmental guarantee 3, 7–8, 61–2
  Arts 114 and 193 TFEU 315–16

conditions required 62–6
proportionality and 309
Environmental Impact Assessments
  13, 23
  Aarhus Convention and
    access to justice 143
    costs 143–4
    direct applicability 144
    procedure 143
  access to information 138
  alternatives 140–141
  cumulative assessments 135
  development consent 133–4
  direct and indirect impacts 138
  EIA Directive
    Aarhus Convention and 143–4
    basic principles 130–134
    cumulative assessment 134–7
    obligations 137–41
    scoping 138–9
    screening 139–40
    splitting of projects 134–7
    transboundary projects 141–3
  European Soil Charter 210–211
  Habitats Directive and 204–6
  incremental projects 135
    case law 135–7
  "material assets" 137–8
  origins 130
  procedural obligations 137
  procedures *132*
  "project" defined 131
  "public concerned" defined 133
  "public" defined 131
  screening 139–40
  scope 138–9
  scoping 140, 141
  soil 210–211
  splitting projects 134–5
  substantive obligations 137
  transboundary projects 141–2
    guidance 142–3
    time frames 142
environmental liability
  case law 153–4
  "damage" defined 151
  "environmental damage" defined 151
  Environmental Liability Directive
    150–156
  international law 156

minimum standards 156
policy rationale 152–3
polluter pays principle 152–3, 156
preventive effect 155
preventive principles 152–3
"socially efficient prevention" 155
strict liability 154–5
Environmental Management and Auditing Scheme (EMAS)
aims 109
registration criteria 110–111
renewal of registrations 111
environmental management systems (EMSs)
Environmental Management and Auditing Scheme 109
international scope 108
ISO standards 108
national scope 108–9
see also Environmental Management and Auditing Scheme
EU Council see Council of the European Union
EU Network for the Implementation and Enforcement of Environmental Law (IMPEL), 71–2
European Chemicals Agency 49–50, 290
European Commission
delivering opinions and recommendations 43
functions 42–3
implementation powers 43
monitoring compliance 43
representation of the EU 43
structure 43
European Environment Agency 48–9
European Investment Bank 47–8
European Maritime Safety Agency 49
European Parliament
form 40
functions
advisory function 40
budgetary and supervisory function 40
decision-making function 40–41
impact on EU policy 42
standing committees 41
duties 41–2

fines 77–9
see also sanctions

genetically modified organisms 50, 299
authorisation procedure 300–302
food products 304–6
GMO Directive 300–302
labelling 302–3, 305
regulatory developments 306–7
traceability 303–4
GMO Directive 300–302
see also genetically modified organisms
green public procurement
legal framework 127–8
targets 126
groundwater 114–16, 227
Groundwater Directive 219, 227
Water Framework Directive 227

Habitats Directive 185–6
alternative solutions test 196–7
appropriate assessment stage 191
content of appropriate assessment 194–5
integrity of the site 191–4
public consultation 195–6
Art. 6(3), 187
alternative solutions test 196–7
appropriate assessment stage 191–6
IROPI exception 197–203
screening stage 188–91
Art. 6(4), 188–203
declassification of sites 203–4
Environmental Impact Assessment Directive an,d 204–6
European Soil Charter and 210
IROPI exception 197–8
absence of priority natural habitat type 198–200
absence of priority species 198–200
compensatory measures 201–3
presence of priority natural habitat type 200–201
presence of priority species 200–201
screening stage 188
"individually or in combination

Index

with other plans or projects" 190
  likelihood of effects 188–90
  significance of effects 190–191
soil 210
Special Areas of Conservation 182, 186
harmonisation
  air pollution 247–52
  chemicals
    Classification, Labelling and Packaging regulation 291–2, 294–5
  minimum harmonisation 233–41
  negative harmonisation
    trade standards 310
  noise pollution 233
    EU self-certification 234
    EU type approval 233
    EU type examination 234
    EU verification 234
  positive harmonisation
    trade standards 310
  trade and harmonisation of standards
    Cassis de Dijon case 310
    community pre-emption 311–12
    Compassion case 312–13, 315
    exhaustive effect of legislation 311–12
    Lomas case 314
    minimum harmonisation 311
    Motte case 314
    negative harmonisation 310
    positive harmonisation 310
    proportionality 316
    Van Bennekom case 313, 314
heads of power *see* competences
high level of environmental protection principle 3, 8–9
  application 11
  CJEU 11
  Environmental Action Programmes 10
  TFEU 10–11
    balancing economic and social development 11
    cost/benefit analyses 11
    taking different situations into account 11
  human rights 12–13

"imperative reasons for overriding public interest" (IROPI) exception 188
  Habitats Directive 197–8
    absence of priority natural habitat type 198–200
    absence of priority species 198–200
    compensatory measures 201–3
    presence of priority natural habitat type 200–201
    presence of priority species 200–201
implementation of legislation
  conferral of implementing powers 70
  examination procedure 70–71
  executive federalism 69–71
  improvement of 71
    non-legal instruments and measures 71–3
indirect aid 171
  border tax adjustments 172
  Chemial Farmaceutici case 173–5
  energy taxation 171–3
  non-discrimination principle 173
  Outokumpu Oy case 171–3
    impact 173–5
Industrial Emissions Directive (IE Directive)
  access to justice 94
  best available techniques 114, 118–19
  groundwater 227
  IPPC recast 23, 34, 112
  permitting 112–13
    obligations of member states 113–18
infringement procedures 75
  bad application 76
  fines 77–9
  non-communication 76
  non-conformity 76
  reforms under Lisbon Treaty 77
integrated pollution prevention and control (IPPC), 216

Best Available Techniques Reference
    Guides 268
  emissions 112–13
  IPPC Directive 23, 31, 34
  recycling 265, 267
  see also Industrial Emissions
    Directive
integration principle 19, 22–3
  aims 23–4
  Alands Vindkraft case 319–22
  broad interpretation 23
  internal market integration strategy
    23
  narrow/vertical interpretation 23
  procedural integration
    Environmental Impact
      Assessments 23
    sustainability impact assessments
      23
  substantive integration
    animal welfare 24
    energy 24
    shipments of waste 23–4
invasive alien species 213–14

Kyoto Protocol 253, 261, 324

labelling 119–20
  chemicals 293–4
    Classification Labelling and
      Packaging of Substances and
      Mixtures Regulation 290–291
    harmonisation 294–5
    obligations 292–4
  eco-label 120
    legislative framework 120–123
    Environment Public Health and
      Food Safety Committee 41
  EU energy label 60, 123
    distance selling 126
    legislative framework 123–6
  genetically modified organisms 299,
    302–5
  motor vehicles 262
  treated articles 298
legal principles 17–19
  general principles 19
  integration principle 22–3
    aims 23–4
    broad interpretation 23

internal market integration
  strategy 23
narrow/vertical interpretation 23
procedural integration 23
substantive integration 23–4
polluter pays principle 18
  aims 37
  implementation 36–9
  origins 36
  soft-law instruments 38
precautionary principle
  CJEU case law 29–31
  criticisms of application of
    principle 31
  implementation 31–2
  lack of legal definition 28–9
  Maastricht Treaty 28
  prevention principle and 33
  Rio Declaration 28
  risk assessment and management
    criteria 32
prevention principle
  implementation 34–5
  known risks 34
  precautionary principle compared
    33–4
procedural principles 18–19
  access to environmental
    information 83–92, 96–100
  access to justice 93–5, 101–7
  public participation 92–3, 100
proportionality principle 21–2
rectification of damage at source
    principle 35
  implementation 35–6
specific principles 19
subsidiarity principle 19–20
  application 21
  criteria 20
  enforcement 20–21
  proportionality and 20
substantive principles 18–19
sustainable development
  Brundtland Report 24, 26
  constitutional dimension 26
  definitions and interpretation
    24–7
  social dimension 26
  Stockholm Declaration 24
  threats to 27

lex specialis 61
  access to information and 89, 98
  GMO Directive 89
  Regulation 1367/2006, 98, 101
Lisbon Treaty (2007), 3–4, 6, 60, 253
  Committee of the Regions 45–6
  decision-making procedures 66–8
  delegated and implementing acts 52
  infringement proceedings 77, 78
  Regulation 1367/2006, 101
  solidarity clause 60–61
  subsidiarity 20

Maastricht Treaty (1992), 2–3, 4, 6, 13–14
  Committee of the Regions 45–6
  Economic and Social Committee 46–7
  precautionary principle 28
  qualified majority voting 62
  subsidiarity 20
marine environment 216, 229–30
motor vehicles
  emissions 247–50
    climate change policy 261–3
  noise pollution 234–7

nature conservation *see* biodiversity
noise pollution 231
  agricultural and forestry tractors 236
  aircraft 240–241
  Environmental Noise Directive 231–3
    implementation 233
  minimum harmonisation 233
    EU self-certification 234
    EU type approval 233
    EU type examination 234
    EU verification 234
  noise mapping 232–3
  noise at work 237–8
  outdoor use equipment 238–40
  sector specific regulation
    2- and 3-wheel vehicles and quadricycles 236–7
    agricultural and forestry tractors 236
    aircraft 240–241

  minimum harmonisation 233–41
  noise at work 237–8
  outdoor use equipment 238–40
  vehicle motors 234–5
vehicle motors 234–5
non-discrimination principle 12, 32, 129, 173–4
PreussenElektra case 321–2, 324

ozone concentrations
  air quality 244, 246–7

packaging *see* Classification Labelling and Packaging (CLP) regulation; labelling
permitting and licensing procedures 112
  best available techniques 114
    determination of 118
    "emerging techniques" 118–19
    exchange of information for member states 119
  Industrial Emissions Directive 112–13
    best available techniques 114, 118–19
    obligations of member states 113–18
    integrated pollution prevention and control approach 112–13
    role and responsibilities of member states 113–14
    applications 114–15
    compliance 116–17
    emission limits 115
    incidents and accidents 117
    inspections 117
    maintenance and surveillance obligations 115–16
    measures relating to non-normal conditions 116
    obligations to supply competent authority 115
    reconsideration of permit conditions 116
    release monitoring requirements 115
    transboundary obligations 116–17

policy objectives 8–9
  high level of environmental
    protection 8, 10–11
  improvement of quality of
    environment 8, 12
  promotion at international level
    13–14
  protection of human health 13
  right to the protection of the
    environment 12–13
  sustainable development 8, 9–10
polluter pays principle 18
  aims 37
  Deutsche Bahn case 167
  environmental liability 152–3,
    156
  implementation 36–9
  origins 36
  soft-law instruments 38
  state aid and 167, 168–9
    transitional period 169–71
precautionary principle
  criticisms of application of principle
    31
  ECJ case law 29
    burden of proof 30–31
    limitations to application of
      principle 29–30
  lack of legal definition 28–9
  Maastricht Treaty 28
  prevention principle and 33
  Rio Declaration 28
  risk assessment and management
    criteria
      cost/benefit analyses 32
      examination of scientific
        developments 32
      non-discrimination 32
      proportionality 32
  secondary law examples 31–2
prevention principle
  examples 34–5
  known risks 34
  precautionary principle compared
    33–4
primacy principle 4, 55, 56, 73
  direct effect principle compared
    74–5
procedural principles
  application 95–6

access to environmental
  information 96–100
access to justice 101–7
public participation 100
implementation 82–3
  access to environmental
    information 83–92
  access to justice 93–5
  public participation 92–3
see also Aarhus Convention
proportionality principle 7, 21–2
  Amsterdam Treaty (1997), 20
  Committee of the Regions 46
  environmental guarantee and 309
  precautionary principle
    risk assessment and management
      criteria 32
  subsidiarity principle and 20
  trade and harmonisation of
    standards 316
protection of human health 77, 83–4,
    117
  air quality 243–4
  emissions 246
  bathing water 225
  drinking water 224–5
  Environment Public Health and
    Food Safety Committee 41
  EU labelling 119
  European Chemicals Agency
    Committee for Risk Assessment
      49–50
  genetically modified organisms 58–9
  Habitats Directive 187–200
  marine environment 229
  polluter pays principle 38
  proportionality 31
  REACH Regulation 277, 284,
    286–9
  TFEU 7, 8–9, 13
public participation *see* Aarhus
  Convention; procedural principles
public procurement 126
  green public procurement targets
    126
  legal framework 127–8
  performance and function
    requirements 128–9
  small and medium-sized enterprises
    128

Index

qualified majority voting 2, 67–8

REACH regulation 277–8
  authorisations 286–90
  exempted substances 279
  registration of substances 278
    actors/parties concerned 281–3
    chemical safety assessment and risk management measures 284–5
    evaluation 285–6
    exempt substances 279–81
    importers 282
    information required 283–5
    manufacturers 281
    process 285
    producers 282
    quantities 278–9
    representatives 282–3
    substances concerned 278
    technical dossiers 283–4
rectification of damage at source principle 35
  implementation 35–6
refusal of access to information
  appeals 91–2
  grounds for refusal 88–9
Regulation 1367/2006 98, 104
  case law 104–7
  implementation of Aarhus Convention 105–6
  locus standi, EU's relationship with 104–5, 107
  scope of judicial review 104–7
right to the protection of the environment
  human and fundamental rights distinguished 13
  Rio Declaration 12–13
  TFEU 12–13

sanctions
  criminal penalties 158–60
  manufactures and air pollution 249, 258
  trade sanctions 308, 323
  see also fines
secondary law
  Art. 288 TFEU 5
  binding acts 5
  decisions 51
  delegated and implementing acts 52
  directives 50–51
  horizontal legislation 53–4
  non-binding instruments 5
  other legal instruments 52–3
  recommendations and opinions 51–2
  regulations 50
shared responsibility principle
  noise pollution 231–2
  soil contamination 206–7
    European Soil Charter 209–10
    Biodiversity Thematic Strategy 210
    Common Agricultural Policy 211–12
    Environmental Impact Assessment Directive 210–211
    Habitats Directive and 210
    resource efficiency roadmap (2011), 212
    Strategic Impact Assessment Directive 210–211
    Soil Thematic Strategy (STS)
      identification or problem areas 208
      mitigating action 208
      objectives 208–9
      private ownership and 209
      transboundary nature of soil degradation 209
    strategic impact assessment directive 210–11
Soil Thematic Strategy (STS)
  identification or problem areas 208
  mitigating action 208
  objectives 208–9
  private ownership and 209
  transboundary nature of soil degradation 209
sources of law
  ECJ case law 5
  Environmental Action Programmes 6
  international law 5
  primary law 4
  secondary law 4–5
Special Areas of Conservation (SACs) 182, 186

Special Protection Areas (SPAs) 184
state aid
  compensation 163
  Deutsche Bahn case
    equal treatment principle 166–7
    international law and 166
    polluter pays principle 167
    relevant secondary law 164–5
  indirect aid 171
    border tax adjustments 172
    Chemial Farmaceutici case 173–5
    energy taxation 171–3
    non-discrimination principle 173
    Outokumpu Oy case 171–5
  polluter pays principle 167, 168–70
  preferential tariffs 162–3
  regulatory framework 161–2
  threats to competition 163
  whether state aid or not 162–3
Strategic Environmental Assessments (SEAs)
  characteristics of plans and programmes 147–8
  Environmental Impact Assessments compared 144–5
  European Soil Charter and 210–211
  guidance 149
  relationship with Environmental Impact Assessments 145–7, *146*
  screening 147
  soil 210–211
  transboundary consultations 148
subsidiarity principle 19–20
  application 21
  criteria 20
  enforcement 20–1
  noise pollution and 231
  proportionality and 20
supremacy principle *see* primacy principle
sustainable development 3, 8–10, 12–13
  Brundtland Report 24, 26
  constitutional dimension 26
  definitions and interpretation 24–7
  integration principle 22, 145, 147–8
  social dimension 26
  Stockholm Declaration 24
  threats to 27

trade 308
  Alands Vindkraft case 322–4
  Essent I case 320–324
  Essent II case 324–6
  harmonisation of standards 310
    Cassis de Dijon case 310
    community pre-emption 311–12
    Compassion case 312–13, 315
    exhaustive effect of legislation 311–12
    Lomas case 314
    minimum harmonisation 311
    Motte case 314
    negative harmonisation 310
    positive harmonisation 310
    proportionality 316
    Van Bennekom case 313, 314
  internal market 308
    case law 309
    exhaustion and the pre-emptive effect 309, 311–12
    proportionality 309
    Treaty law 308–9, 315–16
  international law 308
    climate change measures 309
    scrutiny of EU law and policy 309
    World Trade Organization 309
  mutual recognition 310–316
  PreussenElektra case 318–20
  restrictions on use of lawfully marketed products 326–8
  Mickelsson case 328–9
transboundary issues
  Air Quality Directive 245
  EIA Directive 141–3
  permitting and licensing procedures 116–17
  river basins 218
  soil degradation 209
  Strategic Environmental Assessments 148
  water legislation and policy transboundary river basins 218
Treaty of Nice (2001), 3
Treaty on European Union *see* Maastricht Treaty
Treaty on the Functioning of Europe 4, 5, 7–8
  access to justice

Art. 263 TFEU 101–4
  direct concern 102
  individual concern 102
  non-privileged applicants
    101–2
  Plaumann test 102–3
  privileged applicants 101
division of competences 5–6
environmental guarantee 315–16
integration principle 22–4
precautionary principle 28
prevention principle 33
subsidiarity and proportionality
  19–22
sustainable development 24–5

unanimous voting 2–3
United Nations Conference on the
  Human Environment (Stockholm
  Conference), 1–2, 12, 24, 33
United Nations Economic
  Commission for Europe
  Convention on Access to
  Information Public Participation
  in Decision-Making and Access to
  Justice in Environmental Matters
  see Aarhus Convention
United Nations Environment
  Programme (UNEP), 1–2

vehicles *see* motor vehicles

waste legislation and policy 264
  Arco Chemie case 273–4
  charges for waste disposal and
    treatment 270–271
  "circular economy" 272
  EU law **275–6**
  evolving policy 264–5
  General Union Environment Action
    Programme 269–70
  OECD influence 264
  Palin Granit case 274
  producer responsibility 271
  Shell case 274
  sustainable materials management
    270
  thematic strategy (2011), 268–9
  thematic strategy on prevention and
    recycling of waste (2003), 265
    Best Available Techniques
      reference guides 268
    IPPC Directive and 267
    tradeable waste rights 267
    waste prevention targets 265–7
  "waste" defined
    case law 273–4
    Waste Framework Directive
      272–3
water legislation and policy
  adaptation to climate change 221
    droughts and water security
      222–4
    floods 221–2
  bathing and swimming water 225–6
  Blueprint to Safeguard Europe's
    Water Resources 216–17
  drinking water 224–5
  groundwater 227
  legislation and policy 215–17
  marine environment 229–30
  Water Framework Directive 216
    chemical environmental quality
      standards 219
    common implementation strategy
      220
    integrated river basin management
      217–20
    key terms and concepts 217–18
    member state responsibilities 218,
      219–20
    objectives and standards 218
    timescales 217, 218
    transboundary river basins 218
  water pollution 228
Wild Birds Directive 183–4
  derogation 185
  killing or capture 184
  member state responsibilities 185
  Special Protection Areas 184